MARATHA HISTORIOGRAPHY

MARATHA HISTORIOGRAPHY

(Based on Heras Memorial Lectures)

A.R. KULKARNI

Foreword by

IRFAN HABIB

MANOHAR
2006

First published 2006

ISBN 81-7304-687-5

Published by
Ajay Kumar Jain for
Manohar Publishers & Distributors
4753/23 Ansari Road, Daryaganj
New Delhi 110002

Typeset by
InoSoft Systems
Noida

Printed at
Lordson Publishers Pvt. Ltd.
Delhi 110007

Distributed in South Asia by
FOUNDATION BOOKS
4381/4, Ansari Road
Daryaganj, New Delhi 110002
and its branches at Mumbai, Hyderabad, Bangalore, Chennai, Kolkata

To
Professor J.V. Naik
A Friend Indeed

Contents

PART III: MARATHA HISTORIOGRAPHY IN MODERN TIMES: THE INDIAN APPROACH

Foreword

My distinguished friend Professor A.R. Kulkarni has graciously asked me to contribute a Foreword to his detailed study of the evolution of Maratha historiography. As he explains clearly, what he is concerned with is not the historiography of Maharashtra, but that of a particular phase of its history, when, owing mainly to political developments, notably the Maratha empire of the eighteenth century, the region's history intertwined exceptionally closely with that of the country as a whole. Traditionally, the phase is taken to begin with the construction of Shivaji's 'swarajya' in the latter half of the seventeenth century, and the end of the Peshwa's regime in 1818.

There is a second boundary, which Professor Kulkarni also sets. He is not concerned with Maratha historical sources themselves, notably the narratives known as *bhakhars*; his concern is strictly with modern historiography, the application of critical methods of research being taken as its hallmark. Since these methods, in their most developed forms, came to us from the West, it is natural that Professor Kulkarni should give considerable space, in the beginning of his work, to Europeans who investigated Maratha history, from the early Portuguese biographer of Shivaji, Cosme da Guarda, to the nineteenth-century British historian of the Marathas, Grant Duff, whose *History of the Mahrattas* was published in 1826. Professor Kulkarni, in effect, offers us a fascinating story of 'Orientalism', as it has actually been applied in a particular field, where not just prejudice (whose presence in Orientalism in general is so heavily underlined by Edward Said), but also an increasing use of rational tools, shaped the historians' approach.

We see from Professor Kulkarni's detailed study how these techniques, notably the use of historical texts and archival materials, were adopted by Indian historians, whose point of view was necessarily different from those of their Western practitioners. Maharashtra occupies a unique position in the history of modern historiography since here the shift took place with extreme sharpness. On the one hand were historians like V.K. Rajwade, K.N. Sane, V.V. Khare and D.B. Parasnis, who so lovingly collected and used archival sources (and about whom I first read, as an MA student, in Jadunath Sarkar's sensitive sketches in his *House of Shivaji*). On the other, there were those who, using a larger canvas, created new reconstructions of Maratha history, such as Justice M.G. Ranade, Jadunath Sarkar himself, G.S. Sardesai and S.N. Sen, whose works one could read in English. Here in Professor Kulkarni's book we have authoritative accounts of the work of these scholars and others (mainly writing before Independence), with due attention paid to the differences in approach found among them. One major feature of Professor Kulkarni's study is the impartiality with which he treats the positions taken by the various participants in the controversies of the past. The small points are also often illustrative of changing attitudes: for example Sarkar, finding how his occasional use of the informal 'Shiva' in the early editions of his biography of Shivaji, irritated some of his readers, shifted to 'Shivaji' in the later editions of his book.

Professor Kulkarni has given some space in his last chapter for the post-Independence phase. He has refrained, however, from details here, probably because he felt contemporary historians cannot be treated with the same freedom, as those of previous generations. In a characteristic act of modesty, he omits to mention his own work (except in the Bibliography). It is, therefore, incumbent on me to point out that Professor Kulkarni himself initiated an important trend when he explored social and economic conditions for understanding the nature of Maratha political history. One needs to recall his

Maharashtra in the Age of Shivaji, 1969, and then his trilogy, (1) *Medieval Maharashtra*, (2) *Medieval Maratha Country*, and (3) *The Marathas*, published in 1996. His intensive study of records relating to Indapur were part of a project which led to his illuminating essay on the pre-colonial Deccan village, which he presented in his Address as the General President of the Indian History Congress at its New Delhi session in 1992. There have been other scholars in this field, whom Professor Kulkarni duly mentions, notably two from Japan, the late Hiroshi Fukazawa and Professor Hiroyuki Kotani. The fact is that due to the richness of records collected with unique dedication by successive generations of scholars, Maharashtra is probably the region where the most intensive studies of economic conditions, at least for the eighteenth century, can be undertaken; and Professor Kulkarni, the doyen of Maratha historians today, has done pioneering work here on his own.

It was in 1943 that, as a schoolboy, I heard Professor D.V. Potdar, the dominant personality of the 'Poona school', speak at the Aligarh session of the Indian History Congress, of which he was one of the founders. At the next session of the same Congress at Aligarh, in 1960, I met the late Shri G.H. Khare, self-effacing and modest, a scholar alike in Marathi and Persian, and in later years the main spirit behind that unique institution, the Bharat Itihas Samshodhak Mandal. My friendship with Professor Kulkarni, had its beginnings too at that session; and now through his pages, memory revives once more of some of the *savants* of Maratha historiography, whom I was privileged to see and others whose writings I read.

It is fitting that the generations of dedicated scholars who collected archives, pored over records and reconstructed Maratha history, should rcccivc so affectionate and impartial a treatment as Professor Kulkarni has provided us with. All of us should feel deeply grateful to him for fashioning such a fitting tribute to his precursors.

June 2006 IRFAN HABIB

Preface

> The most intriguing subject of history is neither the study of history, nor history itself, but rather the study of the history of historical studies.
>
> CARL BECKER

The term 'Maratha history' as it is used now is misleading. It is not the history of the people of the Maharashtra region alone, but the history of the Indian subcontinent with which the Marathas were directly or indirectly associated. Grant Duff, the first historian–administrator of the Marathas to attempt a comprehensive history, has admitted unequivocally that the British wrested political power in India with the overthrow of the Marathas in 1818. It was perhaps this political supremacy of the Marathas, which had its beginnings in the seventeenth century and was at its zenith in the eighteenth century, that induced many foreign and Indian scholars to make an in-depth study of the rise, growth, decline, and fall of Maratha power. Maratha historiography is not merely a study of regional history but essentially an intrinsic part of the historiography of the Indian subcontinent.

This study attempts to make a brief assessment of the contributions of eminent historians to various aspects of Maratha history. Historiography, or the history of history writing, 'the most intriguing subject' as Carl Becker, the American historian remarks, as an independent branch of historical study is of relatively recent origin. Indian universities are now introducing it in their history courses.

It is certainly interesting to know why historians hold different or even conflicting views about a particular event in history. This may be due to the discovery of new sources, or a significant reinterpretation of the earlier material used by other historians, or even due to their preconceived notions about the history of a people or of human societies. G.R. Elton in this respect writes, 'Historians' personalities and private views are a fact of life like the weather. . . . They cannot be eliminated, nor should they be. The historian who thinks that he has removed himself from his work is almost certainly mistaken'[1] (*The Practice of History*, London, 1970, p. 134).

The study of history is an intellectual pursuit, an activity of the reasoning mind. 'A professional historian,' states Elton, 'in disseminating historical knowledge fulfils a useful social function' as he or she helps a 'good many people' who 'simply want to know about the past for emotional or intellectual satisfaction' and 'to know the past better' (ibid., pp. 60–8).

It is often argued that history does not exist until it has been reconstructed and written down by the historian. It can, therefore, be said that as the historian's own intellectual and cultural environment is inevitably reflected in his writings and interpretations, a study of the historian himself will certainly add to a better understanding of his historical writings and methodology.

It is from this point of view that an attempt is made here to present a fairly detailed account of the development of Maratha historiography, a subject that has so far not received its fair share of attention. R.C. Majumdar, the distinguished historian, in his Heras Memorial Lectures on 'Historiography in Modern India', offered a brief survey of historical writings on India in the context of historiography in Europe, and also pointed out a few shortcomings in the studies on Indian historiography (Majumdar, *Historiography in Modern India*, Bombay, 1970, p. 2). Taking a clue from his lectures, I have endeavoured to study Maratha historiography, which I think is necessary for a proper understanding of Indian historiography.

Another incentive to undertake this project was a letter of appreciation of my paper on Grant Duff, presented at a seminar at the School of Oriental & African Studies, London University in 1968, by Sheila Sakalov Grant (the great-granddaughter of the historian) whom I had met in London. She wrote, 'I found it (that is, my assessment of Duff's *History*) very interesting. I admire the meticulous scholarship displayed. . . . It is a great moment when history and historians, especially suddenly become free of emotional and political bias and can write what they believe to be true "without fear or favour". Indian historians certainly seem to be very advanced in this, and you yourself are doing very important and valuable work'.

This letter was as encouraging as it was challenging. I do not know how far or how successfully I have responded to this challenge. I am quite aware of my limitations, but being involved in teaching and researching this subject for a number of years, I thought it my moral responsibility to place before discerning scholars of history whatever I have learned and tried to understand all these years for their scrutiny, and also to encourage young scholars to undertake further studies on this subject.

It is pertinent to mention here very briefly the earlier works on this subject. Maha Mahopadhyay Datto Vaman Potdar, the noted Maratha historian, gave a brief resumé of historical research and writings in a Marathi booklet entitled *Marathi Itihas va Itihas Samshodhan* (Pune, 1935). However, it does not fulfil the requirements of a systematic study of Maratha historiography. It simply enumerates the works written in Marathi on Maratha history.

However, one may find a few stray articles both in Marathi and English that appeared in certain edited volumes or a few biographies of historians such as G.S. Sardesai and Jadunath Sarkar.

C.H. Philips in his edited volume *Historians of India, Pakistan and Ceylon* (1963) includes some articles on historians associated with India. Yet J.B. Harrison in his article 'Portuguese Historians of India' does not even mention the name of Cosme da Guarda, a seventeenth-century historian of Shivaji. The volume does not include any article on the pioneering work of James Cuninghame Grant Duff, *A History of the Mahrattas*, published in 1826, which appeared within a period of eight years after the fall of Maratha power in 1818.

It simply makes a passing reference to some anecdotes about its publication. However, the volume does include one article, 'Modern Historical Writings in Marathi' by V.G. Dighe (pp. 473–80), a hurried account of some Marathi sources and historical works of modern historians, particularly G.S. Sardesai.

S.P. Sen edited a volume entitled *Historians and Historiography in Modern India* (Calcutta, 1973), which contains articles on Jadunath Sarkar, Balkrishna, M.G. Ranade, K.T. Telang, V.K. Rajwade, D.B. Parasnis, V.V. Khare, G.S. Sardesai, and Grant Duff; the last two individuals alone are the historians who wrote comprehensive histories of the Marathas.

Jadunath Sarkar, a biographer of Shivaji, has reviewed in his book *House of Shivaji* (Calcutta, 1963) the pioneering works of Maratha scholars, namely, K.N. Sane, V.K. Rajwade, V.V. Khare, and D.B. Parasnis, who made valuable contribution to the collection and publication of Marathi historical source material.

S.R. Tikekar in his small book *On Historiography* (Bombay, 1964) offers a brief review of the works of Jadunath Sarkar and G.S. Sardesai.

Thus, it can be said that a systematic work on Maratha historiography was a desideratum. When I was invited by the Heras Institute of Indian History and Culture, St. Xavier's College, Mumbai in 1982, I seized this opportunity to attempt to fill the gap in the field of historiography. This was in a way an attempt to address the shortcomings mentioned by R.C. Majumdar in his Heras Memorial Lectures of 1970.

The contribution of India to historiography is often underestimated. It was believed for a fairly long time that India had no historical literature of any worth, and that the study of Indian history was a gift of the foreigners. However, the vast amount of historical literature produced in various languages of this subcontinent bears an eloquent testimony to the traditions and ideas that Indians entertained about their own history all through the ages. A.K. Warder in his *An Introduction to Indian Historiography* (Bombay, 1972) has rightly observed that each country of the Indian subcontinent has its own historiographical tradition though these derive from the universal ancient Puranic history. The Hindu view of 'universal history' as depicted in their Puranas or epics underwent certain changes with the advent of the Turks, the Mughals, and the European powers, and it came to be seen as 'regional' during the medieval period. During the Muslim period, the concept of contemporary history became dominant in historical writings, and numerous histories of various dynasties generally known as *tawarikhs* were produced.

The rise of Maratha power in the medieval period gave an impetus to historical writings in the regional languages as well as in Sanskrit. Warder gives a brief account of the historiography of Maharashtra, particularly under the Bhonsales, the House of Shivaji, and afterwards (ibid). A number of chronicles called *bakhars*, in which one finds a happy blending of the Hindu and Muslim traditions of historical writings, were produced in Marathi during the course of time. But as the *bakhars* could not be considered histories in the strict sense of the term, the era of history writing proper, based on authentic sources and scientific methods, began only in the late nineteenth century in Maharashtra.

The early historical accounts of the Marathas were presented mainly by the foreigners who were in charge of the administration of the newly acquired territories of India. They were anxious to know more about the land and the people of the country under their control. They followed the maxim that if one wants to govern a people, one must know them and one can know them only through their histories. This induced many Westerners to involve themselves in writing the histories of India.

Among the foreigners, the British, being more successful as conquerors than others, addressed themselves to the task of preparing historical accounts of India. Thus, we find individuals such as Mountstuart Elphinstone, John Briggs, John Malcolm, Grant Duff, James Tod, and Mark Wilkes, to mention only a few, devoting themselves to the writing of histories of the areas that they had to govern.

Warder in this respect rightly observes, 'Practically all existing Indian histories written in English can in fact be adequately characterized as "imperialist" historiography in the sense that it reflects the outlook of the foreign and alien invaders as conquerors of India' (ibid.).

In view of the multiplicity of languages, traditions, and customs, and the varied types of documents, the writing of the history of India became an arduous task. One cannot, as James Mill did, boast that one could write the history of India without visiting this subcontinent. Elphinstone, who spent the formative period of his life (1795–1826) in India and a major part of it in Maharashtra, was a modest man and was quite aware of the difficulties involved in attempting to chronicle an authentic history of India (Philips, op. cit., p. 223).

Elphinstone has thus rightly pointed to the equipment needed for writing the history of India. Foreign historians, therefore, could not do full justice to the histories that they attempted for lack of the necessary equipment.

The present work on Maratha historiography is essentially a resumé of the contributions of eminent historians, both foreign and Indian, with special emphasis on the trends in historical writing from the seventeenth to the twentieth century.

The volume is divided into three parts:

Part I deals with the foreign approach towards the history of the Marathas, which includes the assessment of the historical works produced by the Portuguese, the German, and mainly the British historians.

Part II is devoted to the archival movement in the Bombay Presidency prior to the independence of India, with special reference to the restrictive colonial policy and the emergence of the popular revolt against it. To the British, Maratha history was a 'hot subject', particularly in the early nineteenth century. They believed that the Marathas had not forgotten that they had been masters of this land in the recent past and reduced to their present low position by the British. Thus, with a view to preventing them from reviving their past glory as an inspiration for future generations, the British adopted a restrictive archival policy preventing any free access to the state archives. This attitude of the British led Maratha scholars to launch a movement for the collection, preservation, and publication of historical source material preserved with the important Maratha families in the region. The pioneering work in this direction made by K.N. Sane, V.K. Rajwade, V.V. Khare, D.B. Parasnis, and many others is discussed in this section.

Part III, the last section first examines the early Indian approach to Maratha history with special reference to the Marathi *bakhars*, i.e. chronicles and the writings of M.G. Ranade, an assessment of modern historiography, and discusses the contribution of eminent historians such as G.S. Sardesai, Jadunath Sarkar, Surendra Nath Sen, T.S. Shejwalkar, V.G. Dighe, V.S. Bendre, and many other scholars. It also takes cognizance of the work done on Maratha history in the USA, Britain, Germany, Australia, Japan, and other countries.

I am highly indebted to the Heras Institute of Indian History and Culture, St. Xavier's College, Mumbai, and particularly its former Director, late Fr. (Dr) John Corriea Alfonso, S.J., who provided me a platform to present my research in the field of Maratha history. The present volume is an expanded version of the three lectures that I delivered under the auspices of the Heras Institute in 1982. I am grateful to my friend Prof. Dietmar Rothermund formerly of Heidelberg University, Germany for his observations on the first part of this study. I can never forget my dear esteemed friend and colleague, late G.N. Sharma of Dr B.R. Ambedkar Marathwada University, Aurangabad, who meticulously went through a major portion of my manuscript and made valuable suggestions to improve it. I am equally thankful to my friends Prof. B.N. Kulkarni of S.P. College, Pune, Prof. J.V. Naik of Mumbai University, and Dr Arun Tikekar, the historian–journalist, for their unstinting cooperation in the preparation of this work. I am extremely grateful to Prof. Irfan Habib for his Foreword to the book. I am also thankful to Radhika Seshan, Sumitra Kulkarni, and my wife Vijaya for their help in proofreading and preparing the Index.

I am extremely obliged to Shri Ramesh Jain, of Manohar Publishers & Distributors, New Delhi, for publishing the volume.

Pune A.R. KULKARNI
10 November 2004

[illegible] Rajwade, V.V. Khare, D.B. Parasnis and others is discussed in this [illegible]. [illegible] the early Indian [illegible] in Marathi history [illegible] modern historiography, and the [illegible] Indian historians such as [illegible] the history of [illegible] Britain, Germany, Australia, Japan, and other countries.

I am highly indebted to the Heras Institute of Indian History [illegible] College, Mumbai, [illegible] Dr. [illegible] who provided me a platform to present my research [illegible] history. The present volume is an expanded [illegible] of the three lectures that I delivered [illegible] in 1982. I am grateful [illegible] Department of [illegible] University [illegible] on the first part of this study [illegible] friend and colleague [illegible] Dr. B.R. Ambedkar Marathwada University, [illegible] Prof. [illegible] for their [illegible]

I am [illegible] Delhi, for [illegible]

[illegible]

PART I

FOREIGN HISTORIANS OF THE MARATHAS

1

Cosme da Guarda: The Portuguese Historian

Rise of the Maratha power in the seventeenth century and the advent of the Europeans, excepting the Portuguese on the west coast of India who had come earlier at the end of the fifteenth century, is a strange coincidence of history. The Portuguese, who had already acquired some political power in India, and the other European powers like the British, the French, and the Dutch, who were aspiring for it, viewed with great concern the rapid growth of Maratha power since its establishment in the seventeenth century. This concern of the foreign powers regarding the fortunes of Maratha power apparently prompted them to learn more about the Marathas, who were likely to be their competitors or rivals in the course of time. This seems to have been the reason behind the genesis of European writing on the Marathas in some form or the other since the 1690s.

The Portuguese were the first among the Europeans to acquire territorial possessions on the west cost of India. Contemporary Marathi records refer to them as *phirangis* and their state as *phirangan*. However, during the period of Shivaji (1630–80), the Portuguese had become a declining power in India, and hence had to remain content with defending their small territories by soliciting the favours of the Marathas or the Mughals, depending on political exigencies.

The earliest known biography of Shivaji, the founder of Maratha power, was written in Marathi between 1694 and

1697, at the instance of his son Rajaram, by Krishnaji Anant Sabhasad, a contemporary of Shivaji. Cosme da Guarda, the Portuguese chronicler, was the first foreign biographer of Shivaji, whose work in Portuguese entitled *Vida de celebre Sevagy* or *The Life of the Celebrated Shivaji* was compiled in 1695 with a view to satisfying the curiosity of Europeans about the Maratha leader. It was published posthumously in 1730.[1] Shivaji had already been introduced to Europeans by contemporary European travellers and officials such as Jean de Thévenot (1665–7), Barthelemy Carré (1668–73), John Fryer (1672–81), François Bernier (1659–67), Tavernier (1640–66), Dellon (1669–76), Niccoloi Manucci (1653–1701), and François Martin (1668–1706). Cosme da Guarda, however, was the first European to write a complete life story of Shivaji for European readers.

Authentic biographical details about Guarda are still unknown. He claimed that he was born in Marmagao, Goa, but this seems to be in doubt.[2] However, from the minute details of Shivaji's life narrated by him, it appears that he evidently moved about freely in Shivaji's territories, and that he may have acquired a working knowledge of some Deccani languages, namely, Urdu, Persian, and Marathi and its dialects. While preparing the narrative on Shivaji, he evidently spared no effort in consulting all the then available records concerning the Maratha hero and other related matters.

When Guarda's biography was published in 1730. Maratha power was in its ascendancy, under the leadership of Chhatrapati Shahu and his dynamic Peshwa, Bajirao I. The Portuguese were, therefore, anxious to know more about the rise and growth of Maratha power in the Deccan. Perhaps this curiosity of the Portuguese led to the publication of this biography, which had been lying in the archives since 1695. Soon it became very popular among Portuguese officers. The manuscript was censored before its publication, and the expert to whom it was referred opined that though it was not possible to verify the truth of all the statements, on the whole the narrative appeared to be correct and accurate.[3] The so-called expert was a Portuguese officer who was not qualified to sit in judgement over the correctness and accuracy of the account of the career of Shivaji. Guarda's information about Shivaji's early life, particularly about his birth and birthplace, has been rejected by historians such as V.K. Rajwade and P.S.S. Pissurlencar as incorrect and baseless.

Guarda must have written this biography while he was in the Deccan. Clearly, he must have collected information about Shivaji from various people. His information, however, is incomplete and unreliable at many places. But from the point of view of historiography, this work has its own value. Guarda attempted to present the image of Shivaji as it prevailed among the Maratha people during his period. Being a staunch Roman Catholic, his testimony of the achievements of Shivaji, a pagan, is of greater significance. It appears from Guarda's account that the Portuguese held a very high opinion of Shivaji's love of justice, his keen interest in the welfare of his subjects, his generalship and statesmanship.

Guarda's biography is not a history of Shivaji in the strict sense of the term. It is essentially a chronicle similar to Sabhasad's *bakhar* of Shivaji, and hence the events are neither chronologically arranged nor do they cover the entire life story of Shivaji. It seems that Guarda himself was not unaware of this deficiency in his writing.

In the twenty chapters of the biography, Guarda discusses the major events in Shivaji's life such as his birth and early career, his major encounters with the Adil Shahi kingdom of Bijapur under the command of Afzal Khan, his inroads into the Konkan, his night attack on Shaista Khan, the Mughal commander, his sacking of Surat, his surrender to the mighty Mughal army under Mirza Raja Jai Singh, his visit to Aurangzeb at Agra and and his miraculous escape from captivity, his encounter with the Portuguese at Marmagao, and lastly his death.

It is really surprising that Guarda did not write much about the relations between Shivaji and the Portuguese except at one place, where he describes Shivaji's invasion of Marmagao. In this respect, it must be remembered that Guarda was the only historian who wrote about the naval battle between Shivaji and the Portuguese at Marmagao. This account has been corroborated by some unpublished records preserved in the Lisbon archives. This naval enterprise of Shivaji, however, proved to be abortive and Shivaji expressed his sincere regrets to the Viceroy of Goa. He pleaded, according to Guarda, that it was not his intention to offend the Portuguese for whom he had always entertained great respect. In this connection, Guarda writes,

> It cannot be described how the Viceroy rose in the estimation of Sevagy on account of the treatment he had accorded him, and Sevagy liked him so much that he always praised his valour, judgement and courtesy. The Viceroy had great credit with Sevagy and enjoyed his respect as long as he was the India and even after he had ceased to govern.[4]

This reference is to Antonia de Mello de Castro, who was appointed Governor of India in 1662, and was soon elevated to the position of Viceroy. Apart from this incident, no other reference dealing with the relationship between Shivaji and the Portuguese is mentioned by Guarda.

Shivaji was coronated as a sovereign ruler—Chhatrapati—in 1674, and he thereby declared his sovereign authority over his dominion. But this important event in Shivaji's life does not find any place in Guarda's biography. In fact, Portuguese records do not take cognizance of this major event. Pissurlencar, the Goan historian, says that official correspondence from 1669–77 is not available in the Portuguese archives, and therefore we do not find any reference therein to Shivaji's coronation.[5] A young scholar from Goa, T.R. de Souza in an unpublished paper, has tried to explain this silence on the part of the Portuguese regarding the coronation of Shivaji. He writes:

> The silence can be explained only as an intended blackout. This is not difficult to believe. The fanaticism of the Portuguese had always considered the Hindu religious rites as devilish, and any public celebration of these was banned within the limits of the Portuguese jurisdiction. Hence the coronation ceremony performed by Hindu priests, and attended by them in large numbers, was surely regarded by the Portuguese as a grand pagan act, which they could neither approve nor talk about without feeling guilty of blasphemy or fearing the stern hand of the Inquisition.[6]

After his coronation, Shivaji led an expedition into the Carnatic, which also does not find a place in Guarda's biography. He also does not discuss in detail the relations of Shivaji with other European powers.

However, the political inaccuracies in his biography are compensated for by his minute observations on the intelligence system of the Marathas, a comparison between the Maratha and the Mughal armies, a description of Raigad, the fort capital of Shivaji, the camp life of the Mughals, etc.

Guarda has tried to present a contemporary picture of Shivaji. He has not only faithfully recorded popular and prevailing opinions about him, but has also depicted the character of Shivaji with an admirable degree of fairness. 'Sevagy's name,' he writes, 'however had already become so terrible that it was very seldom that anybody dared to defy him.'[7] At another place he observes:

> Such was the good treatment he accorded to people and such was the honesty with which he observed the capitulations that none looked upon him without a feeling of love and confidence. By his people, he was exceedingly loved; both in matters of reward and punishment he was so impartial that while he lived he made no exception for any person; no merit was left unrewarded; no offence went unpunished. . . . He was naturally loved by all men of valour and good conduct . . . with such a procedure of justice, without consulting any jurist, he made his subjects ever happy and his fame rose to such a height that throughout Industan it became as dreaded as it was cherished.[8]

Unwittingly, he also gives a clue to solving the controversial subject of the birth date of Shivaji. According to him, Shivaji was twenty-nine years old in the year 1660. This date comes closest to the birth date advocated by the new school of Pune historians, who have accepted 1630 as the year of Shivaji's birth based on the evidence of *Shivabharat* and *Jedhe Shakavali.*[9]

The love that Shivaji received from his soldiers has been expressed in these words, 'He prized the lives of his soldiers above all the interests of the world.'[10] Shivaji gave protection to all needy persons and tried to maintain justice in his dominion. Guarda writes:

> He gave frequent audiences even to the most wretched of (*mais tristes*) his subjects and to all he administered equal and impartial justice. He ardently wished that there should be peace and order among his people, and he did his best to ensure that they might all live in abundance. He

did not enact many laws, but his orders were strictly obeyed. . . . He never permitted any feud or strife and least of all robbery, and for any of these offences (the culprit) paid with his life. If in any of his stations or provinces any native wanted to molest a traveller and if the latter invoked (the name) of Sevagy all (his troubles) came to an end, and such was the respect (he enjoyed) and such was the fear his subjects had (of him).[11]

The portrait of Shivaji that emerges from the writing of Guarda compares well with the description of the character of Shivaji that we find in contemporary Marathi chronicles and other records.

Thus, Guarda's biography of Shivaji, despite all its limitations and inaccuracies, occupies a place of some importance in the field of historical writings on the Marathas in general, and by foreigners in particular. It is significant also as a contemporary source of information on Shivaji, enabling the historian to understand the assessment of the activities of Shivaji through the eyes of a contemporary foreigner, who was by no means obliged or inclined to be generous to a native ruler.

Notes

1. S.N. Sen (ed.), *Foreign Biographies of Shivaji*, 2nd edn., Calcutta: K.P. Bagchi & Co., 1977, pp. 2–4.
2. P.S.S. Pissurlencar, 'Shivaji Maharajanche Ek Portuguese Charitrakar', *Vividhajna Vistar*, vol. 6, 1919, p. 55.
3. Sen, op. cit., p. 3.
4. Ibid., p. 112.
5. P.S.S. Pissurlencar, *Portuguese–Marathe Sambandha*, Pune: Pune University, 1967, p. 112 (henceforth referred to as PMS).
6. T.R. de Souza, 'The Impact of Shivaji's Power upon the Administration and People of Goa', paper presented at the seminar on 'Chhatrapati Shivaji as a Nation Builder', Delhi, 1975.
7. Sen, op. cit., p. 40.
8. Ibid., pp. 59–60.
9. Ibid., p. 61.
10. Ibid., p. 66.
11. Ibid., p. 121.

2

Early British Historians

The British began to take a keen interest in Indian politics with their first major victory in the Battle of Plassey (1757) followed by the Battle of Buxar (1765), ultimately resulting in the acquisition of the diwani rights of Bengal in 1765 from the titular head of the Mughal Empire, Shah Alam. The Third Battle of Panipat (1761) had also dealt a severe blow to Maratha supremacy in the north.

The East India Company was essentially a body of merchants that always placed trade above politics. The Company's policy over the issue of sovereignty versus commerce was the subject of debate in England, in which leading economists also participated. It was argued that 'sovereignty and commerce could be successfully married but only when those in control were prepared to implement compensatory strategies for Bengal'. Adam Smith, the chief exponent of the classical school of economists, held the view that the government of an exclusive company of merchants was perhaps the worst of all governments for any country.[1] It was believed by economists that commerce and sovereignty were incompatible, and serious doubts were raised about whether sovereignty would advance commerce or destroy it.[2]

Early British administrators, both civil and military, developed a desire to know more about India and Indians, through their histories. This was particularly true of the Marathas and their history. As the Marathas were one of the immediate impediments in the way of British ambitions of establishing their own sovereignty in India, some British officers sought to learn more about the Marathas through a study of their history. They could foresee that sooner rather than later the governance of the Maratha territories would pass into their hands, and realized that the acquisition of knowledge of these territories would be a necessary preparation for their future responsibilities.

CAPTAIN JAMES KERR

Captain James Kerr was the first British administrator to present an account of the Marathas in English, in 1782.[3] His narrative cannot be regarded as an independent work on the Marathas, but is simply a translation of a Persian manuscript compiled by his munshi, or Persian teacher, at his instance. One hardly gets any biographical details of Captain Kerr and his suitability for writing, or even translating, a manuscript relating to the Marathas.

To Kerr, the Marathas were only a tribe of not very ancient origin, and he thought that his native munshi was well informed in the general history of this country, and was 'a man of integrity, intelligence, and observation'. But from the 'narrative' before us, one can see that Kerr was backing the wrong horse. He says that he had given to the munshi, the 'strictest injunctions to be careful' in not misleading him, and that under his own inspection all necessary information was collected from the Persian manuscript, supported by 'oral traditions and the best-received accounts of the more recent times'.

Kerr has, however, made it clear that 'a narrative of this kind cannot be expected to be always very exact in the detail, either with regard to time, or the less important circumstances'. He was not himself keen on publishing this 'narrative', but he says that 'a few friends and respectable characters in the literary world here' induced him to do so with the assurance that 'such a narrative at this time would not be unacceptable or uninteresting to the public', however imperfect it might be. He also mentions the purpose of this 'narrative', that is, 'as a general knowledge of this subject seems wanted, and the humble attempt now made to communicate that knowledge may lead and induce to more minute researches by others, whose opportunities of information have been or may be more favourable to success than such as I pretend to'. With all humility, Kerr confesses that, while presenting this 'narrative' to the public, he would not 'intrude on the historian' but confine himself only to the role of a translator.

As regards his scholarship in Persian, it seems that, besides taking regular lessons from his munshi, he had also studied *Persian Grammar*, written by Sir William Jones, the author of *Life of Nadirshah*, published in 1773, and was also well acquainted with the *Dictionary of Persian and Arabic*, and *Arabic Grammar* by Richardson. He also mentions contemporary works such as Robert Orme's *A History of the Military Transactions of the British Nation in Indostan (1745–61)*, published in three volumes between 1763 and 1778; Alexander Dow's *History of Indostan*, which he must have consulted while translating the Persian manuscript.

Besides, Kerr had stayed in India for ten years and was well acquainted with the people of the country. In this respect, he sounds a note of warning against the 'native character'. He urges precaution against 'a prevailing servility of spirit' among the native inhabitants from whom the best information might naturally be expected. However, he says, 'With a view to pleasing their master, they often give wrong information which would never satisfy the European enquirer, whose air is truth.' He had learnt of this trait of the native character, he claims, through personal experience and repeated observations. As he was collecting oral traditions for his narrative, he thought that one should be on guard against this disposition of the natives.

Kerr also mentions the titles of some Persian manuscripts consulted by him or his teacher while preparing the narrative. Firishta's *Tarikh-i-Firishtah (Gulshan-i-Ibrahami)*, i.e. *History of the Muslim Power in India*, was consulted for the first part of his account, dealing with Rhumba and Sumbha who had settled in Satara. One does not know whether he consulted the original Persian *Tarikh* (presented to Ibrahim Adil Shah of Bijapur in 1609–10) or its first English translation by Alexander

Dow done between 1768 and 1772. Without giving any details, he mentions two more works, a 'Persian manuscript, which treats particularly of Allumageer's conquests . . . and the history of Bahadur Shaw, son and successor to Aurangzeb'. It is rather difficult, and also futile, to verify this account with the authorities that he has mentioned.

Kerr's account of the Marathas begins with the history of Rhumba, the first Maratha chief, a native of Udaipur (Rajasthan) who had settled in Satara. The entire story of Rhumba and his son Sumbha is unintelligible. It is difficult to identify Rhumba and Sumbha with Maloji and Shahaji. The details given by Kerr also do not tally with historical facts.

The narrative ends with the assassination of Peshwa Narayanrao in 1773. In the concluding passages, however, Kerr narrates the history of the Bhat family of the Peshwas up to 1775, when Raghunathrao, a frustrated member of the Peshwa's family, sought British help and joined the British camp.

This particular incident perhaps led Kerr to make an assessment about the rise and rapid progress of Maratha power and its future in the opening paragraphs of his narrative. He writes:

> Chance and fortune have contributed more to its rapid rise and progress than either the wisdom of its founder or the plans of his successors. . . . It would be judged a presumptuous prediction, and unauthorised by appearances at this period, to say that they have already arrived at their highest pitch of power, and that it would not be at all extraordinary if they are shortly seen losing their influence in India, as quickly as we know they have acquired it.[4]

Kerr's narrative, though the first among British contributions to Maratha historiography, cannot be taken seriously as an authentic and scientific work on Maratha history as it is full of inaccuracies and is not based on authentic historical source material.

Nevertheless, it would be interesting to know how the contemporary historians of India who wrote on the Marathas after Kerr assessed his contribution. Robert Orme, who published his work on Indian history during the same period as Kerr, does not take much cognizance of it. In response to Kerr's assertion that Persian manuscripts 'are the only historical guide to this subject', Orme's comment is, 'We had compiled all we know of Sevagy and after him, of the Morattoes, until the year 1689, before Mr Kerr's work was published, and have changed nothing in consequence but rest on our own enquiries.'[5] This shows the little importance Orme attached to Kerr's narrative.

M.C. Sprengel, a German historian of the Marathas, in his book published in 1785 reveals that he was aware of Kerr's narrative, and wrote a long note about him in the preface to his book and also referred to it in the course of discussion of certain events of Maratha history.[6] He writes:

> No doubt Mr James Kerr, an Englishman, attempted the history of the Marathas mostly based on such sources as writers in Europe could not question, that is on sources from Persian manuscripts dealing with old and new revolutions of Indian Empires of which many were to be found in Hindustan. But as has been generally observed in the following pages, Mr Kerr along with his anonymous authorities is not a sure guide to this history. He sets dates, persons and events topsy turvy, or even passes over the most important (historical) facts.

Robert Orme (1728–1801)

While surveying the work of British writers on Maratha history, one cannot ignore the work of Robert Orme, the author of *Historical Fragments of the Mughal Empire of the Morattoes and of the English Concerns in Indostan*, published in London in 1782. The fact that this work later went into two more editions shows that it was appreciated by contemporary readers.

Robert Orme, the son of John Orme, a surgeon attached to the East India Company, Bombay, was born in June 1728 in Anjengo, near Travancore, in Kerala. At the age of eight in 1736, he was sent to Harrow, and later was shifted to another school near London with a view to obtaining some training in commercial pursuits. In 1742, he returned to India to serve in Jackson & Wedderburn, a mercantile firm based in Calcutta. During this period he lost his parents as well as his only brother, William. In 1743, he was appointed as writer in the civil service of the Company in Calcutta, where he remained for nearly nine to ten years. During the course of his service he applied himself with indefatigable energy to promoting the interests of his employers and studying at all convenient seasons the institutions as well as the state of the municipal government of the town. It was during this period that he collected a good deal of source material, which he used in his subsequent historical writings. He wrote his first essay, 'General Idea of the Government and People of Indostan' in 1752 when he was attached to the Madras office. He developed a close friendship with Robert Clive, who was his contemporary in Madras. In 1753, he returned home along with Clive and stayed there nearly for one year. His knowledge of India influenced the authorities of the East India Company, and he was asked to join the Madras government as a member of the Governor's Council in 1754.

The two Eurupean powers that were developing their trade and commerce in the Carnatic[7] during this period were the French and the English. The outbreak of the Austrian War of Succession (1740–8), in which both England and France were involved, also placed the two mercantile companies in India technically in a state of war. This led to the three Carnatic wars fought between the English and the French between 1746 and 1760. The French were finally defeated in the Battle of Wandiwash. Orme was in Madras during the last Carnatic war, which he calls the War of Coromandel. As a member of the Governor's Council, he took an active part in directing the military operations in the Carnatic from 1755 to 1759. It is said that in some of the most critical junctures of that war his abilities as a politician and statesman were particularly prominent. Pleased with his services, the Court of Directors appointed him as the eventual successor to the Governor of Madras, but he did not continue in India long enough to succeed to that honourable station.

He arrived in London in 1760, and devoted himself to the writing of *History of the Military Transactions of the British Nation in Indostan from the Year 1745*, which he completed in three volumes between 1763 and 1778. (To these volumes is prefixed the description a 'dissertation on the establishments made by Mahomedan Conquerors in Indostan'.) These three volumes, running into 1,175 pages in royal-size, deal mainly with the War of Coromandel and the War of Bengal that the British fought between 1745 and 1761; this was essentially a work of contemporary history.[8]

In 1770, Orme was elected a Fellow of the Society of Antiquaries, and the Court of Directors gave him free access to the Records of the India House. He was appointed the official Historiographer of the Company on a salary of £400 per annum. Though he was closely associated with Clive while he was in India, this friendship was practically dissolved after 1769. He was a contemporary of Samuel Johnson, and was full of praise for him. He used to say, 'I do not care on what subject Johnson talks, but I love better to hear him talk than anybody.' Perhaps it was this admiration for Johnson that led Orme to imbibe an ardent desire to study classical literature. He had developed a good taste for painting and occasionally used to write poems. In the course of his life he had collected a number of documents, which are now preserved in the India Office Library, London.

In 1782, Orme wrote his 'most laborious work', *Historical Fragments*, popularly known as *Fragments*. Its first two editions were published in 1782 and 1805 in London; after a gap of a century, the third edition was published in 1905 in Calcutta. *Fragments* was his last work; he died on 13 January 1801, at the age of seventy-three.[9] His *Fragments* must be considered an early account of the Marathas. It begins in the year 1659 and ends in 1689, the most significant period in the history of the Deccan in general and of the Marathas and the British in particular. Most of the book is devoted to the activities of the Marathas in the Deccan. He called this account *Fragments* in the hope of obtaining more details about this important period in the 'History of the East'. The editor of the second edition (1805) writes:

> We are not without hopes that some of the many in India who have the means, will supply the portions of information which are deficient in these *Fragments*, and must otherwise always continue out of our reach. The knowledge is well worth the enquiry, for besides the magnitude of

the events, and energy of the characters, which arise within this period, there are no States or Powers on the continent of India with whom our nation have either connexion or concern, who do not owe the origin of their present condition to the reign of Aurangzeb, or to its influence on the reigns of his successors.

About his account of Shivaji, it is further mentioned in the editorial,

His account of the famous Sevagy, the founder of the present nation of the Marottoes, is extremely curious and interesting. As a preparatory work to 'Fragments' he renewed his acquaintance with the Portuguese, Spanish, Dutch and Italian languages through Mr Boughton Roufe, now Sir Charles Roufe Boughton, Bart., his friend, who had a high reputation for oriental learning, supplied him extensive translations of *Ain-e-Akbari*, Ferishta and Persian manuscripts.[10]

Orme made every effort to collect all possible source material on the period of Shivaji, as he considered these years to be the most eventful in the history of India. In this connection he wrote on 26 June 1779:

If any portion of history wants more attention than others, it should seem that a period of revolution in the state or the progress of the foundation of a new one demand the strictest investigation. Sevagy was the founder of the Morratoe Dominion, in the Peninsula of India, and hitherto we have no account, either sufficiently accurate or sufficiently connected, to follow his life.[11]

Orme begins his *Fragments* with the Rajas of Chittore, who claimed descent from Porus, a king in ancient India. The Afzal Khan episode of 1659 is a significant event in Maratha history as it gave Shivaji an opportunity to measure his strength against a mighty Deccani power, i.e. the Adil Shahi of Bijapur. Orme, therefore, begins his narration with this event, and states that Shivaji stabbed Afzal Khan with his own hand by a device, it is said, that could be used with deadly effect, without arousing the least suspicion.[12]

He then narrates the subsequent military exploits of Shivaji, and also describes the extent of Shivaji's kingdom in 1667, just after his escape from Aurangzeb's captivity in Agra.[13] He also tells us how the Company acquired the island of Bombay, and describes Shivaji's relations with the English, particularly with reference to the plunder of the Rajapur factory. He also mentions Shivaji's attack on the Chauthia Raja of Ramnagar, and his demand for *chauth* from the Portuguese, which they had hitherto been paying to the Raja of Ramnagar.[14] The purpose of Shivaji's coronation in 1674 finds a special mention in this book.

> He had long been entirely independent of any other power, but the ceremony sanctified by the Brahmins was intended not only to insult the Mogal, and the two other Mahomedan kings with whom he was at war, but especially to authenticate to his own people his title and the succession as king of the Morattoe nation.

Orme also describes the extent of Shivaji's territory in 1674 and says that the Marathi language was extended 'along the coast from the island of Bardez to the river Taptti'.[15] The main source of information for the description of Shivaji's coronation was the report of Henry Oxenden, who was present at Raigad. Subsequent writers on Maratha history have relied mainly on this English source, particularly on the coronation of Shivaji and on the plunder of the Rajapur factory and on Shivaji's demand for reparations.

Rumours and anecdotes were quite rampant in those days, and Orme recorded them in his *Fragments* without verifying them. He mentions that in 1676 it was reported and believed that Shivaji was ill, at Rairee, and that he was rumoured to be dead,[16] but in the same breath he tries to explain the long stay of Shivaji at Raigad in 1676. He further writes, 'It was the prelude of the most important operation of his life which our lights are very insufficient to explain.'[17] This refers to Shivaji's Carnatic campaign of 1677–8, about which Orme could not say much for paucity of records. He observes, 'The want of contemporary records has disabled us from acquiring any regular account of Sevagy's expedition into the Carnatic, although on ground in which the arms and interests of our own nation have late years taken so much concern.'[18]

Orme's interest in the early history of the Carnatic was quite obvious, as he wrote at length on the military activities of the British in the Carnatic from 1745 to 1761. It seems that he was not aware of the existence of *Memoirs* and *Journals* of

François Martin, who served the French East India Company for forty years and took a keen interest in Carnatic affairs. His *Memoirs* (1664–96) deal extensively with Shivaji's expedition into the Carnatic. Perhaps the Anglo–French rivalry did not allow him to consult the French archives in Paris or Pondicherry. After making a brief reference to Shivaji's rapid successes in the Carnatic, he rightly mentions that the increase in Shivaji's power excited the indignation of Aurangzeb.

Orme discusses at length Shivaji's encounter with the Siddis, and how he tried to subdue them. According to him, Shivaji expired on 5 April 1680 (though Indian historians place this event on 3 or 4 April) at the age of fifty two.[19] His lengthy estimate of Shivaji deserves special notice. He writes about the origin of the Bhonsle family, the religiousness of Shivaji and his staunch championship of Hindu gods; his private life was simple, even to the point of parsimony; his manners devoid of insolence or ostentation; as a sovereign he was humane and solicitous about the well-being of his people, as soon as assured of their obedience.[20] After giving an account of Shivaji's military organization, Orme writes:

> Sevagy possessed all the qualities of command. . . . In personal activity he exceeded all generals of whom there is record. . . . He met every emergency of peril, however sudden and extreme, with instant discernment and unshaken fortitude; the ablest of his officers acquiesced to the eminent superiority of his genius; and the boast of the soldier was to have seen Sevagy charging sword in hand.[21]

The portrait of Shivaji presented in *Fragments* shows that Orme was overwhelmed by the personality of the Maratha leader. In his estimate of Shivaji, he writes:

> Thus respected as the guardian of the nation he had formed, he moved everywhere amongst them with unsuspicious security and often alone, whilst his wiles were the continual terror of the princes with whom he was at enmity, even in the midst of their citadels and armies. Whenever we shall obtain a history of his life written in his own country, he will doubtless appear to have possessed the highest resources of strategem, joined to undaunted courage, which although equal to the encounter of any danger, always preferred to surmount it by circumvention, which if impracticable, no arm exceeded his in open daring. Gallantry must lament that it should once have been stained by the blood of assassination.[22]

Such is the candid and considered opinion of a British historian about the founder of Maratha power with whom the British had to deal with in the seventeenth century and with his successors in the eighteenth. Orme also quotes Aurangzeb in support of his praise of Shivaji. He writes:

Aurangzeb could not suppress the emotions of his joy on hearing of Shivaji's death, nor the justice due to his character which he had denied during his life. 'He was,' he [Aurangzeb] said, 'a great captain and the only one who has had the magnanimity to raise a new kingdom, whilst I have been endeavouring to destroy the ancient sovereignties of India; my armies have been employed against him for nineteen years and nevertheless, his state has been always increasing.'[23]

Orme did not forget to give the boundaries or extent of Shivaji's kingdom at the time of his death, a description that is more or less accurate. 'The whole at a general amount may be estimated 400 miles in length and 120 miles in breadth.' This refers to the Swarajya territory, and the area 'at the distance of 300 miles' acquired in Carnatic was in addition to it. He states further that all these territories had been 'acquired by his own abilities from an origin of little note, and left at his decease a permanent sovereignty, established on communion of manners, customs, observances, language and religion, united in common defence against the tyranny of foreign conquerors, from whom they had recovered the land of their own inheritance'.[24]

Orme's *Fragments* closes with the execution of Sambhaji, whose character has been depicted by him on the basis of some chronicles. It therefore naturally includes certain popular accounts about Sambhaji, such as his attempt to poison Shivaji, his addiction to women, particularly the story of a Brahmin girl, Godavari, whose dwelling was on the side of the rock (of the Raigad fort) to which Sambhaji used to descend at night,[25] and that after capturing him Aurangzeb offered him rank and service if he turned Muslim, to which Sambhaji gave a spirited reply, 'If you would give me your daughter in marriage.'[26]

Orme gives a graphic account of the military achievements of Sambhaji against the Mughals and the Portuguese, but also laments that this 'young man possessed all the courage and activity of his father but little of his discretion or foresight'.[27] He has exaggerated Sambhaji's addiction to women in these words:

That propensity to women which wisdom of his father Sevagy seems to have early foreseen as the germ of Sambhaji's destruction had increased with his manhood and power. It wasted not his time in allurements of dalliance, but his variety was insatiable, and every beauty he heard of became the object of his acquisition, despite all parental and religious resentments.[28]

Kalusha Kabji, a minister of Sambhaji, was believed to be the spy of Aurangzeb and the 'procurer of his pleasures', who finally laid a trap to help the Mughals capture Sambhaji.[29] Untold miseries were inflicted on Sambhaji, and after a humiliating procession, he was executed brutally in public. However, Orme rightly observes that his death did not produce 'the expected effect of submission from any part of the Morattoe government, which it only animated to continue the war'.[30]

Orme's *Fragments* ends with this remark: 'Our narrative must now resume as well as it can the English concerns in the Empire from the end of 1685.' Thus we find that though Orme intended to write about the concerns of the Mughals, the Marathas, and the English in India, his major focus was on the Marathas, the most formidable rising power in the Deccan, a cause of alarm both to the Mughals and the English. From the concluding remarks of the first section, which covers only a period of thirty years (1659–89), it seems that Orme had a plan to narrate the history of the subsequent period in the next section. This he could not do though he lived for nearly eighteen years after the completion of the first section either because of waning interest or, what is more likely, because he could not get enough source material to continue the narrative. Had he completed the second section, it would have been a valuable and objective contribution to the history of the growth and decline of Maratha power till the close of the eighteenth century.

Orme, the historiographer of the East India Company, was strikingly scientific in his study of Maratha history. The lengthy notes appended to the volume bear eloquent testimony to the amount of labour involved in preparing *Fragments*. Contemporary scholars have described it rightly as 'a most laborious work'. For a text of 209 pages (third edition), notes running into 142 pages are appended. These notes discuss at length the sources consulted and give explanations wherever necessary, particularly regarding places and persons, that would help the reader, especially the European reader. Among the Persian documents available in Europe mention has been made of *Alamgirnama*, as well as the accounts of the travellers who visited India during the seventeenth century such as Tavernier (1640–66), Bernier (1659–67), Thévenot (1665–7), Carré (1668–73), Dellon (1669–76), Dr Graft (1640–87), Haye (1676), Fryer (1672–81), and Manucci (1653–1708). About the travellers who have made reference to Shivaji or the Marathas, Orme writes a general note saying, 'The narration of all the travellers who were on the western side of India during his (Shivaji's) life, after it became an object of fame, speak more or less of his exploits.' About Carré, the French traveller who visited India (Surat) in 1668, and again in 1672, Orme writes, 'He admires Sevagy's character with enthusiasm. Compares him to Gustavus Adolphus and Julius Caesar and ascribes to him all the qualities of a consummate hero and sovereign.' About John Fryer, he writes, 'Our attention to what Fryer says of him first led to the discovery that Sevagy was the founder of the present nation of the Morattoes.' He further states that except for Fryer contemporary travellers or records did not 'ever call the people or armies which Sevagy governed or commanded. The Morattoes are always called Sevagy's people, or the troops of Sevagy'.[31]

Orme also refers to certain historical narratives that were available to him. He mentions *Histoire de Sevagi* by Pierre D'Orleans, a Jesuit, published in Paris in 1688, an account composed on the basis of an earlier one written in Goa. This history of Shivaji, according to Orme, 'does not give a single date, and only a few facts without precision, and better known before'.[32] Similarly, Alexander Dow's *History of Indostan from the death of Akbar to the complete settlement of the Empire under Aurangzeb*, published in three volumes in London (1768–72), makes casual references to Shivaji from 1663 to 1669, and refers to him as the prince of Konkan. Orme's opinion of Kerr's *Narrative* has already been mentioned. Besides these published sources, Orme gained information about Shivaji and the Marathas from the contemporary records compiled by the East India Company; the earliest record mentioning Shivaji dates to 1673.

Of course, references to Shivaji could be traced right from 1659 in the Factory Records of the Company. The Company's estimation of Shivaji underwent a good deal of change, shifting from earlier descriptions of him as a 'raider', 'plunderer', 'rebel', or 'grand rebel' to later descriptions of him as the 'greatest diplomat of the eastern part of the known world' by the time of his coronation in 1674.[33] When Orme wrote on Shivaji he had perhaps only the report of the English ambassador, Henry Oxenden, who had attended Shivaji's coronation. For he writes, 'Could we have discovered the whole series with the collateral branches of correspondence from the year 1650, the *Fragments* we now publish would have acquired some authentic additions; but the labour would have exceeded the conception of any of our readers excepting the keeper of the records at the India House.'[34]

This 'discovery of the whole series' pertaining to Shivaji was made in course of time by the Bharat Itihas Samshodhak Mandal, Pune, which published a volume in 1931 entitled *English Records on Shivaji (1659–82)*.[35] B.G. Paranjape, during his stay in London for his bar at law degree in 1928–9, made this selection from the Factory Records and the Orme Collection in the India Office, and wrote an introduction to it. Paranjape has paid glowing tributes to the efforts of Orme, as Record Keeper, in collecting material on Shivaji, which served as the foundation for subsequent studies on the Maratha leader. This volume includes extracts from the Orme Collection, vols. 114, 174, 263, 268, etc. Orme was so absorbed in his project on the life of Shivaji that he collected information not only from English sources but also from sources in other

European languages such as Portuguese, Dutch, and French. He wrote to Charles Malet, the Resident at the Peshwa's Court (1786–97), asking him to get for him a portrait of Shivaji and the early history of Shahaji and Shivaji.[36]

In the light of the account of Maratha history presented by Orme after consulting all sources available to him, it would be interesting to learn what contemporary historians thought of his work. M.C. Sprengel, who published his study in 1785 seems to have been very deeply influenced by Orme's account of Shivaji in his own volume, *The History of the Marathas*. Sprengel commented on Orme's work in his book as he had done in the case of Kerr's *Narrative*. This means that he had accepted it as the standard work on the Marathas then available.

Scott Waring, who published his *Maratha History* in 1810, refers to Orme's work with the highest regard. He notes that Orme was the first historian to manifest any interest in the history of the Marathas. However, in his evaluation of *Fragments* he expresses regret for the type of material that Orme had to use for his work. He writes:

> Unfortunately, his materials were very defective and frequently incorrect, and as he did not unite a knowledge of the Asiatic languages with his other attainments, he sometimes places too great a confidence in suspicious authorities. He has however concentrated, in a small compass, a most valuable mass of information, nor is it to be omitted that he has pointed out almost every European author who has written on the subject.[37]

Grant Duff, who published his comprehensive *A History of the Mahrattas* in 1826, was quite aware of the difficulties that his predecessors had to face in collecting the necessary material. He writes:

> The difficulty in obtaining the requisite materials also hitherto deterred most of our countrymen from venturing on a subject where the indefatigable Orme has left his *Fragments* as a monument of his research accompanied by an attestation of the labour which they cost him.[38]

R.C. Majumdar, while discussing historiography in Europe, made an uncharitable remark about Orme's work in his *Historiography in Modern India*. He says:

His ideas on the Mughals and the Marathas were derived partly from personal investigation but mainly from hearsay and secondary sources. Being a foreigner he could not form any clear conception on the subject and his statements are not of much historical value.[39]

But when one goes through the text as well as the exhaustive notes prepared by Orme, and appended to this book, one cannot agree with the sweeping remarks of Majumdar. B.G. Paranjape, has rightly pointed to the interest of Orme in the sources of Maratha history and the pains that he had taken in collecting and arranging them. For want of proper source material, and also because of his lack of knowledge of Asian languages, Orme's account of the Marathas could not be as accurate as it should have been, but his objectivity and sympathetic approach could hardly be denied. He was writing in a period when 'history' was yet to achieve the status of a scientific discipline. In view of the efforts made by Orme to underline the importance of the Marathas in Indian history, he deserves a place in the 'history of historical studies' by Europeans on Maratha history.

NOTES

1. William J. Barber, *British Economic Thought and India (1600–1858)*, Oxford: OUP, 1975, pp. 76–7.
2. Ibid., pp. 98, 115–25.
3. Captain James Kerr, *A Short Historical Narrative of the Rise and Rapid Advancement of the Mahrattah State to the Present Strength and the Consequences it has Acquired in the East*, written originally in Persian and translated into English by an officer in the East India Company's service (Captain James Kerr), London, printed by J. Nichols, 1782.
4. Kerr, op. cit., p. 1.
5. Robert J. Orme, *Historical Fragments of the Mughal Empire of the Morattoes and the English Concerns in Indostan,* London: C. Nourse, 1782.
6. M.C. Sprengel, *History of the Mahrattas up to the Last Treaty with England (17 May 1782)*, Frankenthal, Gesels 2nd edn., 1791.
   Unpublished English translation by R.N. Chapekar in the BISM Library Pune. It has been quoted at several places in this book. Henceforth referred to as *Chapekar.*
7. In eighteenth-century records 'Carnatic' indicated a large area of Tamil Nadu, particularly the Arcot district, and a small portion of Andhra Pradesh and present-day southern Karnataka.

8. This work, although a major contribution to historical writing, does not fall within the purview of this study on Maratha historiography.
9. Robert J. Orme, *Historical Fragments of the Mughal Empire of the Morattoes and the English Concerns in Indostan*, London, 1782. It contains 234 pages, along with an index, notes, and two maps. The second edition London, contains a long write-up on Orme and a photograph of his statue. 1805. The third edition, Calcutta, 1905, p. 309 contains notes running into 142 pages, along with an index, and a brief life sketch of Orme. It was reprinted from the original edition of 1782. The references in this book are to this edition of 1905.
10. *Fragments*, op. cit., p. xiii.
11. Shiva Charitra Karyalaya, *English Records on Shivaji (1659–1682)* with Introduction by B.G. Paranjape, Pune, 1931, no. 533, vol. II, p. 327. See also nos. 533–41 of vol. II, pp. 327–51.
12. Orme, op. cit., 1905 edn., pp. 4–6.
13. Ibid., p. 17. About Shivaji's escape from Agra, he mentions the use of covered baskets, and writes: 'A boat, as for common passages, was waiting at the extremity of the city. They passed the river unsuspected, when Sevajy giving the boat-man money, bid him go and tell Aurangzeb that he had crossed Sevajy and his son across the Jumna.'
14. Orme, op. cit., pp. 34–5.
15. Ibid., pp. 51–2.
16. Ibid., p. 69.
17. Ibid., p. 74.
18. Ibid., p. 78.
19. Ibid., p. 113.
20. Ibid., p. 114.
21. Ibid., pp. 118–19.
22. Ibid., pp. 119–20. Orme's reference to 'Shivaji's life written in his own country' indicates that he had by then not come across any contemporary chronicle (*bakhar*) of Shivaji, particularly the one compiled by Sabhasad.
23. Ibid., p. 120.
24. Ibid., pp. 120–1.
25. Ibid., p. 69.
26. Ibid., pp. 126–7.
27. Ibid., p. 69.
28. Ibid.
29. Ibid., p. 206.
30. Ibid., p. 209.
31. Ibid., pp. 7–17 (pt. II).
32. Ibid., op. cit., p. 17 (pt. II).
33. H.K. Sherwani and P.M. Joshi (eds). *History of Medieval Deccan*, Govt. of Andhra Pradesh, Hyderabad, 1973, vol. I, p. 579.
34. Orme, op. cit., p. 20 (pt. II).
35. Shiva Charitra Karyalaya, *English Records on Shivaji (1659–1682)*, with an Introduction by B.G. Paranjape, Pune, 1931, p. 45.
36. Paranjape, op. cit., Introduction, p. 1.
37. Edward Scott Waring, *History of the Mahrattas to which is prefixed, An Historical Sketch of the Deccan. Containing a short account of the Rise*

and Fall of the Mooslim Sovereignties Prior to the Era of Mahratta Independence, John Richardson, Royal Exchange, London, 1810, p. 191.

38. Grant Duff, *A History of the Mahrattas*, revised and annotated edition with an introduction by S.M. Edwardes, London: Oxford University Press, 1921, vol. I, p. lxxxvi.
39. R.C. Majumdar, *Historiography in Modern India*, Bombay: Oxford University Press, 1970, p. 7.

3

Marthias Christian Sprengel: The German Historian

Marthias Christian Sprengel (24 August 1746–7 January 1803) was perhaps the first European historian to attempt an exclusive history of the Marathas. He was professor of history and librarian at Halle University, Germany. He had no opportunity to visit India, nor was he conversant with Asian languages, yet he was prompted to attempt a history of the Marathas purely from an academic point of view. He writes:

> The history of the Marathas, a race, that of all Indian races has become known in our times by the conquest of the decaying Empire of the Great Mongals; by the prestige and importance which it attained so briskly and by the fall which followed even so briskly has yet found no historian.[1]

Sprengel had earlier been mainly interested in the study of current history, particularly Amercan and Indian histories. He had published a book on Hyder Ali in 1784, mainly a tribute to his achievements as the ruler of Mysore. Sprengel's *History of the Marathas*, was first published in 1785, its second edition appeared in 1791, followed by a third in 1814. Whether the 1814 edition was really a third edition or not is not quite clear.[2] But the very fact that it was published twice within the lifetime of the author speaks for the popularity of this book among German readers and perhaps a few other Europeans.

Sprengel's *History* covers the period up to 1782, the year in which the Marathas registered their first and last victory against the British in the First Anglo-Maratha War by signing the Treaty of Salbye on 17 May 1782 between Mahadji Shinde and Anderson on behalf of the British. The Marathas once again raised their head after suffering a crushing defeat at Panipat in 1761, and re-established themselves as the controllers of the Indian political scene under the able leadership of Peshwa Madhavrao I and then under the administration of Nana Phadnis and Mahadji Shinde. The Marathas who were then challenging British colonial power must have attracted the attention of Sprengel, who was first of all a student of American history, and presumably could not have missed the parallel between the struggle of the Americans for freedom from British colonialism and of the Marathas against British power. He aimed at presenting an impartial account of the rise of Maratha power, the structure of their state, and their encounters with the Mughals and the Europeans. He explains the plan of his work on Maratha history and the extent to which he succeeded in the following terms:

> Whatever I have collected here about the Marathas and have sought to unite a whole is of two-fold nature. In the earlier period of history of this people, especially regarding its origin, its gradual ramification in Hindostan and in the Deccan before Nadir Shah's invasion, the reader will find here collected the most important historical data which writers accessible to me have observed on these events, either casually or purposefully.[3]

Sprengel collected material for his history from various languages, including English, German, French, Dutch, Italian, and Latin, though most of his source material was drawn from English-language sources. It included short historical monographs such as those of Kerr, Orme, and Sullivan and the reports, annual registers, pamphlets, narratives, correspondence of the East India Company and travelogues. He gives a long list of sources in non-English European languages that he consulted for his monograph. From his exhaustive notes and references given in the Appendix, which runs into about thirty-three typed pages, the reader gets an idea of the amount of labour put in by him in writing his history. Sprengel observes:

> In the writing of this history, which according to my design is to obtain everything what we in Europe know at present of the Marathas and of

the most important revolutions of this people and what we can know of them up to the time when John and his Company founded in Calcutta shed light on this dark part of Indian history, I have left no work untouched where I could expect to find something on the Marathas and the changes in their state.[4]

He further states:

Out of respect for general Indian history, I have set in order and coherence this fragment mostly disconnected, often loose in merit, widely different. Indeed, I have not always attained my objective. I could not give the complete sequence of the events and fill the gaps which occasionally obscure the history of this people. However, I could and would invent nothing pragmatically where my guides and predecessors kept silent.[5]

Sprengel paid much attention to the regional aspects of Maratha history. He provides a general description of the Maratha country and examines its strategic importance. His main source of inspiration on Shivaji was Orme's *Fragments*, but his account of Shivaji as compared to that of Orme appears to be more systematic. Sprengel stresses Shivaji's qualities as an unrivalled military leader, simple in his own habits, but generous in his expenditure on military adventures and fortifications, full of religious, zeal and relentless in the pursuit of his enemies. Shivaji, according to Sprengel, was born in 1629, and was coronated in 1674. He gives a good account of Shivaji's coronation, but immediately after this he writes, 'Old Shahaji was unexpectedly arrested.' This is an instance of anachronism, for Shahaji had died in 1664, and had in fact been arrested by the Adil Shah of Bijapur in 1648–9. Sprengel gives details of Shivaji's Carnatic expedition and mentions that Shivaji died on 5 April 1680 at the age of fifty-two and states that he was 'immolated on the pyre with the usual ceremonies of the Rajputs. He then gives an account of the career of Sambhaji. One can see in these accounts that Sprengel was under the influence of Orme, particularly in his treatment of the last days of Shivaji and of the capture and execution of Sambhaji. The factual mistakes in these accounts may be attributed to the paucity of authentic material available in those days.

Sprengel does not give any details of the most glorious period of Maratha history, i.e. from the execution of Sambhaji in 1689 to the death of Aurangzeb in 1707, a period during which the Maratha patriots heroically resisted and foiled the Mughal army which used all its might for more than twenty-five years to wipe out the Marathas from the political map of India. This lacuna in Sprengel's *History* may be due to various reasons. Orme's historical narration ends with the execution of Sambhaji, and as he had no faith in the *Narrative* of Kerr, and was unable to get authentic local sources, he presumably must have avoided entering into the details of this period. Sprengel observes that the history of this people during their subjugation consists of a few fragments which cannot be narrated in an orderly and connected manner'.[6]

As regards the presentation of history, he writes, 'To make conquests of the Marathas to some extent comprehensible to the readers, conquests which make their history particularly attractive to lovers of history and to arrange chronologically, as far as it is possible, various events important but incoherent, should be highlighted in a book narrating the history of these people who so heroically defended the 'Swarajya' against the Muslims and the Mughals.

Sprengel arranges the history of the subsequent period into three phases: (i) the fall of the Persians (Nadir Shah) in Hindustan, 1739; (ii) the defeat of the Marathas at Panipat, 1761; and (iii) the treaty concluded with the English at Salbye in 1782. His information on Bajirao I is not accurate as he writes that 'this Peshwa ruled the Maratha state so long as Shahu lived and even for sometime under his successors. He confuses Bajirao I with Balaji Bajirao at some places.

Sprengel has drawn heavily from the Karnataka Reports for his information after the year 1756, which mainly deal with the relations of the British and other European powers with the Marathas. Orme's three-volume history of the military transactions of the British between 1745 and 1778 was readily available to him for consultation. However, his account of Indian affairs in the north is very sketchy, and even his reference to the Third Battle of Panipat is too brief.

He could give more details of the First Anglo-Maratha War because of the availability of information in English. The parliamentary reports concerning the war helped him in describing in detail Anglo-Maratha relations leading to the war and the subsequent peace. As he was more interested in current history, it was but natural for him to focus his attention on current affairs and treat the earlier history as a backdrop.

But it seems that Sprengel was not satisfied even with the information on current events. About the history of the eighteenth century, he writes:

> Although we are the contemporaries of most of these events we cannot describe them chronologically and synchroniously. We in Europe can give less information regarding the most recent domestic events in Hindostan than that regarding earlier ones. The local wars and conquests of the Europeans, especially those of the Englishmen, had perhaps become an interesting subject for historians of India.[7]

Sprengel, who wrote this history keeping an eye on German readers, seems to be quite aware of the limited equipment available to him for writing the history of people with whom he was not personally acquainted, and that too with the help of the limited sources at his disposal. He frankly expresses his feelings in the preface. He writes:

> With a few and yet very faulty sources of the history of the Marathas, I am not sure whether I deserve thanks of the German readers for the history of this people outlined in the following pages; whether my work can hope to arrest the attention of the German public, and whether I have not undertaken a work which perhaps lies beyond my powers. This thought and even more the difficulties confronted during the execution of the work, to make up the gaps in the ancient and modern history—a work in which I have been always fortunate—to arrange a few unimportant and incredible fragments which I found in writers of widely diverse merits bearing on my subject or their; to patch up their contradictions and bring the whole comparatively to coherence, would have always impelled me to give up my work notwithstanding the pains, time and money spent over it and to leave the honour of becoming an historian of distinguished but unknown people to research-workers more worthy and more fortunate. Because there is always an unceasing development in the realm of history, to have collected everything available of the known and little known matters, to work up an uncultivated field of history critically, impartially and purposefully is a true gain for the history of the world and further on account of my acquaintance firstly with the history of India, obtained and presented in print, I could not believe to be undertaking a completely futile work. Therefore all the

difficulties explained beforehand and the approval of competent judges of my efforts done hitherto have encouraged rather than discouraged me in this section of history.[8]

This justification and confession of Sprengel is an eloquent testimony to his earnestness in undertaking this task of writing the history of the Marathas. A similar sense of modesty is found in the preface of Grant Duff's *History of the Marathas* as well as in his private correspondence, which will be discussed later. About his own work Sprengel says:

A comparison of this history with an earlier work in the historical portfolio of 1782 will best show how these sources, truly copious but laborious to investigate, have been utilised by me; and whether the history of the Marathas has gained by my investigations and collection of what I have thought, read and collected.[9]

It is really unfortunate that those who wrote on the Marathas, particularly the British historians Scott Waring (1810) and Grant Duff (1826), did not take any cognizance of Sprengel's *History*. About the importance of this German history of the Marathas, Sheelavati Ketkar writes:

The impression one gets on reading this book is that while English writers on the subject had ampler materials, as they had the chance of gathering information on the spot, this writer uses the existing material with greater critical acumen, and that the book is written with that zeal and care which characterises the proverbial German Professor.[10]

Dietmar Rothermund observes that the main feature of Sprengel's History is its objective and detached style. Sprengel used mainly British sources, but he did not narrate the events from a British point of view, nor did he give much prominence to Mughal history, although most of the indigenous sources quoted by the British writers were Mughal sources. Rothermund describes Sprengel as an early precursor of the school of 'autonomous' history, which aims at presenting an independent history of the countries subjected to colonial rule. The advocates of autonomous history have fought valiantly against the old protagonists of colonial history. According to Rothermund: Sprengel's methods may not be up to the mark of modern historiography, but his motivation was certainly as strong as theirs. Sprengel did portray an adequate picture of the political organization of the Marathas, their relations with neighbouring powers, their diplomacy, their military ventures, etc. In short, he did not consider the history of the Marathas as a marginal affair which is of interest only to the extent of their interaction with European powers.[11]

We may agree with Rothermund's assessment of Sprengel's contribution to historical writings on Marathas, when he says:

> As a pioneering venture the book is very impressive indeed. It is his straightforward narrative which is not burdened by gratuitous comment or rhetoric. Sprengel reminds us of Orme whom he greatly admired, but he was better than Orme in his grasp of essential features, leaving out much of the details of battles or intrigues which were of no immediate importance for the further course of events.[12] He considered only such events which were of direct relevance to Maratha history. Sprengel's approach was not that of a specialised historian of the Marathas, but that of a curious, enthusiastic and intelligent observer.

On the whole, while writing his history in a general way Sprengel did not lose sight of historical methodology. While comparing Sprengel with Scott Waring, Rothermund observes:

> In this he showed a better judgement than later writers like Scott Waring who did not provide much more information than Sprengel did although he was able to consult Maratha documents. Scott Waring copied Orme to a large extent and did not have such a good sense of judgement as Sprengel had who always used his sources without getting carried away by their detailed descriptions of minor events.[13]

Sprengel was more interested in acquiring a bird's eye view, outlining the main course of events with a shrewd appraisal of the relative weight and importance to be attached to each event. Rothermund, in his concluding remarks, says, 'Judged by the standards of the time, Sprengel's *History of the Marathas* is a good piece of historical writing and deserves a place of honour in Maratha historiography.'[14]

NOTES

1. Dietmar Rothermund, *The German Intellectual Quest for India*, New Delhi: Manohar, 1986, p. 25.
2. Ibid., p. 25.

3. R.N. Chapekar, Translation of Sprengel's German book into English, a typed copy preserved in the BISM Library, Pune, see Preface.
4. Ibid., Preface.
5. Ibid.
6. Ibid., p. 75.
7. Ibid., p. 81.
8. Ibid., Preface.
9. Ibid.
10. Sheelvati Ketkar, 'History of the Marathas (in German) by Sprengel M.C.', *BISM Quarterly*, vol. 4, no. 1, 1923–4, p. 107.
11. Rothermund, op. cit., p. 25.
12. Ibid., p. 30.
13. Ibid.
14. Ibid.

4

Later British Historians

EDWARD SCOTT WARING

Nineteen years after the publication of Sprengel's history, Edward Scott Waring, a servant of the East India Company working in the Poona Residency Office for a period of about seven years, published his *Maratha History* in 1810 in London.[1] The chief merit of his work is that he uses the available Marathi sources for the first time on a large scale.

Scott Waring's history appears to have been written mainly for a limited circle, mostly the servants of the East India Company, as we find a long list of names of some distinguished persons appended to this book. It is not clear whether there was any literary or other society of which these dignitaries were members. It includes the names of Elphinstone, Thomas Munro, the Raja of Tanjore, etc. The book is dedicated to 'The Chairman, Deputy Chairman and Directors of the Honourable East India Company, the liberal Patron of Oriental literature by their obedient servant, Scott Waring'. As this book did not see a second edition or any reprint after 1810, it may be inferred that Scott Waring wrote this book for private circulation among the members of some society or club, or that it did not gain sufficient popularity, to warrant a reprint or a second edition. He does not seem to be quite confident about his own work, as he writes in the preface:

The bark however is now launched, the sails are loosened, and whether it be buffeted about at the mercy of the waves, or sail securely to its destined haven, I must submit . . . yet I feel anxious to deprecate the judgement of some partial friends, who anticipated more information than I fear they will receive, and whose disappointment therefore will be commensurate with their expectation.[2]

Scott Waring was attracted towards the subject perhaps due to his long stay in Pune, the capital of the Marathas, and his easy access to the source material in that city, which must have helped him to understand the rise and growth of Maratha power. He writes, 'I was attached for seven years to the Embassy of Poona, and of course had greater opportunities of gaining information on many points than usually fall to the lot of other persons'. Besides, he was witness to the decline of Maratha power. He says, '. . . the Mahrattas were once a mighty nation, How they rose, and how they fell, may surely challenge enquiry'.[3]

He begins his history with a long historical sketch of the Deccan running into 52 pages, in which he describes the geography and history of the region before the rise of the Marathas. The second part, which forms the core of this book, consists of seven chapters (pp. 53–189), and deals with the history of the Marathas from Shivaji to the assassination of Peshwa Narayanrao in 1773. Scott Waring does not go beyond that period because he feels that 'the history of the Mahrattas since that period is sufficiently known (as the book was published only in 1810), that all the leading features exist in a variety of publications, and that I could not have written without the *recentibu odiis* or without strong prepossessions'.

The British Residency in that city started functioning in 1786 with the appointment of Sir Charles Malet as the British Resident in the Peshwa's Court in that city. We do not have any biographical details about Scott Waring, but as he claims that he spent seven years in that city, he must have been there some time between 1772 and 1810. The period of active British involvement in Maratha politics began with the appointment of Mostyn as British envoy in 1772, when the Peshwa Madhavrao I was on his deathbed. Scott Waring ends history with the death of Madhavrao in 1772, perhaps with a view to maintaining objectivity as the British had involved themselves directly in the internal politics of the Marathas by supporting the cause of Raghobadada, the uncle of the deceased Peshwa. The last part is an Appendix (pp. 101–279) containing 48 notes giving details of the authorities used by him in support of his statements.

Scott Waring's untiring labour in preparing this history is evident from the exhaustive notes supplied by him in the Appendix. He was not sure whether he could fulfil the expectations of his readers, but at the same time he wrote: 'I must assume the merit of having considered my subject most fully and of having spared no pains to procure every possible record that could add greater interest to my work or justify the favourable opinion of my friends.' Being employed in the Residency at Pune, he had easy access to historical records, particularly Marathi records, to which he attached more importance in his account. But he complains about their 'extreme conciseness' and also of 'their want of those striking incidents which can alone render any history a favourite with the public'. He, therefore, consoles himself with the hope that to the students of Indian history it may not be altogether unacceptable and it will show them 'what the Mahrattas possess upon this subject'. He further says, 'However much I regret the scantiness of my materials and the paucity of striking events I must still congratulate myself that my enquiries have not often led me to consult Persian authorities.'[4]

It is difficult to understand Scott Waring's aversion to Persian sources. It may be due to his lack of adequate proficiency in that language or to his doubts about their credibility. However, a true historian of the Marathas, particularly of their political history, cannot afford to ignore the Persian sources. He may discard them only after convincing himself of their falsity or unreliability. He must have consulted Ferishta, perhaps with the help of a munshi as he considered him 'almost the only historian who merits the praise of impartiality and accuracy. He died before the era of Mahratta independence, and his mantle has not fallen on any of his brethren.[5]

Scott Waring believed that contemporary Muslim historians could not be impartial or objective towards the Marathas. He claimed that they 'view with animosity and anguish the progress the Mahrattas have made in the conquest of their fairest provinces; and which of late years must have been aggravated by the bondage of their king, the unfortunate representative of the house of Timoor'. He, therefore, felt that one could hardly expect anything fair or favourable towards the Maratha character from such historians.

His attack on the Persian sources was in the extreme. He did not approve of their selection of facts and disliked their style. He writes:

The facts that they give are garbled and perverted, while the slightest circumstance against them is seized upon and extended to an immeasurable length. Their style is also a subject of just reprehension. Their forced and unnatural images, their swelling cadences, and modulated phraseology are as disgusting to a discriminating taste as they must be inimical to historical truth. For in a history composed in verse, something will be sacrificed to measure, and much to rhyme. Although the Persian histories be not written in verse, yet they partake of all its faults. They abound in quaint similies and forced antithesis, while the redundancy of their epithets distract and bewilder attention. If this judgement to the Persian scholar seems harsh, I refer him to the history of the late Nizam of the Deccan, or if he objects, to the undisputed master of this prurient style, the celebrated Abul Fazl.[6]

As against this severe assault on the Persian historians, Scott Waring was surprisingly very sympathetic towards the Maratha historians, who were essentially chroniclers, in spite of the fact that there was growing animosity between the Marathas and the English even during the period when he was writing his history. He was full of praise for the plain, simple, and unaffected style of the Maratha historians, although some people would not consider them historians. Perhaps he was referring here to the Marathi *bakhars* or chronicles. A characteristic feature of Maratha historical writing, according to Scott Waring, was that 'victory and defeat are briefly related; if they pass over the latter too hastily, they do not dwell upon the former with unnecessary minuteness. They do not endeavour to bias or mislead the judgement, but are certainly greatly deficient in chronology and in historical reflection.'[7]

Scott Waring has drawn upon the Marathi chronicles to a great extent, but could not state with certainty that he had done full justice to them as he was aware of his 'own incompetency and his ignorance of the deficiency' of his material. However, he is happy that he was the 'first to present the reader with a connected history of the Mahrattas, derived from original sources, and sources till lately not known to have existed'.

He knew that some parts of Maratha history had been published, but none of them were 'derived from their own annals and consequently neither of them is so copious nor so authentic'. Obviously, he was referring to the histories of Orme and Kerr. He was not aware of Sprengel's *History*, which had appeared much before his own *History*. Perhaps being in German, it was not available to either Scott Waring or Grant Duff, who were then in India busy with their own historical writings. So both of them could claim that they were the first to undertake the study of the history of the Marathas. To be the first in a particular field is certainly a matter of pride, and Grant Duff, who wrote the complete history of the Marathas, also confessed to the same feeling later.

Scott Waring divided the history of the Marathas proper into seven chapters in Part II of his book. He traces the etymology of the word Maratha and the origins of Shivaji. Whenever a reference has been made to a Marathi manuscript, it invariably means a Marathi *bakhar*. Scott Waring mentions how the goddess Bhavani revealed the concealed treasure to Maloji, how the marriage between Shahaji and Jijabai took place, and how Shivaji was born at Shivneri in 1626–7. From this description it is quite clear that he must have secured some *bakhars* and simply rendered them into English. But which *bakhars* were likely to be available to him before 1810? From the available data about the period of the *bakhars*, one can say that the *bakhars* he consulted were possibly those of *Sabhasad* (1697), *Chitragupta* (1759), and *91 Qalmi bakhar* (1780).

In his Appendix, Scott Waring mentions that for the Shivaji and Sambhaji periods, he consulted four 'Mahratta histories', i.e. *bakhars*, out of which one was kept at Rairi, i.e. Raigad, and, according to him, that was more authentic than the others. The *Rairi bakhar* is also known as *91 Qalmi* (articles) *bakhar* which was compiled by Dattaji Trimal Waqnavis of Shivaji's times, between 1685 and 1713. This manuscript was translated into English by Frissel in 1806 and was published in Forrest's Selections from *Bombay Archives - Maratha Series*, vol. I (1885). But the original Marathi manuscript was lost and what we get at present is a copy prepared by Khando Ballal Malkare in the eighteenth century. The *bakhar* has been edited and published by three eminent scholars in historical journals, namely D.B. Parasnis in the *Bharatvarsha*, V.K. Rajwade in the *Prabhat* and K.N. Sane in the *Kavyetihas Samgraha*. Its Persian version *Tarik-i-Shivaji,* preserved in the British Museum and India Office Library, London, was rendered into English by Jadunath Sarkar and published in *Modern Review* in 1907. We find some articles missing in each edition. V.S. Wakaskar, a Maratha scholar from Baroda, published all its versions together in 1930 under the title *91 Qalmi Bakhar.*

From the early account of Shivaji and particularly of his birth, it is quite obvious that Scott Waring consulted mainly this *91 Qalmi bakhar* and simply rendered it into English. Perhaps he had secured a copy of Frissel's translation of 1806.

The account of Shivaji's coronation is mainly based on the travelogue of John Fryer. In a footnote he says, 'See an excellent account of Sevajee's coronation in Fryer who received it from an eyewitness Mr Oxenden. Fryer is the only contemporary traveller with Sevajee whose account of the Mahrattas is in any way authentic.' This statement of Scott Waring may be true as far as the coronation is concerned, but at times we find him relying on hearsay accounts, particularly about the administration of Shivaji. Scott Waring has also quoted Orme quite often in his *History*. In addition to the political history of the Shivaji period, Scott Waring also discusses the form of Maratha government, the military system, religion, etc. As regards the death of Shivaji, he writes in one of his notes (no. 21)[8] that Persian manuscripts attribute it to the prayers of a Muslim devotee, and a Marathi *bakhar* to Shivaji's wife. (p. 215).

About the character of the Marathas based on his study of history and the observations of Monsieur Anquetel du Perron, Scott Waring writes:

> The Mahrattas are a hardy, brave and active people, short but well made, and industrious and peaceable subjects . . . the Mahrattas, though rude, are cunning, independent yet mean, brave still treacherous, and without the polish, still possessing the vices of the most refined courtier.[9]

Scott Waring did not neglect the cultural aspect of Maratha history. He devoted about ten pages to describing the language, customs, and festivals like Dasara, for which he drew material from a manuscript called *Vrata Raj* or 'Royal Duties' preserved in the library of the Peshwas. He also consulted another work called *Rajkosh*. About these two books he writes in his notes that they are in the Sanskrit language and were obtained from the Peshwa's library and read with his kind friend, Mr Goware, perhaps a Sanskrit pandit from Poona. He gives further details about *Vrata Raj*, which was composed in Sanskrit at Banaras by Vishwanath Bhatt 'of the tribe of Chitpawan (or inhabitants of the Konkan) in the year Vickramajeet 1658 or AD 1602'. This book is designed to show the religious duties imposed on a monarch during each day in the year and the relation such duties hold with their temporal prosperity.'[10]

The *Rajkosh* was an account in which 'the Yavana or Mooslim terms are subjoined to the Sanskrit offices'. This *Kosh* can be identified with the famous *Rajvyavahar Kosh* of Raghunath Hanmante composed at the instance of Shivaji at the time of his coronation.

For the period of Sambhaji, particularly regarding the account of his arrest and his dialogue with Aurangzeb concerning marriage with his daughter, Scott Waring relies on Orme's *Fragments*. But the subsequent period covering Rajaram, Tarabai, and the Maratha War of Independence has been hurriedly dealt with, for he could not get authentic material on this period, nor could he draw from Orme whose history closes with the death of Sambhaji. Even for the period from the arrival of Shahu in 1707 to the year 1760, his treatment of the subject is very sketchy. He had secured two *bakhars* of Chhatrapati Shahu that covered the history of the first three Peshwas. One of these seems to be the *bakhar* compiled by Govindrao Khanderao Chitnis between 1742 and 1782. It begins with a brief account of Sambhaji and Rajaram and later deals with the career of Shahu up to his death. The other *bakhar* mentioned by him cannot be identified. Perhaps it was a copy of the same. This *bakhar* seems to have been begun in 1742 and completed in 1782. Scott Waring is perhaps referring to these two *bakhars* of Shahu written at different dates. He mentions also the *bakhars* written on the 'unfortunate expedition to Hindoostan, which ended in the battle of Panipat; one of these is written by the great Malharrao Holkar addressed to the Peshwa'. This seems to be *Holkarachi Thaili* or *Malharrao Holkarachi Thaili* written in 1762–3, which mainly represents the case of Malharrao Holkar who had fled from the battlefield of Panipat in 1761. As against this, the *Bhausahebachi bakhar* represents the case of the Shindes who fought vigorously till the end.

The *bakhars* dealing with this event are mainly *Holkaranchi Thaili* (1762–3), *Nana Phadnisache Atmacharitra*, *Bhausahebanchi bakhar* (1762–3), and *Shrimant Bhausaheb anchi Kaifiyat* (1762–3). As these *bakhars* were compiled before the publication of *History*, it may be presumed that when he refers to Marathi manuscripts in support of his account of Panipat, it may be one of the *bakhars* mentioned above. A reference has also been made to an article published in the *Asiatic Researches*, vol. III of the year 1799. This article is nothing but the translation of the Persian account of the Battle of Panipat and of the events leading to it by Kashiraj Pandit, an eyewitness to the event. In the context of Panipat, he quotes, for the first time, a letter from Malharrao Holkar, who wrote pressing letters to the Jats requesting them to join him against their common enemy, i.e. the Abdali.[11] The last chapter briefly narrates the history of Madhavrao and the assassination of Narayanrao Peshwa. For this, Scott Waring says that he consulted two manuscripts of Madhavrao and Narayanrao each, a Maratha account of the Raja of Berar, the Gaikwads, and the Shinde and the Holkar families. Perhaps he is referring to the *Karinas* or *Hakikats* or *Kaifiyats* of these Maratha sardars preserved in the library of the Peshwa.

He divides his authorities into two categories. The first includes the published works of historians, and the second, as he puts it, 'such authorities as I believe are exclusively my own'.

The first category includes the works of Robert Orme, Captain Jonathan Scott's translation of Ferishta, Col. Dow's *History of the Mahrattas*, which he says is scanty, imperfect, and incorrect, Howell's account which he considers barren, Major Rennell's *Memoirs*, being a sketch of the Marathas, John Crawford's short account of the Marathas, and the accounts of Kerr, Tone, Elias Habesci, a traveller, and others.

William Henry Tone, an Irishman who entered Maratha service in 1792–6 in Poona, has been referred to by both Scott Waring and Grant Duff for his pamphlet, *Some Institutions of the Mahratta People*. He was killed in 1802 in action near Maheshwar while serving the Holkar.[12] Scott Waring gives some additional information about Tone in the Appendix to his book. He writes that Tone published at Bombay some letters on the state of the Marathas addressed to Col. Malcolm. These letters, according to Scott Waring, contain some valuable information on the present state and the manners of the Marathas. (Perhaps these letters were later published in book form under the title *Some Institutions of the Marathas*.) Tone was an officer in the service of Shinde, the *bais* (ladies) of Shinde, and Holkar, and had he possessed sufficient knowledge of the Eastern languages, few persons would have been better qualified to have written the history of the Marathas.[13]

In the second category Scott Waring includes original unpublished source material from Persian as well as Marathi and Sanskrit. A reference has already been made to the Marathi sources consulted by him. Among the Persian sources consulted, he first mentions Syed Ghulam Husain Khan Tabataba's Persian history *Siyar-ul-Mutakherin* (View of Modern Times), which describes the history of India between AD 1707 and 1780, to which the 'the author has added a critical examination of the English Government and policy in those countries, as far down as the year 1780'. Written in 1780 as a contemporary source, *Siyar* has its own importance. The author Syed Ghulam Husain was an Indian nobleman of high rank, who wrote both as 'actor and spectator'. His study contains an account in general of the reigns of the last seven Mughal emperors of India and the details of the rise and fall of the families of Siraj-ud-Daula and Shuja-ud-Daula, the last nawabs of Bengal and Avadh, in particular.

Siyar first attracted the attention of Warren Hastings (1772–85), who got it translated into English by M. Raymond, a French renegade who had assumed the name of Hajee Mustafa. He translated the manuscript in three volumes under the pseudonym *Mota Manus*. It was subsequently translated once again by John Briggs. Scott Waring says that 'his English is bad, but the work contains most useful information with a tolerable sketch of Maratha History'.

The preface claims that it is written in the most charming style, embracing the century immediately preceding the final assumption of the sovereignty of India by the British Crown. From the point of view of Indian historiography of the medieval period, Prof. R.C. Majumdar writes, 'This book may be regarded as the latest and at the same time the best history of India written by an Indian before the modern historiography made its influence felt in this country. History, in his opinion, gives us a glimpse into the most glorious part of the creator's performance.'[14] All foreign and Indian historians writing partly or fully on Maratha history have consulted this work.

Besides *Siyar*, Scott Waring also consulted a Persian history of the Marathas written in 1786 by Ali Ibrahim Khan, a judge of Benaras, Khafi Khan's *Muntakhab-ul-Lubab* (1735), anecdotes of the Southern Court by a Muslim observer in the year 1781–2, *Life of Nizam Ali Khan* in Persian translated by Hollingberry (a work written at the court under the patronage of the prince, full of the most palpable falsehoods), Aurangzeb's operations in the Deccan, i.e. *Nuskha-i-Dilkasha,* written by a Bundela chief (Bhimsen Burhanpuri), and two Persian letters of Aurangzeb, one to Azam Shah and the other to Kambaksha.

In the Appendix Scott Waring presents a statement on the six subas of the Deccan made out from Maratha records shortly after the campaign of Cornwallis. It resembles the one that Parasnis has published in vol. X of his *Bharatvarsha* under the title *Subhe Dakshan va Hindusthancha Zada* of the Shahu period. Scott Waring must have found this document in the Peshwa's library.[15]

This brief review of the contents and the sources consulted by Scott Waring for his history of the Marathas reveals the amount of labour involved in the production of this work. But in spite of this labour, Scott Waring's *History* did not attract much public attention. Grant Duff's *History*, although not much known during his lifetime, became the standard work on Maratha history for almost a century. It became controversial when Maratha scholars started exposing the shortcomings in his *History* late in the nineteenth century. Such attention was never paid to Scott Waring's *History*, and scholars both European and Indian did not take this work seriously. Thus, it possesses value only as a step in the historiography of the Marathas though its intrinsic value cannot be underestimated. In 'Maratha Historical Literature', a paper presented to the History section of the Bombay Branch of the Royal Asiatic Society in 1905, Parasnis sums up Scott Waring's contribution as a historiographer: 'Scott Waring treats his materials with great discrimination and impartiality, and his work stands preeminent as the first attempt to deal with Maratha history in a spirit of justice and fairness.'[16]

James Mill (1773–1836)

James Mill did not contribute anything special to Maratha history as such, but as his was the first comprehensive history of India written by a Briton, and as it continued to influence British administrators in India for a fairly long time, it would be worthwhile to examine his views on Indians in general and Marathas in particular.

James Mill was the first British historian to offer a comprehensive treatment of Indian history. It was he who for the first time made a formal division of Indian history into Hindu, Muslim, and British periods. His chief interest being in the study of civilization, he devoted only 'cursory attention' to the political history of India.

He started working on Indian history in 1806 without having any first-hand or long-term acquaintance with India or her languages. When challenged about his knowledge of

India or his qualification to undertake such a gigantic task, he said, 'A man who is duly qualified may obtain more knowledge of India, in one year, in his closet in England, than he could obtain during the course of the longest life, by the use of his eyes and his ears in India.'[17] He added further that the essential qualification for the historian of British India was a most profound knowledge of the 'laws of human nature', of the 'principles of human society', and a comprehension of the practical play of the machinery of government, and stated that these insights could be acquired only in Europe. According to him, Hindu society at its peak had managed to rise only a short distance above the level of barbarism.[18]

If this was the attitude of Mill towards Hindu society, one could hardly expect anything in detail or of value on the Marathas from him. In fact, when he had started working on his *History*, the only major power left in India were the Marathas with whom the British had to struggle for supremacy over India. Mill based his account of the Marathas mainly on secondary sources as he was not interested in giving a detailed account of the history of medieval India.[19] His statements, therefore, are not supported by authentic historical evidence.

After tracing the history of the Bhonsale family of Shivaji in about ten pages, he concluded the history of the founder of Maratha power by saying, 'Sevagee breathed his last in his fortress of Rayree on 5th April 1682 of an inflammation in his chest, at the early age of 52, having displayed a fertility of invention, adapted his ends, and a firmness of mind in the pursuit of them which have seldom been equaled, probably never surpassed.'[20] The most glorious period in the history of the Marathas, from the death of Shivaji to the death of Aurangzeb in 1707, during which the Marathas heroically resisted the imperial army has been disposed of in six or seven pages. The Third Battle of Panipat (1761) has been very hurriedly mentioned, the treatment of the First Anglo-Maratha War in which the British were defeated was very casual, whereas the Second Anglo-Maratha War, in which the British fought with the Shindes and the Holkars and finally imposed the subsidiary alliance on the Marathas, has been elaborately treated in the last volume. Commenting on the shortcomings of Mill's *History*, Grant Duff wrote to Elphinstone on 21 January 1822, that the work displayed 'an inclination to find fault when he does not fully understand, a total want of genius, and the want of an Indian spirit or the knowledge of what pervades over public services generally'.[21]

Vishnushastri Chiplunkar, in his essay on *History* written in 1874–5, after making remarks about the equipment of Mill for writing the *History of India*, observes that if the English reading public formed a low opinion about Indians and their civilization, one could hardly blame them, i.e. the readers.[22]

In his critical assessment of Mill's *History*, one of our leading historians, R.C. Majumdar, observes that Mill had supreme contempt for the early Indologists and European travellers who praised Indian civilization. He further says, 'It would be difficult to name another book written by one possessing eminent qualifications as a historian, in which so much prodigious labour has been misdirected to produce a historical work which by any canon of criticism does not deserve the name.'[23]

Mill's *History* has, however, been praised by Lord Macaulay as 'the greatest historical work which has appeared in our language since that of Gibbon'.[24] It was first published in 1817 and reprinted in 1820, 1826 and 1840.

It is quite obvious that a work based mainly on secondary sources, unsupported by first-hand knowledge of the civilization and languages of India, and lacking actual experience of Indian life and conditions on the part of the author, could hardly provide a satisfactory account of the Marathas, who were the predecessors of the British in India.

Mill received praise for his monumental *History* in the early days from persons such as Macaulay, Ricardo, and Bentham. Individuals like Elphinstone, and Grant Duff who had lived in India did not openly criticize Mill's *History*, perhaps due to his position in the East India Company. Macaulay, who had compared Mill's work with that of Gibbon, was disillusioned after his visit to India and modified his opinion of Mill: 'Mr Mill's book, though it has undoubtedly great and rare merit, is not sufficiently animated and picturesque to attract those who read for amusement.'[25] Elphinstone's work, although it was superior to Mill's study as the treatment of the Hindu and Muslim parts was concerned, did not succeed altogether in erasing the impressions about Hindu civilization created by Mill. To add to this, Elliot and Dowson, through their monumental series in eight volumes, *History of India as told by its own Historians*, covering the period of 600 years, from the eleventh to the seventeenth centuries, demolished the reputation of greatness of the Muslim rulers, and thus the total impact of Mill and Elliot resulted in 'pushing into the background the more sober, more sympathetic and objective interpretation of Elphinstone'.[26]

NOTES

1. Scott Waring, *History of the Mahrattas, to which is prefixed a historical sketch of the Deccan containing a short account of the Rise and Fall of the Mosslim Sovereignties prior to the era of Mahratta Independence*, London: John Richardson, Royal Exchange, 1810.
2. An attempt to compile the history of the Marathas, it seems, was made by Sir Charles Malet, the Resident at the Court of Poona, as a reference is found to in the Fort William India House Correspondence, vol. 17, but the full MS is not traceable and it was never published. So the first published work bearing the title *Maratha History* was that of Scott Waring, published from London in 1810. See also Scott Waring's Preface.
3. Scott Waring, op. cit., Preface, p. viii.
4. Ibid., p. viii.
5. Ibid., p. viii.
6. Ibid., p. ix.
7. Ibid., p. x.
8. He refers to one Marathi MS that attributes Shivaji's death to Soyarabai (no. 21). But the *bakhar* that he consulted most extensively, i.e. the Rairi *bakhar*, does not mention it. In another note (no. 22), he mentions the articles possessed by Shivaji at the time of his death—which included grains, clothes, arms, metals, coins, etc. It is obvious from this that he knew of the Sabhasad *bakhar*, and that his account of the legacy of Shivaji is based on it.
9. Scott Waring, op. cit., pp. 104–5. Also no. 17, Appendix.
10. Ibid., pp. 100–9; n. 20, p. 214.
11. Scott Waring, op. cit., p. 155.
12. *The Dictionary of National Biography*, p. 95.
13. Scott Waring, op. cit., p. 193.
14. R.C. Majumdar, *Historiography in Modern India*, Bombay: OUP, 1970, p. 5.

15. Scott Waring, op. cit., nn. 38–9, pp. 237–71.
16. *JBRAS*, vol. 22, 1904–7, p. 170.
17. James Mill, *The History of British India*, vol. I, p. xv, London, 1817. See also Vishnushastri Chiplunkar, *Nibandhamala*, New Edition, Pune: Chitrashala, 1917, pp. 92–3.
    See also J.S. Grewal, *Muslim Rule in India*, New Delhi: Oxford University Press, 1970, pp. 64–97.
18. William J. Barber, *British Economic Thought and India 1600–1838*, Oxford: OUP, 1975, p. 128.
19. Grewal writes, '. . . he attempted to give a summary of the works of Alexander Dow, Jonathan Scott, Francis, William Franklin, Robert Orme, and Ghulam Hussain', op. cit., p. 90.
20. Mill, op. cit., vol. II, p. 358.
21. MSS EUR, F 88, Grant Duff to Mountstuart Elphinstone, 21 January 1822.
22. Chiplunkar, op. cit., p. 93.
23. Majumdar, op. cit., p. 14.
24. C.H. Philips, *Historians of India, Pakistan and Ceylon*, Oxford: OUP, 1961, p. 219.
25. Ibid., p. 224.
26. Ibid., p. 226, 'Grewal, however, writes, "The timely appearance of Elphinstone's, *History of India* in 1841 proved to be a decisive blow to Mill's pretensions to be a sound historian of Muslim India"', op. cit., p. 97.

5

Mountstuart Elphinstone

Mountstuart Elphinstone did not write the history of the Marathas, but influenced its writing. He arrived in India in 1796, the year in which Bajirao II assumed the robes of the Peshwaship. He was associated with the Maratha country and people for nearly a quarter of a century. He stepped into the land of the Marathas at the turn of the nineteenth century as assistant to the British Resident at the Peshwa's court in Pune, and remained in this region till his final retirement from the Company's service in 1827, interrupted in 1808 for a couple of years when he led the British Mission to Kabul. When he came to Pune, the Maratha power was crumbling, and he not only presided over its liquidation, but also achieved the settlement of the territories conquered from the Peshwas.

His long association with the Maratha country and its people had a profound influence on him as can be seen from the notes in his diary made in 1816. He writes, 'It struck me this, in talking after breakfast about the revolutions in Poona, that an interesting history might be produced which is rapidly passing away.'

However, his preoccupation with heavy administrative duties led him to defer this thought. He writes, 'To remedy this (i.e. uneasiness arising after retirement), I have thought of writing a Maratha history, or a history of the fall of the Mughal empire and the rise of ours.'[1]

He did carry out his plan, but instead of a Maratha history, he produced a book on the history of Hindu and Muslim India in 1841, covering a vast period of Indian history from the earliest times to the Third Battle of Panipat in 1761. It was praised as a great work for which he was acclaimed as the Tacitus of modern India.[2] His esteemed friend, Sir T.E. Colebrooke, published a posthumous volume of Elphinstone's history, *The Rise of the British Power in the East* (1887), which was based on his notes and journals. It is true that he could not dislodge James Mill, who published his *History of India* in 1817 and which was reprinted twice before Elphinstone's book came out, and continued to remain in the public mind even after the publication of Elphinstone's study. Mill's *History* was essentially a plea for the continuance of British rule in India. Elphinstone, like other contemporary historians such as Grant Duff, James Tod, and John Malcolm, took a sympathetic view of Indian society and people and did not indulge much, like the Utilitarians, in condemning their Hindu or Muslim predecessors.[3] The British were writing histories with a view to knowing the people whom they were destined to rule. It was essentially a search for the vital elements in the social, economic, and political structure of the country that could be adapted by the new rulers so as to carry on the existing system without unnecessary 'innovations'. Elphinstone was clear in his mind about the future of British rule in India. He wrote to his friend Sir James Mackintosh, 'I am afraid the belief that our Indian Empire will not be long-lived is reason and not prejudice. It is difficult to guess the death it may die; but if it escapes the Russians and other foreign attacks, I think, the seeds of its ruin will be found in the native army, a delicate and dangerous machine, which a little mismanagement may easily turn against us.'[4]

Elphinstone admitted that Mill's *History* was 'masterly' yet 'misguided', 'setting out to revolutionise India on abstract principles. . . with characteristic under-emphasis'. After reading it when it first appeared, he said that the ingenious original and elaborate work of Mr J.S. Mill left 'some room for doubt and discussion'. He further stated that 'the excellence of histories derived from European researches alone does not entirely set aside the utility of similar enquiries conducted under the guidance of impressions received in India, which, as they arise from a separate source, may sometimes lead to different conclusions'.[5] He had a good grasp of the overall development of Indian history and the difficulties involved in presenting it to the European reader, who was not likely to evince any interest in India's antiquity. He observes, 'To write India's early and medieval history would require great knowledge and a very philosophical and reflecting mind. If suitably executed, it would be a most important work.'[6]

With a view to emphasizing its importance to European readers, Elphinstone suggests, 'It must be made up by connecting with the general history of the species, and this requires a thorough knowledge of the principles of human action. The style also must be condensed and animated, and the reflections striking and profound.'[7]

This sums up Elphinstone's framework of research methodology and his attitude towards Indian history. It is clear from his correspondence with Captain James Grant Duff, that he had given much thought to the nature and scope of Maratha history, the authenticity of Persian, Marathi and other sources, and the places from which the source material could be obtained. But as he was too busy with administrative duties, he could not find the necessary leisure to write a history of the Marathas. He, therefore, encouraged others like Grant Duff, Tod, Erskine, and Briggs to write histories or translate historical works into English.

The brief sketch of Maratha history that he incorporated in to his monumental *Report on the Territories Conquered from the Peshwas*, submitted in 1819, shows not only his acquaintance with but also his mastery over the details of Maratha history.[8] Of course, the picture of Maratha history in 1819 was hazy and hence there are some factual mistakes in his 'hasty view of the history of the Marathas'.[9]

Elphinstone had developed a great fascination for the Marathas, particularly after 1810 when he joined the Residency at Pune. In 1814, he wrote to his friend Edward Strachey in London that he would continue to collect material and write it (that is, his Maratha history) during his old age.[10] However, he did not disclose his intention of writing a history of the

Marathas till the middle of 1819. He was preparing the ground for it, as can be seen from the instructions given to James Grant Duff, the Political Agent at Satara, that he should collect documents of historical significance from the areas under his charge. But Grant Duff could not attend to this task till the middle of 1819 because of the heavy duties of his new job. He was very apologetic that he could not comply with his master's demand for old letters or records.[11] When, however, Grant Duff succeeded in collecting a number of old documents of historical significance, he was greatly impressed by the information therein and thought of putting it together and presenting a connected account of the Marathas.[12] He was aware of his limitations for undertaking such an arduous task and was not quite sure about the reaction of Elphinstone to his 'floating idea' of writing a history of the Marathas. Grant Duff's letter of 19 July 1819 reminded Elphinstone of his cherished but deferred idea of writing a history of the Marathas. Elphinstone was, however, delighted to learn that somebody else was coming forward to give shape to his ideas, and without pausing a moment to review the qualifications of Grant Duff for such a stupendous and complicated task, he wrote back to him instantly by return of post, 'I am delighted with your progress in historical collection, and still more with your intention of putting them in order. I certainly advise you most earnestly to do so.'[13] With Elphistone's blessings and later with his guidance and help at every stage, Grant Duff completed his history of the Marathas before he left Satara in January 1823, and published it in England in 1826. However, while preparing the draft of his history, Grant Duff constantly felt that Elphinstone was the proper person to do justice to such an undertaking. He wrote to Charles Grant, a friend, in 1821, that Elphinstone had at one time an idea of writing a Maratha history and lamented that it was a pity that official business had interfered and prevented him from even arranging and initiating his plans.[14]

Vishnushastri Chiplunkar, while commenting on Grant Duff's *History of Mahrattas* as well as the works of other British historians such as Robert Orme, James Mill, John Malcolm, Meadows Taylor writing on Indian history, expressed his regret that an intelligent and wise person like Elphinstone, who had earned the love and respect of the people of Maharashtra and had the best knowledge of this country, did not himself apply his mind, like Colonel Tod, to writing the history of the Marathas.[15]

Elphinstone not only encouraged Grant Duff to write a history of the Marathas, but also got himself involved in giving shape to it. In 1818, Maratha history was a closed chapter. It was, therefore, possible for a historian to view it as a whole, and so he could impress upon the mind of Grant Duff that 'the wholeness of your subject is one of its greatest beauties'. He had visualized the nature and scope of Maratha history. In this respect he writes, 'It would embrace the downfall of the Mughal empire and the rise of our own as well as that, which is its professed object to treat. It must be well thought over and told.'[16]

This means that Elphinstone, like James Mill and other Britons, had visualized the history of the Marathas only in the context of the Mughal and British periods of Indian History, and not as the history of an independent people from whom the British had wrested power. Grant Duff's *History of the Mahrattas* (1826), however, which was compiled under Elphinstone's supervision and sent to the press only after his approval, accorded an independent status to the Marathas. But Elphinstone, whose history of India was published in 1841, did not modify or change his views about the status of the Marathas in Indian history.

He devoted the last two books, i.e. XI and XII (pages 603–753) of his *History* to Aurangzeb and the successors of Aurangzeb respectively. Out of these 150 pages, he devoted about fifty pages to discussing the activities of the Marathas during the period of Aurangzeb and his successors up to the Third Battle of Panipat in 1761. For this purpose, he drew widely on Grant Duff, though he often referred to the authority of Khafi Khan.[17] Grant Duff also drew heavily on Khafi Khan for reconstructing the early history of the Marathas.

While tracing the early history of the Marathas, Elphinstone laments that 'the early Mahometan writers do not seem to have been aware of the Marathas . . . the word Maratha first occurs in Ferishta in the transactions of the year AD 1485 and is not then applied in a general sense.'[18] Elphinstone, however, has used the term 'Maratha nation' in connection with Shahaji's son, whose family were afterwards to play an important part as the founders of the Maratha nation.[19]

Elphinstone begins his account of the Marathas with a description of the Maratha country and people. He defined Maharashtra as a country 'lying between the range of mountains which stretches along the south of the Narmada, parallel to the Vindhya chain, and a line drawn from Goa, on the sea-coast through Bidar to Chanda, onwards. That river is its boundary on the east, as the sea is on the west.'[20] In his account of the Maratha nation, he writes, 'Though the Marathas had never appeared in history as a nation, they had as strongly marked a character as if they had always formed a united commonwealth.'[21] He describes the physical features and the character of the Marathas and compares them with those of their contemporaries, the Rajputs. His long stay in India, from 1796 to 1827, and that too during the most formative period of his life, enabled him to form an accurate assessment of the Maratha people, which Grant Duff was unable to achieve, in his lengthy opening chapter entitled 'Preliminary observations, etc.'[22]

While comparing the Marathas and the Rajputs, Elphinstone writes:

> They (the Marathas) are small sturdy men, well made, though not handsome. They are all laborious, hardy and persevering. If they have none of the pride and dignity of the Rajputs, they have none of their indolence or their want of worldly wisdom . . . A Maratha thinks of nothing but the result, and cares little for the means if he can attain his object. For this purpose he will strain his wits, renounce his pleasures, and hazard his person; but he was not a conception of sacrificing his life, or even his interest, for a point of honour.[23]

However, Elphinstone makes it clear that his analysis of the Maratha character applies chiefly to the soldiery to whom more bad qualities might fairly be ascribed. The ryots according to him, were 'sober, frugal and industrious, and, though they have a dash of the national cunning, are neither turbulent nor insincere'.[24]

It seems that Elphinstone was aware of the controversy regarding the Rajput origins of the Marathas to which Grant Duff has not referred to at all. In this respect, he writes, 'If any Maratha had a claim to Rajput descent, it was the family of Jadu (i.e. Jadhav). The name is that of one of the Rajput tribes; it was borne at the first Mohometan invasion by the Raja of Deogiri, the greatest prince in the Deckan; and it is not improbable that the protector of Maloji (who was deshmukh of a district not far from Deogiri) may have been descended from that stock.'[25]

He narrates in detail the early activities of Shivaji (born in May 1627), based mainly on Grant Duff. He agrees with Grant Duff about the difficulty in accounting for and tracing the early rise of Shivaji, and the 'astonishing rapidity with which he extended his power'. He confesses that his account of Shivaji is a mere abstract of Grant Duff's volume, whose clear and animated account of Shivaji he had inserted into his own text (i.e. Elphinstone's *History*).[26] As he did not have enough time to verify all the facts and as there was a paucity of original materials, he falls into serious errors. For instance, he writes on the authority of Grant Duff that Shahaji remained for years a prisoner in Bijapur. In fact, Shahaji was arrested on 25 July 1648 and released on 16 May 1649, after securing the necessary assurances from Shivaji.[27] Elphinstone gives the details of the Afzal Khan episode and charges Shivaji with Khan's assassination, but at the same time says that 'during his whole career . . . Shivaji was never personally guilty of any useless cruelty'.[28]

Elphinstone condemns *bakhars* and *tawareekhs* as 'gossiping' and 'gasconading' accounts respectively. But in his account of Shivaji's escape from Agra, one can clearly see that he drew upon the Marathi chronicles, mainly the accounts of Shivaji by Sabhasad and Chitnis and also of Khafi Khan, perhaps due to his entire reliance on Grant Duff. He also praises the military and civil administration of Shivaji, and says that 'the most minute attention to economy pervaded every department of his service'.[29]

By citing examples from history, he explains how Aurangzeb's bigotry created general disaffection among the Rajputs, and how 'every Hindu in the Deccan became at heart a partisan of the Marathas'.[30] Such interpretation of historical facts is lacking in Grant Duff's account of the hostility of the Marathas towards the Mughals. Elphinstone could visualize the history of India as a whole, and then determine the role of the Marathas in its shaping.

After narrating briefly but accurately the achievements of Shivaji up to 1674, Elphinstone discusses the motives behind his coronation, and gives an account of it based on Henry Oxenden's report. Shivaji did not survive long after his coronation and died after a brief illness on 5 April 1680. Elphinstone gives a very balanced and objective account of Shivaji's character in one small but very effective paragraph, which may be compared with the lengthy estimate of Shivaji given by Grant Duff. He writes:

> Though the son of a powerful chief, he had begun life as a daring and artful captain of banditti, had ripened into a skilful general and an able statesman, and left a character which has never since been equalled or approached by any of his countrymen. The distracted state of the neighbouring countries presented openings by which an inferior leader might have profited, but it required a genius like his to avail himself as he did of the mistakes of Aurangzeb, by kindling a zeal for religion and, through that a national spirit among the Marathas.[31]

Elphinstone's account of Sambhaji was based mainly on the *bakhars* and also on Orme's *Fragments*. He gives a spirited account of the heroic resistance of the Marathas to the imperial forces for nearly a quarter of a century. Compared to his brief analysis, Grant Duff's one full chapter on this topic appears to be quite insipid.[32] He writes, 'Strong as was the animosity of the Marathas, their chance of resistance appeared to be very small . . . without the pervading genius of Shivaji, the Marathas would never have been formed into a nation; but now, when all were animated by one spirit, the nature of the people, and their mode of war, required that it should be left to operate by individual exertions.' The plan best adapted to them was

> to bend before a blow, to offer nothing tangible for the enemy to attack, and to return to the charge with undiminished vigour whenever it suited them to take the part of assailants. . . . The armies of Santaji and Dhanaji,

though under the control of those chiefs, acted much on the same system (i.e. to enrich themselves at the expense of the Mogul's subjects) the Marathas spread, at once, in all directions, and the whole Deckan was filled with fire and rapine, terror and confusion.[33]

In this connection Elphinstone's letter to Grant Duff regarding the exploits of Santaji and Dhanaji is a very significant one.[34] (It will be discussed in more detail in the section on Grant Duff.) As Grant Duff could not follow the suggestion of his master, his account of the most glorious period of Maratha history is dry and indifferent. He gives a fine analysis of the Maratha success against the Mughals. The pomp of the emperor's camp equipage, the total relaxation of discipline, and the grossest abuses that had crept into the military department of the Mughals have been compared with the simplicity of the Maratha camp and the Marathas, 'the little active men, accustomed to hard work and hard fare'. He writes, 'Their usual food was a cake of millet with perhaps an onion; their dress a small turban, tight breeches covering their thighs, and a scarf or sash rolled round their middle. When their body was not bare, it was covered by a light cotton tunic.'[35]

Elphinstone has rightly pointed out that dissensions among the Marathas ultimately led to the murder of that 'dazzling star', Santaji Ghorpade, and set off the process of the decline of Maratha power. While appreciating the Maratha efforts, he did not forget to praise the efforts of Aurangzeb, who, in his declining years when he faced difficulties, misfortunes and discouragement nevertheless, retained his vigour, and alone conducted every branch of his government in the most minute detail.[36] Elphinstone gives us a fine portrait of Aurangzeb and tells us how he surmounted all difficulties and fought against the Marathas till his death in 1707. He writes, 'The impassable streams, the flooded valleys, the miry bottoms, and narrow ways caused still greater difficulties when he was in motion, compelled him to halt where no provisions were to be had, and were so destructive to his cattle as sometimes entirely to cripple his army.'[37]

One could hardly find elsewhere than in Elphinstone's *History* a better and more appreciative account of Maratha tactics and strategy, based on the Bundela Narrative (as given in Scott Waring's *History of the Deccan*), by which the grand army of the Mughals was hard-pressed. He writes:

> At times they plundered up to the very skirts of the camp, intercepted the supplies, carried off the cattle, cut up the foragers, insulted the pickets, and made it impossible for anyone to show his head out of the lines without a powerful escort. If any ordinary detachment was sent to check them, they repelled or destroyed it. If a great effort was made, they vanished; and perhaps did not appear till they had plundered some distant town, and left time for their pursuers to weary themselves by forced marches in a wrong direction. They now treated the power of the emperor with derision.[38]

Such descriptions of the movements of the Marathas are also found in the Marathi chronicles and records.

After a careful study of the 'hundreds of letters of Aurangzeb' and a French traveller Gemelli Careri's (1651–1725) personal observations, Elphinstone concludes, 'With all his bigotry, he was not superstitious, . . . of all the kings of India, Aurangzeb is the most admired among the Mussulmans.'[39]

In the next book XII, running into seventy-eight pages entitled 'Successors of Aurangzeb', Elphinstone summarizes the course of Maratha history from 1707 to 1761 in about twenty pages. Shahu, who was released from Mughal captivity in 1707, became the Chhatrapati of the Marathas after defeating his rivals, supported by Tarabai, the widow of Rajaram,[40] in a civil war. Elphinstone praises Balaji Vishwanath (the founder of the brahman dynasty of the Peshwas) for his services to Shahu, who was firmly established on the Maratha throne, and gives an outline of his complicated revenue policy. He remarks that this intricate policy 'threw the Maratha chiefs entirely into the hands of their Brahmin agents and strengthened the Peshwa's power by increasing that of his caste'.[41] However, he does not mention anywhere the important *sanads* of *swaraj*, *sardeshmukhi*, and *chauth* and *babati*, which he obtained from the Mughals in 1719.[42] About the treaty that Balaji concluded with the Mughals in 1719, he says, 'Saho was content, in his intercourse with the Mogul court, to acknow ledge himself a vassal of the empire.'[43] It was but natural for him to devote more attention to the career of Peshwa Bajirao I (1720–40) as he came in conflict with the Mughals in the north and their protegé, the Nizam, in the Deccan. Here he uses Grant Duff and also the chronicles of the Peshwas, but it must be admitted that Grant Duff surpasses Elphinstone in his appreciation of Bajirao I.

By 1740, the Marathas had relegated the Mughals to the background, and therefore the historian turned his attention to the activities of the Marathas. Elphinstone seems to be quite aware of the controversy regarding the authenticity of Shahu's testament. He writes:

> It was no less than an assertion that the raja had signed an instrument, transferring all the powers of his government to the Peshwa, on condition of his maintaining the royal title and dignity of the house of Shivaji through the grandson of Tarabai. It is said that this important deed was executed at a secret interview between Balaji and the raja but whether the signature (if genuine) was obtained by persuasion or fraud, when the deed was produced, and how far authenticity was admitted at the time, are left in an obscurity which is rendered more mysterious by the conduct of Balaji and Tarabai in circumstances which will appear in the sequel.[44]

In the footnote to the above statement, however, Elphinstone clearly states: 'I have no facts relating to this revolution but what are given by Grant Duff, but I have been led to conclusions somewhat different from that author, both with regard to the reality of Ram Raja's descent and the bonafide consent of Saho to the transfer of the sovereignity.'[45]

By 1759–60, Maratha power was at its zenith: 'Their frontier extended on the north to the Indus and the Himalaya, and on the south nearly to the extremity of the peninsula; all the territory within those limits that was not their own, paid tribute.'[46] The Panipat episode, based mainly on Grant Duff, who had relied heavily on Kashi Raja's eyewitness account as well as the *Seir-ul-Mutakherin* of Mustafa, has been dealt with in great detail. About the defeat of the Marathas, he writes, 'Never was a defeat more complete, and never was there a calamity that diffused so much consternation. Grief and despondency spread over the whole Maratha people; most had to mourn relations and all felt the destruction of the army as a death blow to their national greatness.'[47] Elphinstone thinks that the history of India as ruled by Indian powers practically became a closed chapter by 1761. He leaves the task of writing the history of the Indian empire to British historians. He writes:

> The actors in the last transactions having now all left the state, the history of the Mogul empire here closes of itself. Its territory is broken into separate states; the capital is deserted, the claimant to the name of emperor is an exile and a dependent; while a new race of conquerors has already commenced its career, which may again unite the empire under better auspices than before.[48]

Both Elphinstone and Grant Duff have treated the Marathas with sympathy in spite of their political animosity. Their acquaintance with the land and the people of the Maratha country has made their account of the Marathas more sober and rational as compared to those of James Mill or those European authors who drew their information mainly from the Persian sources. It is for this reason that Elphinstone cannot be altogether ignored while tracing the evolution of Maratha historiography.

Elphinstone, being a modest man, hesitated to write history in spite of his equipment and the constant encouragement of his friends because he felt that to write India's early and medieval history would require great knowledge and a very philosophical and reflective mind. If suitably executed, it would be a most important work. Eager to rectify Mill's *History* and driven by a sense of duty, he started working on the Hindu and Muslim periods of Indian history in 1834, gave it up for sometime, took it up again in 1836, and completed it by 1841.[49] It was very well reviewed in the leading British magazines and was declared the best 'history of India to appear in English'.[50]

From the point of view of Maratha history, Elphinstone's *The Rise of the British Power in the East*, is not of much significance. It seems that he was reluctant to write about the British conquest of India, which was, according to him, 'well digested by Mill'. Philips has aptly pointed out that though 'he had already confessed that in the matter of style he did not feel equal even to Mill', in truth he found writing about the British conquest difficult. His *History of British Power in the East*, therefore, could go as far as Warren Hastings' governor-generalship, and thus remained incomplete.[51] In the preface to this book, which was edited by Edward Colebrooke, it is mentioned that 'he had commenced some further chapters on the early relations of the British Government with the Marathas, on the affairs of the Rohillas, and on Hastings' treatment of the Raja of Benares, but they are mere Fragments'.[52] It begins from the close of the fifteenth century, i.e. the advent of the Portuguese, and ends in 1780. The treatment of the Marathas in this volume is peripheral to the main focus. The main theme of this volume is the rise of British power in India against native and other European powers in the fifteenth century.

Being a product of the Romantic school of history, Elphinstone had a sympathetic and appreciative attitude towards the antiquity of India; he was quite liberal but at the same time he could not altogether overcome his imperial prejudices. His views on the Marathas clearly reveal his limitations as a historian.

Notes

1. J.S. Cotton, *Mountstuart Elphinstone and the Making of South Western India*, Oxford: OUP, 1892, p. 212.
2. R.C. Majumdar, *Historiography in Modern India*, Bombay: OUP, 1970, p. 17.
3. C.H. Philipis (ed.), *Historians of India, Pakistan and Ceylon*, London: OUP, 1961, p. 223.
4. Sir T.E. Colebrooke, *Life of Mountstuart Elphinstone*, London: J. Murray, 1884, vol. II, p. 72, letter dated 2 July 1819.
5. Philips, op. cit., p. 223.
6. Ibid., p. 223.
7. Ibid.
8. A.R. Kulkarni, 'Mountstuart Elphinstone and Maratha History', *Bengal: Past and Present*, July–December 1970, pt. II, no. 168, pp. 203–4.
9. G.W. Forrest, *Selections from the Minutes and other official writings of the Honourable Mountstuart Elphinstone*, London, 1884, p. 264.
10. MSS EUR, F 128, Box 7, no. 4, Elphinstone to Strachey, dated 5 December 1814.

11. MSS EUR, F 88, G.D. to M.E., dated 15 July 1819.
12. Ibid., G.D. to M.E., dated 19 July 1819.
13. MSS EUR, F 88, M.E. to G.D., dated 20 July 1819.
14. MSS EUR, F 88, G.D. to Charles Grant, dated 20 April 1821.
15. V.K. Chiplunkar (ed.), *Nibandhamala*, New Edition, Pune: Chitrashala Press, 1917, p. 615.
16. MSS EUR, F 88, M.E. to G.D., dated 20 July 1819.
17. Mountstuart Elphinstone, *The History of India: The Hindu and the Mahometan Periods*, 7th edn., London, 1889, p. 600.
18. Ibid., pp. 616–17.
19. Ibid., pp. 581–2.
20. Ibid., p. 614. Compare Grant Duff, *A History of the Mahrattas*, 26th edn., London, 1921, pp. 3–4.
21. Elphinstone, op. cit., p. 615.
22. Grant Duff, *A History of the Mahrattas*, 6th edn., Oxford: OUP, 1926, pp. 1–33.
23. Elphinstone, op. cit., pp. 615–16. Compare this with the views of Jadunath Sarkar, 'Shivaji and His Times', 5th edn., Calcutta, 1952, pp. 6–13.
24. Ibid., op. cit., p. 616.
25. Ibid., p. 617.
26. Ibid., pp. 619–20, fn.
27. Elphinstone, op. cit., p. 621, Grant Duff, op. cit., vol. I, p. 114, and Jadunath Sarkar, op. cit., p. 399.
28. Elphinstone, op. cit., p. 623.
29. Ibid., pp. 628–9; Grant Duff, vol. I, pp. 166–9; compare with *Chhatrapati Shivaji Raje Yanchi Bakhar* by Krishnaji Anant Sabhasad (ed. S.N. Joshi), Pune, 1960, pp. 50–1; *Sapta Prakaranatmak Charitra* by Malhar Ramrao Chitnis (ed. R.V. Herwadkar), Pune, 1967, pp. 156–60.
30. Ibid., p. 638.
31. Elphinstone, op. cit., p. 647; compare with Grant Duff, vol. I, pp. 228–31.
32. Ibid., pp. 656–63; Grant Duff, op. cit., vol. I, pp. 278–311.
33. Elphinstone, op. cit., pp. 656–8.
34. M.E. to G.D., dated 20 April 1822.
35. Elphinstone, op. cit., pp. 659–60.
36. Ibid., pp. 665–6.
37. Ibid., pp. 665–6.
38. Ibid., p. 669.
39. Ibid., pp. 699–700.
40. The second son of Shivaji, who held Maratha power during the period of Shahu's imprisonment; he died in 1700.
41. Elphinstone, op. cit., pp. 699–700.
42. Grant Duff (ed.) vol. I, pp. 339–41.
43. Elphinstone, op. cit., p. 699.
44. Ibid., p. 728.
45. Ibid., fn. 11, compare with Grant Duff, op. cit., vol. I, pp. 440–3.
46. Ibid., p. 744.
47. Ibid., p. 752.
48. Ibid., p. 753.

49. Philips, op. cit., p. 224.
50. J.S. Grewal, *Muslim Rule in India*, Calcutta: OUP, 1970, p. 130. For a detailed account of Elphinstone's assessment of Muslim rule in India, see Ch. IX of this book.
51. Philips, op. cit., p. 224.
52. Mountstuart Elphinstone, *The Rise of the British Power in the East*, ed. Colebrooke, London: John Murray, 1887.

6

James Cuninghame Grant Duff

Captain James Cuninghame Grant Duff, the first historian to write a comprehensive history of the Marathas, was born on 8 July 1789, in the Scottish family of John Grant of Kincardine Neil in Banff. His mother Margaret Miln Duff succeeded to the estate of her brother William Duff of Eden, Banffshire, and was thereupon obliged to assume the name of Duff under the entail in 1824.[1] His father died in 1799 and the family moved to Aberdeen (Scotland), where Grant Duff joined the Marischal College. He gave up his education and went out as a boy of sixteen to India. He was ship wrecked on his way near Cape St. Rogue, was all but drowned by the upsetting of a boat off the Cape of Good Hope, where he first saw shots fired in anger, and broke his arms between that place and Bombay. He accepted a cadetship in the Bombay Military Service, and after successfully completing his preliminary training, secured a commission as ensign on 23 April 1807. He was assigned to the 1st Bombay Native Infantry, also known as the Bombay Grenadiers. He attracted the attention of Mountstuart Elphinstone, the Resident at Poona since 1811, and was admitted into the band of workers (including Captain Pottinger, John Briggs, William Chaplin and others) popularly known as the family of Elphinstone, in the subsequent period.

He had 'most handsomely' volunteered his services in the famous battle of Kirkee fought in November 1817, along with Colonel Burr and Captain Ford of the East India Company. Though he was a subordinate officer to Colonel Burr, it appears that it was due to his sagacity and promptness that the calamity of a crushing defeat was averted.[2] This must have brought him still closer to Elphinstone. He thus became not only a devoted servant, but also a counsellor of Elphinstone in the course of time.

He became captain in 1818 and was selected by Elphinstone for the office of the Political Agent and Resident at Satara (11 April 1818), an independent state carved out of the territories conquered from the Peshwas. His son writes that Duff 'was governing the Satara State, a country equal in extent to about a third of Scotland with nearly absolute power'. He was to administer the state strictly according to the instructions issued to him, and was asked to secure the support of the Raja without introducing any innovations in the state. He entered into a treaty with the Raja of Satara on 25 September 1819 regarding the management of the transactions of the state for a specific period, and also entered into separate agreements with the feudatories of the Raja. He was to train the Raja and his officials before handing over the responsibility of the state to him in 1822. He remained in that position for four years (1818–22), and after surmounting all the difficulties in his way, he left the Raja whom he regarded as 'the most civilized Maratha', after establishing 'excellent order' in the State.[3] As Political Agent his remuneration was fixed at Rs. 2,000 per month plus Rs. 1,500 allowances per month plus the cost of the establishment of his office.

It was here in Satara that he collected all his source material for writing his Maratha history and also prepared its first draft, before leaving the shores of India. His son, however, disapproved of this activity of his father, which was, according to him, 'unhappily superadded'. The double labour ruined his health, and in January 1823 he left India. Wisely or unwisely, he determined within the next year or two that he was quite unfit to return thither, or indeed to take up any work of a serious kind at home.[4]

His services as an administrator were appreciated by the people, and 'Grant Saheb' became a household name in Satara.[5] A glowing tribute has been paid to him by a British official who wrote, '. . . at 25 years of age, with no previous training (he) was sent to govern a kingdom with absolute power, and who did govern it so wisely and firmly that he literally changed wilderness into a fruitful land'.[6]

After his mother's death in 1824, he succeeded to the Duffs' estate. He married in 1827,[7] Jane Catherine, the charming daughter of Sir Whitelaw Ainslie, the author of '*Materia Medica of India*, and settled down at Eden, devoting himself partly to field sports, but chiefly to improving his property according to his plans. He retired from the Company's service on 12 May 1827. He got some estate from his wife's side also, and thus became James Cuninghame Grant Duff in 1850.

He spent the rest of his life as a country gentleman, devoting most of his time to agriculture, cattle breeding and planting. He had acquired some practical knowledge of farming, and bought some 'miserable working land in addition to what he had inherited'.[8] He loved touring. In his lengthy letters to Elphinstone he wrote about his sojourns in Europe and discussed contemporary politics. He began feeling weak in 1852, as he writes, 'I am afraid I may not very long pursue my bodily activity.'[9] He died six years later, on 28 September 1858.

Grant Duff's wife was a very domineering woman. His first son, Mountstuart Elphinstone Grant Duff did not hold a good opinion of him though he owed his own eminent position to the good offices of his father. Grant Duff left behind him two sons and a daughter, Alice Jane. Mountstuart Elphinstone Grant Duff, held responsible positions under the Company and the Crown. His second son, Ainslie Douglas Ainslie, adopted the surname of his mother.

Grant Duff evinced a great interest in the Raja of Satara even after his retirement. He wrote to the Raja in 1828, 'Administer justice impartially, assess your lands lightly, and make the Resident your friend by your good conduct.'[10] The Raja, too, often expressed his deep gratitude towards him. Grant did not like the British policy of deposing the Raja in 1839, and the final annexation of the state in 1848. He held the view that British statesmen should not be swayed by any consideration except simple, straightforward honesty.[11]

The History of the Mahrattas was Grant Duff's only contribution to historical writing. He did not revise it, or publish its second edition. He worked on his draft in the light of the suggestions made by his friends, and requested John Murray to undertake its publication. He writes that, 'the whole will be comprised in two moderate sized quartos of not more than 200,000 words in each volume'.[12]

Murray consulted some experts and told Grant Duff that he would publish his work provided he altered its title to 'The Downfall of the Mughals, and the Rise of the English.'[13] Grant Duff refused to do so, and went to Sir James Mackintosh, who helped him in getting his history published through Longman & Company, and in six weeks' times *A History of the Mahrattas* saw the light of day.[14]

Elphinstone had once thought of writing a history of the Marathas. Perhaps his own *Report on the Territories Conquered from the Peshwas* (1819) induced him to pursue the historical part of it in more detail. But 'it was a pity that official business interfered to prevent even arranging his plans'.[15]

The mantle of writing the Maratha history thus ultimately fell on the shoulders of Grant Duff, who was unaware of the plans of Elphinstone till he expressed them in reply to his letter in which he wrote about his 'floating idea' of writing a Maratha history.[16] He thus set himself to give effect to his 'floating idea' during his stay at Satara.

Collection of Material for the Maratha History

While holding the charge of the newly created Satara Raj as its Political Agent and Resident, Grant Duff was convinced that the Marathas, who had played such an important role in the seventeenth and eighteenth centuries in India, had not been properly introduced to the European public. He found that the earlier attempts at presenting a history of the Marathas were either too brief or deficient or incomplete at several stages, perhaps for want of the necessary source material or because of lack of access to it. As Maratha power had become extinct by then, it was possible for one to take a wide and sweeping view of the entire history of the Marathas from their rise, expansion, decline, and fall with the help of numerous sources in different languages. He also felt that as the rulers of the Maratha country, it was obligatory on the part of the East India Company and its officers to become fully acquainted with their predecessors, who had controlled the destiny of this country directly or indirectly for more than two centuries. In the preface to his *History* he writes: 'The want of a complete history of the rise and progress and decline of our immediate predecessors in our conquest, the Mahrattas, has long been felt by all persons conversant with the affairs of India; in so much, that it is very generally acknowledged, we cannot fully understand the means by which our own vast empire in that quarter was acquired until this desideratum is supplied.'[17]

However, when he undertook to 'supply this desideratum', he was not quite aware of the difficulties involved in working out this history, which aimed to present a reasonably good and authentic account of the various phases of Maratha history. In the eighteenth century, the Marathas had practically become an Indian power, and the nature and scope of Maratha power had so enlarged that it was difficult to keep track of Maratha activities on several fronts, connect them with a common purpose, and present a consistent account of them.

It is true that Grant Duff was neither highly qualified, nor a trained historian. Basically, he was a soldier, who had become an administrator by force of circumstances, and entered the field of history by sheer accident. He was a self-made historian, as is revealed from his extensive correspondence with Mountstuart Elphinstone and other contemporaries regarding methodology, use of historical material, fixing their authenticity and chronology, and other problems of historical writings.

Elphinstone had asked him to keep an eye on historical material, perhaps for his own history, while discharging his duties as Political Agent at Satara. For a long time the immediate problems of the state prevented him from paying any attention to this request of the commissioner. But during the rainy season of 1819 he sat for three nights and ransacked the archives of the Raja of Satara, where he found a treasure of documents all highly useful for writing the history of the Marathas. He enumerated the documents dating from 1649 to 1725, including original letters from Shahjahan, Aurangzeb and his successor, the Sayed brothers, the grants to the Marathas from Muhammad Shah, the letters of the Peshwas, etc. He found certain histories from antiquity to the present times written by Chitnis. After taking stock of the material, he wrote, '. . . a long time ago I had a floating idea of throwing some light on Maratha History. The possession of such materials and some other sources of information enable me to authenticate a great deal of what immediately concerns this country.'[18]

When this floating idea of writing a Maratha history occurred to him, he was not yet sure whether he would be able to carry it to its logical end. He was aware of his limited equipment, and hesitated to make his desire public. He wrote to Elphinstone, 'There is as important a consideration as can occur in a man's life and I am not asking advice after I have made up my mind. Tell me candidly if you think I ought to undertake it. If so, I should like to keep my purpose private.' He thought that Elphinstone would dissuade him. But that was not to be. On the contrary, he got an encouraging reply immediately. Elphinstone wrote, 'I am delighted with your progress in historical collection, and still more with your intention of putting them in order. I certainly do advise you most earnestly to do so.'[19]

Thus the 'floating idea' began to take shape, and before he sailed for England in January 1823, he had before him practically the complete draft of his history duly corrected by Elphinstone, William Erskine, John Briggs, and Vans Kennedy.

It seems that Grant Duff had issued a circular, probably in 1819, in which he appealed to those who possessed *bakhars, kaifiyats*, copper plates, old *sanads* and *watanpatras*, *inampatras*, and *hakikats* in Marathi, Persian or Sanskrit about the rulers of North India, of the Baridshahi, Nizamshahi, and Adilshahi dynasties and of the Marathas, to hand over these documents to him.[20]

He was fortunate in getting original material from the Raja of Satara, the Chitnis family, and a number of other persons, some of whom were eyewitnesses to certain events. He was aware of the difficulties experienced by his predecessors, 'the indefatigable Orme' of *Fragments*, and Scott Waring of *The History of the Marathas* (1810). He confessed that 'circumstances placed me in a situation which at once removed many of the obstacles which those gentlemen encountered, and threw materials within my reach which had been previously inaccessible'.[21]

He spared no pains in collecting, copying, and translating *bakhars* and other documents into English in order to authenticate his statements. Balajipant Natu, his native assistant in Satara, was helpful to him in persuading the Raja to lend his records, arguing 'that these would be printed in Vilayat and that his name would be made known to Europeans'.[22] Yet it appears from the Raja's diary that all documents were not made over to Grant Duff. The Raja warned his officials that they should not leave any documents with the Political Agent, and that a list of all documents shown to him should be maintained.[23] However, Grant Duff managed to secure most of the documents from the Raja. He wrote to Elphinstone, 'Maharaj really has not got any documents of importance to the history. What he has have been in my possession.'[24]

Grant Duff's approach to the study of these documents seems to have been scientific. He did not accept a document or a chronicle without challenging its authenticity. The extracts published from the Raja's diary bear out this fact.

Grant Duff knew Marathi, but it is doubtful whether he could follow the Marathi documents written in the Modi script. He had acquired a number of Marathi chronicles from the Chitnis family as well as from the Deshmukhs and Deshpandes of various villages. Wherever he refers to Marathi manuscripts in his book, it is invariably to a Marathi *bakhar*. Unfortunately, he does not indicate the name of the manuscript supporting the statement. This is a serious omission in his writings. At first, he considered the Chitnis *bakhar* to be a mass of nonsense, though not despicable as it stated some important fact.[25] He told Chitnis that his *bakhar*, which simply glorified the Maratha hero, creates a suspicion in the mind of the reader.[26] Nevertheless, he used this *bakhar* extensively, as after a year or so the same *bakhar* appeared to him 'on the whole most valuable, as it gives a good account of Sivaji's expedition into the Carnatic, but is in general defective in the early details we wish to get'.[27]

He compares the Marathi *bakhars* with the Persian *tawarikhs* and arrives at the conclusion that 'the laudatory accounts of the Muslims are false in many respects. The accounts written by the Hindus are only half-truths'.[28] The person who was appointed to translate the *bakhars* into English was warned that he should do so only after consulting Balwantrao Parasnis and comparing these with the old notes.[29] He refers to a *bakhar* in the possession of Khatao Deshpande dealing with the history of Maharashtra from Shalivahan to Ramdev Rai. He got a copy of Shivaji's life from the Raja of Kolhapur. This is probably the Sabhasad *bakhar*.

However, like Scott Waring, his predecessor in this field, he was also excessively enamoured of the graphic accounts of the chroniclers, both Hindu and Muslim, and based his history mostly on them. It seems that Elphinstone had noticed this trend in his writing as he advised, Grant Duff: '. . . get at facts and combine them with judgement so as to make a consistent and rational history out of a mass of gossiping *bakhars* and gasconading Tawareeks.'[30]

Rajwade, the noted Maratha historian, discussed this history of Grant Duff as nothing more than a revised edition of the *bakhars* from which it had drawn its chief material. When Duff's volume was translated by Captain David Capen and Baba Sane into Marathi in 1829, it is surprising that its title was *Marathyanchi Bakhar.*

Duff consulted a number of original documents. When he took possession of the archives of the Raja of Satara, in November 1818, he found copies of grants, Shivaji's letter to Ekoji, the ruler of Tanjore, Aurangzeb's letters, etc. He found the original letters of Chimnaji Appa and Brahmendra Swami at Poona, and yet complained that the Poona Daftar had supplied nothing for several years after 1720.[31] He discovered that some records of the period from Sambhaji to Shahu were lost either at Raigad when taken by the Mughals or had been burnt when Satara was looted by Parsuram Bhau Patwardhan.[32] He did not suspect that perhaps the Raja had concealed something from him. He was convinced that the records had really very little useful information to reveal. All the papers not shown to him were mere trash according to his advisors Balajipant Nath and Balwantrao Chitnis.

The Marathi documents were not only difficult to translate, but also the labour involved in the task, according to him, was not always worthwhile. He writes, 'It is one peculiar evil of the work in which I am engaged that out of papers of ten elbows long there are perhaps ten useful lines.'[33]

Grant Duff was quite aware that no authentic history of the Marathas, especially its earlier portion, could be satisfactorily narrated without consulting the Persian sources. He consulted Ferishta, Khafi Khan, Abul Husain Qazi's history of Bijapur, Mir Ibrahim's history of Bijapur, Nurulla's history of Ali Adil Shah II, *Mohmud Nama*, by Maula Zahur, a historical poem called 'Ali Nama' composed by Nasarat, a history of Bijapur written by Syed Moideen Pirzada in 1821, etc.[34] Ferishta and Khafi Khan were useful to him in narrating the early history of the medieval Deccan. He did not agree with Briggs, who was translating Ferishta, as his account went beyond 1596. But as Ferishta had died in 1626, one can understand Briggs's contention.[35] He attached more importance to Khafi Khan's *Muntakhab-ul-lubab*, and was anxious to procure a good copy of this manuscript. He had one imperfect copy, which he regarded as highly useful in assisting inquiries, but whose accuracy he was inclined to doubt in many particulars. About Khafi Khan he writes, 'After reading the translation of Ferishta and collecting every scrap of written legend to be had in this country, I found an immense blank from the year 1600 to 1650, which Khafi Khan enables me to fill up much better than I expected.'[36] Mahaumad Hanif of Aurangabad had given him a good copy of Khafi Khan, and a Syed from Bijapur had told him about his authenticity, that, on the whole, he was a good historian for the Mughals but 'that he is a partial writer on the side of Shahjahan, and altogether wrong in a part of what he states regarding Beejapur'.[37] However, he was inclined to follow Khafi Khan's account in preference to any other, though it was unduly different from Hindu accounts in some points. According to Grant Duff, up to the time when Shivaji commenced his career, Khafi Khan was, an authority, and hence there was no reason to doubt him than a Marathi *bakhar*.[38]

Muntakhab-ul-lubab was written in 1735, and it has now been rejected as an authentic source for the history of the seventeenth century. Besides this, from the authorities quoted by Grant Duff, it appears that he was not aware of the existence of the *Alamgir-namah*, the *Masir-i-Alamgiri*, and the *Akhbarats*.

Anyone who reads the views of Grant Duff on the Chitnis *bakhar* and Khafi Khan can easily see the impact of these two secondary sources on his *History of the Mahrattas*.

In addition to these *tawarikhs*, Grant found certain Persian documents in the Raja's archives, including a few original letters of Shahjahan (1649), Aurangzeb and his successors (1656–1707), and Sayed Hussain Ali Khan (1718), the three grants made by Muhammad Shah to the first Peshwa in 1719, and a number of letters from 1719 to 1725.[39]

Grant, while in the Bombay Native Infantry, had acted as the Persian interpreter of his regiment. It was perhaps his knowledge of Persian that had attracted the attention of Elphinstone. It is, however, doubtful whether he was able to read Persian manuscripts. In fact, the vast amount of Persian material that he collected was created problems for him, and his advisers insisted on him consulting the Persian sources. Elphinstone asked him to study Muslim histories and memoirs from north India, the Hyderabad records, and the *Siyar-ul-Mutakherin,* translated by Mustafa, 'which is worth its weight in gold'.[40]

Briggs, who read the first six chapters of Grant Duff's manuscript dealing mainly with the Muslim period in the Deccan, advised him to revise his chapters in the light of certain Persian authorities. Duff expressed his inability to carry out this suggestion as he was anxious to finish the writing of this work before leaving India. He complained, 'I am getting stronger in authorities, but the size is tremendous, the subject tedious, and if the labour is sickening to me, it will be appalling to the reader.'[41]

It appears from the correspondence between Duff and Elphinstone that the former had not only access to original records, but had also personally collected a number of manuscripts and documents from various sources. It's not known what happened to this personal collection of Grant Duff. It was believed for sometime that he had carried the whole of it with him, and that it had unfortunately caught fire in the course of his sea voyage. But Grant Duff wrote regularly to Elphinstone about his journey, and nowhere does he mention any kind of mishap. Justice K.T. Telang carefully examined the records of the Literary Society of Bombay, as it was claimed that had deposited them there, but in vain.[42] Neither the India Office Library, London possesses these papers, nor does the National Register of Archives, London make any reference to it.[43]

Dajisaheb Saranjame, a clerk in the Inam Commission constituted by the company's government to settle the claims of land grants by the erstwhile Maratha government, had circulated a rumour that Grant Duff, in league with Elphinstone, had destroyed his collection of historical records. He claimed to have found evidence supporting his statement in the office of the Deccan Commissioner, Pune. He maintained that he had personally seen an exchange of letters between Grant Duff and Deccan Commissioner. It is absurd to think that Elphinstone and Grant Duff, both great lovers of history would destroy such valuable source material that they had collected over long years with great difficulty and preserved at considerable expense.

N.J. Kirtane, a junior student at the Deccan College, presented a critical paper on Grant Duff's *History* in 1868, in which he made the above-mentioned charge against the Briton. However, he confessed in 1882 that it was based on the oral information supplied to him by Dajisaheb Saranjame, and that most of the documents referred to by Grant Duff were traceable, and that the rumour of the destruction of the original records by him was baseless.

S.M. Edwardes, in his Introduction to Grant Duff's *History* mentions in a footnote that the Bodleian Library at Oxford

University possesses 'A Catalogue of J. Grant Duff's Library to be sold along with that of J. Adams on July 6, 1888.' On personal examination by the author, the reference was found to be misleading. The person J. Grant mentioned therein was not the historian Grant Duff, but a medical professional.[45]

Among the European records, Duff relied more on the English records from Bombay and Calcutta than on the French, the Dutch, or the Portuguese. He consulted the Portuguese records while describing the siege of Bassein. He had sought confirmation of certain dates from the Viceroy of Goa. As regards the English records dealing with the Treaty of Wadgaon (1780), he writes, '. . . all the English transactions will require reflection, prudence, and moderate, though just, opinions'.[46] Elphinstone had asked him to consult the dispatches of Mostyn, Malet and Palmer, Anderson's letters from Scindia's camp, Barry Close on Baji Rao, his own letters to the Bombay and Bengal Governments giving the account of recent times, the *Asiatic Researchers* for accounts of Panipat, Parliamentary records, etc. He says further that the plots, intrigues, conspiracies, and combinations from the time of MadhavRao's death till Bajirao's accession might be easily obtained from the Reports of Malet and Palmer.[47] He was prepared to procure copies of these records for Duff, provided the latter was prepared to pay for them. Duff gave a list of documents that he desired to obtain from Bengal and agreed to spare Rs. 1,000 for this job.[48] He seems to have been at home when dealing with the English material. It is perhaps due to this that the last part of his *History* gives more details than the earlier one. Rajwade says that Duff has disposed of the history of about 150 years in 475 pages, whereas the history of 22 years (1746 to 1796) occupies 200 pages. In other words, it describes the English activities in Maharashtra in greater detail than the activities of the Marathas.[49]

Duff also consulted a number of scholars, eyewitnesses to certain events, while preparing the draft of his *history*. His manuscript was read by Elphinstone, William Erskine of Bombay, John Briggs, the collector of Khandesh, Vans Kennedy, the secretary of the Literary Society, Bombay, and others. He requested some of his Indian assistants to write accounts of certain historical events. Mention may be made here of the voluminous history of his times prepared by Balaji Pant Natu, his first native assistant at Satara.[50] When his friends delayed in supplying him with the necessary material he got annoyed with them, and wrote in despair, 'I expected some assistance from them, but they do not seem inclined to afford it. I shall have something less to say in the preface . . . I will show them, I can make something of it without their aid.'[51]

HISTORIAN AT HIS DESK

The narration of the rise and fall of Maratha power presented a number of problems. First, there was a lack of adequate and authentic materials. Second, the period of Shivaji and his times could not be satisfactorily described due to a paucity of authentic state papers. With the rise of the Peshwas in the eighteenth century, the scope of Maratha activities was widened, and the narrative becomes much more complicated. For a full understanding of eighteenth-century Maratha history, one has to carefully study the activities of the Mughals, the Nizam, the Nawabs in the South, the Rajas of Mysore, the Marathas in Malwa, Gujarat and Karnataka, the factions among the Maratha Sardars, namely Dabhade and Gaikwad, Bhonsle and Pratinidhi, Shinde and Holkar, and the relations with the Siddis, the Europeans, etc. In view of the limited time at his disposal, it was not possible for Grant Duff to undertake a careful scrutiny of these problems. He was not interested in narrating these events. He writes, 'I am exceedingly horrified by events on events, so many characters and so many interests, and with all so little interesting to the reader, that nothing cheers me except that I see or fancy I see what no one alive knows.[52]

It was this idea of doing pioneering work in an unknown field that prompted Grant Duff to undertake this stupendous task. However, his earlier enthusiasm waned with the progress of his work. He could not keep pace with the increasing amount of material and the suggestions made by his friends.

He became confused and lost, and writes, 'I cannot find out what I meant to express.'[53] Elphinstone had, however, clearly defined to him the nature and scope of Maratha history. He writes, 'A Maratha History would embrace the downfall of the Mughul Empire and the rise of our own as well as that which is its professed object to treat. It must be well thought over and then told.'[54] Grant had, of course, no time for all this. Elphinstone was attracted towards Maratha history at least for one reason, that is, as he puts it to Grant Duff, 'The wholeness of your subject is one of its greatest beauties.'[55]

The relationship between Elphinstone and Duff was that of a supervisor and his pupil. The exchange of letters between the two throws much light on the ideas of history and research methodology prevailing in the early nineteenth century. As a historian and as someone interested in Maratha history, Elphinstone had carefully thought over the problem of presenting it. He used to go through Grant Duff's chapters carefully and make useful suggestions (which Grant Duff calls censures), regarding their improvement and additional reading. Grant Duff regarded these suggestions as not only useful but also necessary to save him from future shame.[56] He thought that these censures gave him much stronger encouragement than he had ventured to hope.[57]

Elphinstone wanted to develop the history of the Marathas on certain specific lines. He asked Grant Duff to introduce more material on the manners of the Marathas, and add material on the people and their leaders to enable readers to understand their motives and modes of action. He recommended Grand Duff to adopt the model of Bernier, the European traveller of the seventeenth century, 'of mixing history and travels which is required in recording the transactions of a distant nation'.[58] He cited an example from Maratha history, and said, 'When you bring Shivaji and Shaista Khan together, contrast in a few touches the luxurious magnificence and pride of the Mohammedan with the hardy, bold and crafty character of the half-naked Maratha.'[59]

Elphinstone insisted that Grant Duff should make his history more readable and interesting. He felt that Grant Duff did not pay much attention to the reader, who he took for granted as being well acquainted with Mughal history, and having the ability to pick up a story after frequent interruptions, or to turn back and search for the broken thread. He wrote, 'You must connect causes and effects so that the relation may be seen, without appearing to explain too much or to undervalue the worthy reader's understanding.'[60] He further suggested that Duff should continue his method of arranging the facts and polishing his style and alter it, if necessary, after ascertaining the public taste in Europe. He cited the example of Gibbon, who wrote his first quarto seven times and was scarcely satisfied even then.[61] He suggested that Duff should study the approved authorities to avoid confusion, and show his manuscript to a literary man or a professed writer, which would enable him to meet the eye of the public.[62]

It is interesting to note that Elphinstone recommended the use of anecdotes 'which could not only make description picturesque, but also grease the wheels of the narrative'. At the same time, he warned him that 'all jokes and sly bits of every description should be cut out as they are unsuited to history'.[63] He recommended a plain and simple style for a historian. He urged that scenes and events should be painted as they appear to a plain man and in plain language. He warned Duff, 'You are ruined, if you assume a stately, formal style.'[64]

Elphinstone was aware of the shortcomings of Duff's work. Yet he was full of praise for the latter's efforts. He emphasized the value of the proposed work in these words, 'This book is excellent and satisfies curiosity on many points still unknown. All the seeds of the Maratha greatness are laid open to the complete satisfaction of the reader. I have no doubt whatever that the *Maratha History* will be a valuable and even a popular work.'[65] He wrote to Colonel Barry Close, 'It would be an excellent history; Shivaji, Sambhaji and Rajaram now stand in full light, as simplified and intelligible as Hyder and Tipu.'[66]

Duff showed his gratitude to his teacher by deciding to dedicate his book to him. On this Elphinstone said, 'I am much flattered by your proposed notice of me in your publication. I wish I saw it in print.'[67] He suggested to the authorities of the ship by which he was sailing that in case of any mishap on his way, his baggage containing his draft and notes be sent to Elphinstone. Grant Duff's *A History of the Mahrattas* begins with a note of dedication and ends with profound tributes to the achievements of Elphinstone in western India.[68]

In spite of Elphinstone's characterization of it as a valuable and popular work, Duff's *History* was not received with enthusiasm when it was first published in 1826. It was not submitted to any principal reviewers, nor were efforts made to promote its sale. Even the East India Company did not purchase the usual number of copies. It was in those days mainly read by the revenue officers of the Company posted in western India.[69]

John Briggs and Vans Kennedy who read Duff's manuscript did not consider it satisfactory. Elphinstone believed that Duff's *History* was rich in facts, beyond all previous studies, and that his views were always judicious and correct.[70] Yet even he did not like Duff's treatment of the subject. He wanted Duff to appreciate the spirit behind Maratha activity. He urged him to seek some object behind the narration rather than provide a dry enumeration of facts. Justice Ranade has described the period 1689–1707 as a time of heroic resistance, a period of the Maratha war of independence.[71] However, Grant Duff could not grasp the line of thinking suggested by Elphinstone. He complains, 'The Marathas are such actors for the page of history and there is such a dreary sameness in the detail of the progress, of the confusion they created, that it is the total want of interest in them which makes you wish for some object on which to fix attention.'[72]

When the volume was published in 1826, it was not prominently noticed by the critics. N.J. Kirtane was the first to criticize Grant Duff, forty-two years after the publication of his work. He first congratulated Duff for his stupendous work and than proceeded to point out a few shortcomings in his *History*. His main point was that Grant Duff did not utilize fully the materials that his position had enabled him to avail of. His study, according to Kirtane, is a dry narration of the various campaigns of the Marathas.[73]

Vishnushastri Chiplunkar, who wrote about eight or nine years after Kirtane, was inclined to be more sympathetic towards Duff. When he heard that John Murray had refused to publish Duff's *History* without any change in the title of the book, he commented that the utterances of Murray indicated how indifferent the British were to the history of Indians. All that he had found correct and authentic had been included by him without favouritism towards the English or malice towards the Marathas. He did not belong to that category of scholars who are always anxious to exhibit their knowledge, which is often vague, and who are always eager to establish the superiority of their nation in knowledge and morals. In short, the *History* of Duff would appear unbiased and acceptable even to the Marathas as it did not provoke them by casting aspersions on their religion or morals.[74]

Justice Ranade's *Rise of the Maratha Power* was a powerful reply to Duff's views. He emphasized the moral basis or significance of the rise of Maratha power, which was not, as thought, like a conflagration in the forests of the Sahyadri.[75]

Similarly, Rajwade, pointed out a number of omissions and factual mistakes in Duff's history. He rejected this work as being incomplete and unauthentic since it was mainly based on secondary sources like *bakhars* and *tawarikhs*. In his opinion, Duff was not equipped for the task of being a historian. He felt that had a gifted historian like James Mill, or Gibbon, or Mommsen undertaken to write the history of the Marathas, he would have achieved wonders with the material that Duff had been fortunate to secure.

Rajwade, however, admits that Duff's account of Maratha *history* is more systematic than that of the *bakhars*. He says that as his account is old and incomplete, it should be rejected on the following grounds:

1. It is based mainly on the *bakhars*, *tawarikhs*, *kaifiyats* and some minor sources, which are unauthentic and secondary in nature. To that extent, his history is incomplete and unreliable.
2. He did not exploit fully the archival material at Satara and Poona, which lay at his feet. Rajwade shows the

omissions in Duff's *History* with the help of documents later published in *Kavyeitihas Samgraha* of Sane and *Aitihasik Lekh Samgraha* of Khare.

3. He did not possess the necessary equipment to write this history.
4. He was a foreigner and had no interest in the history of the Marathas. His intention was to present a factual account of Maratha history to his European readers.
5. The purpose of Duff's *History* was to glorify the achievements of the British, which were comparatively insignificant at that time, and to suppress the deeds of the Marathas. His general survey, which emphasizes mainly the military operations of the Marathas, creates an impression on the mind of the reader that the Marathas were plunderers who could not aspire for the sovereignty of India, that there was no peace and order in India during the eighteenth century, and that these blessings, namely peace and order, were the gift of the British, who wrested power from the Marathas.[76] Rajwade concludes that Grant Duff did not go into the larger issue of the objective method, or moral consideration, behind the expansionist activities of the Marathas, and as a result his partial and prejudicial view of the Marathas remained uncorrected for a long time.

It must be admitted at the outset that the points raised by Rajwade are valid and are of a fundamental nature. It is true that Duff treated the Anglo—Maratha contests in great detail, particularly that which occurred between 1798 and 1818. But perhaps this was so due to the large number of records pertaining to this period available to him and also due to his personal involvement in this last phase of Maratha history. It must be noted that Grant Duff aimed primarily at compiling a political and military history of the Marathas, and even this was a stupendous task. The exclusion of larger philosophical considerations was due to limitations of time and energy, which cannot be conclusively attributed to racial or colonial prejudice. Rajwade accused Grant Duff for what he had not done, particularly his neglect of the metaphysical aspect of Maratha history. His criticism of Grant Duff's *History* may be accepted as valid. But at the same time, while evaluating his work, the circumstances in which he was writing, the time available to him for his work, and the availability of sources may also be considered. Rajwade was reviewing Duff's *History* more than seventy years after its publication, when many more new sources were available and known due to the tremendous efforts of Maratha researchers, including Rajwade himself. It may be said that in spite of its shortcomings, Grant Duff's *History of the Marathas* still remains a pioneering work on Maratha history, which cannot be ignored by research scholars.

V.V. Khare

The Bharat Itihas Samshodhak Mandal, Pune, launched a movement in 1918–19 to enumerate the mistakes in Grant Duff's *History*. Vasudeo Vaman Khare also known as Vasudeoshastri Khare, the reputed editor of the *Aitihasik Lekha Samgraha*, published a few mistakes from Duff's *History* in *The Maratha*, an English periodical founded by Lokmanya B.G. Tilak. However, Khare ultimately gave up this effort as futile and a sheer waste of time. The mistakes pointed out by Khare mainly refer to certain dates of the movements of the Peshwas, or some place names and persons. In this respect Khare wrote, 'This is no history but a *bakhar.* Most of the dates are wrong. Places, personalities and their characters, deeds and names are also wrong at many times.'[77] However, he respected the efforts of Grant Duff and appreciated his inquisitiveness, industry, and sincerity.

Sir Jadunath Sarkar, in the introduction to his *Shivaji and His Times*, simply pointed out how his own work marked an advance on Duff's work as far as source material was concerned. He stated that he had not only used original materials unknown to Duff but had also made a minute and careful study of the material known to him.[78]

No British historian has so far critically studied Duff's contribution to historical writing. Professor C.H. Philips, while assessing the contribution of Elphinstone to Indian history, writes, 'It (*Maratha History*) is a straightforward, sympathetic account, invaluable in that it is based on material that has long since disappeared, a classic account though never, in fact, much read.' G.D. Bearce considers it a pioneering study, yet not a very successful scholarly work. He describes it as 'an apology for an imperial undertaking'. He writes, 'What he told was the account of how a people, through many wars and revolutions, whose history was marked by violence, treachery and ignorance, had arrived at the gate of British Rule. The outcome of this development was the justification of British conquest.'[79]

It would be unfair to impute motives to Grant Duff. It is true that his main object in writing this history was to introduce the Marathas, of whom the public had yet but imperfect information.[80] He had no ill-will towards the Marathas. He identified himself with the Marathas, when he wrote, 'Briggs is a Mughal or Pathan, and me a *ghureeb Maratha manoos*,'[81] or 'He is a Pathan Toork that slaughters kine, and I am a Maratha *manoos* as can fight or flee.'[82]

Grant Duff was aware of his limitations. He was not a trained historian, as he confessed, 'Notwithstanding all I have done, and all I have chalked out, I am perfectly sensible of my inability in many respects for the task of authorship.'[83] He had realized that the history of the Marathas was a great subject, and that he should not climb higher than that point from which, if he did fall, he stood little chance of breaking his neck.[84]

His style was subjected to more criticism. This problem of style had always disturbed him. He wished to maintain a plain style with no learned professions or anything that he could not support.[85] His defective style may be attributed to the nature of the subject under study, the type of source material he had to handle, and the limited time at his disposal to collect and digest the numerous materials.

Grant and the Romantic School

According to some historians, Grant Duff's deep interest in the Maratha past as well as his sympathy towards them is an indication of a romantic trait in his nature. This is especially true of his fascination for the Ghats of Maharashtra and the ruins of Bijapur, which he found imparting a feeling of melancholy, and the elegant and graceful architecture of splendid mosques and palaces. 'When viewed as mere ruins, the remains of that city, as they at present exist, are exceedingly grand, and as a past wholly far exceed anything of the kind in Europe.' He appreciated the extraordinary 'power of music' over the Indian mind and heart, and stated that 'some of the Hindoostanee airs are beautiful'.[86] Professor J.S. Grewal observes.

> Grant's appreciation of the Marathas was informed in the last resort by his Romantic sense of nationality. For him the Marathas possessed a distinct genius and character; for all their shortcomings, they deserved admiration for their qualities as a nation. Their hardihood and patience, energy and love of enterprise, their glorious exploits, their love for their *watan*, their national sentiment, their attempt, however partial, at 'vindicating their civil and religious liberties', these were the aspects of their history which compelled sympathy and appreciation. Inferior in civilization they may have been; despicable, never.[87]

However, on the basis of these stray references it is difficult to assign Grant to any school of history. He belongs to that phase of historical writing in which administrators assumed the role of historians. In their view, the administration of a country and its people demanded first of all knowledge of their history, society, manners and culture. Administration, as they rightly held, was no lifeless mechanism but an organic unit of society. How else could administrators govern a people whom they did not know or care to know? It is quite evident from the correspondence between H.E. Goldsmid of the Bombay Civil Service and Grant Duff that Maratha history was read mainly by the revenue officers for carrying out their administrative duties. The earlier histories of India or its regions written by British administrators believed that 'if you want to govern a people you must know the people and you could know them only by understanding their history'. Perhaps it was this spirit that motivated Grant Duff to write the first comprehensive history of the Marathas.

Publication of History

Duff took a great risk in publishing his work. Before it went to press, it cost him upwards of £1,700 and he could get back about £ 2,000 only. It means that he got only about £ 300 from the sale of his book. His publisher, John Murray, had already told him that '. . . people in India don't buy, they read but borrow, and it would be long before the *Mahratta History* would be bought as an outfit book'. The members of the Court of Directors were generous enough to buy forty copies of his book, as he writes, 'which they would have done equally, had it been a *Mahratta Vocabulary*'. He laments further, 'I do not suppose any Director or aspirant of that period even opened the *Mahratta History* after they become Directors.'[88] In 1840, it was suggested to him by Goldsmid that a revised edition of the book should be published, but neither the publisher recommended it nor did Duff himself show any willingness to undertake the trouble of revising it. Its second edition was published in 1863; the third edition appeared in 1873, the fourth in 1878, the fifth from Calcutta in 1921, and the last one was published by the Oxford University Press with an introduction by S.M. Edwardes in 1921.

The Associated Publishing House, New Delhi, brought out the seventh edition of Grant Duff's *History*, in two volumes, in 1971.[89] This edition is edited by J.P. Guha, who taught English at Hans Raj College, Universityof Delhi. His editorial note attacking Rajwade and G.S. Sardesai, and glorifying Grant Duff, indicates Guha's scant knowledge of the subject. He has taken no pains to correct, or explain the statements of Duff, by adding footnotes like S.M. Edwardes did in his 1921 edition. Guha has too high an opinion of Duff's work and writes, 'Indeed Duff's is a mirror in which each reader can see his own reflection.' His charges against Rajwade and Sardesai are uncalled for.[90]

Marathi Version

The Marathi translation under the title of Duff's volume *Marathyanchi Bakhar* has also gone through six editions. It was translated into Marathi in 1829–30 by Captain David Capen with the help of Baba Sane. Earlier, Briggs had persuaded Pratap Singh, the Raja of Satara to get the work translated into Marathi. His letter of 20 August 1827 says:

I trust your Highness has received his book (Duff's History of the Mahratta Empire), which your Highness should procure to be translated by decree into the Marathi language, after which it might be struck off on lithography (Chhap) at Bombay, which would obtain as great a name for your Highness in the east as your friend Captain Grant Duff has established himself in Europe by compiling his excellent history.[91]

Conclusion

Grant Duff's *A History of the Mahratta*, published in 1826, has not lost its significance even to this day as the first comprehensive history of the Marathas and as a landmark in Maratha historiography. S.M. Edwardes of the Indian Civil Service, who was the editor of the sixth annotated edition (1921) and provided a highly informative and critical introduction, has aptly pointed out 'two circumstances' that might have contributed to the 'permanent value of Grant Duff's literary achievement, the first being his own personal experience of the people about whom he wrote and his natural impartiality; and the second, the advice and criticism of his friend and official chief Mountstuart Elphinstone'.[92]

In support of the first circumstance, he cites an extract from the *Calcutta Review*, which says:

Grant Duff lived among them (the Marathas) for years, understood their peculiar character, and without any pretension to commanding talent, seems to have combined the chief qualifications necessary to be a good Political Agent. He was industrious, impartial and benevolent . . . He studied men and manners in the camp, the cabinet, and in the peasant's field, as well as in the dusty records of his office. He examined the past that he might understand the present. . . . His book is written with the candour and the gentlemanliness of the accomplished soldier, combined with the kindliness to be expected from a disciple of Mountstuart Elphinstone. . . The record of that portion of Maratha history that came under Grant Duff's personal observation appears to us to possess the rare merit of thorough impartiality. . . Truth was his grand object. He sank no point by which it might be ascertained or illustrated; but while doing so, he uniformly treated his opponents with unassuming candour.[93]

Elphinstone was at once Duff's sponsor and critic. The exchange of letters between them from 1819 to 1823 'testify to the constant interest which he took in the preparation of the work'. He taught him methodology, the style to be followed in a subject like history, the assessment of source material, and several other relevant matters, about which references have already been made earlier. It is because of this 'circumstance' that 'it is not surprising that Grant Duff's work takes place in the very first rank of historical composition'.[94]

Duff's *History* did not attract much attention while he was alive. He did not care much for the fate of his book. He could imagine how John Bull would yawn at his *History*.[95] However, the services rendered by him to the cause of Maratha history in particular, and to the historiography of modern India in general, can hardly be denied. It was not only an advance over the study of Scott Waring, who wrote his volume in 1810, but it also stimulated a critical study of Maratha history in India by scholars, including G.S. Sardesai, C.A. Kincaid, D.B. Parasnis, Sir Jadunath Sarkar, Surendra Nath Sen, and many others, who enriched the subject by their painstaking and critical studies.

D.B. Parasnis, while surveying Maratha historical literature (1904), makes an appropriate note of this work in these words:

The most notable book of this period is, however, Grant Duff's *History of the Mahrattas*. In spite of later researches, Grant Duff is still the paramount authority in the subject of Maratha History. His work fully deserves all the eulogies heaped upon it by successive writers. For patient research and judicious statement it stands pre-eminent among the works on Maratha History. Whatever additions and improvements may be made by later writers, Grant Duff's work stands on its own pedestal and can hardly be surpassed. It cannot be denied that want of familiarity with the Maratha language and such other causes have led to some errors and defects which later investigations may be able to correct.[96]

NOTES

1. This biographical note is based mainly on an unpublished and incomplete autobiography of Mountstuart Elphinstone Grant Duff, the son of Grant Duff, who subsequently became the governor of Madras. I am indebted to Mrs Sheila Sokolov Grant, the great-granddaughter of Grant Duff, for making available this manuscript. Besides this, the 'Memoir of the Author' by S.M. Edwardes in his introduction to the sixth edition (1921) of Grant Duff's *History of Mahrattas*, has also been consulted.
2. MSS EUR, F88, Box 90—Mountstuart Elphinstone to Grant Duff (henceforth referred to as M.E. to G.D., etc.), 24 April 1822.
3. Sir T.E. Colebrooke, *Life of the Honourable Mountstuart Elphinstone* (2 vols.), 1884, vol. II, p. 188.
4. Unpublished, referred to in n. 1. Italics mine.
5. D.B. Parasnis, *Mahabaleshwar*, p. 41.
6. Leslie Stephen, *Life of Sir James Fitzjames Stephen*, London, 1895, p. 171.
7. According to S.M. Edwardes, 1827. See Introduction to *The History of the Marathas*, vol. I, p. xxxiii. Perhaps this date is correct, as Grant Duff must have married only after the publication of this book, i.e. after 1826.
8. G.D. to M.E., 14 October 1852.
9. Ibid., 4 June 1852
10. *J.I.H.*, vol. XV, pt. 2 (1936), p. 227(5).
11. G.D. to M.E., 10 January 1849.
12. I am indebted to John Murray & Company, London for making available this letter of Grant Duff, 17 January 1826.
13. James Grant Duff, *A History of the Maharattas*. Revised annotated edition (6th edn.) in 2 vols., with an introduction by S.M. Edwardes, Oxford: OUP, 1921, vol. I, Introduction, p. xxxix.
14. James Grant Duff, *A History of the Mahrattas* (in 3 vols.), London, 1826, printed for Longman Rees, Orme, Brown and Green, Paternoster Row.
15. G.D. to Charles Grant, 20 August 1821, see also Duff, op. cit., Introduction, p. xxxviii.
16. G.D. to M.E., 19 July 1819, MSS EUR, F 88, Box 6B18.
17. Duff, op. cit., Introduction, p. lxxxvi.
18. G.D. to M.E., 19 July 1819.
19. M.E. to G.D., 21 July 1819.
20. Deccan College Maratha History Museum, Rumal No. I, File No. 6: 24. This circular is incomplete, and its author and date are not known. Yet from the nature of its contents and the place where it was found, it is clear that it must have been issued by Grant Duff in 1818–19. See also Grant's letter to H.E. Goldsmid, 30 January 1846, where he writes, 'I began to collect materials at his (Mr. E's) and Sir Thomas Munro's suggestion lest we should lose the only chance of recovering the records of a very extraordinary power, the history of which was known in a very superficial manner.' Duff, op. cit., Introduction, p. xxxviii
21. Ibid., Introduction, p. xxxvi.
22. G.S. Sardesai (ed.), *Selections from the Peshwa Daftar (SPD)*, vol. 42, Bombay, 1934, p. 25.

23. Ibid., p. 20.
24. G.D. to M.E., 15 July 1819.
25. Ibid.
26. Sardesai, op. cit., *SPD*, vol. 42, p. 26.
27. G.D. to M.E., 25 June 1820.
28. Sardesai, op. cit., *SPD*, vol. 42, p. 31.
29. Ibid., p. 29.
30. M.E. to G.D., 20 April 1822.
31. Ibid.
32. G.D. to M.E., 15 July 1819.
33. G.D. to Hutchinson, 1821.
34. Duff, op. cit., vol. I, p. 80. For references to Persian sources also see vol. I, pp. 323, 324, 337. See also G.D. to Gordon, 15 February 1821.
35. G.D. to M.E. March 1822. Compare this with the 'Life of the Author' given in the first Volume of the translation of Ferishta by Briggs.
36. G.D. to Gordon, 15 February 1821.
37. Ibid.
38. G.D. to Erskine, 20 February 1821.
39. G.D. to M.E., 19 July 1819.
40. M.E. to G.D., 24 April 1822.
41. G.D. to M.E., 22 June 1822.
42. K.T. Telang, *Gleanings from Maratha Chronicles*, Ch. XIII, Appendix to *Rise of the Maratha Power* by M.G. Ranade, Bombay: Bombay University, 1961, p. 136.
43. The author contacted one of the descendants of Grant Duff, Mrs Sheila Sokolov Grant, his great-granddaughter, Woodbridge, London, but could not trace any historical records or papers of Grant Duff, except a few family photographs and an incomplete autobiography of his son, Mountstuart Elphinstone Grant Duff.
44. A.R. Kulkarni, *James Cuninghame Grant Duff*, Pune, 1970, pp. 213–14.
45. Grant Duff, op. cit. (1921), Introduction, p. lxxx.
46. G.D. to M.E., 12 April 1822.
47. M.E. to G.D., 24 April 1822.
48. The India Office Library, London has preserved all these notes of Grant Duff under the title Grant Duff Papers.
49. V.K. Rajwade (ed.), *Marathyanchya Itihasachi Sadhane (MIS)*, vol. I, Wai, 1898, Introduction, p. 32.
50. Duff, op. cit., vol II, pp. 470 fn.
51. ——, G.D. to M.E., 8 July 1820.
52. ——, G.D. to M.E., 29 May 1822.
53. ——, Ibid.
54. ——, M.E. to G.D., 21 July 1819.
55. ——, M.E. to. G.D., 4 January 1823.
56. ——, G.D. to M.E., 21 March 1822.
57. ——, Ibid.
58. ——, M.E. to G.D., 21 March 1822.
59. ——, Ibid.
60. ——, M.E. to G.D., 1 April 1822.
61. ——, Ibid.
62. ——, M.E. to G.D., 5 January 1822.

63. ——, Ibid.
64. ——, M.E. to G.D., 8 April 1822.
65. ——, Ibid.
66. ——, M.E. to Close, 5 May 1822.
67. ——, M.E. to G.D., 4 January 1823.
68. ——, Duff, op. cit., vol. II, p. 534.
69. ——, Ibid., vol. I, Introduction, p. xi.
70. ——, M.E. to G.D., 4 January 1823.
71. ——, M.G. Ranade, *Rise of the Maratha Power*, p. 104.
72 ——, G.D. to M.E., 22 April 1822.
73. ——, A Review of Grant Duff's *History of the Marathas* by N.J. Kirtane, Pune, 1968, 2nd edn., 1894; 3rd edn., 1926.
74. Vishnushastri Chiplunkar (ed.), *Nibandhamala*, New Edition, Pune, 1917, pp. 102, 610–11.
75. M.G. Ranade, op. cit., p. 10.
76. V.K. Rajwade, *Aitihasik Prastavana*, Pune, 1928, pp. 26–31. See also A.R. Kulkarni, op. cit., pp. 226–8.
77. *The Maratha*, a periodical, Pune, 30 May 1915, p. 183 and 4 September 1916, p. 417.
78. Jadunath Sarkar, *Shivaji and his Times*, 6th edn., Calcutta, 1961, Preface, p. 1.
79. G.D. Bearce, *British Attitudes Towards India*, London, 1961, p. 266.
80. ——, G.D. to Charles Forbes, 9 December 1820.
81. ——, G.D. to M.E., 12 August 1820.
82. ——, Ibid., 31 August 1820.
83. ——, Ibid., 12 October 1820.
84. ——, Ibid., 2 August 1829.
85. ——, Ibid., 31 March 1822.
86. J.S. Grewal unpublished thesis 'Muslim Indian History', presented to the University of London, 1962. Ch. 10, 'The Marathas and James Grant Duff', pp. 316–17.
87. Ibid.
88. Duff, op. cit., vol. I, Introduction, p. xi.
89. J.P. Guha, *Grant Duff's History of the Marathas*, 7th edn., in 2 vols., New Delhi, 1971.
90. ——, Ibid., see his Editorial Note.
91. A.R. Kulkarni, op. cit., pp. 203–5.
92. Duff, op. cit., Introduction, p. xxxv.
93. Ibid.
94. Ibid., p. xxxvii.
95. G.D. to M.E., 27 April 1827.
96. D.B. Parasnis, 'Maratha Historical Literature', in *JBBRAS*, nos. 60–2, vol. 22, 1904–7, p. 171.

PART II

THE ARCHIVAL MOVEMENT: COLLECTION OF SOURCE MATERIAL

7

The Archival Movement in the Bombay Presidency: Colonial Policy (1818–1947)

The pioneering work in Maratha historiography, as has been pointed out in Part I, was mainly done by Europeans, namely the Portuguese, the English, the French and others, between the seventeenth and the nineteenth centuries. The Indians during this period did not go beyond historical chronicles, the only tool of conducting a dialogue with the past. This was partly due to the lack of a tradition of history writing, and also due to the restrictive colonial policy followed by the British Government regarding the use of archival material for historical purposes. The state papers were collected by the East India Company from the Peshwas and the village and pargana officials and other papers were kept under lock and key by the government and were used only for administrative purposes.

An attempt is made in Part II of this book to trace the archival movement in the Bombay Presidency and to provide a survey of the tireless and extraordinary efforts made by Maratha historians in launching a popular movement for collecting private records, as well as bringing pressure on the government to open the 'archives' to the public.

The archival movement in the Bombay Presidency between the years from the loss of Maratha political power in 1818 and the attainment of Indian independence in 1947 is a sordid story of the inelastic, inflexible imperial archival policy of the British against which Maratha intellectuals had to make an all-out effort to establish their right to use the archives and their right to publish historical material. However, we have to acknowledge, in retrospect, our indebtedness to the rulers for jealously safeguarding our archival material until it passed into our hands. The resistance of the rulers in this respect was an unintented benefit to the cause of historical research. This was aided and carried forward by the labours of our pioneering scholars and historians. It was thus possible to present a connected account of the history of India in general and especially the history of the Maratha people.

The British had humbled the Marathas and wrested power from them in 1818. Though this was an accomplished fact, a relation of trust between the two was yet to be established. The Marathas were still suspect in the eyes of the British and the memories of the Maratha Wars had yet to be effaced. While this was so, the Marathas could not but look wistfully at their past, recollect with sadness their lost power and eminence, and seek to restore and revive it by an appeal to history.

G.W. Steevens was a British traveller who visited Poona in 1899 when anti-British feeling was at a higher pitch because of the recent murders of Mr Rand and Lt. Ayerst on the Jubilee night arranged in honour of Queen Victoria, on 25 June 1897, by the Chapekar brothers, who were later hanged. His observations regarding the rebellious Maratha's are very interesting. He writes:

> Other provinces of India were ceded to us or conquered from alien lords; the Marathas lost their all in war . . . the Marathas have never forgotten how high they were less than a hundred years ago and who it was that brought them low. They lost more than others, and they feel the loss more. For others we were a change of masters, we brought them down from masters to slaves.[1]

This explains why the British treated Maratha history as a 'hot subject', containing explosives harmful to the foundation of the empire, and sought to bar historians from any access to state papers, and also why Maratha history was full of explosive material, which, if not hidden and guarded from public view, might lead to the loss of their hard-won gains and undermine the very foundations of their empire, and hence why access to state papers was strictly barred. As we have remarked at the outset, this, contrary to what the rulers might have expected, led to protest against British archival policy and to the rise of a school of nationalist historians.[2]

Archives under the British

When the East India Company conquered Maratha territories from the Peshwas in 1818, Mountstuart Elphinstone, the Resident at the Poona court, applied himself to the task of organizing the scattered records of the Huzur Daftar at one place, and assigned the job of preparing a preliminary report on the nature and contents of the state records to his colleague, Capt. John Macleod.[3] The Huzur Daftar was a very extensive establishment under the control of Huzur Phadnavis (Phadnis), in which about 200 clerks were employed in the several departments of the various branches of the state administration. It was mainly a repository of the income and expenditure records of the state and several other money transactions, 'excepting only the private affairs of the prince, or such accounts as it suited not the interests of individuals in power to have on record'. It was a complete daftar till the time of the last Peshwa, Bajirao II, and Nana Phadnis, the *karbhari* or the manager of the Peshwa, government, had kept it in order since he enjoyed supreme authority over it (1774–96).

The Daftar, which was in a state of the utmost disorder, and was kept at different places, was moderately complete up to 1730 and was nearly complete from, 1763 to 1796, as pointed out by Capt. Macleod in his preliminary Report of 15 September 1819. A salient feature of this Daftar, according to him, was that 'the series of accounts of the districts and villages afford a view of the comparative state of cultivation and improvement and assessment of the country at different times'.[4]

Thus, the concern of the British, as it is clear from Macleod's remarks, was to know more about the revenue administration of the Marathas rather than their history.[5] William Chaplin who succeeded Elphinstone as the Commissioner of Deccan in 1819 rightly pointed out in his Memorandum on the Pune Daftar (9 May 1826) that the utility of the Daftar of the Peshwa was for reference on a great variety of subjects connected with the territory of the Bombay Government.[6] It was for this purpose that priority was given to the organization of the Daftar by the new masters.

William Chaplin had entrusted the management of the Records to the sardars and jagirdars of the Deccan, and A. Bell acted as their Agent for managing the Huzur Daftar. All the Records, amounting to nearly 3,500 bullockcart-loads, were kept in the Nana Phadnis Wada, and five Amanatdars[7] were appointed to help the Agent in registering and arranging the Daftar.

The Agent, A. Bell, knew well that the Records were referred to by others 'on points requiring elucidation in the public administration'. Nevertheless, in 1836 he wrote to the Chief Secretary to the Bombay Government:

> As all the valuable and useful papers have long since been abstracted and the frgments can now be of little use in the management of the country, I venture to recommend that they may be locked up and the key kept with the Agent, who can either personally attend, or depute some trustworthy person to open the Daftar whenever a copy of any paper may be required.

The Amanatdars, however, asked for an extension of two years for completing their work, and the Government accepted this request as they 'thought it desirable to have a complete registry of the Records to prevent frauds'. The Government appreciated the work of the Amanatdars, who had taken sufficient care and trouble while discharging their duty and the neatness and the cleanliness with which the Records were arranged.[8]

R. Mills, the Agent who succeeded A. Bell, suggested that as most of the valuable papers were abstracted, the fragments should be either burnt or sold, as the cost of preservation would be much higher than the importance accorded to them. He further stated that if they were sold, they would fetch Rs. 1,000 which would 'fully cover the expenses of the establishment required and leave a little for the benefit of Government'.[9] The committee appointed by the Government held the view that until all the valuable documents were arranged properly, and the useless fragments destroyed, the arrangement of the Daftar could not be considered as complete. The Government was always worried about the expenses involved in maintaining the Daftar. It was, therefore, suggested that in order to minimize the cost of maintenance, the Daftar, after the completion of the arrangement, should be transferred to the various districts of the Government to which they belonged, and a general register of all documents be kept in Pune and Bombay.

Mills was informed that 'many objections exist to the sale of such documents and that to burn them without at least a partial inspection would be a measure to be regretted'.[10] He was also censured for the delay in submitting the report of the committee.

H.E. Goldsmid, Superintendent of the Revenue Survey in the southern Maratha country, complained that the Carnatic papers were not received by him and expressed his fear that they might be tampered with, and therefore warned the Government that any delay might result in the loss of many thousands of records. The new Agent, John Warden, requested the Government to spare the services of Goldsmid for arranging the Daftar. He, with his 'indefatigable energy, quickness and clearness', prepared within a short period a report on the present state of the Poona Daftar. He was further requested to complete the examination of the entire Daftar relating to the Maratha territory.

Goldsmid in his observation strongly resented the suggestion to close the establishment made by the former Agent, Bell, and reiterated the importance of the Records for settling the just claims of the affected persons, and how they had as a result formed a favourable opinion about the fairness and equity of the Government. He was unhappy with the original lists prepared by the Amanatdars. He was also critical of the appointment of 'outsiders' in the Department by removing local persons who had a thorough knowledge of the arrangements of the Records and were, as he called them, 'walking indexes'.[11] While admiring the work of the Amanatdars for putting the Records in order, he also pointed out the chief defects in their system regarding the identification of papers, classification and separation of important papers from useless ones, etc. He discovered immense quantities of loose papers scattered in different rooms and closets, exposed to damage from damp and vermin. He also pointed out the dangers involved in transferring the selected papers to the headquarters of different *zilas* (districts).[12]

The Amanatdars set aside the arrangement of Macleod of 1819, and within a period of seven years of their office (1835–41) catalogued two-thirds of the Peshwas' papers. The original nucleus of the Daftar comprising about 1,300 bundles expanded in the course of time due to accretions of records from the offices of the Poona Resident (1818), the Deccan Commissioner (1818–26), the Agent for Sardars (up to 1856), the Angres of Kolaba (1790–1840), the Konkan Daftar from Ratnagiri (1751–1818), the Satara Rajas (1703–1840), the Satara Resident (1818–48), Karnataka and Gujarat, and lastly the Jamav Daftar, and the papers collected by the Inam Commission.[13]

Between 1851 and 1860, the *ferists* or handlists of all the *rumals* (bundles), with the contents of some of them, were prepared. The issue of classification and indexing of records was again reopened by the Government of India in 1868, but Col. Etheridge, the Alienation Settlement officer, categorically rejected it as a sheer waste of time and money. His suggestion that after the completion of all the original work a small establishment of 'practised hands' to manage the working of the Poona Daftar be maintained was accepted by the Government. He stated that 'skilled hands will turn up anything, but the whole Maratha Government Record Office is a labyrinth and chaos to the unskilled'.[14]

In 1875, presuming that the records in the Daftar were classified and indexed, the Government of India asked Col. Etheridge to prepare a complete list of the records for publication, to which he replied that 'any system of complete indexing was impossible and unnecessary'.[15] In 1886, Robertson, the then Commissioner, C.D. put forth a project for printing the more valuable parts of the Peshwa's Diaries. The project was sanctioned by the Government, and Govind Chimnaji

Vad, the Alienation Assistant to the Commissioner, who was put in charge of this project, transcribed and translated thirty-two volumes of extracts from the Peshwa's Diaries and other papers in the Poona and Satara Daftars. The Deccan Vernacular Society requested the Government in 1897 that they be entrusted the work of editing and printing these volumes. This was accepted by the Government, but due to excessive cautiousness and the discouraging archival policy of the Government only one volume relating to Satara could see the light of day. The society was also assigned the job of editing and publishing the Chitnisi letters, i.e. the correspondence of the Peshwa's Officers.[16]

The official correspondence regarding the publication of the Diaries by the Deccan Vernacular Society is a telling example of the delaying tactics employed by the Government in the matter of publishing any material relating to Maratha history. The extracts were selected by Vad, a government official, yet the condition put on the society was, 'The Commissioner, C.D. should determine the form in which the selection should be printed, that he should inspect and approve the annotations made by the society, and that 30 copies of each of the printed volumes should be supplied to Government for their use free of cost.'[17] Out of these thirty gratis copies, ten copies were sent to the Secretary of State for India, London. A copy of Ranade's 'Introduction' to the Peshwa's Diaries was also sent to the Under Secretary of State, London. The society was instructed not to sell the Diaries as an authorized government publication. The proofs were to be corrected by the Commissioner, C.D. He certified on 23 December 1903 respecting the first volume that the proof sheets were inspected in his office before final printing and found to contain no anomalies.[18]

Justice Ranade as President of the Deccan Vernacular Society had taken the initiative in getting these Diaries of the Peshwa's. He wrote an exhaustive introduction to the first volume of the Diaries and sent it for the approval of the Government. The official noting in this respect states:

Although the publication of the Diaries has been undertaken by the Deccan Vernacular Society as a private enterprise, yet it is acting under the sanction and with the permission of Government, and the Introduction, if published with the Diaries, will be regarded as being approved by Government, as an accurate and authoritative exposition of the effect and the contents of the Diaries. It is really an essay written with the object of exhibiting the rule of the Marathas in the most favourable light possible and is coloured throughout with the personal opinion and bias of the author. Any introduction of the kind ought to have been approved by Government before being given to the public.[19] (26 March 1901)

While forwarding the Introduction to the Secretary, Government of Bombay, for perusal, the Commissioner, C.D. stated: 'I see no objection to its being prefaced to the selection' (18 February 1901). However, by a resolution, he was requested to inform the Secretary of the Deccan Vernacular Translation Society that 'Government would prefer that the selection from the Peshwa's Diaries should be published separately from the paper prepared by the late Honourable Mr. Justice Ranade'[20] (1 May 1901).

The Government, in its authority, even went to the extent of issuing instructions regarding the title page of the Diaries. It was resolved that the heading 'Selections from the Records of the Government of Bombay' should be omitted and that, after the words, 'printed and published' should be inserted the words 'with the permission of Government'[21] (30 October 1901).

It is difficult to understand the rigid attitude of the Government of Bombay and of the Government of India regarding Ranade's Introduction to the Peshwa's Diaries regardless of the fact that some competent British officials had praised it. The Governments were perhaps scared that Ranade's emphasis on the use of the Daftar for historical purposes might lead to a public demand for free and open access to these records. It was interpreted that Ranade was justifying Maratha rule and thereby indirectly criticizing British rule. In his Introduction, Ranade had pointed out how the earlier historical works of English historians like Grant Duff and others, including the Marathi *bakhars* (chronicles), had harped only on political events, ignoring the conditions of life of the people and the efforts that were made by the state towards the improvement of the society and economy. Ranade wrote:

These State Diaries . . . are simply invaluable and though they have their own defects, in the absence of better materials, they shed a flood of light upon the real movements and the hopes and fears, the strength and weakness, of the people for over a century, and for purposes of instruction and guidance, they far outweigh in value the narratives of wars and conquests, dynastic changes and revolutions, which take up so much space in our ordinary histories.[22]

Ranade was not motivated by any prejudice or animus—direct or indirect—against British rule in his historical writings. In fact, his aim, as he has mentioned in his Preface to *Rise of the Maratha Power*, was 'to remove many misapprehensions . . . and, above all, to enlist the sympathy of the representatives of the conquering British power in the fortunes of its worsted rival'.[23]

It has been rightly pointed out that the British were not merely 'history conscious' but 'history-friendly'.[24] They were quite aware of the value of the Poona Daftar for historical purposes. Nevertheless, they doggedly withheld historical records from public view; they still preferred to treat the Poona Daftar as an 'Alienation office' rather than as a storehouse of source material for a comprehensive history of the region as well as of the subcontinent. The Government purposely created the impression that they had published almost all the information available from the Maratha records for historical purposes through their printed selections and in the research conducted by historians. Regarding the publication of the Peshwa's Diaries, A.C. Logan, Acting Commissioner, C.D., remarks, 'What these selections were has been observed that they comprise only a small fraction of the documents in the office . . . there lies an unworked field for greatly amplifying and perhaps correcting the brief sketch of Maratha internal administration which Mr Ranade has attempted.'[25]

A.M.T. Jackson, ICS, Collector of Nasik, who was later appointed as the Officer on Special Duty responsible for calendering the Peshwa's Records in 1907, had made it quite clear how valuable the original state papers were for students of history and how the new school of historians, from Von Ranke onwards, had drawn from the collections of state papers. He remarked, 'Every civilized Government now admits students of history to search its archives.' After pointing out the present stage of research in Maratha history, he observed, 'No Government in India owns a collection of vernacular state papers that approaches in interest and importance those of the Poona Daftar and it is, I venture to think, the duty of Government to make them available to all students of Indian History.'[26]

However, his basic stand on the historical writings of Maratha intellectuals was not very different from the general attitude of the Bombay Government towards this subject:

> Government are aware that a school of thought has grown up in the Presidency which looks back to the rule of the Peshwa's as a sort of golden age and seeks eagerly for evidence in support of this belief. Even Mr Ranade was not free from the patriotic bias and gives a somewhat one-sided picture of Maratha rule through looking too exclusively, at its best period, under Madhavrao. A selection made by adherents of this school of thought is likely to give too bright a picture of the period and therefore to encourage political dreams which can do no good either to the dreamers or to the Government.[27]

To avoid the danger of 'bias' or 'prejudice', Logan suggested in his report of 1905 that:

> An officer endowed with critical acumen and the historical sense should be appointed to examine the records systematically for historical purposes and compose a large volume of valuable information. . . . The book prepared on these lines would be both a history in itself and a guide to future historians who might desire to delve still further into the originals.[28]

Jackson, however, did not approve of Logan's suggestion, arguing that, 'a work prepared by a Government officer would be suspected of equal bias on the other side, unless it could be published along with its evidence'. Only a complete publication of the whole of the evidence will suffice to lead the student to the true view that the Maratha administration was on about the same level as that of the Plantagenets in England, and was good or bad according to the character of its leading officials.[29]

Jackson, had suggested to the Government as early as 1901 the preparation of a calendar on the lines of the English Record Office about which he had collected some information while he was on leave in London. According to him, the most important papers for the history of the Peshwa's Government were the Diaries (the day books) and *Ghadnis* (a ledger of revenue matters), which he argued deserved priority in the scheme of calendering. The Diaries provided the indispensable chronological framework that which a historian requires, and the extracts from the *Ghadnis* would give additional details of the transactions referred to in the Diaries. The rest of the Records like the *Prant Ajmas*, the *Chitnisi Daftar*, etc., could be taken up later as the means and the editors became available. Jackson suggested that though the Government need not pledge at once to the whole undertaking, it was desirable both for political and historical reasons to calendar and publish the records. The editor of each section was expected to write an introduction that would give a sufficient account of the organization of the Peshwa's Government to make the Diaries intelligible and also to note the evidence from the Diaries on doubtful points of history with reference to Grant Duff and the Marathi chronicles.[30]

It appears from the forwarding remarks of Logan (8 June 1907) that he was not much in favour of the suggestions regarding calendaring and the appointing of editors for selecting and publishing the records. He remarked that in view of the work already done by G.V. Vad and Purushottam Mawaji, there was no immediate need for an editor. C.A. Kincaid, the Collector of Pune, to whom the suggestions of Jackson were referred for comments, remarked, 'Calendaring was after all only intended to facilitate examination of the originals, which were in many files, being rapidly eaten away, by white ants, and even the ink was gradually disappearing.' He further suggested that the cost of appointing a full-time special officer might be spent in printing all the files and then the originals might be destroyed.[31]

Jackson was appointed as officer on Special Duty for calendaring documents in the Pune Daftar in September 1908. He was to select those records that would prove to be of sufficient value to students and historians and those that would be helpful in revising Grant Duff's *A History of the Marathas*. The Government anticipated that the work would require five years and that it would cost about Rs. 2 lakh. Jackson accepted the appointment for one year, and submitted his estimate of the cost of calendaring and publishing the records. But he was murdered by the revolutionaries on 23 December 1904 before he could take up his new assignment.

The Main Issues: Policies of the Home Government and the Government of India

The main issues before the Government of India on which the archival movement was concentrated in the last decades of the nineteenth century, and particularly before the First World War respecting the Archives were calendaring all the archival material, publishing it, and lastly, opening the Archives to the public. The founding of the Indian National Congress, the introduction of the Reforms Act of 1909, and the move for access to the Records and the publication of historical material as a part of the general national movement, forced the Government to take a serious view of archival matters. Officers like Logan and Jackson had already realized that the use of the Pune Daftar could not be confined only to the problems of alienation, but could also be used for historical study and political purposes.

H.G. Stokes of the Foreign Department of the Government of India and Dr E. Denison Ross, the officer in charge of the Records and of the three main Records Offices, namely Calcutta, Madras and Bombay, were chiefly concerned with two problems in 1909: (1) the preparation of calendars of the old records of all the three centres, and (2) the preparation of lists of such records in the Bombay Presidency and the publication of selections therefrom.[32] The problem of calendaring had been under consideration by the Government of India since 1861. The Secretary of State for India suggested that the calendars, instead of being limited only to the papers of 'historical interest, should contain every document, whatever its value'. When Denison Ross consulted the Bombay Government in this respect, he got the impression that they had the least enthusiasm for the scheme of calendaring the Records. They did not want their scheme for the Peshwa Daftar to be disturbed, and regarded calendaring as a work of supererogation.[33]

It was held by the Government of India that the public had no right of access to the Records, but private research scholars, on payment of fees and agreeing to certain conditions, could be allowed to consult the records and get their copies with the express sanction of the officer and publish them with his permission. The Government were of the opinion that there was no general and genuine historical interest in India by 1910, and that there were only 'political pamphleteers' and no historians. While agreeing to give conditional access to bona fide students and research scholars, it was at the same time decided that it would be undesirable to throw open the records to the public before press-lists and indexes had been completed and the contents of the Records settled and listed. It was regarded as 'unwisdom' to provide material 'which may be used against Government either politically or otherwise. The Government of India is not old enough to throw open its archives in the manner suggested with impunity for all concerns'.[34]

When it was pointed out that the records in London 'are the same' as those in India, the Secretary replied, 'But the public is different.'

> There is in India no aristocracy of erudition, no school of history, no historical research; scientific use of evidence, and critical scholarship are barely understood and seldom achieved. . . . The encouragement and opportunities which the opening of the records would afford to frivolous and impertinent writers, unscrupulous journalists and the like would be disastrous to the Government.[35]

It is quite obvious that the Department of Education of the Government of India underestimated the intellectual activities and potential of Indians and completely ignored the Maratha historians of the stature of Justice Ranade, Rajwade, Khare, Sane, Parasnis, among others. Ranade's *Rise of the Maratha Power* (1900), 'Introduction' to the *Peshwa's Diaries* (1900), and *Currencies and Mints under the Maratha Rule* (1899) remain historical contributions of outstanding interest and importance. V.K. Rajwade, a pioneer of the nationalist school of historians, started in 1898 his series '*Marathyanchya Itihasachi Sadhane*' (Source Material of Maratha History), in which he not only published source material but also wrote lengthy and critical introductions; he also critically examined in the very first volume (1898) Grant Duff's *History of the Marathas*. He founded the Bharat Itihas Samshodhak Mandal, Poona, in 1910 with a view to providing a platform for historians on the lines of Ranke's seminars. The writings of Ranade, Rajwade, Khare, Sane, Parasnis, and others display an 'aristocracy of erudition, and critical scholarship' which A.F. Scholfield's eyes could not see in India but found only in the works of the historians of the West. It is clear that his eyes refused to see and take note of the writings and activities of Indian historians of the time who were animated by a genuine interest in the past, a spirit of patriotism, and concern for the country's future. It is hard to understand how a government with a reputation for 'eternal vigilance' failed to sense the ideological climate of the times.

This is confirmed by the reply of the Department of Education, Government of India to the Secretary of State of India in reply to the latter's dispatch of February 1914 regarding the question of allowing private individuals access to unpublished records:

> We recognise fully the force of the proposal sent by your Lordship for our consideration. Conditions in India are however different from those prevailing in England, and after careful consideration, we are of the opinion that the disadvantages of the change will out-weigh the possible benefits. (4 February 1915)[36]

Towards a New Policy

The political situation in India from the 1910s onwards began deteriorating because of the repressive policy of the Government of India. The Morley-Minto reforms of 1909 failed to satisfy the political aspirations of the Indians. When the First World War broke out in 1914, and Turkey joined the anti-British camp, Indian Muslims also turned anti-British. The Press Act of 1910, the Defence of India Act of 1915, and the growth of revolutionary organizations in India and abroad, compelled the British to take cognizance of the growing unrest in India on all fronts. Montagu, who took over as the Secretary of State for India in 1917, was sympathetic towards Indians. He criticized the attitude of the Government of India as 'too wooden, too iron, too inelastic, too anti-diluvian, to be of any use for the modern purpose we have in view'. His liberalism and belief in the progressive realization of responsible government in India had its effect on the official archival policy as well. Ramsay Muir was asked to work out a scheme for the improvement of the management of archival records for the purposes of historical research. He visited the different Records offices in India, consulted many concerned people, and wrote to Sir E.D. Maclagan, keeper of Records of the Government of India, a demi-official letter on 7 December 1917 saying:

> In dealing with the historical records of India, I strongly feel that we ought not to limit our view to our official archives. After all, they are only a section of the material even for the British period, and the Imperial Government ought to have in view the history of India as a whole, and not merely of the British administrative system. There are vast stores of historical material of Indian origin still available which ought to be properly treated before they are lost, and it seems to me to be the duty of the Imperial Government to ensure as far as possible that the whole body of evidence for the history of India is properly safeguarded and is treated systematically on a sound plan.

Ramsay Muir recommended the setting up of a Historical Materials Commission and made valuable suggestions regarding the duties of this body. One of the duties that he suggested, was the selection 'from among the historical teachers or graduates of the universities and colleges of India, the men who should be asked to undertake the editing, and where necessary the translation of various series of archives'.[37] He observed how the archives in different provinces were in different languages and how an Indian from one province was unable to understand what was written in another language in another province.

The Historical Records Commission, 1919

The Government of India was generally guided by the policies of the British Government. When the Royal Commission of Records in England abandoned the policy of preparing press-lists as too meagre, the Government of India followed suit and decided that calendaring was too slow, too elaborate, and too expensive. The restrictive policy was thrown overboard, and they decided that 'the best method of rendering the records accessible to the public' was by,[38]

1. preparing a list of the volumes or bundles accompanied by a descriptive handbook;
2. calendaring of certain documents; and
3. reprinting in full of certain specific documents.

As a part of this policy, the Indian Historical Records Commission was set up in March 1919 as a permanent body of expert advisers. Jadunath Sarkar, B.K. Thakore, and L.F. Rushbrook Williams were nominated to the first Commission by the Government as non-official members. The Madras and Calcutta Records offices were represented on the Commission, but the Bombay Government, in spite of their large collection of archival material, did not find any official representation on the body. This was perhaps due to the restrictive policy of the Bombay Government regarding access to private individuals to the Records office. J.L. Rieu, Secretary to the Government of Bombay, General Department stated:

> The Government of Bombay are opposed to the giving of general permission to search and examine such of its records as date back beyond a certain period as there is no guarantee that even records bearing a comparatively remote date do not contain documents or information, the disclosure of which to the public would be prejudicial to the interests of the state . . . these precautions are especially necessary in the case of the important historical records bearing on the relations between the Peshwa's Government and the British Government, which cover a period extending from the year 1750 onwards.[39]

The Historical Records Commission and the Bombay Presidency Archives

B.K. Thakore, of the Deccan College, Pune, the non-official member of the Commission, moved a resolution at its very first meeting in Simla in 1919 that the body should request the

Government of Bombay to produce a volume on the source material of Maratha history (seventeenth and eighteenth centuries) with the help of the University of Bombay and the Bharat Itihas Samshodhak Mandal of Pune, and other local bodies and public-spirited individuals. It was also mentioned in the resolution that if the Government of Bombay accepted the proposal, the Commission would request the Government of India to contribute to the production of the volume at one rupee a page.[40] The Bombay Government accepted this resolution and entrusted the task to Prof. H.G. Rawlinson of the Deccan College, Poona, who, with the help of Prof. R.P. Patwardhan, Elphinstone College, Bombay, after overcoming many hurdles, published it in 1929 as a Government publication. It must be remembered here that the first volume that was published includes records up to the death of Shivaji, i.e. the seventeenth century, comprising two parts: (i) Maratha Sources, and (ii) Foreign Sources. The material is drawn mainly from literary sources, family papers, travelogues, English records and translations of Persian texts, and not from the State Archives.[41] The Bombay Government must have readily accepted this proposal, as it did not touch the sensitive period of Anglo-Maratha relations. The second volume dealing with the eighteenth century was never published.

The Pune School of History, however, did not appreciate the work of the Commission respecting the Maratha Archives. D.V. Potdar, in his capacity as Secretary, Bharat Itihas Samshodhak Mandal, Pune, criticized the domination of Jadunath Sarkar and G.S. Sardesai in the Commission, who were pressing the Commission against the adoption of the original plan of arranging and organizing the Peshwa Daftar on historical principles as an aid to the writing of history. Potdar objected to the publication of select documents from the Peshwa Daftar and the Poona Residency Correspondence by the Bombay Government. This publication was prepared under the general editorship of G.S. Sardesai, who was appointed as the Historical Research Officer at the Peshwa Daftar, while Jadunath Sarkar, who was regarded by the Poona historians as the very incarnation of Grant Duff, carried out the actual work of selecting the documents on behalf of the Commission. Potdar appealed to the democratic Government of Bombay, set up under the Act of 1935, to abandon the old policy of depending entirely on the advice of Sarkar–Sardesai regarding the Peshwa Daftar, to remove all restrictions regarding access (of which he was also a victim), and to give up the practice of charging fees from scholars for consulting the Archives.[42] Questions were also raised in the Council on the working of the Peshwa Daftar. As Potdar was taking a keen interest in the activities of the Commission, he was nominated to it by the Government as the representative of the Bharat Itihas Samshodhak Mandal, Pune, in 1942.

V.G. Dighe, a noted Maratha archivist, however, praised the work of the Commission. According to him, from the point of view of Maharashtra the achievement of the Commission was 'focusing the attention of the Bombay Government on the importance of the Peshwa Daftar for historians, and constantly urging for the assessment of the Daftar from the experts, preparation of lists, publication of Residency Records, etc.' As a consequence of this, the Government published forty-five volumes of selected documents of the Peshwa Daftar and fourteen volumes of the Poona Residency Correspondence.[43]

Sardesai–Sarkar

Notwithstanding differences of opinion among historians, the contribution of Sarkar–Sardesai and of the Commission need hardly be exaggerated. Sardesai's services as Historical Research officer were sought by the Government through Jadunath Sarkar, who regarded him as 'the eminent historian, so highly praised by Kincaid'. There were no complaints against him in the sessions of the Council, says the official noting and adds further that he was persuaded to take up the assignment against his own personal inclinations in the interest of the public work.[44]

Sardesai, however, was not entirely free to select and publish extracts from the Peshwa Daftar. Whenever the press copy was prepared, the Government of India sought a clearance certificate from the Commissioner, C.D., who was in charge of the Alienation office. He had to forward the press copy with the note, 'The selection has been carefully examined in my office before being sent to the press for printing with a view to ensuring that nothing objectionable administratively was being published.'[45]

Sardesai had to seek permission for everything, even on minor matters such as whether R.P. Patwardhan could go through the proofs in the absence of Rawlinson with a view to improving the English.[46] It seems that there was some difference of opinion regarding the title of volume no. 14 of the selections, whether it should be 'Maratha Conquests in the North' or 'Expansion of the Maratha Empire in the North', as suggested by the editor. The Commissioner, however, suggested that it should be 'The Incursions of the Marathas into the North or Northern India'. Sardesai did not accept, and the original title was retained. He resented this sort of direct interference as it amounted to a drastic change in the very interpretation of history.[47] He was not prepared to forego as editor, and he had made this stand clear to the Government earlier. He wrote:

> While on the one hand I must not divulge any official information in the papers in the Alienation office, I have on the other hand a certain duty to perform towards that large expectant public of India who are interested in historical research. . . . By agreeing to do research work here, I think I do not lose my individual liberty to say what I think is right.[48] (21 November 1929)

A reviewer of the first seventeen volumes called PRC, under the title 'Notices of Books', wrote: 'They confirm in a striking degree the general accuracy of Grant Duff, but they make many doubtful points clearer and afford a personal touch about many individuals, particularly the founders of the Sindia, Holkar, Patwardhan and Pawar families.'[49] The same reviewer had similar words of praise for the accounts of the battles of Panipat and Udgir.

Jadunath Sarkar expressed his satisfaction with the work of Sardesai in his letter of 14 June 1931 to W.F. Hudson, Governor of Bombay in these words, 'This series is doing a service to the country's history which any civilized government may be proud of.'[50]

NOTES

1. G.W. Steevens, *India of Yester Years,* London, 1899 (rpt, 1984), pp. 271–2.
2. J.H. Voigt, 'British Policy towards Indian Historical Research and Writing (1870–1930)', *Indian Economic and Social History Review*, vol. III, no. 2, Delhi, June 1966, p. 138.
3. Huzur Daftar is the record of the transactions of the Government as registered by the officers. It was later on known as the Peshwa Daftar, the Alienation office, and now as the Pune Archives.
4. 'Selections from the Records of the Bombay Government', no. XXX—New Series I: *Correspondence exhibiting the Nature and Use of the Poona Daftar and the Measures Adopted for its Preservation and Arrangement since the Introduction of the British Rule*, Bombay, 1836, p. 1 (henceforth referred to as *P.D.*), pp. 1–4.
5. Macleod wrote a note on the Maratha revenue system under Nana Phadnis, perhaps while organizing the Huzur Daftar. See India Office Library, London, MSS EUR, D-32, Erskine Collection. Thanks to Dr Stewart Gordon for bringing this to my notice.
6. *P.D.*, pp. 4–8.
7. The Amanatdars were: (1) Balajipant Narayan Natu, the Pradhan Amanatdar; (2) Ramachandra Pandurang Dhunduri; (3) Moro Trimbak, the native judge; (4) Naro Shankar, Daftardar to the Revenue Commissioner; and (5) Visaji Gopal, Daftardar to the Principal Collector of Poona—*P.D.*, pp. 23, 26. See also *Aitihasik Samkeerna Sahitya*, BISM, 1947, vol. 7, Letter nos. 37, 38, pp. 46–9.

   The Peshwa Daftar was earlier in the Shanwar Wada (palace), but when the palace was set on fire, it was removed by the order of Chintopant Deshmukh to the houses of Govindrao Kale, Babaji Naik, and Babaji Naik Baramatikar, where they remained in complete disorder. Till they were removed by Elphinstone first to the house of Khasgiwala and subsequently were housed in Nana Phadnis's palace till 1890, when they were finally removed to the new building specially constructed for this purpose.
8. *P.D.*, pp. 8, 17, 27, 34.
9. Ibid., p. 30, 11 June 1841.
10. Ibid., p. 34.
11. Ibid., p. 44. 'Elphinstone preferred local people as officers. But Chaplin, who was in Carnatic for some time, brought Carnatic persons from the ceded districts and gave them high positions. Mr Warden finds some danger in introducing either the eminent persons or supporters of the last Peshwa in the Archives as they might find the means benefiting their friends and injuring their enemies.' *P.D.*, p. 41.
12. *P.D.*, pp. 49–50. Report, 11 February 1845.
13. 'Note on the Alienation Office, Poona, compiled for the Committee appointed by Government Resolution No. 6099 dated 27th July 1905', prepared by A.C. Logan, Acting Commissioner, *P.D.*, pp. 1–2 (henceforth referred to as Logan).

    The Committee appointed by the Government of Bombay under the Acting Commissioner, A.C. Logan, was asked (1) to examine and report on the present condition of the papers in the Alienation office; (2) to submit proposals for future supervision, for the rearrangement of the daftar, and for the preparation of the indexes; and (3) to consider whether the future Alienation establishment could undertake the duty of supervising the arrangement and indexing of records in other offices.

Logan's exhaustive report giving a descriptive account of the Alienation office is still considered an authentic guide to the Poona Daftar.

14. Logan, pp. 3, 6.
15. Ibid., p. 6, 13 April 1876.
16. Ibid., p. 39.
17. Maharashtra State Archives (MSA), Bombay, Revenue Department (henceforth referred to as RD), vol. 68 of 1904, General Resolution (GR) No. 949, 4 February 1897, p. 303.
18. Ibid., pp. 284, 287–8, 291, 297.
19. RD, vol. 90 of 1901, p. 145.
20. Ibid., p. 161.
21. Ibid., p. 173.
22. M.G. Ranade and K.T. Telang, *Rise of the Maratha Power and Other Essays and Gleanings from Maratha Chronicles*, Bombay: University of Bombay (rpt. 1961), pp. 173–4.
23. Ibid., Preface, p. 1.
24. Voigt, op. cit., p. 141.
25. Logan, pp. 38–9.
26. RD, vol. 37 of 1908, p. 413, Jackson's letter to the Secretary to Government, Revenue Department, 25 May 1908.

    'The study of the history of the Maratha period in this Presidency is still in the medieval stage. We are dependent upon the *Bakhars* or chroniclers, some of whom wrote to glorify particular persons or families, while others had very imperfect means of knowing the facts. It is true that Messrs. Telang and Ranade have drawn attention to the mass of materials that awaits the historian in the Poona Alienation office, but no one has yet seriously undertaken to publish more than a small fraction from it.'

    A.M.T. Jackson was a student of Indology and interested in promoting the cause of Sanskrit. He was, therefore, liked by Indian intellectuals, but the repressive measures against the anti-British activities of revolutionary organizations like the Abhinava-Bharat founded by V.D. Savarkar were resented by patriotic-minded people. He was shot dead in a theatre in Nasik, on 21 December 1909, at 9.30 p.m. where he had gone to attend a performance. Anant Kanhere, a young revolutionary of Aurangabad, and his associates Krishnaji Karve and Vinayakrao Deshpande were arrested and later hanged.
27. RD, vol. 37 of 1908, pp. 413–14.
28. Logan, pp. 38–9.
29. RD, vol. 37 of 1908, p. 414. Logan objected to the comparison between the Peshwas and the Plantagenets of England who ruled between AD 1154 and 1485. Logan remarked, 'No more unhappy comparison could be made than that which Jackson suggests between the sordid despotism of the Peshwas and the rule of the noble Plantagenets who founded the constitution of England.' See RD, vol. 37 of 1908, 8 June 1907, pp. 417–18.
30. RD, vol. 37 of 1908, pp. 417–18.

31. Ibid., p. 419.
32. National Archives of India (NAI), New Delhi, Home Department, Public Branch, 'A' Proceedings, April 1910, nos. 1–5, Notes, p. 1.
33. Ibid., p. 2.
34. NAI, Foreign Department, General Branch, 'B' Proceedings, March 1910, nos. 261–3, Note dt. 24 November 1910, signed by H.G. Stokes and H. Adamson.
35. NAI, Department of Education, General Branch, 'A' Proceedings, June 1914, nos. 1–2, Note dt. 28 April 1914, signed by A.F. Scholfield.
36. NAI, Department of Education, General Branch, 'A' Proceedings, February 1915, nos. 7–9, Letter from the Government of India to the Secretary of State for India, no. 2 of 1915, para 4.
37. NAI, Department of Education, General Branch, 'A' Proceedings, April 1918, nos. 1–17, Notes, pp. 19–22, Letter of Ramsay Muir to Sir E.D. Maclagan, 7 December 1917.
38. NAI, Department of Education, General Branch, 'A' Proceedings, August 1919, no. 12, Resolution no. 77, 21 March 19191.
39. NAI, Department of Education, General Branch, 'A' Proceedings, February 1915, no. 7, 'Letter from the Government of Bombay, no. 7460, 22 September 1914. In 1750, the Peshwa and the British had signed a treaty of mutual help against the Angres. However, the bone of contention between the two was Vijaydurg, the marine fort, which the British wanted to keep with them to establish their control over the westcoast.
40. S.N. Sen, *Indian Historical Records Commission: A Retrospective, 1919–1948* New Delhi: Government of India, 1948, pp. 19–20.
41. The Resolution of the Commission IX, item 16 of Agenda of the meeting held at Simla in June 1919, R.P. Patwardhan and H.G. Rawlinson (eds.), *Source Book of Maratha History*, vol. I Bombay, 1929. (Reprinted with an Introduction by P.M. Joshi and A.R. Kulkarni, under the auspices of the Indian Council of Historical Research, by K.P. Bagchi & Co., Calcutta, 1978.)
42. D.V. Potdar's article in *Sahyadri* (Marathi periodical), vol. 9, no. 1 (January 1939), pp. 71–5.
43. Dr V.G. Dighe's article in *Lokshikshan* (Marathi periodical), Year 9, vols. 6–7, December 1938–January 1939, pp. 420–9.
44. Pune Archives (PA), Poona, File July 1929 to June 1933, July 1929.
45. PA, Selection from Peshwa Daftar, File, pt. VI, September 1930–January 1933, p. 387.
46. Ibid., p. 418.
47. Voigt, op. cit., p. 144, quoted by Dr Voigt, A. Mackie, Commissioner, C.D. to Sardesai, 10 November 1930.
48. Ibid., p. 144. Draft of a letter by Sardesai, 21 November 1929, quoted by Dr Voigt from the Alienation office, Poona, File 1929–31. [I could not trace these two references in the above-mentioned file.]
49. P.A., Sarkar–Sardesai Government File, July 1929–June 1933, p. 426. [The name of the journal in which the reviews were published is not mentioned.]
50. Ibid., p. 551.

8

The Popular Movement: Early Historians of the Marathas

The spirit of the Indian Renaissance found its echo in the pride of Maratha intellectuals in their historical heritage. It has already been pointed out how the assault of N.J. Kirtane, a junior student of the Deccan College (1868), on Grant Duff's *A History of the Marathas* (1826), and later V.K. Rajwade's virulent attack on the same work (1898), aroused the interest of Maratha scholars in the history of their ancestors. When it was found that the Pune Archives in the possession of the British were closed to the public, Maratha historians started a parallel movement for the collection and preservation of historical materials from old families, closely associated with the rise, decline and fall of Maratha power. Their aim was to present a correct and comprehensive history of the Marathas from the point of view of the Marathas themselves as against the biased and prejudiced works of British historians.

Vishnushastri Chiplunkar (1850–82), who has been described as the Shivaji of the Marathi language, in his well-known essay entitled *Itihas* (history) exposed the biases of British historians like T.B. Macaulay and James Mill as well as the works of missionaries by critically examining their prejudiced views and derogatory remarks against the Marathas.[1] He pointed out that Morris's *History of India*, which was then prescribed as a textbook in India, allotted only about thirty to thirty-five pages for the history of India up to 1739. The Mughal rulers hardly got five pages. Morris's account of Shivaji, whom he considered, a robber, includes a detailed description of the Afzal Khan episode and contains a number of anachronisms, such as dating Shivaji's coronation ten years earlier, dating the murder of Afzal Khan three years later, and placing the execution of Sambhaji during the lifetime of Shivaji. Chiplunkar also cited some of the typical questions set by the Bombay University for the B.A. examination in History, for instance, (a) Write the genealogy of the Peshwas, (b) When, where and among whom was the Third Battle of Panipat fought? What were its consequences?

Chiplunkar criticized the utter neglect of the history of the Marathas by British historians as well as the teachers at the universities. Neverthless, he was very sympathetic towards Grant Duff, who had sacrificed his fortune to get his monumental work on the Marathas published. He castigated the Indians for having forgotten their glorious past and for having developed an inferiority complex. The English language, he said, was superceding the mother tongue of Indians; Indians were not proud of their country, religion, customs and traditions, and had thus orphaned themselves. He lamented that the erudite essay of N.J. Kirtane on Grant Duff had been ridiculed by intellectuals and had remained unnoticed in the printing press for nearly seven years. He then made a fervent appeal to the public to collect all historical material irrespective of its significance or insignificance and preserve it for posterity so that an authentic history of the Marathas could be written which would serve as a source of information for generations to come.[2]

While reviewing the efforts of *Kavyetihas Samgraha*, a periodical devoted to literature and history, Chiplunkar visualized three periods of Maratha history to be covered in three volumes. The first period, which may be described as 'Shivaji and his times', would cover such topics as the condition of people in the pre-Shivaji period, Shivaji and his times, Shivaji and his associates Mavales, his civil, and military administration, the Mughals, saints like Ramdas and Tukaram, the valour of the Prabhu community, etc. The second volume would cover the period between Sambhaji and Shahu, i.e. from 1680 to 1748. After the death of Shahu, the range of Maratha history widens, and it becomes a history of the whole subcontinent because the Marathas everywhere occupied pockets of territory in different parts of the country. The third volume would deal with the period that witnessed Maratha power at its zenith, and also the period of its decline and fall. Chiplunkar argued that history does not mean glorifying the valour of Shivaji, or Bajirao, or Yashwantrao or the diplomacy of Nana Phadnis. It must also take into account the judicial and revenue systems, arts and crafts, money and banking, medicine, literature, forms of popular entertainment such as tamasha or the vocal music of Venkat Narsi, the courtesan of the Peshwas, sports like wrestling, etc. History should also deal with social relations between father and son, husband and wife, religious beliefs and festivals, learning, dress, diet, and so on. He further stated, that the history of the Marathas would remain incomplete as long as we do not get from it every sort of information about the Marathas. Chiplunkar was thus ahead of his age as far as historiography is concerned.[3]

Chiplunkar's appeal calling for the collection and preservation of historical documents did not go unheeded. Sane, Khare, Rajwade, and Parasnis, may be described as the four pillars of the mansion of Maratha history, who devoted their lives to collecting *bakhars*, family records, paintings, copperplates, coins and various articles, which may be regarded as the documents of Maratha history essential for reconstructing a comprehensive history of the Maratha land and its people.

Kashinath Narayan Sane (1851–1927)

Kashinath Narayan Sane, a contemporary of N.J. Kirtane of the Deccan College, entered the Bombay Government education service after graduating in 1873 and held different positions in the department. He opted for voluntary retirement in 1908 in protest against the government's denial of his legitimate claim to promotion as educational inspector. Nevertheless, the government did recognize his sincere service and conferred on him the title of 'Rai Bahadur'.[4]

Sane was very deeply impressed by the appeal of Kirtane and Chiplunkar regarding the collection and preservation of historical documents. He started a periodical called *Kavyetihas Samgraha* in 1878 in cooperation with Chiplunkar and Balaji Janardhan Modak with a view to publishing Marathi historical records, and Sanskrit and Marathi poems. Sane was in charge of the section dealing with historical records. The periodical lasted only for eleven years, but during this brief period it published 6,300 pages worth of material, which include twenty-two historical works, mainly *bakhars* (chronicles) and 501 letters, and a few Sanskrit and Marathi literary works. About the achievements of the periodical, Sane stated with great pride: 'This work marked the revival of the national spirit in Maharashtra after the setback and despair following the disaster of 1817. . . . A feeling of national pride was kindled. Everywhere there was awakened the desire to publish old historical works and letters.[4] The *Kavyetihas Samgraha* not only aroused the pride of the Marathas in their own language, land and religion, but also inspired historians like Khare, Rajwade, Parasnis and others to launch a movement for the collection, preservation and publication of historical documents.

About Sane, it may be said that the 'age of *bakhars*' dawned with him, though he also published a few family papers in his periodical. He emphasized the publication of *bakhars* first as they were compiled in the common man's language and therefore it was easy to carry history to the masses. Thus, about eighteen *bakhars*, including *kaifiyats*, were brought to light by him through his periodical. His critical editions of two *bakhars* on the life of Shivaji by Krishnaji Anant Sabhasad and Malhar Ramrao Chitnis, the *Bhausahebanchi Bakhar* and the *Peshwa Bakhar* by Sohani, are still regarded by scholars as standard editions. He collected most of the manuscripts during his travels as a school inspector in the districts under his charge. He was quite aware that the *bakhars* did not have the status of histories, but neverthless believed that they could be treated as sources of information in a limited way. He published the *bakhars* without altering or modifying their text but only provided relevant details of their location. If two or more manuscripts of the same *bakhar* were found, he examined their contents and edited only that version that he considered most authentic and complete, indicating the differences in the texts of other versions of the *bakhars* in footnotes. He tried to establish the authenticity of *bakhars* by citing corroborative evidence from authentic historical records, wherever possible. Thus, his critical edition of Chitnis's *Life of Shivaji* running into 376 pages, contained 114 pages of footnotes. His erudite critical editions of *bakhars* were highly praised by scholars such as R.G. Bhandarkar, Gopal Hari Deshmukh popularly known as Lokhitwadi, D.V. Potdar and Jadunath Sarkar.[5]

Sane was actively associated with the Bharat Itihas Samshodhak Mandal, Pune, since its foundation by Rajwade in 1910 and was its president for some years. He died at the age of seventy-six, on 17 March 1927 at Kalyan. (A list of his contributions to history and historical research is provided in the appendix to this chapter.)

Vasudeo Vaman Khare (1858–1924)

Vasudeo Vaman Khare popularly known as Vasudeoshastri Khare was one of the pioneering research scholars of the post-Panipat period of Maratha history. He was a nationalist historian, a contemporary of Sane, Tilak, Agarkar, and Kelkar, who devoted his entire life to the unearthing of the priceless historical documents in the possession of the Patwardhans of Miraj, a prominent noble family enjoying the patronage of the Peshwas in the post-Panipat period.

Khare was born in Guhagar (Konkan) on 5 August 1858, in to a poor Chitpawan brahmin family. He began learning traditional Sanskrit under the well-known Sanskrit scholar of those days, Pandit Anantacharya Gajendragadkar of Satara. After completing his studies in Sanskrit, he left Satara for Pune where he secured a teaching job on a salary of Rs. 15 per month in a school. Later he joined the editorial section of the history journal *Kavyetihas Samgraha*, founded by K.N. Sane, where he came into contact with reputed Marathi scholars like Chiplunkar, Modak, Sane, Jinsiwale, and others. In fact, he was advised by Krishnashastri, the father of Vishnushastri Chiplunkar, to learn English, become a pleader, and then as a hobby write in Marathi, as one could not earn a living by producing volumes in Marathi. But Khare did not pay much heed to this piece of advice.

Khare's talent and potential were recognized by B.G. Tilak and G.G. Agarkar. They persuaded him to join the New English School, which they had founded in January 1880. It was Khare who suggested the name *Kesari* for the newspaper founded by Tilak and Agarkar in 1881 and also the motto, beginning with 'Gajali Shreshta', a Marathi version of a Sanskrit verse praising the lion, Kesari, the symbol of *Kesari* to this day.

From Pune Khare shifted to Miraj in November 1880 to join the Miraj High School as a shastri on a monthly salary of Rs. 30. Greatly attracted by the project of working at the Miraj Archives, he made the town his permanent home even on this modest salary, declining better prospects elsewhere, including a job offering Rs. 35 per month. He mastered the English language and read carefully the writings of Macaulay, Scott, Byron, Goldsmid, Grant Duff, Murray, Mill, and Elphinstone. He also studied the histories of Rome and Greece, and even translated Byron's epic poem 'Ocean' into Marathi under the title 'Samudra'. He established himself as the best Sanskrit teacher. In the course of time he earned the favour of the Chief of Miraj and was granted entry into the archives of the Patwardhans of Miraj. As Jadunath Sarkar has aptly observed, 'Khare's employment at Miraj and settlement in that town was a divine dispensation to all lovers of Maratha history. Here was the work and here was the man.'[6] The importance of the Patwardhan archives for reconstructing the history of the Marathas can hardly be exaggerated. The Patwardhans had been in the service of the Peshwas from the time of Nanasaheb till the end of during Maratha power. They rose to prominence in the days of Nana Phadnis, fought many wars during the last phase of Maratha power, and served the Maratha state in various capacities. Miraj had thus become a centre of great political activity in the post-Panipat period. The agents of the Patwardhan chiefs, stationed at the Pune darbar, regularly sent newsletters to their masters or relatives giving a day-to-day account of the happenings at the Pune court. This corpus of historical letters thus formed a priceless treasure trove of raw materials for the study of Maratha history. The Patwardhans joined hands with the British against Bajirao II to save their homes at Miraj, Kurundwad, Tasgaon and Jamkhandi, parts of the southern Maratha country, from the ravages of war. As the Patwardhans withdrew from the Anglo–Maratha contest, their homes and particularly their archives remained intact.

Khare found a variety of original records at Mirajmala where he worked for nearly five to seven years from 1893. From the 300 *Rumals* (bundles) of records, chronologically arranged and well preserved, he selected nearly four lakh letters, copied many of them with the help of a *modi* scribe appointed by him on a monthly salary of Rs. 7 or 8, and published about 30,000 letters in his historical journal *Aitihasik Lekh Samgraha* in twelve volumes, each running on average to 500 pages. He had read almost every letter in the archives of Mirajmala, but published only one out of every 500 letters that he had read. He also examined the records of Ichalkaranji jagir, the private papers of the *watandars*, and also a few relevant records from the Pune archives.

Khare was well equipped to undertake scholarly research. He knew how to select relevant records from a mass of historical documents, determine the importance of each record by comparing it with other records, fixing its date, establishing the correlation between different records, and simultaneously preparing introductory notes on them. Fixing the dates of letters written before 1774 was a difficult task for researchers. The earlier letters mentioned the date and month according to either the Muslim or the Hindu calendar, without mentioning the year, which the scholar had to fix by analysing the contents of the letters. Sometimes the letter writer did not indicate even the date or month of the record. The next step after fixing the date was to arrange the records chronologically and thematically. With his analytical mind, keen observation, and constant reading, he was able to discover evidence in confirmation and corroboration in support of his findings in other contemporary records. This aptitude for research was partly inherent and partly cultivated by him. He has clearly laid out the method of his study of historical documents in the first volume of *Aitihasik Lekh Samgraha*, published in 1901.

Khare has made out a case for the authenticity and utility of the Patwardhan records for the post-Panipat history of the Marathas in his introduction to the first volume. He maintains that about twenty or twenty-five persons from the house of the Patwardhans shed their blood in several campaigns of the Marathas, particularly in the south, and one gets details of the movements of the army—sieges, plunders, pitched battles, chasing, raiding—in the various dispatches sent by the sardars or their clerks who were actually involved in these campaigns. Gopalrao and Parashuram Bhau were the two noteworthy warriors from the Patwardhan family, and numerous letters of their period—a period of crisis—were available to Shastri. One finds numerous references to the Maratha luminaries of this period, including Sakharam Bapu Bokil, Nana Phadnis, Trimbakrao Pethe, Mahadji Shinde, Tukoji Holkar, the Bhonsales, the Gaikwads, and the Ghorpades, as well as the enemies of the Marathas, mainly Haider Ali and Nizam Ali.

It is true that the records published by Khare are mainly political in nature, but a few of them do shed some light on the socio-economic conditions of the times. The *behadas* (budget) of *saranjam* assignments of revenue for military service, *jabitas* (rules mainly for collection of revenue), decisions of village panchayats, market rates, pensions of soldiers, forms of punishments, expenses incurred on pilgrimages to Kashi, etc., provide valuable material for the socio-economic history of eighteenth century India.

Khare took every precaution to make the documents intelligible to the reader. He explained old and obscure works in footnotes. As the Marathi language was an admixture of Persian, Urdu, Portuguese, Kannad, and English words, the original Marathi words often appear in a corrupt form and need explanation for identifying persons and places. He had collected a number of atlases, descriptive books of places, chronologies of old families, gazetteers, ephemera and various reference works in English and Marathi. He had carefully studied the geography of the Maratha country in particular and India in general. He presented the old records in a style that makes them interesting and worth reading.

A distinguishing feature of Khare's volumes are the exhaustive notes attached to each group of letters. In fact, these notes are essentially histories based on the documents of a particular period. His argument in this respect was that most people read only the introductory remarks rather than the archaic letters. He was satisfied even if people only read the notes, to which he, as a nationalist historian, attached great importance as a means of creating national awareness and a knowledge of their glorious past. His son later published only the introductions to the first four volumes under the title *Marathi Rajyacha Uttarardha*, vol. I, which was essentially a history of the post-Panipat period, written in a lucid style.

Sane, as has been mentioned earlier, emphasized the publication of *bakhars*, but both Khare and Rajwade rejected the *bakhars* as legendary accounts compared to the more authentic documents housed in the archives. He believed that a sound structure of Maratha history could be erected on the firm basis of authentic records without which one would not get the real picture of social and political conditions.[7] Like Rajwade, Khare, too understood the importance of collecting and preserving of the records of the historical families lest they should be lost forever. However, Khare was fortunate in getting all the records that he wanted at one spot and did not have to wander, like Rajwade, from place to place.

He started his journal *Aitihasik Lekha Samgraha* in June 1897 with an annual subscription of Rs. 3 and fixed the price of individual numbers at 5 annas. He promised to print 500 pages per year through his journal. It was indeed a courageous step for a teacher getting a small salary of Rs. 30 per month. The journal ceased publication after three years during which period the first three volumes appeared. However, the next three volumes appeared over a period of ten years, from 1901 to 1911, due to various financial and domestic problems. Khare spent about thirty-five years of his life on historical research, out of which twenty-eight years were taken up for the completion of twelve volumes.

The Patwardhan chiefs did not give any financial support to Khare for the publication of their archives. The manager of the Mirajmala archives, however, gave him all the relevant information, particularly on Nana Phadnis on whose life Khare wrote two books. He also succeeded in obtaining permission to publish from the political agent of the southern Maratha country. But the necessary funds were not forthcoming. He appealed to people for help by subscribing to his journal. Even the reviewers of his volumes used to make a fervent appeal to the public for support for Khare's work. The cost of production of a volume of 500 pages was roughly Rs.1,500, and the total collection by way of subscription was hardly Rs. 500 to 600 only as the membership did not go beyond 100 or 125. To make both ends meet, he required at least 200 new members. His monthly income was about Rs. 45, on which he had to support his wife and four children. With a view to devoting his entire time to research, he opted for premature retirement in 1913 and his pension was fixed at Rs. 15 per month.

His friend T.S. Karkhanis, the proprietor of the Maharashtra Natak Mandali suggested that he should write plays for his theatre company, which would help him to cover the expenses of supporting his family as well as the cost of publication of his historical volumes.

In all he wrote six plays, namely, *Gunotkarsha* (1885), *Tara Mandal* (1914), *Krishna Kanchan* (1917), *Chitra Vanchana* (1917), *Shiva Sambhav* (1919), and *Ugramangala* (1922). His last play, *Deshkantak*, which he wrote practically on his deathbed, was published posthumously, in 1930. He was quite successful as a playwright, and his historical play *Shiva Sambhav* (Birth of Shivaji) is popular to this day.[7]

Tilak had fully realized the importance of Khare's work and the patriotic duty of supporting nationalist historians at all costs. He would make some time in his busy schedule of political activities to attend the historical discourses at the Bharat Itihas Samshodhak Mandal, Pune. While addressing a meeting of the Mandal in May 1915, he reviewed the works of the historians of France and Germany and maintained that any rising nation should first research its history. In an editorial in *Kesari*, he wrote:

> No purpose would be served only by reciting the names of your ancestors. The modern age demands evidence for everything that you say.

Nobody would listen to your gossip. Your ancestors surrendered your kingdom and if you lose your history, your successors would destroy your religion and there would be every possibility of effacement of the very name of Maharashtra, or the destruction of Maharashtra. So no longer neglect your history henceforth.[8]

Rajwade was enraged when he learned that the Patwardhans were indifferent to Khareshastri's efforts to publish the Patwardhan archives. He curtly wrote in one of his Introductions.

While Vasudeoshastri Khare should sell out his household for publishing the records of the Patwardhans, and the Patwardhans of Miraj, Sangli, Jamkhindi should not take even cognizance of it is really annoying. Should we say that Shivaji the Great, Damaji Gaikwad or Parashurambhau Patwardhan etc. were the grandfathers or great grandfathers of the historians, and quite unrelated to the chiefs of the princely states. . . . What a great crime that these chiefs and inamdars ancestors should go into oblivion? This Bharatdesh is known as the worshipper of the ancestors, and now what a shameful treatment is accorded to them.[9]

Khare's major contribution to Maratha historiography were the twelve volumes of *Aitihasik Lekha Samgraha*, published between 1897 and 1924, covering the historical material from 1760 to 1800 in 6,483 pages. One finds a good deal of material on the Maratha activities in the Deccan in most of the volumes. His desire to take the history up to the end of Maratha power was fulfilled by his son Yashwantrao Khare, who added three more volumes to the series covering the period from 1810 to 1818 in 1,600 pages, between 1925 and 1948.

With the help of material available in the Mirajmala, Khare wrote two books on Nana Phadnis, *Nana Phadnisanche Charitra* (1892) and *Adhikaryog* (1908). He edited the *bakhar* of the house of the Patwardhans called *Harivamshachi Bakhar* (1909) composed by Balkrishna Harihar Patwardhan, a long essay on *Maloji and Shahaji* (1902), and a critical introduction to N.C. Kelkar's book *Marathe va Ingraz* (1918), which has been acclaimed as the best analytical essay on the causes of the decline and fall of Maratha power. As a historian he was true to his discipline and never wrote anything to please anyone by hiding the truth. When the chief of Ichalkaranji entrusted to him the records of his jagir for the writing of its history, Khareshastri made it clear to the chief that he would write or present a true history, without omitting any 'scar or blemish' as it emerged from the sources, and would never flinch from expressing his views, inferences and conclusions as strictly deduced from the sources, and that he would be free to write what he felt was true and correct. The chief of Ichalkaranji readily accepted this condition, and Khare produced a volume of 530 pages entitled *Ichalkaranji Samsthancha Itihas va Ichalkaranji Daftaratil Nivadak Patre Yadi* (1913). Besides presenting a consistent history of the Ichalkaranji Jagir of the Ghorpades, and introducing relevant original material, Khare Shastri critically discussed at length the origin and decline of the Maratha confederacy, which, as Justice Ranade has rightly pointed out, was at once both the source of strength and weakness of the Maratha state. The two pamphlets, namely *Miraj Prakaran* (1898) and *Haider Ali var Tisri Swari* (1901), which were first serially published in his journal, mainly form a part of the history of the Patwardhans.

Khareshastri did not spare anyone who made inaccurate, false and prejudiced historical statements. The historians of Maharashtra were dissatisfied with the only comprehensive history of the Marathas then available, that is, the study by Grant Duff, and they started finding fault with it right from 1868. The Bharat Itihas Samshodhak Mandal undertook the task of correction and revision, and Khare was entrusted with the responsibility. He was acknowledged as the most critical and analytical historian of the early nineteenth century and had impressed his peers by his commitment to historical veracity and scrupulous fidelity to archival sources. Khare had read an essay on the errors in Grant Duff's history in 1916, which was published in a summary form in the English weekly *The Maratha*, of the *Kesari* group.[10] He pointed out the errors in the dates of events and names, and the deeds and characters of certain historical personalities, as well as certain misstatements in Grant Duff's history, with the help of the new material that he had discovered in his researches at Mirajmala. In view of these numerous mistakes, he concluded, like Rajwade, that Grant Duff's study was not a history, but rather a chronicle of the Marathas. But while assailing Grant Duff for his acts of commission and omission, Khare at the same time praised the Englishman for his inquisitiveness and thirst for knowledge, his efforts in collecting source material, and the sacrifices that he had made.[11]

A.B. Latthe of Kolhapur wrote an article[12] on the tomb of Parashuram Bhau Patwardhan, who had fought his last battle against the Chhatrapati of Kolhapur at Pattankudi in September 1799. Latthe, perhaps with a view to pleasing Chhatrapati Shahu Maharaj of Kolhapur, made certain unhistorical statements about Parashuram Bhau Patwardhan and his funeral based on Balaji Prabjakar Modak's *History of Kolhapur*. In fact, Khare had earlier torn to pieces Modak's statements regarding Parashuram Bhau Patwardhan's last battle by citing authentic evidence, and Modak had gracefully accepted the criticism and apologized for his mistake. But Latthe did not stop at this. He proceeded to make certain derogatory remarks against Parashuram Bhau, and Khare wrote a series of six articles in the newspaper *Dnyan Prakash* (November and December 1914) in response and exposed Latthe thoroughly.

In his famous introduction to N.C. Kelkar's monograph on the relations between the Marathas and the English, Khareshastri maintained that the main causes of the downfall of the Marathas were lack of experience of proper administration through political institutions, lack of discipline, lack of reforms in the military system, a loose and ineffective central administration, dissensions among the Maratha sardars, and perhaps the social barriers of the age-long caste system. He did not hesitate to highlight the defects in the Maratha character, particularly the complete absence of patriotism, the inability to work together as a group, selfishness, and utter dependence on others. These defects were more prominently visible in the eighteenth century and finally led to the destruction of Maratha power. As a nationalist historian, Khare appealed to the people to shed these shortcomings and build a new and enduring swaraj.

As has been pointed out earlier, Khare's major contribution to the history of Maharashtra, particularly of the forty years between 1760 and 1800, was the publication of the twelve volumes of *Aitihasik Lekh Samgraha* (1897–1924). Out of these, the first four volumes running to 2,000 pages are devoted entirely to the period of Madhavrao I, who had to undertake the uphill task of restoring the lost prestige of the Marathas, which had been shattered by their defeat at the Third Battle of Panipat (1761). The next five volumes (5–9) deal exclusively with the activities of Mahadji Shinde and Nana Phadnis, the two great pillars of the Maratha state between 1773 and 1795. The two major events of this period were the First Anglo-Maratha War and the Battle of Kharda against the Nizam, and in both the Marathas registered victory. The remaining three volumes (10–12) narrate the sordid tale of the last phase of Maratha history, from the assumption of the peshwaship by Bajirao II (1796) to the death of Nana Phadnis (1800).

Khare had a strong desire to complete his project, carrying it up to the end of Maratha power in 1818, and had collected all the relevant original material but did not live long enough to realize his dream. This task was left to his son Yashwantrao, who published this material between 1926 and 1948 in three volumes, bringing Maratha history up to 1818. Thus, all these fifteen volumes cover the history of the Marathas from 1760 to 1818 in 8,443 pages. Khare did not want to waste a single moment while working on his volumes.

An interesting incident throws light on Khare's living conditions and reveals his total absorption in his work. His wife had to go to Konkan for a few days and before leaving she left a certain number of wicks for the oil lamp in the house. As it happened, she stayed away longer than she had planned, and the wicks were exhausted. Khare ingeniously pulled out the thick yarn from his carpet, which was his seat while at work, and used it as wicks for the oil lamp. Khare's research continued without let-up, but when his wife returned she found a shrunken and disfigured carpet. Two yards of the carpet had been burnt during the night-long lucubrations of Khare. While this loss must have meant much to his wife, it was trivial in the eyes of Khare when compared to the gain in knowledge.

Jadunath Sarkar observes about Khare: 'His *Lekh Samgraha* will stand as a model for other workers among historical archives and editors of documents. His introductions are most helpful to the reader and are admirably concise and free of irrelevant digressions.'[13]

Khareshastri had to struggle hard to get each volume published. There was no response from the public, the rates of printing had doubled, the prices of paper had trebled, and so he had to appeal every time to the public for help. During the preparation of the twelfth volume, which covered a period of aboout nine months in 1800, Khare became seriously ill, and his liver was damaged by jaundice. Proper medical treatment and rest might have restored his health but he preferred to die while working rather than wasting time in rest. He became anaemic and did not possess the necessary strength to sit and work even for a short while. He had realized that death was approaching but he continued working on the volume so as to get it ready before his end. He used to sit, taking support on both sides, and worked nearly ten hours a day and thus completed the press copy of the volume. The last chapter, nearly 200 pages long, that he wrote was on 'Shinde's, Departure to the North', and he handed it over to his son. He looked quite happy and smiled with satisfaction at having accomplished his life's mission. He then rested his neck on the pillow and breathed his last. The joy of his life lay in his work and the reward of his work was the joy of working—this was perfectly true in the case of Khare.[14] When his health began to deteriorate he requested his doctor to prolong his life by five to six years so that he could bring the history of the Marathas up to the Treaty of Bassein (1802). The doctor retorted that there should rather be a 'treaty' between Khare and his health so that he could write down the dry details of the Treaty of Bassein, and that this could wait until he regained his health. Though he was suffering miserably, Khare once told a student that God had given him 'splendid health, splendid energy and splendid power of application for sixty-five years' and that he was prepared to surrender his body at any time as per God's dictate.[15] And so he surrendered his body on 11 June 1924 at 9.00 a.m.

In his obituary on Khare, N.C. Kelkar, the editor of *Kesari* wrote (17 June 1924) that his historical research was so substantive and well arranged that it could easily be equated with that of any Western-educated scholar. Although he was not well placed in life like the historian Parasnis, nor able to move from place to place like V.K. Rajwade in search of historical material, Khare's research was systematic, scientific and thorough. He did not have an invaluable and rich collection such as Parasnis had, nor the flight of imagination and the quickness of comprehension of Rajwade. However, Khare surpassed them with his unbiased and analytical mind and his power of sustaining the interest of his readers. His style was simple and his work was systematic and clear.

As Rajwade said, a nation does not produce very often a man of the status of Khare, an individual who possessed an enormous fund of information. He did everything unaided and it was his determination and strong will power that enabled him to carry out his project to its end. D.V. Potdar, who was very close to Khare, remarked that he was a shastri in the traditional sense, a sincere teacher, a humorous storyteller, poet, popular playwright, and a research scholar of proven merit. He will be remembered by all for his multifaceted personality, yet at heart he was a research scholar of history.

Jadunath Sarkar, on the basis of material supplied to him by J.M. Bhat the brother of the biographer of Khare, wrote:

> Though for the greater part of his life he was forced to live in poverty, what fortune denied to him was supplied by his innate contentment and simplicity. A self-respecting man, he would never stoop to abject means to enrich himself. Gifted with high brain power as he was, he never shunned hard work. He preferred silent work to platform speeches. His labours at the history of the past did not blind him to the present, and he kept in touch with current literature and newspapers. He was social in his manners, and never was a man more witty and humourous in private talk.[16]

Notes

1. V.K. Chiplunkar (ed.), *Nibandhamala*, New Edition, Pune: Chitrashala Press, 1917, pp. 61–107.
2. Ibid., pp. 104–7.
3. Ibid., pp. 486–7.
4. Jadunath Sarkar, *House of Shivaji*, Calcutta: M.C. Sarkar, 5th edn., 1955, p. 206.
5. R.L. Lohkar, 'K.N. Sane- A Research Historian', in *Samshodhak*, Year 57, vols. 1–3, March–April 1989, Dhule.

6. Sarkar, op. cit., p. 303.
7. D.M. Bhat, *Vasudeo Vamanshastri Khare: Chavitra and Grantha Parichaya* Miraj: Author, 1929, pp. 103.
8. *Kesari* (newspaper) 18 May 1915, Pune. Khare's article on Grant Duff.
9. M.B. Shah (ed.), *Itihasacharya V.K. Rajwade Samgraha Vangmaya*, vol. 10, *Introductions* Dhule: Samshodhan, 1998, p. 449.
10. *The Maratha,* 30 May 1916, p. 183 and 4 September 1916, p. 417, Pune. Khare's article on mistakes in Grant Duff's history.
11. A.R. Kulkarni, *James Cuninghame Grant Duff*, Pune: Pune University, 1971, pp. 233–7.
12. A.B. Lathe, 'Purashuram Bhau Patwardhan Yanchi Samadhi', *Manoranjan,* Pune (Monthly) May 1914.
13. Sarkar, op. cit., pp. 304–5.
14. Bhat, op. cit., p. 173.
15. Ibid., p. 174.
16. Sarkar, op. cit., p. 305.

APPENDIX

Historical Works Edited by K.N. Sane

(A) Bakhars and Kaifiyats

1. *Peshvyanchi bakhar*, by Krishnaji Vinayak Sohani, five editions, 1878–1925.
2. *Bhausahebanchi bakhar*, by Krishnaji Shyamrao, five editions, 1879–1932.
3. *Khardyachya Swarichi bakhar*, 1885.
4. *Shivaji Maharajyanchi bakhar*, by Chitragupta, 1888.
5. *Panipatchi bakhar*, by Raghunath Yadav, 1885.
6. *Thorale Shahu Maharaj Yanche Charitra*, by Malhar Ramrao Chitnis, 1893.
7. *Shakakarte Shri Shiva Chhatrapati Maharaj Yanche Saptaprakarnatmak Charitra*, by Malhar Ramrao Chitnis, 1924.
8. *Shrimant Chhatrapati Dhakate Ramraje va Dhakate Shahu Maharaj Yanchi Charitre*, by Malhar Ramrao Chitnis, 1884.
9. *Shrimant Chhatrapati Sambhaji Maharaj ani Thorale Rajaram Maharaj Yanchi Charitre*, by Malhar Ramrao Chitnis, three editions, 1882–1915.
10. *Shrimant Narayanrao Peshwe Yanchi bakhar*, 1887.

11. *Senapati Dabhade va Gaikwad Yanchi Hakigat*, 1887.
12. *Holkaranchi Kaifiyat*, 1886.
13. *Bramhendra Swami urfa Bhargava Baba Yanche Charitra*, 1882.
14. *Shiva Chhatrapatinche Charitra*, by Krishnaji Anant Sabhasad, four editions, 1878–1923.
15. *Bhausahebanchi Kaifiyat*, 1887.
16. *Sashtichi bakhar*, 1882.
17. *Nagpurkar Bhonsalyanchi bakhar*, by Kashiraj Rajeshwar Gupte, 1885.
18. *Jayaramswami Vadgaonkar bakhar*, 1889.
19. *Marathi Samrajyachi Chhoti bakhar*, 1889.

(B) Letters, Historicai, Kavya, etc.

1. *Nagpurkar Bhonsalyanchi Kagadpatre* (in cooperation with Vaman Daji Oka), 1889.
2. *Pantapradhan Yanchi Shakavali*, 1883.
3. *Patre Yadiche Pustak*, 1887.
4. *Rajniti*, by Malhar Ramrao Chitnis, 1887.
5. *Selections from Peshwa Diaries*, vol. 9, 1911.
6. *Shrimant Narayanrao Peshwe* (Kavya), by Pandurang, 1887.
7. *Shri Shivakavyam* (Kavya), by Purushottam Pandit, 1887.

Historical Writings of Vasudeo Vaman Khare, Published in the Volumes of Aitihasik Lekh amgraha

1. January 1760 to May 1763. Last days of Nanasaheb Peshwa to Peshwa Madhavrao's contest with the Nizam.
2. May 1763 to December 1764. Madhavrao's activities from the Battle of Raskhasbuvan with the Nizam to the siege of Dharwad fort.
3. December 1764 to October 1769. Madhavrao's Karnatak campaign: Haider Ali to the attack on the Bhonsales of Nagpur.
4. October 1769 to August 1773. Last phase of Peshwa Madhavrao's career to the brutal assassination of Peshwa Narayanrao.
5. August 1773 to July 1775. Barbhai politics to the beginning of the revolt of the imposter.

6. August 1776 to April 1778. Suppression of the revolt of the imposters, Karnatak campaign, Mahadji Shinde's attack on Kolhapur, return of forces from Karnatak.
7. April 1778 to April 1784. Morobadada Phadnis's conspiracy, relations with the English, the Treaty of Salbye, peace with Kolhapur.
8. May 1784 to February 1791. Tipu Sultan and the Marathas—the tripartite alliance between the Nizam the Marathas and the English against Tipu.
9. March 1791 to November 1796. Maratha–English in Karnatak, return of Mahadji Shinde from the North and his conflict with Nana Phadnis Battle of Kharda, deaths of Mahadji and Peshwa, defeat and arrest of Patwardhan.
10. December 1796 to December 1798. Peshwa Bajirao and his relations with the Maratha confederacy.
11. September 1798 to February 1800. Continuation of the affairs discussed in vol. 10: revolt of Chatur Singh, conflict with Karvir.
12. March to December 1800. Besieging Karvir, death of Nana Phadnis, Daulatrao Shinde.

    Total number of pages 6,843.

13. The last 3 vols. of *Aitihasik Lekh Samgraha*, published between 1926 and 1948 by Khare's son Yashwantrao carried the study of Maratha history from 1801 to 1818, pages 1,600

Grand total of pages 8,443

Miscellaneous

1. *Maloji and Shahaji*, 1920	40 pages
2. *Adhikar yoga*, 1908	140 pages
3. *Nana phadnisanche Charitra*, 1892–1927	283 pages
4. *Ichalkaranji Samsthancha Itihas*, 1913	530 pages
5. *Harivamshachi Bakhar* (ed.), 1909	105 pages
6. *Marathe va Ingraz* (Introduction), 1918	37 pages
7. *Marathi Rajyacha Uttarardha*, vol. I, 1927	285 pages
	Total 1,420 pages

9

Vishwanath Kashinath Rajwade (1863–1926)

Vishwanath Kashinath Rajwade, the doyen among the historians of Maharashtra, was a multi-faceted personality. Besides being a distinguished historian, he was also adept in linguistics, grammar, lexicography, literature, geography, epigraphy, paleography, sociology, and many other disciplines. He was born into a Chitpavan brahman family in a small village called Varsai (district Raigad) on 23 June 1863. The family originally held the surname Joshi, but due to its long association with the royal palace of Shivaji, people used to call them Rajwades.[1] The family later shifted to Pune, where V.K. Rajwade's father practised law. Rajwade's education was mainly done in Pune under the care of his uncle, as his father died when he was still young.

Rajwade was formally registered as a student at the Deccan College, Pune, in 1884 but he was mostly a self-taught man. During the period of his stay at the Deccan College, he took advantage of the college library, developed an interest in a variety of subjects such as economics, ethics, political science, philosophy, psychology, theology and so on. His college career was interrupted mainly by financial problems. He could get his B.A. degree only after a long gap, in 1891. He used this long period of seven years to equip himself academically and to acquire physical fitness. After his graduation, he enrolled for postgraduation but did not pursue it.

He started his career as a teacher in a school, but the teaching profession did not suit his temperament, and he gave it up within a period of three years. He got married at the age of twenty-five (in 1888) but lost his wife when he was thirty (in 1893). He had two children from her, but the first child died within two months of his birth, and the second died immediately on her birth along with her mother in 1893. He did not marry again and devoted the rest of his life to research and the pursuit of knowledge.

Rajwade in his youth had been greatly influenced by the writings of Vishnushastri Chiplunkar, the editor of *Nibandha Mala*, a Marathi journal, of K.N. Sane, the editor of *Kavyetihas Sangraha*, and of Parashurampant Godbole, the editor of a book of old poetry entitled *Navaneeta*. He writes that Chiplunkar saved him from falling prey to the English language Sane's publications made him aware of the historical past of his own country; and Godbole's anthology of old poetry made him proud of the language of the land, i.e. Marathi. These three stalwarts inculcated in him the love of country, language, and culture.[2]

While in college he had translated Plato's *Republic* into Marathi. He had read many classics in English, and was amazed by the fund of knowledge contained in them. The influence of Chiplunkar made him a protagonist of the Marathi language; he had taken a vow that he would not write in English. However, he earnestly wished to make available the treasures of the English language to Marathi readers, and thus started a journal in 1894 called *Bhashantar*, i.e. translation. The purpose of this journal, according to him, was to translate the works of ancient and modern European and Asian authors on such subjects as psychology, logic, metaphysics, economics, history, law, political science, etc., with a view to introducing them to Marathi readers. Rajwade was a great optimist and believed that his ambitious programme would succeed in due course. In spite of financial losses he continued the journal for thirty-seven months, and published fifteen complete translations of Plato, Edmund Burke, Thomas Paine, Plutarch, John Stuart Mill, Bacon, Abul Fazl, Ferista, and eight incomplete translations of the works of Aristotle, Gibbon and others.[3] The immediate cause of the closure of *Bhashantar* was the outbreak of the plague epidemic in Pune.

One of his major interests of study in college was history. He had perused most of the historical works on India written by British historians, and was convinced that they, when compared to other European historians, were not at all qualified to write Indian history. The reading of Grant Duff's *History of the Marathas* (1826) convinced him further about the ignorance of British historians of Indian history. He, therefore, decided to correct the 'horrified errors' in Grant Duff's volume with the help of the historical material published by K.N. Sane, and at the same time devoted himself to the task of collecting historical material and publishing it with introductions,wherever necessary. He carried this work, begun in 1898, until his death in 1926.

Rajwade's contributions to the study of history may be examined from many angles, namely, (i) collection of scattered source materials from various places and family records; (ii) selecting important documents and publishing them in volumes with exhaustive introductions; (iii) publishing lengthy or brief articles in journals with a view to introducing new material or discussing controversial issues and critically examining the views expressed by fellow researchers; and (iv) lastly, but most importantly, after critically examining the ideas, particularly those of nineteenth century European historians, developing his own views on various aspects of historical research and thereby revolutionizing the historical method.

I. Collection of Source Material

The researchers in history had no easy access to the state archives preserved mainly in Bombay and Pune. None of the pioneers in historical research, namely Sane, Khare, Parasnis, and Rajwade, had an easy task; but compared to that of the others, Rajwade's task was more arduous, if not insuperable. Sane, Khare, and Parasnis, could obtain most of the material at one or two places, but Rajwade had to travel throughout the country, and even outside, and had to suffer all sorts of hardships, privations, humiliations, and financial difficulties in his hunt for historical source material, particularly from family sources.

Rajwade had given much thought to this most important aspect of historical research. In one of his introductions he writes, 'Afghanistan, Iran, Lisbon, Paris, London, Amsterdam are the places outside India where there is every possibility of getting historical documents. A search for documents carried out by Briggs, Grant Duff, Mackenzie should be made in London itself.' He had made a long list of 113 places in India where one could find historical material relating to Maratha history. These places include Ayodhya, Benares and Aligarh (in UP); Panipat (in Punjab); Bundi, Kota, Bhopal, Gwalior, Dewas, Dhar, Maheshwar, and Indore (in MP); Jaipur, and Ujjain (in Madhya Pradesh); Aurangabad, Beed, Bhiwandi, Chandvad, and Satara (in Maharashtra); Talikot, Srirangapatnam, Mysore, Ramdurg, Bijapur, and Bidar (in Karnatak); Hyderabad (in AP); Surat (in Gujarat); Tanjavur and Gingi (in Tamil Nadu).[4]

He had frequently visited almost all the places included in the lists particularly those which were in Maharashtra. In 1890, he had also visited Kabul along with some merchants and had stayed in a monastery of the Mahanubhav sect of Maharashtra. During the course of his travels over three decades, he came across a number of people of different temperaments. It was often difficult for him to bear his travelling and maintenance expenses. It is said that he used to get a share of alms collected by the disciples of the saint-poet Ramdas, of whom he was a great admirer. With a view to getting accurate information about historical places, he had to frequent forests, valleys, mountains and several inaccessible places. He was helped in all his efforts, not only by the followers of the Ramdasi sect, but also by poor school teachers and clerks in villages. It would only be fair to describe Rajwade as a veritable 'scholar Gypsy', to borrow Matthew Arnold's memorable phrase.

Rajwade's work of collecting records was not very much appreciated while he was alive. A great novelist of Maharashtra, who was known for his historical novels and often regarded as the Walter Scott of Maharashtra, Hari Narayan Apte, scorned this collection of records and dismissed it as of no importance. Rajwade was underestimated by many as a 'a mere collector'. Those who possessed historical documents looked upon him with great suspicion, and others refused or hesitated to permit him to dig into their family archives. Sometimes he used to get irritated by the attitude of the people who had no respect for their own history. He felt sorry that a man of limited means like Vasudeoshastri Khare could not get any financial help from the Patwardhan sardars, whose historical records he was selecting and publishing on his own. He remarks with bitterness: 'They (the Patwardhans) are now enjoying their ancestors' jagirs . . . Khare has a greater moral right to their estates than the present members of the family.' It was a matter of great disgrace, he felt, that the several princes, sardars, jagirdars, and others who were eating the fruits of the labour of their ancestors showed such scant respect for their history. Why should poor research scholars take all the trouble of collecting and publishing the documents of such people, who are indifferent to their own history and forgetful of their ancestors? He, however, reconciled himself to this bitter reality with the thought that though the successors of great heroes of history may sleep, researchers should keep awake and keep themselves their great deeds alive for the sake of posterity.[5]

Jadunath Sarkar, though critical of Rajwade in many respects, expressed his appreciation of his work in these words:

> The greatest discoverer, the exclusive devotee without the life-long searcher, the most fruitful collector of the raw material of Maratha history. . . . Rajwade devoted all thoughts, all passions, all interests of a long mateless professionless life to the ceaseless exploration of all possible and impossible 'find-spots' of historical records, amidst hopelessly defective means of transport, discomfort, privation and lack of helpers, in the teeth of ignorant suspicion and hostility neglect and inertia from a local public whom he had to humour, coax, educate, and when necessary delude. But his life's mission was achieved. He alone revolutionized historical methodology in the Deccan and—by that example—in other parts of India as well. . . . He was our pioneer par excellence . . . the most daring, the most indefatigable, the most extensive and continuous digger in our historical realms of gold.[6]

II. Publications

Rajwade was keen on publishing selected documents from the collections that he had made. During the course of travels he used to make copies of important documents on the spot, if the owner was not willing to lend them. Sometimes he had to pay for certain manuscripts. He had hardly any money of his own that he could invest in printing the documents. He started a historical series called *Marathyanchya Itihasachi Sadhane* (Source Material of Maratha History) and published twenty-two volumes in his lifetime, between 1891 and 1926. Subsequently, four volumes under the same title were published between 1941 and 1947 by the Rajwade Samshodhan Mandal, Dhule, where he had deposited his collection before his death.[7]

It would be interesting to know in Rajwade's own words the hardships and financial strains that he had to undergo during the course of publishing these records, from 1898 to 1905:

I started the work of collection of reliable historical sources in 1890 and published the first volume of *MIS* in 1898. It was first printed in Shri Vitthal Printing Press, Pune, but unfortunately the same was destroyed in fire along with the press. I suffered a loss of about Rs. 1,000/-. The Printing Press of Sahakar printed it for the second time but as it was full of printing mistakes, there was no alternative but to dispose it of as waste paper. The third print of the same volume was brought out at Wai in the Modvritta Printing Press in 1898. Shrimant Balasaheb Patwardhan of Miraj State gave a donation of Rs. 400/- for its publication, and the balance of Rs. 600/- of the total cost was met from the sale of the books. Meanwhile, the search for documents and their collection was continued. The 4th volume of *MIS* was brought out by Vasudeo Joshi at Chitrashala Press, Pune (1900). The 2nd, 3rd, 5th, 6th, and 8th, in all five volumes of *MIS*, were published in the *Granthamala* at Kolhapur (1900, 1901, 1902, 1903, 1905 respectively) by Professor V.G. Vijapurkar who bore the entire cost of publication. He used to give me 50 copies of each volume free of cost for my labour and work. I sold them to meet my travel expenses partially. I got Rs. 600/- from selling these complimentary copies; got donations of Rs. 500/- together from the Chief of Ichalkaranji State, Pandoba Shiralkar and Ravaji Bhide. Besides this, my other friends gave me a loan of Rs. 600/- to meet my travel and other expenses. Thus I have spent about Rs. 3,600/- for the above work. I have yet to pay an amount of debt of Rs.1500/-. Some people charge interest, some do not. People ask me how I maintain myself and also meet my travel expenses, and hence I have given this information, in which I am least interested. My moneylenders have never pressed me for repayment of their loans, even in their difficulties. But I cannot forget the fact that I am indebted to them. (para 71)

My research publications extend over 4,400 pages, which have cost me Rs. 5,000/- . . . I have incurred a debt of Rs. 1,500/- and I suffered loss on account of it. (para 72)

Rajwade says further that, if for such a small work of four volumes he had to incur a debt of Rs. 1,500, the publication of the remaining documents, hundred times bigger in volume, would cost him more than one and a half lakh of rupees. By 1905, he had 1,200 important manuscripts and 40,000 to 50,000 historical documents in his collection, which deserved immediate publication in the interests of authentic history. He was advised by his friends, who were willing to help him financially, to be cautious in proceeding with the publication of this additional material. Who but twenty or twenty-five serious students of history would take an interest in the publications? Three or four hundred might simply glance at them out of curiosity and put them aside. But Rajwade considered such advice as short sighted, and he continued to publish whatever he could till his death. He says, 'The extent of the work is vast. Attempt will have to be made for the collection, search and publication of source material. It may cost lakhs of rupees and would require help of hundreds of experts working in this field' (para 73).[8]

Rajwade was fully aware of the fact that the publication of historical material was not one man's job. There should be a body of experts who could undertake such a venture. He suggested setting up expert historical research associations as in Europe. He also suggested that donations should be collected from the rich for the setting up of a small committee of experts, who could devote themselves to the collection and publication of sources. The Government could also finance such work on the advice of a committee of experts. He was, however, not enthusiastic about seeking government aid for this project as he feared that it might lead to government interference. It was his view that this work was to be carried out impartially by an independent body of devoted scholars or independent institutions and research bodies. He expressed his views in 1905, and followed up by founding the Bharat Itihas Samshodhak Mandal (BISM) in Pune in 1910 with the support of a few friends, as the renowned historian Ranke had done in Germany.

III. Introductions, Articles and Notes

Rajwade is known for his introductions to a few volumes of his series *Marathyanchya Itihasachi Sadhane* (*MIS*). He wrote long introductions to vols. 1, 2, 3, 4, 6, 8, 10, and 11 and to the two historical manuscripts edited by him, namely, *Radha Madhav Vilas Champu* and *Mahikavatichi Bakhar*. His introductions did not always deal with the main subject matter of the volume he edited, but they are discourses on various aspects of history. It would, therefore, be interesting to note briefly the contents of these introductions.[9]

Vol. 1 of the *MIS* contains in all 304 documents throwing light on certain campaigns of the Marathas, including the Third Battle of Panipat in 1761, covering a period between 1750 and 1761. It was published in 1898. The introduction to this volume running into 127 pages analyses the contents of the documents of the volume subject-wise, and also critically examines at length the shortcomings, and prejudices about the Marathas contained in the *History of the Marathas* by Grant Duff. He also expresses his views about the writing of the history of a nation, particularly of the Maratha nation, which, according to him, should take note of its physical and metaphysical aspects. This introduction brought Rajwade into the limelight, and was praised by many as an extraordinary piece of historical writing. T.S. Shejwalkar alone, of all the Maratha historians, demurred on the ground that the charges levelled against one of the parties—Govindpant Bundele—were, according to him, not justifiable.

The introduction to vol. 2 of the *MIS* deals with the chronologies (*shakavali*) of the Peshwas and Fatehsingh Bhonsale of Akkalkot, covering the period from 1714 to 1761. It was published in 1900. He points out the inconsistencies and mistakes in the *shakavalis* and points out further faults in Grant Duff's *History*. He maintains that so long as research scholars do not avail themselves of the opportunity of consulting original source material, they will have to accept Grant Duff entirely and would never be able to see any of his mistakes and inaccuracies. He praises the work of Nilakantha Janardhan Kirtane, the first critic of Duff (1868), and Kashinath Narayan Sane, the editor of *Kavyetihas Samgraha* (1878). An important aspect of this introduction is that it establishes two main features of eighteenth century Maratha history, particularly since the release of Shahu from the custody of the Mughals. They are (i) acceptance of Mughal Vassolage by the Marathas; and (ii) the creation and spread of feudalism in Maharashtra and Greater Maharashtra i.e. the expansion of Maratha power in the north.

Vol. 3 of *MIS* containing 568 documents covers the period from 1700 to 1760. It deals with the correspondence of some historical families. It was published in 1901. The introduction to this volume, running into 97 pages, gives an exhaustive account of the Maratha admirals of the Angres of Kolaba on the west coast, the internal and external aspects of Maratha diplomacy, the growth of feudalism, the role of Brahmendra Swami in Maratha politics, and the importance of the various types of historical records of the eighteenth century, that he had collected in large numbers.

Vol. 4, published in 1900 and reprinted in 1923, contains an introduction, a few Maratha *bakhars*, and a critical examination of the *bakhar* (chronicle) as an authentic source of information. The introduction is important as it critically discusses the views of Justice M.G. Ranade and Rajaramshastri Bhagawat on the concept of *Maharashtra Dharma* and advocates his own interpretation of the term. In this context, he reiterates emphatically that neither the *bakhar* writers nor Grant Duff, whose *History* is based mainly on *bakhars*, are qualified to make any general statements about the history of the Marathas.

However, the introduction to vol. 6 written in 1905 is most important from the point of view of historiography in general and Maratha historiography in particular. This volume of *MIS* contains 624 documents covering the period of Peshwa Bajirao I and his son Balaji alias Nanasaheb (1720–61). The long introduction of 98 pages discusses the difficulties that he had to face in copying and publishing documents, the real nature of human history, the concepts (mostly wrong) of the historians of the West and the East, the scientific method of history writing, the nature of history, and of the sociology and philosophy of history, the meaning of perverted history, the three stages of the development of historical writings, namely, upto 1818, upto 1857, and after 1857, with special reference to the works of Ranade and Telang, the preparation for history writing, the general indifference towards history, the need to found historical research societies, and many other subjects.

MIS vol. 8, covering a long period of Maratha history (1649–1817), was published in 1903. It contains 195 documents from the old family of the Pant Amatya of Gagan Bavada (Kolhapur district), out of which 36 documents belonged to Shivaji's period. The long introduction of 127 pages critically examines the earlier publications of the Deccan Vernacular Translation Society, namely the *Peshwa Diaries*, edited by Vad, Mawaji, Parasnis and others, in fifteen volumes. The introduction is important in many respects as it deals with such subjects as the editing and publication of historical documents, the origin and development of the Modi script, Marathi which is written in two ways, i.e. *Balbodha* in the Devanagari script and *Modi* in a cursive script, the impact of Persian and other languages on Marathi, and several other themes. He underlines the importance of published historical material and urges research scholars to collect documents on Maratha History prior to 1728.

The introductions to vols. 9, 10 and 11 of the *MIS*, published between 1906–9, are very brief and mainly deal once again with the mistakes of Grant Duff, the ethnographic view of history, the difficulties that research scholars have to face while collecting source material, the equipment of the researcher, the present state of publication of historical documents, and such other matters.

Besides these eight introductions, two more introductions of Rajwade are equally important. He discovered an important historical poetic work called *Radha Madhav Vilas Champu*, compiled by a contemporary poet, Jayaram Pindye of Nasik. It was published in 1922, and its long introduction running into 201 pages focuses attention mainly on the career of Shahaji in Karnataka. Besides this, it also discusses a variety of topics connected with the history of Maharashtra prior to the rise of Maratha power under Shivaji. This intorduction could also fruitfully be used by sociologists and anthropologists working on the Maratha country.[10]

Rajwade edited a *bakhar* called *Mahikavatichi Bakhar* and published it in 1924 with an introduction of 110 pages. *Mahikavati* means Mahim, the present-day Mahim suburb of Mumbai, and the *bakhar* essentially deals with the history of the Konkan region or the west coast of Maharashtra from the twefth century to the early decades of the sixteenth century. This was compiled by Keshavacharya and Nayakorao at different stages, but Rajwade has edited mainly the six chapters of Keshavacharya, giving a bief account of the political history of the Konkan with particular reference to the Yadavas of Deogiri. He also underlines the importance of swaraj under Shivaji and the concept of Maharashtra Dharma as the guiding spirit of Maratha power in the medieval period.[11]

Rajwade was a prolific writer. Besides history, he wrote on a variety of subjects like sociology, politics, anthropology, Sanskrit and Marathi literature, epigraphy, linguistics, grammar, lexicography, philology, and so on. He wrote articles of different length, in various journals like *Bhashantar*, *Granthamala*, *Vishwavritta*, *Saraswati Mandir*, *Prachi Prabha Rashtra Dharma*, *Chitramayajagat*, *Prabhat*, *Lokshikshana*, *Vidya Sevak*, *Maharashtra Itihas*, *Rashtrodaya*,and so on. Some of his articles are mostly replies to queries made or points raised in the writings of others, and they are published in the *Kesari, Samartha*, and in the periodicals of BISM, Pune, Satkaryottejak Sabha, Dhule, and the *Samshodhak* of the Rajwade Samshodhan Mandal, Dhule.

Most of his miscellaneous writings are incorporated into three volumes published in Pune between 1928 and 1935. Of these three volumes the first contains his ten introductions to the *MIS* volumes referred to earlier, and the remaining two contain fifty-seven articles on a variety of subjects.[12] In his miscellaneous writings and introductions to various volumes, there are several references to the life of Shahaji, the colonization of Maharashtra, the family of Shivaji, the structure of society during Shivaji's time, the concept of *swaraj* advocated by Shivaji, the formats of royal correspondence and accounts keeping known as *mestaks*, the great famines of the medieval period, Shahu Chhatrapati of Satara, Bajirao Peshwa and his family life, Sardar Kanhoji Angre, the Maratha admiral, and several other issues relating to the Maratha country.

Thus, the total number of volumes of writings on different subjects, according to one estimate, are 76 books and 343 articles spread over 14,650 pages.

Rajwade as an Editor

While appreciating the tremendous work of collection and publication of Marathi sources from various historical families, G.H. Khare, who is adept in the technique of editing, points out a few deficiencies in the method of Rajwade's editorial work. These may have been due to the limited time at his disposal in view of the huge task ahead, the absence of adequate human and financial resources, the hardships and privations he had to suffer during this process of collection and publication, and many other factors. G.H. Khare points out the following lacunae in Rajwade's work:

1. The inability to decipher the Persian script led him leave all the Persian portions of bilingual records of the historical families 'untouched and untraversed'.
2. He did not indicate the source and other details of the material that he had acquired. This prevented future scholars from checking the authenticity of the published documents and also to acquire more material, if possible, from the same source for further research. He did give a few details in some cases, but in other instances, there is complete silence, particularly regarding vols. 9, 12 and 15–22 of his *Marathyanchya Itihasachi Sadhane*.

3. As an editor, he should have fixed the dates of documents, particularly of the seventeenth century, and the documents other than the land grants, which are generally incompletely dated in the original documents. Perhaps for want of easy availability of ephemeris for the records of the seventeenth century, half of the dates fixed by him are incorrect. He could not work out the conversion of Muslim dates into Hindu and Christian dates; the dates fixed by him for the seventeenth century documents are not quite accurate, and in a number of cases, dating was not done at all.
4. For want of proper assistance in copying documents, borrowed from the families on the condition of immediate return, he had to copy them himself and that, too, in the presence of the owner of the records. As no competent persons familiar with the Modi script were easily available, he himself had to do both the jobs of copying and comparing the documents. Besides this, he had to do the proof reading of these documents when printed. As a consequence, the text of old records in their published forms were not as faithful as they should have been, and, therefore, could not be safely relied on in many cases, particularly on their phonology, etymology, etc.
5. As he was not an expert in paleography and inscriptions, he had committed several mistakes in editing them.[13]

This, however, does not belittle Rajwade's contribution to Maratha history. With the help of modern techniques, most of the lacunae can be corrected and the material can be used for research.

The Spirit of the Age

History, according to some historians, is dominated by the ideas and thoughts of an 'age' or an 'epoch'. This is called 'the spirit of the age' or an 'epoch-making idea' by European historians, who regard it as the very soul of history.

Rajwade also subscribes to this idea and maintains that this idea or thought would alone enable our present and future generations to remember the achievements of our ancestors. While analysing the concept of historical events, he argued that every historical event is the result of the combination of place, time and individual.[14] However, while discussing the concept of historical causality he says that it is of two kinds: internal nature and external nature, and further observes that the internal nature is itself ultimately determined by the influence of the external nature.[15]

Rajwade's concept of the spirit of the age seems to be the reformulation of Comte's idea of the three stages of intellectual history, namely, theological, metaphysical, and positive. According to Comte, historical agents internalize the spirit of their age and act accordingly. Historians understand the spirit of the age and interpret historical events, which are the results of time and place.[16]

It has been pointed out that while discussing the concept of the spirit of the age, Rajwade does not estimate the influence of geography on the life of human society, or the changes introduced by the economy and technology on society and its institutions. He also fails to consider which particular change dominates human life at a particular time. These omissions, according to Professor S.V. Puntambekar, make Rajwade's discussion of the concept of the spirit of the age incomplete and limited.[17]

MAHARASHTRA DHARMA

The discussion of historical events and the spirit of the age leads Rajwade to formulate his famous concept of Maharashtra Dharma, which, according to him, dominated the entire course of Maratha history, from AD 1646 to 1796. Rajwade calls this idea of Maharashtra Dharma as the spirit of the age or *Yuga Dharma*. He discusses in detail this concept in his intorductions to the volumes of *Marathyanchya Itihasachi Sadhane*, vol. 1 (1900), vol. 4 (1900), and partly in vol. 6 (1905). Besides this, it is carried further in his lengthy introduction to the *Mahikavatichi Bakhar* (1924).

The term Maharashtra Dharma appears first in one of the earlier Hindu sacred books of the fourteenth century called *Guru Charitra* by Gangadhar Saraswati. It was first used in historical perspective only in the *Mahikavatichi Bakhar*, a history of the Konkan compiled between 1448 and 1678, and then prominently advocated by Sant Ramdas in the seventeenth century in his well-known literary composition called *Dashodha*. He used the term to denote the duty of the people of Maharashtra towards their land and society. Maharashtra Dharma was not different from Hinduism, but Ramdas made it militant and pleaded for the unity of the Maratha people for the spread of Maharashtra Dharma everywhere and thereby establish the independent rule of the Marathas.

The Maratha chroniclers of the early nineteenth century, namely Malhar Ramrao Chitnis of Satara, Khando Ballal Chitnis, and some members of the Chitnis family of Baroda State, had mentioned this concept of Maharashtra Dharma in their chronicles written in 1810 and 1818 respectively.

In the late nineteenth century, Maratha intellectuals, namely Justice M.G. Ranade and Professor Rajaram Shastri Bhagwat, equated Maharashtra Dharma with the Bhagwat Dharma or the Bhakti cult promulgated by the saint-poets of medieval Maharashtra. Justice Ranade further stated that the development of this concept caused a political and social revolution in Maharashtra in the seventeenth century.[18]

However, Rajwade was the most eloquent and strongest supporter of the concept of Maharashtra Dharma, which was the dynamic force behind the activities of the Marathas.

Historical Method

As mentioned earlier, the introduction to vol. 6 of the *MIS* discusses Rajwade's views on history and its methodology.[19] During his college days and in subsequent years, he read most of the contemporary literature on history, its nature, scope and methodology expounded by European historians and later formed his own views and methodology of history. While working on history, he also studied and wrote on a variety of subjects, including sociology, language, lexicography, etc. It is often remarked that had he confined himself only to history, he would have been rated as the equal of European historians like Leopold von Ranke (1795–1886) or Theodore Mommsen (1817–1903).[20]

Rajwade's contribution to the methodology of history was most significant though it was not elaborated in full detail; nevertheless, his writings paved the way for a scientific approach to historiography and thus inspired potential research scholars.

Rajwade was influenced most by the German historian Ranke, particularly by his ideas on the scope and methodology of history. Germany had taken the lead in developing the discipline of history in a number of ways, such as the collection, preservation, and assessment of historical material, and establishing public bodies providing opportunities to potential young research scholars. The various deficiencies and shortcomings that characterized German historiography at the time were removed or corrected by Ranke and his disciples in the nineteenth century.

It would be interesting to note briefly the contribution of Ranke to historiography with a view to assessing his influence on Rajwade. According to Ranke, the purpose of history was to study what had happened and how it happened. He adopted a strictly scientific method in searching for historical facts. Every source, he maintained, should be examined from two perspectives: first, its contemporaneity, and, second, the credibility of the author, his position and his qualifications.

This was necessary, according to him, to determine the historicity of the event. He also recommended the study of auxiliary and ancillary sciences like chronology, geography, palaeography, epigraphy, archaeology, lexicography, linguistics, and philology, to determine the time, place, and importance of a particular source.

Earlier, Ranke had looked at history as 'an endless number of barren notices', but the reading of Niebuhr's *Roman History* changed his mind, and he turned to history with all seriousness not only to satisfy his intellectual curiosity, but also to get reliable and accurate information on a nation's past. In the initial stages, he was attracted towards history by the romantic historical novels of Walter Scott. Simultaneously, he also read the classical works of Herodotus, Thucydides, Livy, Cicero and others, and became aware of the mistakes of fact and the distortion of truth contained in historical fiction. He developed the attitude of looking at the past with detachment and objectivity and establishing the accuracy of historical narrative. He emphasized the importance of narrating events exactly as they had happened. He was not carried away by the prevailing theories of liberalism, Hegelianism, romanticism and positivism. He strongly opposed patriotic bias and developed the technique of the critical study of sources. He held that general histories are useless as sources and believed that historians must use the archives in order to make their work authentic and reliable. Ranke always emphasized the use of original state papers, diaries, historical correspondence, official reports, and other first-hand material. He was thus instrumental in undertaking the publication of documentary source material on nineteenth century Europe. Ranke was essentially a political historian and was fundamentally conservative in spirit.

Nevertheless, it must be admitted that under his inspiration and leadership history became an academic subject that required specialized training and archival research. Editing the source material was considered an important activity of historical scholarship. The scientific publication of historical material revolutionized the social sciences, because this new source material gave new insights into social, economic, political, psychological, philosophical, and other approaches to the study of man's life, the subject matter of all the social sciences. Lord Acton describes Ranke as 'The Columbus of Modern History', he is the high spirit of historicism which means he determines each event, but does not justify it.[21]

A careful analysis of the historical writings of Rajwade reveal that he adopted almost all the scientific techniques and methods of historical research expounded by Ranke and his views on the purpose and nature of history with some modifications. Like Ranke, he also critically studied the writings of earlier historians, Indian and foreign, and pointed out their errors, prejudices and distortion of facts.

Rajwade like Ranke believed that every caste, ethnic group, period and region is inspired by a particular spirit, i.e. the epoch-making spirit of the time. Both looked at history with maximum objectivity and judiciousness. They did not interpret the present in the context of past beliefs, or future aims; they simply aimed at presenting the past as it was. However, he did not accept Ranke's view on the philosophy of history, that is , the belief that God dwells in every historical event.[22]

Rajwade held a broad vision of history, which, according to him, should also include the description of society and institutions besides a chronological survey of events. According to him, a true, total and authentic history ought to present an unbiased account of ideas, institutions, events as well as the life of a community. In this respect, he was nearer to Voltaire (1694–1778) and Gibbon (1737–94) than to Ranke. He rejected Seeley's view of history that history is past politics and politics is present history. He maintained that an account of the past events in the life of a society or country is history, and it is immaterial whether the event occurred just a day before or thousands of years before. Instead, he prefers the Indian view of history as *It-ha-asa*, which holds that whatever had happened is history, and includes the totality of the activities of society.[23]

Rajwade defines history as the description or account of the entire life or activities of a nation in the past. He further says that while presenting history, the historian should be objective, avoid all preferences, and should refrain from making extreme statements. However, he also admits that the historian cannot altogether eliminate the subjective element in his make-up. He necessarily belongs to a particular culture and civilization and shares their spirit and tradition. Approaches to world history differ from individual to individual.[24]

Benedetto Croce (1866–1952), a modern Italian historian, has rightly observed, 'All history is contemporary', i.e. subjective. For Croce, there are no realities other than human experience, which, according to him, is the highest source of knowledge. He liberated history from the control of philosophy, and the clutches of science and declared that history is a higher discipline than philosophy, which is simply the methodology of history, and as regards science, he said that history is its precondition as it offers data for scientific generalizations. R.G. Collingwood had further elaborated on this idea.

History is the reconstruction of the past event in the historian's mind, who is in the present. It is the present experience of the past that goes on in the imagination of the historian that constitutes contemporaneity in history. The subject matter of history is not the past, but the idea of the past that is revived through the sources. To Croce, historicism means the science of history. He also improved the historical method. He suggested the collection of facts, and their interpretation and generalization through the inductive method. He advised against forming a theory first and fitting the facts to suit that theory later.[25]

History in the true sense, according to Rajwade, is that which gives a bare account of past events. There should be no explanation or interpretation of events, no preference, no praise, no condemnation of any event. It is the job of ethics to decide what is good and what is bad in the historical past. In short, he argued that history should be like a chronicle, a better organized one than a *bakhar*, which lacks a sense of chronology and is often pronouncedly subjective.

He discusses the nature of the scientific method with reference to the views expressed by European historians, who considered it from three points of view: chronological, regional, and ethnographic.

The chronological method, Ranke believes, is not always applicable or useful as accounts of several castes or ethnic groups cannot be arranged chronologically. Similarly, the concept of regional history would be applicable only when a particular region is permanently occupied by a certain community or group of people. Ranke views history in broad, universal terms, transcending region and period. Region and period are necessary starting points for the historian but they cannot be his final ends.

Historical events, according to Ranke, fall within the framework bound by space, time, and the individual. He discusses at length the concept of the historical event, which is the result of the action and counteraction of these three main constituent parts of history, and considers history as the sequential arrangement of such events. Truth in history, according to him, means verified and verifiable truth.

Rajwade maintained that history is not created only by the heroes of a nation, but also by societies and by common folk and their actions. History would thus be the history of people and not a mere catalogue of heroes and emperors or a list of dates or a bare recital of events. It would include their religious, social, political, economic, and other activities and would be a mirror of their total life.

History is dominated by the ideas and thoughts of an age or epoch. This is called the spirit of the age, or an on epoch-making idea, by European historians and is regarded as the soul of history.[26]

Henri Berr, a French historian, maintains that a historical fact is caused in three ways: contingency, necessity, and inner logic. Facts do not speak for themselves, but they are related to man and his environment, and it is the main job of a historian to explain the historical fact in relation to man. Rajwade, however, believes that the purpose of history is not to explain such a relationship, and that this is the concern of sociology. He limits the job of the historian to presenting facts as they happened according to the scientific method.

It is true that sociology and history are supplementary and complementary to each other, but history, he maintains, cannot be a part of sociology, since their fields of study are different. The narration of the activities of human society is the field of history, while discussion of the causes and forces governing stability and change in society, the laws governing these forces and the movements of the society, is the province of sociology.

Rajwade does not believe in what is known as the philosophy of history. History can have, according to him, only a method—the conscientious method of factual writing. He also does not believe in the idea of progress as the key and substance of history, an idea which was popular among European historians during the nineteenth century. It was typical of the thinkers of the West to maintain that the Occident alone was progressive whereas the Orient was static and tradition bound. Rajwade would look upon this limited concept of progress as an expression of European conceit and as a false judgement on the Orient.[27]

Rajwade finds fault with the concept of progress for another reason, that is history does not show an undisturbed straight line of progress, It is rather a variegated picture of progress decline, stagnation, an erratic cycle of change. Moreover, looking at history from this angle would give the false impression of a primitive world to start with, which steadily progressed without track or interruption towards its present state. This, too, Rajwade would not accept. The Europeans believed that the East is static and the West alone is progressive. The application of the concept of progress to history thereby implies that the East has no history. The supporters of the concept of progress maintain that human beings constantly make efforts to move from their original lower status to a higher status in society.

Rajwade refutes this argument by pointing out that the examination of past histories does not support the idea of consistent progress in human society throughout the course of history. On the contrary, one finds periods of progress, decline, and static in all stages of human history.

In discussing the science of historiography, Rajwade takes into account the two methods or approaches adopted by European scholars, namely, the a *posteriori* or the inductive method and the a *priori* or the deductive method. He maintains that the deductive method of proceeding from the unknown to the known is useful for sustaining society, and that the inductive method of proceeding from the known to the unknown is useful to understand the progress of society. He prefers the inductive method for the analysis of historical facts. However, he does not altogether discard the use of the deductive method, wherever it is applicable.[28]

Rajwade's view of the nature and scope of history developed over time. In his introduction to vol. 1 of the *MIS* (1898), while criticizing *A History of Marathas* (1826), by Grant Duff he talks of two ways of writing history, namely, *bhautic* (physical) and *atmic* (metaphysical). In this context, he writes that if one wants to review fully the activities of a nation, he has to do so from various angles such as religion, morals, knowledge, society, commerce, agriculture, arts, legal systems, politics involving internal and external efforts, and the progression and regression of society on all these fronts. After considering all these aspects of the life and culture of the people, the historian has to present them chronologically, systematically supported by documentary evidence, and then arrive at a synthetic picture of the whole from *bhautic* and *atmic* points of view. The *bhautic* method, he says, includes the results of the activities of a nation in various fields like religion, morals, knowledge, politics, and so on. The *atmic* method reviews the results of national activities in relation to their causes in an attempt to unravel the relation between cause and effect. The political history of a nation, according to Rajwade, therefore, should consider the application of both these methods. He thus accepts that history is not a bare description of facts and events but rather a search for the causes behind them and a discussion and explanation of their relationship.[29]

This view of history was relegated to the background by him in his introduction to the *MIS* vol. 6 written in 1905, in which he emphatically maintains that the purpose of history is a bare statement of facts. The New School of History advocates that history deals with everything that man has ever done, or thought, or hoped, or felt. It believes, like Rajwade, that the development of all civilizations and institutions cannot be measured by one common yardstick for all time. In view of the divergent views expounded by Rajwade on the purpose of history, it is difficult to decide whether his affiliation was with the Old or the New School of History.

Rajwade says that the scientific method of writing history is the same for both Europe and India. There can be only one method of writing honest and scientific history for all countries at all times. Honesty in history writing is of the utmost importance. Dishonesty in a historian is more serious and unpardonable than lapses in the scientific technique of historiography.

The misrepresentation of any event or fact in history with a view to focusing attention on one's own party, opinion, country, power, or interest is tantamount to dishonesty and what Rajwade calls 'perverted history'. He attacks European historians for perverting the history of India and misguiding readers. It may be more proper, however, to conclude that Rajwade, in spite of vacillating between these views, attained at the end a balance of the two–one appropriate to the technique of historiography and the other to the portrayal of social history, each completing or supplementing the other. He condemns all historical writing coloured by the motive of propaganda on behalf of some institution or ideology. He enumerates a number of historical writings that can be classified as propagandist. The history textbooks for schools and colleges written with a definite purpose and all those works that praise one's own country, idea, language, people, religion, etc., are all propagandist histories, according to Rajwade.[30]

Rajwade and the History of Maharashtra

Rajwade has often been criticized by some as a 'mere collector of sources' and has been dismissed as a 'historian'. Neverthless, his interests in research were many and varied. It is said by some that his major work was in linguistics, and he was designated as 'Itihasacharya' by some because of his well-known introduction to vol. 1 of the *MIS*. According to some critics, linguistics, grammar, lexicography, and history are the main fields of his research. He cannot be considered a historian of the Marathas as his introductions to the *MIS*, vols. 4, 6, and 8 are just a collection of his notes on a variety of subjects; these are not based on serious research, and the only two systematic studies on Maratha history are his discussion on the Battle of Panipat, 1761 (*MIS*, vol. 1) and Brahmendra Swami (*MIS*, vol. 3). These are some of the points raised against Rajwade by his critics. One of the reasons for his withdrawal from the Bharat Itihas Samshodhak Mandal, of which he was the founder (1910), was that he had lost all interest in history by 1915 and had become more involved in sociology and lexicography. These are some of the points raised by Shridhar Vishnu Ketkar, the compiler of *Dnyankosh*, and contemporary of Rajwade in his article in *Vidyasevak*, January 1927, *Raijwade hyanchya jeevan paddhati*. Ketkar remarks further that Rajwade did not consider his work as that of a historian.[31]

Rajwade, did not consider himself a historian, as he said that his only ambition was to publish authentic sources with his interpretations. The use of this material was left to future generations. He also warned the readers of his volumes of source material of Maratha history that they should not treat the documents as history, but rather as sources of history. He hardly had the time to elicit and present a connected account of the history of any period of Maharashtra from the sources that he had collected. Had he any more time, it is likely that he would have utilized it for collecting more material. His first aim was collection, then selection, and lastly the writing of history with their help. He was aware that there was no independent and noteworthy treatise on the History of Maharashtra except that of the general history of the Marathas by Justice Ranade and K.T. Telang, *Gleanings from Maratha History* (he laments that unfortunately both are in English) and that we have no idea of historical cartography. All his time was taken up by the collecting and studying of material, and the writing of history based on this material he left to future generations.[32]

However Rajwade had, given full attention to the nature and scope of Maratha history. To write an authentic Maratha history, he suggests that the historian should observe the following five norms:

1. One should not start writing with any preconceived notions or prejudices.
2. One should not chalk out a plan of writing a full history without collecting adequate and authentic material.
3. If one, in spite of limited material, decides to write a history, one should state clearly the gaps in one's information.
4. Any generalization or statement should be based on adequate and authentic information.
5. No statement should be made on the basis of analogy.

Rajwade makes his ideas clear by citing some examples from Maratha history. For instance, he says, on the basis of a document published by K.N. Sane in *Kavyetihas Samgraha*, no. 404, that we should not jump to the conclusion that the British cabinet system or the like of it prevailed in Shivaji's time. The term Ashta Pradhan Mandal (Council of Ministers) does not denote the number but a group of ministers; Shivaji's system was drafted on the Mughal model and cannot be compared with the cabinet system of Europe.

He enumerates eleven branches of Maratha history: (1) social; (2) political; (3) religious; (4) Cultural; (5) linguistic; (6) expeditions; (7) army; (8) navy; (9) legal system; (10) forts; and (11) revenue system. He suggests the division of the Maratha period into eight phases as below:

1. Prior to 1646
2. 1646–1680 = Struggle for independence
3. 1680–1707 = End of war of independence
4. 1707–1731 = Establishment of Hindupad Patshahi
5. 1731–1761 = Brahmanpad Patshahi
6. 1761–1796 = Efforts for continuation of Brahmanpad Patshahi
7. 1796–1818 = End of Maratha Empire
8. 1818–1898 = Degeneration of Maharashtra[33]

Rajwade's Style

Rajwade had developed his own style of writing to make it more effective. It could be easily distinguished from those of contemporary historians like K.N. Sane, D.B. Parasnis, and Aba Chandorkar, and V.L. Bhave. Historian D.V. Apte, while analysing Rajwade's style, remarks that he set the format for discussing the problems of all the divisions and subdivisions of history. He hardly ever used decorative phrases or bombastic language. He was concise, clear, and creative in his discourses. His handwriting was neat and clear. His ideas were arranged in clear-cut paragraphs in an orderly sequence.

The use of pithy axiomatic language was a special feature of his style. For instance, at one place Rajwade writes, 'The image of Vithoba of Damaji's times (fifteenth century), standing in a fixed posture, indicates the principle of toleration whereas the flying image of Maruti (Hanuman), the god worshipped by the saint-poet Ramdas of Shivaji's times, indicates the furling flag of the victorious Hinduism.' In this one pithy sentence Rajwade summarizes the difference between the Varkari and the Ramadasi sects of the Bhakti movement in Maharashtra. Similarly, his remark that a small extract from an authentic document is enough to squash the majority opinion of the *bakhars* succinctly points to the importance of the primary sources over the secondary.[34]

Critics of Rajwade

Rajwade made the gathering, the critical editing, and the publishing of first-rate primary source material the mission of his life. He strictly followed the Rankean principle of historical criticism. His mission may be stated in his own words: 'To collect sources of literature (*kavya*) and history (*itihas*) so long as my body does not fail me and publish them in their original form is the only ambition that I have cherished. I have left the task of interpretation of source material to the future generations.'

A few critics, notably T.S. Shejwalkar, could not quite appreciate Rajwade's monumental work. In Shejwalkar's view, it has, instead of rendering help in establishing historical truth, created confusion in the writing of Maratha history. However, after a careful scrutiny one arrives at the conclusion that Shejwalkar's criticism is as absurd as it is malicious.

Rajwade was a *nationalist historian*. He believed that the aims and objectives of the Indian National Congress established in 1885 go well with the concept of Shivaji's Swaraj. Shejwalkar, however, feels that his patriotism was harmful to the narration of true history. He writes:

> The earlier historians, being nationalist in their approach, their writing and presentation of history has become defective, because none of them wrote systematic history after studying all the available historical litera-

ture on the subject. They read a few historical documents on which they could easily lay their hands and based their findings on such scanty material. Rajwade was no exception to this general practice. He has committed a number of mistakes in his writings. The faulty writings of any well-known intellectual generally result in long-term adverse effects on the society. The edifice of history of Maharashtra presently is erected on erroneous foundations and pre-conceived notions which will not endure for long.

Rajwade's analytical introductions to vol. 1 of his *MIS* (1898), were highly appreciated by Professor Vishnu Govind Vijapurkar, the editor of *Granthmala*. He remarked, 'Rajwade was a genius born in our generation'. As against this, Shejwalkar was critical of this very same 'Introduction', because, according to him, Rajwade under-estimated the role of Govind Pant Bundele in the Panipat (1761) episode. He was charged by Rajwade for his dishonesty and negligence in the execution of his duties as a *kamavisdar*. Shejwalkar, in this respect, maintains that the severe criticism of Bundele is unjustified and thatby this Rajwade had laid the incorrect foundations of historical interpretation.

It is true that Rajwade was a 'nationalist' historian, but that does not mean that he was a charlatan or *propagandist*. His method of history was perfectly scientific. Shejwalkar is wrong in his assertion that Rajwade's writings created a wrong *notion of patriotism* in the minds of the common people, that he was adamant in denying his mistakes, and that his thinking was one-sided. His observation—that 'it would be, therefore, harmful to society, if his teachings form a part of the discipline of History in the Universities'—is unwarranted. These bitter remarks of Shejwalkar are exceptional and they would surely not be able to stand the scrutiny of rigorous historical scholarship.

Rajwade's work has generally been appreciated by scholars belonging to different schools of thought. Even the well-known Marxist thinker, Shripad Amrit Dange, was of the firm opinion that no historians, including the Marxists, could afford to ignore Rajwade while writing on the history of India. Prabodhankar Thakare, who was critical of Rajwade's work on Gagabhatta, the high priest at Shivaji's coronation, had to admit that but for Rajwade's collection and publication of sources, Maratha history would not have come to light. He further stated that Rajwade made an inestimable contribution to the cause of Maratha history. It was his honest opinion that it would take centuries before Maharashtra could produce another Rajwade.

D.V. Apte maintains that Rajwade's greatest contribution to Maratha historiography was that he created the feeling among research scholars that the centre of the history of Maharashtra has to be Maharashtra itself. The well-known social thinker and political analyst of modern times, Acharya S.D. Jawadekar, summarizes the contribution of Rajwade in these words, 'Rajwade, it is true, has not written any comprehensive history of the Marathas, or any independent work on the philosophy of history; but his stray articles on historical themes and sound "Introductions" to the volumes of *MIS* (*Marathyanchya Itihasachi Sadhane*) are his greatest *legacy to Maharashtra*.'[35]

He was an ardent follower of the dictum 'No document, no history'. Interpretation of historical facts cannot be based on imagination, but it should be firmly rooted in unimpeachable evidence. The historians of India in general, and Maharashtra in particular, cannot afford to ignore the contribution of Rajwade.

The concept of Maharashtra Dharma as mentioned earlier which made its first appearance in the fifteenth century and was effectively used by Ramdas, a saint-poet contemporary of Shivaji, for forging the unity of the Marathas, was considered by Rajwade to be the formative idea of the epoch. Following the writings of Ramdas, Rajwade maintains that the scope of Maharashtra Dharma is wider than that of traditional Hinduism. It includes Hinduism + establishment of Dharma + protection of Brahmans and cows + establishment of swaraj + unity of the people + leadership. He further says that Hinduism is tolerant (*sahishnu*), but that Maharashtra Dharma is militant (*jayishnu*). This is how he distinguishes Maharashtra Dharma from the Bhakti cult of medieval Maharashtra.

He further maintains that the Maratha campaigns in the north and south of India were not sporadic, as believed by some historians. The Marathas were very systematic and well disciplined in their military campaigns because they were motivated by the high principle of Maharashtra Dharma, which aimed at the protection of the language, culture, and independence of Maharashtra. Grant Duff and some other historians did not understand this high principle or soul of Maratha history, and therefore called Shivaji as the chieftain of robbers and described the Maratha campaigns as sporadic movements for plunder and rapine.

Rajwade could comprehend the events of Maratha history in the world context, and also predict the future trends of historiography based on the analysis of past events. G.S. Sardesai, who was then writing a history of India in Marathi known as Riyasats, requested Rajwade in 1909 to give him suggestions regarding the compilation of the British period of Indian history called the British Riyasat. Rajwade asked him to equip himself by reading certain documents and gave him instructions regarding the treatment of events from 1818 onwards under different stages such as 1818, 1858–9, 1860–77, 1877, the beginning of the reaction to British rule. He also advised Sardesai to study the events in Western and Eastern history, particularly from 1760 to 1907, including the French Revolution, the American colonies (1760–1814), England in Russia and Afghanistan (1800–1880); Bismarck's colonial policies (1873–1907), the rise of Japan, Japan's colonial empire; Japan, America, and France as the possible rivals of England, and England's position in Ireland, India, Australia, and Canada (1890–1907).

The last point that Rajwade made is that 1950 would see the end of the British Empire. It is amazing that this was foreseen as far back as 1909 by judging the trends of world history and the history of our own country. As we all known the Indian Republic came into existence in 1950 after the country had attained independence three years earlier.[36]

Conclusion

This brief resume of the career of Rajwade reveals how he struggled throughout his life for the cause of history. He developed an interest in many other subjects such as linguistics, grammar, lexicography, sociology, epigraphy and so on, and made significant contributions to these disciplines. However, history seems to have been his first love and he spent a major part of his life collecting authentic source materials from historical families and revolutionizing historical methodology. He did follow initially the traditional Indian approach towards the study of history, but at the same time he did not ignore the contribution of western scholars to various fields of knowledge. He strove to secure a happy blending of Indian and foreign ideas in his writings on history and other subjects. He has certainly carved out a niche for himself in the history of Maratha historiography. He, richly deserves the title *Itihasacharya* or the doyen of the discipline of history.

It is true that Rajwade did not produce any comprehensive work on history. But this does not mean that he was not qualified to do so. As he had made the collection of authentic source material the a mission of his life, he hardly had any time to concentrate on history writing. He prepared the ground for future historians by ushering in the 'Age of Records' in Maharashtra. Professor S.V. Puntambekar has, aptly observed that had Rajwade confined himself to the discipline of history, his contribution would have been equal to that of European historians like Leopold van Ranke or Theodore Mommsen.[37]

NOTES

1. V.K. Rajwade, however, does not accept this derivation. According to him, it was the corrupt form of his family *gotra* (genus) *Raiwata*.
2. D.V. Kale (ed.), *Rajwade Darshan*, Pune: Modern Book Depot, 1965, p. 14.

   J.N. Sarkar, *House of Shivaji*, Calcutta, 3rd edn., 1955. When Rajwade met Sarkar, he told him that he should write in Bengali and not in English. A mutual friend, himself a Deccani Brahman, asked Rajwade, 'If Sarkar had written in Bengali, could you have read his histories, or even known his name? 'There was no answer' (p. 282).
3. Kale (1965), op. cit., pp. 24–33.
4. V.K. Rajwade, *Aitihasik Prastavana*, Pune, 1928, pp. 6–7.
5. B.V. Bhat, *Rajwade Charitra*, Dhule, 1946, p. 178.

   G.D. Khanolkar, *Arrachin Marathi Vangmaya Sevak*, vol. 5, Pune, 1963, pp. 104–7.

Kale, *Marathi Sahitya Darshan*, vol. 15, Rajwade, A.V. Griha, Pune, 1964, pp. 36-43.

Rajwade, 1928, op. cit., p. 463.

6. Sarkar, 1955, op. cit., pp. 276–7.
7. P.N. Joshi, *Rajwade Vichar Darshan*, Pune, 1965, Appendix, pp. 268–71.
8. Rajwade, 1928, op. cit., pp. 362–5.
9. Ibid., this section briefly summarizes the contents of each introduction of Rajwade to his series *Marathyanchya Ithihasachi Sadhane* (henceforth referred to as *MIS*), covering pp. 1–471.
10. Rajwade (ed.), *Radha Madhav Vilas Champu*, Pune, 1922, Introduction, pp. 1–201.
11. Idem (ed.), *Mahikarvatichi Bakhar*, Pune, 1924, Introduction, pp. 1–110.
12. Kale, 1964, op. cit., see Appendix, *Rajwade Vangamaya Suchi*, pp. 143–56.

    It gives a complete list of Rajwade's works along with a list of books useful for the biographical details of his life.

    See also M.B. Shah (ed.), *Rajwade Samagra Sahitya*, vol. II, Preface by A.R. Kulkarni, Dhule, 1998, pp. 1–73.
13. S.P. Sen (ed.), *Historians and Historiography of Modern India*, Calcutta, 1973, pp. 202–4.
14. Ibid., Rajwade, *Lekh Samgraha*, vol. I, op. cit., p. 280.
15. Ibid., vol. II, Pune, 1932, p. 3.
16. M.R. Kantak (ed.), op. cit., p. 102.
17. *Aitihasik Charcha*, vol. 16, op. cit., p. 233.
18. Joshi, op. cit., pp. 47–51. See also Shah, op. cit., pp. 33–5; Preface by S. More, pp. 25–30.
19. This section is mainly based on:
    i. *Rajwade Lekh Samgraha*, Pune, 1928.
    ii. *Aitihasik Charcha*, vol. 16, Dhule: Rajwade Samshodhan Mandal, 1947.
    iii. Bhat, op. cit., 1946.
    iv. Joshi, op. cit., 1965.
    v. Kantak (ed.), *Rajwade and his Thoughts*, Pune, 1990.
    vi. Laxman Shastri Joshi (ed.), *Rajwade Lekh Samgraha*, Bombay: Sahitya Akademi, 2nd edn., 1967.
    vii. D.V. Kale, op. cit., 1964 and 1965.
20. *Aitihasik Charcha*, S.V. Puntambekar, op. cit., p. 220.
21. B. Sheikh Ali, *History: Its Theory and Method*, Madras: Macmillan, 1978, pp. 320–25.
22. *Aitihasik Charcha*, op. cit., pp. 224–5.
23. Rajwade, 1928, op. cit., pp. 306–7.
24. Ibid., pp. 313–14.
25. Sheikh Ali, op. cit., pp. 350–7.
26. *Aitihasik Charcha*, op. cit., pp. 232–3.
27. Ibid., pp. 230–3.
28. Rajwade, 1928, op. cit., pp. 339–40.
29. Ibid., pp. 26–31.
30. Ibid., pp. 312–16.
31. Khanolkar, 1963, op. cit., pp. 109–13.
32. Rajwade, 1928, op. cit., pp. 357–58.

33. Ibid., pp. 104–5.
34. M.B. Shah (ed.), 1998, op. cit., Introduction pp. 57–9.
35. Ibid., pp. 62–5.
36. Bhat, 1948, op. cit., pp. 550–1.
37. Ibid., p. 318.

APPENDIX

Contribution of Rajwade to Historiography

Source Material under the title *Marathyanchya Itihasachi Sadhane* (*MIS*)

Vol. No.	*Period*	*Documents*	*Pages*	*Year and Place of Publication*
1.	1750–61	304	540 (Intr. 125 p.)	1898 Wai
2.	1714–61	*Shakavalies*	197 (Intr. 34 p.)	1900 Kolhapur
3.	1700–60	560	623	1901 Kolhapur
4.	Eighteenth century	*Bakhar*	423 (Intr. 133 p.)	1900 and 1923 Pune
5.	1795–8	242	210	1902 Kolhapur
6.	Eighteenth century	624	778 (Intr. 98 p.)	1905 Kolhapur
7.	Eighteenth century	476	440	1904 Mumbai
8.	1649–1817	195	357 (Intr. 127 p.)	1903 Kolhapur
9.	Tanjavur Inscription	–	104	1906 Dhule
10.	1761–1817	665	508 (Intr. 9 p.)	1909 Pune
11.	1691–1760	118	95 (Intr. 9 p.)	1909 Pune
12.	Eighteenth century	380	239	1912 Pune
13.	Eighteenth century	165	166	1918 Pune
14.	Eighteenth century	82	66	
15.	Shivakalin families	453	492	1912 Dhule
16.	Shivakalin families	87	86	1912 Dhule
17.	Shivakalin families	44	54	1913 Mumbai
18.	Shivakalin families	64	95	1914 Mumbai
19.	1779–84	140	140	1914 Mumbai

Vol. No.	Period	Documents	Pages	Year and Place of Publication
20.	Shivakalin families	290	436	1915 Mumbai
21.	Shivakalin families Part I	314	360	1918 Dhule
	Shivakalin families Part II	75	136	1916 Dhule
22.	1792–3	247	139	1917 Mumbai
23.	Khandesh families	101	134	1947 Dhule
24.	Karad–Girje Papers	286	172	1946 Dhule
25.	Bapu Gokhale Papers	265	225	1941 Dhule
26.	Bhamburkar Bhonsale Papers	192	305	1946 Dhule

Vols. 23–6 were published posthumously by the Rajwade Itihas Samshodhak Mandal, Dhule, edited by B.V. Bhat (vol. 24), K.V. Purandhare, S.N. Joshi (vol. 25), and B.B. Bhonsale (vol. 26).

The Bharat Itihas Samshodhak Mandal, Pune has published a place-index volume to *MIS* vols. 1 to 8, 10 to 12, and 15 to 19, under the editorship of G.K. Chamdorkar (240 p., Pune, 1917).

Edited Manuscripts

I. *Radha Madhav, Vilas Champu* also known as *Life of Shahaji*, composed by Jayaram Pinde, edited with an introduction of 201 pages by V.K. Rajwade, 287 p., Pune, 1922.

II. *Mahikavatichi* also known as *Mahimachi Bakhar*, compiled by Keshavacharya and edited with an introduction of 110 pages by V.K. Rajwade, 225 p., Pune, 1924.

Miscellaneous (only historical)

1. *Rajwade Lekh Samgraha*, vol. I
   Historical introduction, 471+33 p., Pune, 1928.
2. *Rajwade Lekh Samgraha*, vol. II
   Miscellaneous Essays, 25+300 p., Pune, 1932.
3. *Rajwade Lekh Samgraha*, vol. III
   Miscellaneous Essays, 32+290 p., Pune, 1935.
4. V.K. Rajwade, *Bharatiya Vivah Samsthecha Itihas*, 118 p.,
   Introduction by Comrade S.A. Dange, Pune, 1976.

10

Dattatraya Balwant Parasnis (1870–1926)

The first and most indispensable condition of historical research is access to original documents. He who collects old state-papers, and other sources of history, therefore, makes research possible, and he benefits unborn generations of students by saving these unique records from destruction and dispersion. If, in addition to this, he prints the records, he confers a still greater benefit and extends that benefit to a wider circle of scholars, which may embrace the whole world.

JADUNATH SARKAR
House of Shivaji, p. 306

D.B. PARASNIS

Rao Bahadur Dattatraya Balwant Parasnis, like his contemporaries, K.N. Sane, V.V. Khare and V.K. Rajwade, had also carved out a niche for himself in the field of Maratha historiography in various capacities. Jadunath Sarkar proclaimed him as 'a benefactor of all earnest students of Maratha history' because, according to him, 'The first and foremost indispensable condition of historical research is access to original documents', and Parasnis not only fulfilled this major qualification, but also served the research community in many respects.[1] He gained access to the original records of the Peshwas, deposited in the Alienation Office (now called the Pune Archives) through the good offices of Justice M.G.

Ranade and some other British friends; collected old state papers from princely States, saved them from destruction and dispersion, and, above all printed them on a large scale and made them available to the students of Maratha history.

Parasnis was born in a middle-class Maratha brahman family on 27 November 1870 at Borgaon, a village in the Satara district. He did not make much progress in his formal education. He could not even complete the matriculation examination of the Bombay University. But since his childhood he showed a keen interest in Marathi literature and Maratha history. When he was hardly seventeen years old, he started publishing a Marathi magazine called *Maharashtra Kokil*, on the model of Krishnaji Narayan Athalye (1852–1927), the editor of *Keral Kokil. Maharashtra Kokil* had a format of sixteen pages, in which Parasnis used to publish the life sketches of historical personalities and other episodes of common interest. The annual subscription of this magazine was one rupee, and it had more than 2,000 subscribers. However, he had to close it down in 1892 for want of funds. Nevertheless, it earned him fame among those Marathi readers who were interested in the history and literature of this region, an interest which had already been nurtured among them by his contemporaries like Sane, Khare and Rajwade.

Parasnis's maiden historical work, *Life of Maharani Laxmibai of Jhansi* (1894), was deeply appreciated by no less a person than Lokmanya Bal Gangadhar Tilak, editor of the *Kesari*. It made Parasnis popular among the common people. But this popularity did not divert him from his first love, that is, the collection and publication of historical manuscripts, records, discussions, notes, and many other relevant things.

His first major effort in this direction was the publication of a periodical called *Bharat Varsha*, in collaboration with a renowned Marathi novelist, Hari Narayan Apte (1864–1919) in 1896; but this effort proved to be abortive as it could not survive beyond a year or so. However, one must admire the tremendous labour that he put in during this brief period in publishing several *bakhars* (chronicles), historical records, genealogies, *kaifiyats*, and several other texts pertaining to

Maratha history. While explaining the programme of his new venture, in the very first issue of *Bharat Varsha*, he underlined the importance of collecting sources before undertaking the stupendous task of writing the history of the Marathas. In this respect he emulated the example of Sane, Khareshastri and Rajwade, who had worked unceasingly for the future 'Indian Carlyle', who could clothe the dry bones of Maratha history with 'flesh, blood and authenticity'.[2]

After the closure of *Bharat Varsha* in 1897, Parasnis had to wait for nearly eight years to start his reputed series called *Itihas Sangraha*, which continued to publish various types of historical matters for nearly eight years (1908–16). *Itihas Sangraha*, like *Marathyanchya Itihasachi Sadhane* of Rajwade or *Aitihasik Lekha Sangraha* of Khare, was a major contribution of Parasnis to historical literature in the early decades of the twentieth century. The wide range of historical material published in *Itihas Sangraha* included a discussion on 'Old Historical Issues' 3 parts; Historical Notes, 7 parts; Miscellaneous Historical Writings, 2 parts, in addition to the publication of nearly 6,000 original items of archival material, which included five volumes of Rajwade's *Marathyanchya Itihasachi Sadhane* (vols. 16, 17, 18, 19 and 22), *Maheshwar Darbarchi Batamipatre* (newsletters from Indore state), 2 vols.; *Life and Letters of Brahmendra Swami* a prominent religious leader, the records of Mahadji Shinde, the correspondence of diplomat Hinge at the Mughal court, and several other subjects. The list of his publications appended to this section bears an eloquent testimony to his tremendous efforts in procuring, editing and publishing historical material in spite of many odds and criticisms from his contemporaries.

Parasnis had cultivated friendship with many princely states, particularly those of the southern Maratha country. He used to supply them authentic historical information on matters relating to their states. Before launching his historical series *Itihas Sangraha*, he had some leisure time, which he spent with Chhatrapati Shahu Maharaj of Kolhapur, who visited London to participate in the coronation ceremony of King Edward VII of England. Parasnis seized this opportunity to renew his contacts with the retired officials of the Bombay Presidency who had settled in London. This helped him in gaining access to the British archives and also securing recommendations from these retired British civil servants to get permission to work in the Alienation Office or Peshwa Daftar of Pune. He also succeeded in collecting some original English documents, which included files of private letters with autographs of British officials like Dalhousie, Henry Lawrence, Nicholson, Ellenborough, Hardinge and others.

Nana Phadnavis, who has been described as 'the wisdom or moderation of the Maratha Government' by the British Resident, Palmer, and as one who 'shines out as the last genius produced by the Maratha nation' by the Maratha historian Grant Duff, had kept his valuable and important private archives at Menavali, a quiet village on the bank of the Krishna river, near Wai in Satara district. He was in the bad books of the last Peshwa, Bajirao II, and when he was removed, he quietly shifted all his diplomatic correspondence to Menavali. But after his death in 1800, it was neglected by his successors and was in a bad shape for a long time. Parasnis, however, was aware of its existence and importance, and he managed to take possession of the entire Menavali Daftar by adopting all sorts of measures, and saved it from major dispersion and destruction. He selected many important papers and started publishing them in his *Itihas Sangraha*.

The Satara Raj was lapsed to the British in 1848, and the huge collection in the Raja's palace was in a state of chaos and confusion. The Raja's collection comprised valuable historical records dating to the days of Shivaji, many old pictures, coins, artifacts and several other things. Grant Duff's *History* was based mainly on the source material preserved in the royal palace.[3] But the successors of the royal house were either disinterested in preserving this historic heritage or were badly in need of money, and they decided to auction it off. When Parasnis heard about the imminent sale of the royal collection of the Satara palace, he became restless. But he had no means, no power, no patronage, no public support to save this treasure from falling into the hands of unworthy buyers. In this respect

Jadunath Sarkar writes, 'But his heart and brain were ceaselessly devoted to acquiring these raw materials of history and ultimately he did acquire many of them with infinite patience and versatility in the choice of means, in concert with a Bombay capitalist (not then broker) named P.V. Mawjee.'[4]

Parasnis, who was always searching for historical documents, then turned his attention to the princely states of Gwalior and Indore, and he spared no efforts in securing them. Rajwade, the great hunter of historical material, had already pointed out how difficult it was to convince the successor of the ruling families about; the importance of this historical heritage. Out of sheer ignorance, they were reluctant to part with the records.

When Parasnis approached the officials of the princely state of Indore for historical records, his request was turned down on lame excuses. He then decided to bring pressure on the state officials from above and appealed to the Government of India through a retired British Political Agent with whom he had cultivated friendship during his visit to London in 1902. This move had its desired effect, and he got permission to examine the Indore records. But Parasnis proved to be unlucky in his efforts. Before he could reach Indore, he got the news that most of the records were destroyed by a sudden outbreak of fire in the royal palace. He urged the Gwalior State to provide him documents pertaining to the career of Mahadji Shinde. He succeeded in getting these and published them in five volumes, mostly in his series *Itihas Sangraha*.[5]

Historical Museum

Parasnis was greatly fascinated by the idea of setting up a historical museum. Perhaps he was inspired by the museums he saw in London, particularly the British Museum, the India Office Library and other archival centre, on his brief visit to England in 1902. When he managed to get his *Itihas Sangraha* on a sound footing, he started working on his idea of establishing a historical museum at Satara. He appealed to the Bombay Government to come forward and give him the necessary financial support 'in the cause of Indian history'. In his letter of 4 December 1912, he pointed to the difficulties of research scholars in getting access to the necessary historical source material at one place for want of a good library and museum. He narrated his own experiences in this respect. He expressed his earnest wish that whatever he had collected over the years should be put under one roof and made available to researchers.

The Government of Bombay responded favourably to his appeal and adopted a resolution to that effect in 1914. But the sudden outbreak of World War I delayed its implementation. The earlier resolution was slightly modified later, and a proposal was made for two separate buildings, one for the archives and another for art pieces. The Government undertook the responsibility of constructing a building for the museum, which was inaugurated by Sir Leslie Wilson, Governor of Bombay, on 3 November 1925.[6] The entire collection of historical records comprising nearly 20,000 Marathi and 5,000 English documents secured by Parasnis, and nearly 3,000 printed volumes in European languages bearing on the history of the seventeenth and eighteenth centuries.

Parasnis had purchased or obtained records from various sources, which included papers relating to Peshwa Madhavrao I and his uncle Raghunathrao, Nana Phadnavis, Sakharambapu, Haripant Phadke, Mahadji Shinde, Parashurambhau Patwardhan, and other personalities of the post-Panipat period. He had purchased in London nearly 5,000 papers of Mc Cartney, the Governor of Madras (1780–5), which cover the period between 1720 and 1818. Later a major part of this collection was purchased by the Bombay Government and loaned to the Deccan College in 1939 for the benefit of Maratha research scholars. The other part of the historical museum was retained by the Parasnis family, and was later sold to the Dr B.R. Ambedkar Marathwada University. It contained mainly old historical paintings, coins, pieces of art, old weapons, portraits of Bajirao, Shahu Maharaj, Shivaji (Rajaram's son), Mahadji Shinde, Nana Phadnavis and many others. This part had not been transferred to the Historical Museum of Satara, because of the sudden death of Parasnis in 1926, and it therefore remained the personal property of the Parasnis family.[7]

Parasnis was not a government servant, but being pleased with his contribution to the study of history, the Bombay Government sanctioned him a pension of Rs. 300 per month with effect from 1922 till his death, and thereafter Rs. 2,400 per annum to his son Amritrao, on its own accord, as a special case. The Government had also supported his magazine *Itihas Sangraha* by subscribing to a large number of copies for schools and other institutions controlled by the Government.

Parasnis and the Peshwa Daftar

Parasnis had already earned a good reputation in government circles. Justice M.G. Ranade, however, was the first person to introduce him to the Peshwa Daftar. The Deccan Vernacular Translation Society of Pune (DVTS) had undertaken the work of publishing some of the volumes prepared by Ganesh Chimanaji Vad from the numerous records of the Peshwas.[8] He had also obtained the approval of the government for their publication. The society, to begin with, agreed to publish the first six volumes running into 5,300 pages, and with the help of Dadasaheb Karandikar, Sahasrabuddhe and Parasnis, all of Satara, the first volume was published by the Sahasrakar Press for the DVTS in 1902–3, and the ninth and or the last volume was published in 1911. Of these nine volumes, Parasnis along with Vad published the first three volumes dealing with Chhatrapati Shahu and Peshwa Balaji Bajirao, and the remaining six volumes were published by Vad with the help of K.B. Marathe, B.P. Joshi, and K.N. Sane. While emphasizing the importance of the publication of these Diaries, Ranade says, 'They furnish the most valuable materials for constructing the true history of the people of Maharashtra during the most eventful period of their annals.'[9]

He adds:

> These State Diaries, kept by responsible officers of the Peshwa's Daftar, are simply invaluable, and though they had their own defects, in the absence of better materials, they shed a flood of light upon the real movements and the hopes and fears, the strengths and weaknesses, of the people for over a century, and for purposes of instruction and

guidance, they far outweigh in value the narratives of wars and conquests, dynastic changes and revolutions, which take up so much space in our ordinary histories.[10]

The DVTS ceased publication after volume 9, but Parasnis with the help of Purushottam Vishram Mawaji edited and published six more volumes, thus making a total of fifteen volumes out of the thirty-two volumes prepared by G.C. Vad. As he enjoyed the confidence of the Bombay Government, he could get all the necessary concessions in archival research from it.[11]

When the Historical Records Commission (HRC) was set up by the Government of India in 1919, one of the projects of the Archives Department was to prepare a handlist of documents in its cell. The HRC at its meeting in 1921 passed a Resolution (no. IX) regarding the handlisting of the Peshwa's records in the Alienation Office of Pune. Mr L.J. Mountford, the then Commissioner, C.D. wrote to the Secretary to the Government, General Department, 'I have consulted Rao Bahadur D.B. Parasnis of Satara, who, Government are aware is a genuine student of Indian History. He has agreed to do the work, but has asked for an interview with me as he thinks the subject is of great importance and requires proper consideration of several delicate points.'[12] One does not know whether any interview between the two ever took place, but the Government of India, in view of the difficulties involved in such handlisting ultimately dropped the idea. The Ferishts (handlists) prepared by the Peshwa Daftar, however, serves the immediate purpose of scholars, and they are still being used by them.

A History of the Maratha People

C.A. Kincaid (1870–1954) an ICS officer, who spent most of his administrative period in Maharashtra, was very much facinated by the history of the Marathas. He was planning to write a history of the Marathas, as he was not satisfied with the earlier historical works in English language, including that of Grant Duff. He approached Parasnis for help in his endeavour and when Parasnis consented to his request he wrote to him on 16 September 1913, 'you have been so generous in your help that I am emboldened to make the proposal. When writing the history, I would, of course, make every acknowledgement of your aid and I would, either dedicate the work to you, or associate you as a joint author whichever you like best.'[13]

The exchange of numerous letters between the two explains the way in which Parasnis was helping Kincaid in his project. He collected a number of Marathi documents and got them translated into English through a competent person, Shankar Keshav Mahabaleshwarkar, and he devoted himself along with Kincaid in collecting printed sources. It took them nearly eleven years to complete the work and its publication in three volumes was spread over a period of seven years from 1918–25.

The plan of work between Kincaid and Parasnis seems to have been as follows: Kincaid would prepare the draft chapter, which Parasnis would go through, and make his corrections, suggestions and comments and then send it back to him. Often the drafts were finalized during long sittings at any convenient place. During these meetings Kincaid would mainly discuss the suggestions of Parasnis made earlier by him on his drafts, and then the draft was finalized.[14]

Kincaid often used to write to Riyasatkar Sardesai for some material or clarification of certain points. This created some doubts in Sardesai's mind about the participation of Parasnis in Kincaid's *History*. Sardesai, on the basis of Kincaid's letters to him, maintains that Parasnis did not participate in writing any part of Kincaid's *History*, as nowhere in the bulky volumes the critical approach, presentation and expression peculiar to Parasnis can be discerned. Besides, Parasnis, according to him, was interested in his own personal gain rather than helping Kincaid in writing a consistent history of the Marathas that would be an advancement over the earlier histories, particularly that of Grant Duff. He further says that he negotiated with Kincaid for a better price for his documents, as he had been under great financial strain since 1917.[15]

However, Kincaid did not deny at any time his indebtedness to Parasnis in compiling his *History*. Overwhelmed by his generous help without which, he would not perhaps have been able to complete his project, he offered Parasnis on his own volition the joint authorship. In his letter of 22 October 1921, while he was busy with the last volume, he frankly admitted that he would not have found any competent person other than Parasnis who could have helped him with such great authority.[16]

EVALUATION

Historian V.K. Rajwade, praises Parasnis whole heartedly for the publication of the Menavali archives and the selections from the Peshwa Daftar with the help of Seth Purushottam Vishram Mawaji. He says further that Parasnis was really a fortunate person in getting support in publishing historical material and also for building up of a historical museum.[17]

However, being a critical scholar, he did not spare Parasnis for the shortcomings in his writings. For instance, he rejected his account of Janjira because the evidence given in support of it was inappropriate, and the chronology was inconsistent. He therefore commented that his essay on Janjira was reduced to that of a *bakhar*.[18]

At another place he accused Parasnis of ignorance of the importance of time factor in history, particularly while fixing the date of the siege of Vasai (1739) and the Treaty that followed it, and as a result he committed the same mistake as that of Grant Duff in his account of Vasai campaign.[19]

While critically examining his article on the relationship between Mastani and Peshwa Bajirao I, Rajwade tore to pieces the letters quoted by Parasnis in his article published in *Kesari*, the newspaper, and pointed out the weak-links in his research. He exhorted him to follow three norms in his historical research, viz., to rely entirely on one's own analysis, not to consider any hearsay evidence and lastly to ensure that the original documents should not be improperly interpreted by citing a reference from a *bakhar*. He further pointed out the strich observance of these three rules would save the scholar from any embarrassment.[20]

Jadunath Sarkar, like Rajwade, Praises parasnis as a benefactor of all earnest students of Maratha history. As a collector of state papers and other sources, particularly the Menavali Daftar of Nana Phadnavis, their editor and publisher, Sarkar claims that Parasnis has certainly rendered an invaluable service to the scholarly world.[21]

However, Sarkar disapproved of Parasnis's early rush into journalism, at the cost of his education at the school level. Had he completed his full college course, Sarkar writes:

> His mind would have been equipped with knowledge of the various sources of information, so necessary for research workers, his mental horizon would have been widened, and he would have gained greater confidence in his own powers as a writer and boldly challenged criticism by producing scholarly works of his own. As it was, he lived and died a collector and publisher, and not a historian, nor even a reliable editor, though the texts he published will remain invaluable to *other* men who will attempt history after him.

He adds, 'It is only by his publication in the Marathi language that Parasnis will live as an author. These form his enduring contribution to Indian history.'[22]

While commenting on the editing and publication of Mahadji Shinde's papers, Sarkar hinted at Parasnis's ignorance of the Persian language and his limited knowledge of Mughal history, which led him to commit many gross errors in his edition, and warned the reader to be on his guard against them.[23]

One may accept most of the views of Jadunath Sarkar, but one rather hesitates to accept the details of Parasnis's financial tangles, which he discusses at length in his article.[24] Sarkar was supported by G.S. Sardesai in his attacks on Parasnis, particularly regarding the publication of the Shinde papers and the setting up of the Historical Museum at Satara. But these issues in no way belittle the contribution of Parasnis to the advancement of research in Maratha history. The efforts of Sarkar and Sardesai to expose Parasnis, particularly after his death, could have been avoided had they taken the trouble of examining his correspondence in the custody of his son.

M.M. Datto Vaman Potdar, a disciple of Rajwade and an ardent student of Maratha history, did not accept the charges made by Sarkar and Sardesai, which create some doubts about Paranisis character.

Parasnis had hardly any enemies. He had earned the good will of Lokmanya Tilak and his contemporaries such as Gopal Ganesh Agarkar and Hari Narayan Apte, the writer of historical fiction. He had cultivated friendship with his contemporary historians like K.N. Sane, Vasudeoshastri Khare, V.K. Rajwade, Jadunath Sarkar, and G.S. Sardesai, most of whom were at once his admirers and critics.

Among the early research scholars, D.B. Parasnis stands on the lowest rung of the ladder. It is true that he did not possess the scientific acumen or critical attitude of mind of V.K. Rajwade, or the editorial skill of Khare, who wrote analytical introductions to the volumes of his *Aitihasik Lekh Samgraha* and presented a succinct account of the post-Panipat period of Maratha history. Parasnis was perhaps placed in a better situation than his contemporaries, which made it possible for him to collect large amounts of source material without experiencing the hardships of either Rajwade or Khare. His friendship with government officials, and the chiefs of the erstwhile princely states, his relations with rich men like Mawaji, and the blessings of Lokmanya Tilak, Justice Ranade, and many others, directly and indirectly helped him in carrying out his mission of collecting and publishing Maratha historical documents.

Parasnis, like Rajwade, was also motivated by the idea of bringing to the notice of the public whatever information they could collect. He was a prolific writer. He took every advantage of the newly established Historical Records Commission and contributed articles on Marathi historical records from 1921 to 1925. He also presented a paper on Maratha Historical Literature at the History Section of the centenary celebrations of the Asiatic Society, Bombay in 1905. Thus, he spared no efforts to direct the attention of scholars towards the rich source materials of Maratha history.

In conclusion, it may be said that the four pioneers of historical research, namely, Sane, Khare, Rajwade and Parasnis, whose careers and achievements are discussed in this section, proved to be the great benefactors of the world of historical scholarship that was to emerge in Maharashtra in the twentieth century. It is true that none of them wrote a comprehensive history of the Marathas, because they were guided by the belief that the collection of authentic source material should precede the writing of history. They preferred to prepare the necessary background for the future historians of the Marathas.

Notes

1. Jadunath Sarkar, *House of Shivaji*, Calcutta; M.C. Sarkar, 3rd edn., 1955, p. 306.
2. *Bharat Varsha*, Pune, a journal edited by D.B. Parasnis, First Issue 1896. Editorial, pp. 1–8. Parasnis quotes the views of an Englishman on Indian history, 'of history, properly speaking she has nothing except the dry bones which some Indian Carlyle may yet clothe with the flesh and blood of authenticity', p. 2.
3. A.R. Kulkarni, *James Cuninghame Grant Duff*, Pune: Pune University, 1971, pp. 133–4.
4. Sarkar, op. cit., p. 310.
5. Published in 1915 in the *Itihas Samgraha*, a historical monthly started by Parasnis in 1908. On this series of documents relating to Mahadji Shinde, please see Jadunath Sarkar's comments in his *House of Shivaji*, op. cit., pp. 319–24.
6. The Government of Bombay, constructed a fire-proof building for the Satara Historical Museum at the cost of Rs. 1,47,411 in addition to Rs. 15,000 for furnishing it. This did not include the cost of land.
7. Sarkar, op. cit., p. 310.
8. Ganesh Chimnaji Vad, a contemporary of Lokmanya B.G. Tilak, Hari Narayan Apte, the Marathi novelist, and Justice M.G. Ranade, joined the services of the Bombay Government on 1878, as *mamlatdar*, after passing his B.A. examination from the Deccan College, Pune. In the course of time he rose to the position of Assistant Commissioner, Central Division (CD), and was transferred to the Alienation Office, also known as Peshwa Daftar (and now as Pune Archives), which was then under the control of the Revenue Department of the Bombay Government. The Government in response to the demand of scholars, prepared a scheme of publishing some of the original records of the Peshwas in 1886, and entrusted this task to Shri Vad, who selected some important documents from the *Rojkirds* or daily records of the Maratha Government and prepared 32 volumes for publication. They were known as the Peshwas' *Rajnishis* or Diaries. The Deccan Vernacular Translation Society, Pune, founded in 1894 offered to publish some of these Diaries, with the help of Justice M.G. Ranade. Parasnis was associated with the editorial work of 9 out of 15 volumes published between 1903–17.

This note is based on *Athavani* of G.C. Vad, by Parvatibai Mahadeo Paranjape, Pune; Lokasangraha Mudranalaya, 1962, and *Rise of the Maratha Power* by M.G. Ranade and *Gleanings from Maratha Chronicles* by K.T. Telang republished by the University of Bombay, Bombay, 1961.

9. M.G. Ranade, op. cit., pp. 173–4.
10. Ibid., p. 174.
11. Government of Bombay, General Department, Resolution 425, 17 October 1921 and Commissioner CD's letter to Parasnis, 30 November 1921 (State Archives, Bombay).
12. No. 914 of 1921. L.S. Mountford, ICS, Commissioner, CD to the Secretary to Bombay Govt. General Department, 15–19 December 1921.
13. Aroon Tikekar, *The Kincaids*, New Delhi: Promilla, 1992, p. 88.
14. Ibid., p. 101. For a detailed discussion on this topic see Tikekar's *The Kincaids*, op. cit., Ch. 5, 'Charles the Historian of the Marathas, pp. 84–121.
15. G.S. Sardesai, *Mazi Sansar Yatra*, Mumbai: K.B. Dhavale, 1956, pp. 148–53.
16. Tikekar, op. cit., pp. 87–8. See also Arvind Tatake, *Samshodhak Saptarishi*, Pune: Inamdar, 1962, p. 96.
17. V.K. Rajwade, *Aitihasik Prastavana*, Pune: Chitrashala Press, 1928, p. 455.
18. Ibid., pp. 166–7.
19. Ibid., pp. 173–4.
20. Ibid., pp. 191–2.
21. Sarkar, op. cit., pp. 306–9.
22. Ibid., p. 308.
23. Ibid., p. 321.
24. Ibid., pp. 313–18.

PART III

MARATHA HISTORIOGRAPHY IN MODERN TIMES: THE INDIAN APPROACH

11

Introduction: Early Approach to Maratha Historiography

It is often said that the art of history writing was a gift of the west to India and that it was unknown to Indians, particularly the Hindus, before the beginning of the nineteenth century. This may be partially true as far as the 'scientific' approach to history writing is concerned. Indians, it can be said, presented their past in their own way and had developed their own method of history writing before the advent of the Turks, the Mughals, and the Western powers in India. The tradition of history writing in Maharashtra in the regional language and in Sanskrit can be traced from the fifteenth century onwards.

The Hindus considered *Itihas* or history as the fifth Veda, and its standard definition according to tradition is: 'Itihas means past events accompanied or arranged in the form of stories (*kathayukta*) and conveying instructions in *dharma* (morals), *artha* (wealth), *kama* (desire), and *moksha* (salvation), i.e. the four ultimate ends of human beings.'[1]

The Hindu view of history is reflected in the Puranas. They provide a comprehensive view of ancient Indian history, a universal history from the origin of the state, or ultimately the origin of the universe, through the earliest recorded kings and eventually the ancient dynasties down to the early fourth century AD.[2] However, this universal view of history was discontinued in the medieval period because of the fragmentation of the Indian subcontinent due to foreign invasions into several independent states and thus history became a contemporary subject. Nevertheless, many indigenous rulers tried to maintain their links with a puranic antiquity while writing their histories in their own way.

The earliest attempt in this respect is to be found in Kalhan's twelfth-century work called *Rajatarangini*, India's best-known example of regional history. Kashmir is the only region of India in which a tradition of historical writing is known to have existed in pre-Muslim times. However, it may be said that though the tradition of historical writing probably did not exist outside Kashmir at that time, Kalhan's attitude towards history was probably shared by most educated men in medieval Hindu India. Kalhan was the son of Champak, a minister of King Harsha of Kashmir. His aim was to write a comprehensive history of Kashmir from the earliest known legends to his own times. He consulted about eleven earlier books of history, inscriptions, grants, edicts, coins, documents, monuments and several other things as he has himself mentioned in his work.[3] Thus, it can be said that Kalhan's *Rajatarangini* is the general history of Kashmir, beginning with the origin of Kashmir, in the Puranic tradition and tracing it up to his own times. The history of Indian historiography, therefore, should begin with this monumental work of Kalhan. From what he tells us about the mission of a historian, it is clear that he knew how to use historical materials properly and realized the importance of the critical study of earlier writings on the subject, the source material relating to history, and many other relevant things. According to Kalhan, 'the first requisite of a true historian is to keep a detached mind, free from bias and prejudice. A historian, like a judge, says he, must discard love (*raga*) and hatred (*dvesha*) while recounting the events of the past, and he adds that such a writer alone deserves praise. In short, Kalhan had a clear conception of historical objectivity.[4]

Maratha Historiography

The rise of Maratha power in the medieval period gave an impetus to historical writings in the regional language Marathi as well as in Sanskrit, presenting the indigenous view of Maratha history, or what we may call the Indian approach to Maratha history. The House of the Bhonsales to which Shivaji, the founder of the Maratha Swaraj, belonged, was the centre of political activities in the sixteenth and seventeenth centuries. This naturally led to the production of various types of historical writings in Maharashtra, and a new tradition of historiography emerged in this region. A brief review of these writings both in Sanskrit and Marathi would give us an idea of the development of historical writings in Maharashtra.

Maratha Historiography: Sanskrit

The early history of Maratha historiography begins with works in Sanskrit, although these are very few as compared to those in Marathi, the *lingua franca* of Maharashtra. Parmanand and Jayaram Pindye are the two major Sanskrit authors who deserve special attention for their pioneering contributions to Maratha historiography in the early period. There are a few other Sanskrit pandits such as Gagabhatta, Nischalpuri, Raghunath Hanmante, Keshav Pandit and some also from south India, who have written on some aspects of Maratha history. Their works basically serve as useful source material for reconstructing the history of the Marathas.

There is very little authentic information about the life of Parmanand, the poet laureate (*kavindra)* of Shivaji, the author of *Suryavamsa Anupuran*, popularly known as *Shivabharat* or the 'Epic of Shivaji'. It appears that Parmanand, the son of Govindbhat, hailed from Nevasa (Ahmednagar district), as he calls himself 'Nidhivaskar' at the end of each canto of *Shivabharat*. He was a *deshastha brahman*, and his original name was Anand, which was changed to Parmanand after he received the title of Kavindra. The earliest reference to Parmanand is found in one of the 'decisions' of the *Dharmasabha* of Rajapur held in 1664. It mentions that Parmanand, along with other pandits from Varanasi, attended the *Dharmasabha*.[5] Rajasthani records describing Shivaji's visit to Aurangzeb at Agra in 1666, mention the presence of Parmanand in Rajasthan during that period. A Rajasthani newsletter says, 'Shivaji has a poet entitled *Kavishwar* to whom he gave a male elephant, a female elephant, one thousand rupees in cash, and a full suit (*sar-o-pa*).'[6]

Parmanand Bava, the saint of Poladpur, whom Shivaji visited before his Panhala expedition of 1673, has been identified with Kavindra Parmanand, the author of *Shivabharat*.[7] Jayaram Pindye, the author of *Parnal Parvat Grihanakhyan*, has also confirmed this fact. These historical facts conclusively prove that Parmanand was a contemporary of Shivaji. However, his name is not to be found in the list of learned brahmans attending the coronation of Shivaji at Raigad in 1674. It means that he was either too old or was not alive by that time.[8]

Parmanand, it seems from the colophon to the first canto, had originally planned to compose an epic entitled *Suryavamsa Anupuran*, or supplement to Puran, in hundred thousand verses. It is written in imitation of *Raghuvamsa* of Kalidas. It was translated into Tamil in course of time under the title *Shivabharat*, which was accepted by the Maratha scholars and it was since then referred to by that name only. In its present form it contains only thirty-one complete cantos and nine verses of canto 32, covering the history of the Bhonsales from the days of Maloji to the capture of Shringarpur (Prabhavali) in 1661.[9]

While Parmanand was in Varanasi, the pandits gathered there, requested him to tell them about the glories of the sagacious King Shivaji. Parmanand then told them how King Shivaji himself had entrusted the job of compiling the history of his house from Maloji, his grandfather, onwards. Parmanand further said that his family goddess Ekvira assured her support to him in the following words: 'Do not worry, Kavindra! You are in my favour. When the king gave you this duty, he was following my directions.'[10] The poet then requested the pandits to listen carefully the great achievements of Shivaji Maharaj which he had composed in the epic form (*anupuran*) at the instance of the king himself.[11]

Jadunath Sarkar dismissed this writing as a laudatory poem, written by a 'Court flatterer' and condemned it as 'literary beggary'. He further described those historians as 'ignorant' who held it 'as a historical source of first-rate authenticity written by a contemporary'.[12]

It cannot be denied that Parmanand in his enthusiasm to glorify Shivaji has presented a highly coloured picture of the character and achievements of the 'hero' of his poem. Nevertheless, it has its importance as a contemporary source and it needs to be evaluated as such. *Parmanand Kavyam*, compiled by Parmanand's son Devadatta and grandson Govind II, is a supplementary work to *Shivabharat*, narrating the career of Sambhaji, with special reference to the events connected with the issue of succession to the Maratha throne after Shivaji's death. The whole poem, it is remarked, has been 'presented like the ancient puranas with a supernatural setting. Thus, the God Siva is introduced, explaining the course of events on Earth to Kali the evil *Kali* age personified.' It seems to have been written by a partisan of Sambhaji to justify his action in disobeying the command of his father. It throws some light on the influence of the Tantrik cult on Sambhaji and the state of religion and society in Maharashtra during that period.[13]

The Bharat Itihas Samshodhak Mandal (BISM), Pune has in its collection a Sanskrit manuscript entitled *Shivakavyam* from the Panchakshari family of Nasik. It was composed probably by a contemporary poet called Sankarshan Sakalkale. It was published by the Mandal in 1974 for the scrutiny of historical scholarship.[14] The manuscript in its present form contains cantos 2 to 17 comprising approximately 1,160 verses. The poet, whose identity is still uncertain, had originally planned to write, like Parmanand, a *Mahakavya*, as mentioned by him in the colophon of some cantos, perhaps at the instance of Shivaji. There is very little historical information in this incomplete manuscript except on the episodes of Chandrarao More of Javali, the fight with Afzal Khan, the Adilshahi general, and an expedition to Kalyan–Bhivandi in Konkan. It also refers to Shivaji's diplomatic relations with one Karna, the Rajput king of Deogiri.

A similar manuscript called *Shiva Nripal Mahakavya* by the same author, Sankarshan Sakalkale, is found in the collection of the Bhandarkar Oriental Research Institute, Pune, containing

2 to 16 *sargas* (cantos), and 1,179 *slokas* (verses). It is currently being processed by the Institute with a view to publishing it in due course. A comparative study of these two manuscripts and other contemporary sources may help us to identify the author and establish the authenticity of the extant manuscripts.

Another Sanskrit work on Maratha history is *Shri Shivakavya* written by Purshottam Panditji Bandhishte in 1821; it was first published in the *Kavyeitihas Samgraha* of K.N. Sane in 1884. Its Marathi translation under the same title was done by Vasudeo Bhaskar Bhave in 1887 from Kolhapur. It was not available to scholars for a long time, The BISM, therefore, got it reprinted in 1943. The present *kavya* covers practically the entire period of Maratha history, ending with the overthrow of Peshwa Bajirao II by the British in 1818. The historical information found therein is more or less in the form of legends, and is therefore of doubtful authenticity.[15]

When Shahaji was placed in-charge of the Karnataka Suba of the Bijapur kingdom, many families migrated to Karnataka and settled there. Shahaji's second son Ekoji formed a small Maratha state in the south with Thanjavur as its capital; the rulers of this branch of the Bhonsales patronized many learned people. These pandits produced some Sanskrit works relating to the Bhonsale family in Karnataka, in the eighteenth century. For instance, *Bhonsalavamshavali* by Venkateshwar, *Sahendra Vilasa* by Ayyavali, *Champu Dharma Vijaya* by Nala, *Sarbhoji Caritra* by Ananta Narayan, another *Bhonsalavamsavali* by Gangadhara, and so on.[16]

Another noteworthy Sanskrit historian of this period is Jayaram Pindyc, born in a village in the Nasik district of Maharashtra. He joined Shahaji Bhonsale in Karnataka and continued to be in the service of Ekoji or Vyankoji, the son of Shahaji, who later became the ruler of the Maratha kingdom at Thanjavur. The two major historical works credited to Jayaram Pindye are *Radha Madhav Vilas Champu* and *Parnal Parvat Grihanakhyan*. Jayaram Pindye was a linguist, professing to know about twelve Indian languages. Of the eleven parts of *Radha Madhav Vilas Champu*, the first five are devoted to the *vilas* or romantic relations between Radha and Madhav or Lord Krishna, and the remaining parts deal with some aspects of the career of Shahaji in Karnataka. According to Jayaram, Shahaji was descended from the Sisodiya branch of the Rajputs, and thus he associated the Bhonsale family with the ancient Solar Dynasty, *Suryavamsa*, and asserts their claim to the legitimate rulership of India, just as Parmanand of *Shivabharat* had done.[17]

Jayaram Pindye's second work, *Parnal Parvat Grihanakhyan*, as it is clear from the title itself, narrates the capture of the Panhala fort of the Adilshahi kingdom in 1673. It is an important source for the reconstruction of Shivaji's military tactics, and for learning about many customs and practices of the royal family.

Mention may also be made of a few more contemporary Sanskrit works, which, for several reasons, may be considered as authentic sources of Maratha history. Among these are: the *Rajvyavahar Kosh* compiled by Raghunath Hanmante, to expunge all alien terms used in the various departments of the administration and prepare a new set of indigenous equivalent terms for Persian works; and the *Vishvagunadarsha Champu* compiled by Venkatadhvari, a Kannada scholar, giving a detailed account of the position of the Brahmans, the Marathas, and other classes in medieval Maharashtra. The last-mentioned work is useful for social history.

Gagabhatta's *Sivarajprashasti* and *Sivakaryodaya* as well as Nischalpuri's *Sivaraj Rajyabhisheka Kalpataru* are contemporary Sanskrit works written on the occasion of Shivaji's coronation in 1674. They are useful for understanding the significance of the coronation ceremony of Shivaji.

Keshava Pandit's two works, *Dandanithi Prakarnam,* and *Rajaram Charitam*, are useful sources for understanding the traditional system of criminal jurisprudence prevalent in Shivaji's times, and the difficulties encountered by Rajaram on his journey from Raigad to Jinji in 1689, respectively.[18]

Historiography: Marathi

Jadunath Sarkar, a biographer of Shivaji and a reputed historian of medieval India, remarks, that 'The Marathas in the seventeenth century were a poor and rude people dispersed through many states and with no literature of their own except folk-songs and religious literature.'[19] But this is an incorrect judgement. Since he was concerned mainly with the history of Shivaji, Sarkar did not take much cognizance of the earlier developments in Marathi literature, particularly historical writings in Marathi, and did not change his opinion till the end. The following brief resumé of the historical writings of the medieval period would, however, prove that Maharashtra had a rich tradition of historical writings during the medieval period.

The historical writings of this period were mainly the accounts of important episodes, *bakhars* or chronicles, ballads, *vamshavalis* or chronologies, *karinas* and *kaifiyats* or statements of the activities of prominent historical families, or of chieftains, biographies of saints, and so on. Most of these accounts are fragmentary, but among them the *bakhars* or chronicles narrating political history, or the achievements of a particular hero, or the house of the ruler, and the accounts of important political events, constitute the major part of historical writings useful for understanding the history of the land and the people of this region.

The term *bakhar* is derived from the Arabic word *khabar*, which literally means news or report. In Marathi, the term denotes some historical work, could be anything from a local history to a universal history of India since ancient times.[20] *Bakhar* is no doubt a form of literature, but it differs from historical correspondence or literature in general in many respects. It was written in prose in Marathi in the cursive script called *modi* during the post-Yadav and pre-British periods at the behest of some persons who were anxious to know about the heroic deeds of their ancestors, perhaps to gain inspiration from them.[21] Nevertheless, these chronicles cannot be taken as substitutes for scientific history. They glorify their heroes, their knowledge of history is limited, and their purpose is also limited—to satisfy the needs of a specific type of reader. As they were written mostly without reference to any historical documents and are based on the memory of the chronicler, one could hardly expect them to offer any sequence of events or discussion on cause and effect. Therefore, the chronicles, which mainly represent the ethnic view of history, can be regarded as source materials in a very limited sense. Historian V.K. Rajwade, maintains that even one small authentic piece of document would be enough to squash the majority opinion of the *bakhars*.[22]

The writing of the *bakhar*, the main theme of which is political history, began in Marathi with the establishment of Muslim rule in this country. It changed our concept of history from 'universal' to 'contemporary' information. However, the *bakhar* writers, though influenced by the *tawarikhs* of the Muslims, did not altogether give up the traditional way of writing historical accounts. The chronicler sometimes begins his account with reference to the four ages of time called *yugas*, which are *Krita*, *Traita*, *Dwapar*, and the last and present one, which is *Kaliyuga*. He then locates the period of the dynasty in the *Kaliyuga*, for which an author was then commissioned to write.

Rajwade has estimated that between 1566 and 1818, about 250 chronicles were produced. The earliest known is the *Shalivahanchi Bakhar* (covering the Satavahana period 220 BC–AD 218), the original text of which must be very old. It was followed by the *Mahunbhav bakhars* and the *Hemadpanthi bakhars* of the Yadav period. The number of *bakhars* given here, seems to be rather inflated, as Rajwade includes in this category all types of historical writings.[23] However, of the extant historical writings that fulfil the basic characteristics of a *bakhar*, there are not many, and about seventy of them have been published so far. Rajwade does not accept them as scientific histories as the *bakharkars* (chroniclers) were ignorant of the basic requirements of historical methodology; yet he does not doubt their sincerity as they did not purposely hide anything that they knew.[24]

The *bakhars* may be generally grouped under the following heads according to their contents:

1. Biographies of Shivaji, Shahu, the Peshwas, and so on.
2. Autobiographies of Nana Phadnis, Gangadhar Shastri Patwardhan, Bapu Kanho, and some important persons.

3. Family *bakhars*: *Peshweyanchi bakhar*, *Kayastha Prabhunchi bakhar*, *Bhonsaval Vamsa Charitam*, *Nagpurkar Bhonsale*, to mention but a few.
4. Major landmarks in history: The battles of Panipat and Kharda, the campaign of Bassein (Vasai), and similar important historical events.
5. *Kaifiyats*: These are the *bakhars* written in defence of the policy of their masters pertaining to some major historical event such as the Battle of Panipat, e.g. *Holkaranchi Thaili* (1761), *Bhausahebanchi Kaifiyat* (1762), *Holkaranchi Kaifiyat* (1927), *Govindpant Bundele Kaifiyat* (1841), and others.
6. *Pauranik bakhars*: These are other than history, e.g. *Samarthanchi bakhar* by Hanumant Swami.

The *bakhars* may be classified period-wise, for instance, the pre-Shivaji period and the Peshwa period.[25]

The number of *bakhars* written in the pre-Shivaji period is very small but writing the history of one's own people seems to have begun in this period. The most prominent historical writing of this period is the *Mahikavatichi bakhar*, which deserves our attention. *Mahikavati* is present day Mahim (a suburb of Mumbai), and the *bakhar* of *Mahikavati* is, in brief, the earliest history of Konkan. It is not a complete history and does not have all the merits of a literary work as may be found in the *bakhars* of the later period, but it must be admitted that it was a sincere effort on the part of its author to record the historical facts about his own people.[26] The term *Maharashtra Dharma*, which was used quite often as a slogan for uniting the people of Maharashtra to establish swaraj for the protection of the land and culture of Maharashtra, was used for the first time in the *Mahikavatichi bakhar.* The *bakhar* narrates for the first time the history of the seven ruling houses of the Konkan, from AD 1138 to the advent of the *Phirangis* (i.e. the Portuguese) in the late fifteenth century in this country. One of the main features of this *bakhar* is that it arranges historical statements in some chronological order. Another distinguishing feature is that, besides narrating the political activities of the rulers, it also gives brief accounts of the administration, land measurement, the military, the nobility of some important places, rivers, and forts of this region. In the opinion of Rajwade, this *bakhar*, when compared with contemporary Muslim histories, offers more consistency in many of the statements about historic events written 300 years after they had accurred.[27]

The volume of Marathi chronicles increased with the rise of Maratha power in the seventeenth century. Shivaji being the centre of all political activity during this period, he naturally became the subject of most of the *bakhars* written and copied in Maharashtra throughout the period of Maratha dominance. Rajwade enumerates seven *bakhars* on Shivaji written between the seventeenth and nineteenth centuries.[28] Of these, two *bakhars* are noteworthy namely, *Shiva Chhatrapatinche Charitra*, by Krishnaji Anant Sabhasad, a contemporary of Shivaji, written between AD 1694 and 1697, and the other *91 qalami bakhar*, by Dattaji Trimal Waqnavis, a contemporary of Shivaji, perhaps written before 1685, but definitely before 1713.[29] The other *bakhars* on Shivaji are: *Chitraguptachi bakhar*, an enlarged version of the Sabhasad *bakhar*, written in 1760–1, and the Chitnisi *bakhar*, written by Malhar Ramrao Chitins, in 1810. It has been condemned by historians like Grant Duff and Jadunath Sarkar, but has been used profusely by others. The remaining *bakhars*, namely, *Shivadigvijaya* (1818), *Shiva Pratap* (1829), and *Shedgaonkar bakhar* (1854), have been rejected by historiansas 'bogus'. Another series of *bakhars* relating to the House of Shivaji by the members of the Chitnis family includes the biographies of Sambhaji, Rajaram, and Shahu. They were written in the nineteenth century.

These *bakhars* on Shivaji and the house of the Bhonsales are mostly based on old scriptures, the Puranic tradition, legends and information orally transmitted from generation to generation; historical records are used in constructing the history of Shivaji and his period only in a limited way. Naturally, they do not fulfil all the norms of scientific research, yet they are quite important as they form a part of historical literature and contain useful information.

The Peshwa period of Maratha history witnessed the expansion of Maratha power in both north and south India. It was, therefore, but natural that a large number of chronicles were produced giving the accounts of individual rulers of this period and their ministers and sardars, and describing major political events, military campaigns, and other events that took place in the eighteenth and early nineteenth centuries.

The chronicles have brought into sharp focus certain crucial events affecting the course of history. For instance, the Third Battle of Panipat, in 1761, a turning point in the fortunes of Maratha power, led about five contemporary chroniclers to write about it in their own way, between a period of two to twenty years after the event. These are the *Panipatchi Bakhar* by Raghunath Yadav, the *Bhau Sahebanchi bakhar*, and the *Shrimant Bhau Saheb Yanchi Kaifiyat*. Kashiraj Pandit, a Maratha brahman who was in the service of Shuja-ud-daulah, the Nawab of Oudh, during this period, gave an account of Panipat, in Persian, *Holkaranchi Thaili*, and a *kaifiyat* written in Marathi in justification of the escape of Malharrao Holkar from Panipat. These chronicles are useful in reconstructing an authentic account of the Third Battle of Panipat.[30]

Historians have generally dismissed *bakhars* as 'gossiping' accounts, yet this has not stopped many of them from using them for writing their own histories on the Marathas. Scott Waring, who wrote the history of the Marathas much before Grant Duff, preferred *bakhars* to the 'gasconading' *tawareeks* of Muslim historians. He wrote in 1810:

> Their (the Marathas') historians (some will deny the name) write in plain, simple and unaffected style, content to relate passing events in apposite terms without seeking turgid imagery or inflated phraseology . . . no attempt is made to make the worse appear the better reason. Victory and defeat are briefly related. If they pass over the latter too hastily, they do not dwell upon the former with unnecessary minuteness. They do not endeavour to bias or mislead the judgement.[31]

While evaluating the place of *bakhars* in Indian historiography, A.K. Warder writes:

> The chronicles such as that of Chitnis and many others (the majority written during the second half of the eighteenth century, perhaps largely as a response to the critical problems of that period) will reveal to us the ideas of history of the rulers and the thinkers of the Maratha State, set

out within the framework of the ancient Indian tradition of historiography. They constitute a direct continuation of the Puranas and of the medieval dynastic histories, sharing the basic assumptions of their predecessors.

Warder further makes an important observation on the state of study of these early attempts at Maratha historiography. He writes, 'So far, little has been done by way of studying them from the ideological point of view. They have been regarded simply as quarries of facts.' He expects a critical analysis of the Indian outlooks prevailing during the critical eighteenth and nineteenth centuries.[32]

NOTES

1. C.H. Philips (ed.), *Historians of India, Pakistan and Ceylon*, Oxford: OUP, 1961, p. 15.

   धर्मार्थ काम मोक्षणामुपदेश समन्वितं ।
   पूर्व वृत्तं कथायुक्तामिंतिहासं प्रचक्षते ।। १ ।।

   V.S. Apte (ed.), *Sanskrit–English Dictionary*, Delhi, 1965.
2. A.K. Warder, *An Introduction to Indian Historiography*, Bombay: Popular, 1972, p. 157.
3. C.H. Philips, op. cit., pp. 57–65. 'The Kashmir Chronicle' by A.L. Basham.
4. Ibid., p. 21. 'Ideas of History in Sanskrit Literature' by R.C. Majumdar, pp. 20–48.
5. S.M. Divekar (ed.), *Shri Shivabharat*, Pune: Author 1927, pp. 14–15.
6. Jadunath Sarkar (ed.), *Shivaji's Visit to Aurangzeb at Agra*, Calcutta, 1963, Introduction, p. 40, letter no. 28, p. 52.
7. G.S. Sardesai (ed.), *Parmanand Kavyam*, Baroda: Gaikwad Oriental Baroda Series, 1952, p. 13.
8. S.M. Pagadi, *Shivacharitra: Ek Abhyasa*, Kolhapur, 1971, p. 194.
9. Divekar op. cit., p. 10; Warder, op. cit., p. 142.
10. *Shivabharat*, op. cit., canto I, verses 31–2.
11. Ibid., verses 36–41.
12. Sarkar, *Shivaji and his Times*, Swedn., Calcutta, p. 394.
13. Warder, op. cit., pp. 144–6. For details, see Jadunath Sarkar, *House of Shivaji*, 3rd edn., Calcutta, 1953, pp. 322–33. See also G.S. Sardesai, op. cit., Introduction, pp. 1–17.
14. R.P. Goswami (ed.), *Shivakavya*, Pune: BISM, 1974.
15. V.B. Bhave, *Shri Shivakavya*, Pune: BISM, 1943. See D.V. Apte's Introduction to this volume for details.
16. Warder, op. cit., p. 147.
17. Ibid., p. 142.

18. A.R. Kulkarni, *Maharashtra in the Age of Shivaji*, 2nd rev. edn., Pune, 2002, pp. 8–9.
19. Sarkar, *Shivaji*, Calcutta, 3rd edn., 1920, p. 445.
20. Warder, op. cit., p. 148.
21. S.N. Joshi (ed.), *Sabhasad Bakhar*, Pune, 1960. Introduction, p. 17; R.V. Herwadkar (ed.), *Marathi Bakhar*, 2nd edn., Pune, 1975, pp. 10–11.
22. V.K. Rajwade, *Aitihasik Prastavana*, Pune, 1928, p. 297.
23. Ibid., p. 349.
24. Ibid., p. 301.
25. Herwadkar, op. cit., pp. 10–19 and 314–20.
26. Ibid., p. 93.
27. Rajwade, op. cit., pp. 71–3.
28. Ibid., pp. 214–20.
29. Kulkarni, op. cit., p. 10.
30. T.S. Shejwalkar, *Panipat*, Pune, 1946, pp. 104–41.
31. M.R. Kantak (ed.), *Rajwade and his Thoughts*, Pune, 1990, p. 90.
32. Warder, op. cit., p. 151.

12

Justice Mahadeo Govind Ranade (1842–1901)

Justice M.G. Ranade can aptly be described the father of modern Maratha historiography. The publication of Grant Duff's *History of the Marathas* in 1826, like the historical writings of other European writers, had found a place in the school curricula in the Bombay Presidency. Grant Duff's *History* had already been translated into Marathi in 1829 by Capt. David Capen (1793–1869), a military servant of the East India Company, with the help of one Baba Sane. Subsequently, D.A. Isdale, a teacher at the English School of Pune, of which Capt. Candy was the Superintendent, had summarized Grant Duff's original work in English for teaching history in schools, in a dialogue form in 1840. It was translated into Marathi by a student of the English School, Kushaba Limaye, under the title *Maharashtra Deshache Varnana ani Itihas Yancha Prashnotaravaliroop Grantha*, and was printed at the Government Press housed at Vishrambag Vada (the former palace of the Peshwa), in Pune. Between 1840 and 1868 this booklet of 75 pages ran into eleven editions.

The changing political situation in India, particularly after the 1857 Revolt, and the establishment of the Indian National Congress in 1885, made the younger generation aware of their past. As far as Maratha history was concerned, the indictment of Grant Duff by N.J. Kirtane in 1868, as noted earlier, emphasized the need for writing a history of the Marathas from the Indian viewpoint. But the authentic source materials required for writing such a history were locked and sealed in the government archives to which access was denied to Indian scholars. As a protest against this restrictive policy of the British, Indian scholars started collecting material from the his-torical families, as noted earlier in the chapter on the Archival movement. Nevertheless it was felt for some time that the time was not yet ripe for writing history for want of an adequate collection of source material. However, in the last decades of the nineteenth century, some scholars thought that without waiting further for adequate source material, a new history of the Marathas needed to be written to replace the distorted, incomplete and biased accounts of the Europeans, particularly of Grant Duff. Justice Ranade took the lead in presenting a correct picture of the Marathas, and thus emerged his classic work, *Rise of the Maratha Power*.

A Historian in the Making

Ranade had a fascination for Shivaji and the Marathas right from his early school days. He wrote an essay on 'The Civil Administration of Shivaji', in which he compared the English system of administration with that of Shivaji, and concluded that the Maratha system was superior. Sir Alexander Grant, the principal of the School, scolded him for this audacity and suspended his scholarship for six months. Perhaps, this very first punishment taught him the lesson of self-control, which he followed for the rest of his life.[1]

In his matriculation examination at Bombay University (1859), he wrote another essay on 'The Rise and Progress of Maratha Power'. He was then reading English books on history, and naturally his views were moulded by those text-books. However, he was happy to get an opportunity to write a history of his own country, which was to him a pleasing task. His essay, it appears, created an impression that he accepted, though indirectly, the charge of plundering, levelled against the Marathas by European historians, as he concluded his essay with these words, 'Thus was this empire founded by robbers and strengthened by robbery too.'[2]

Ranade was hardly seventeen years old when he wrote this essay. However, the opening remarks of this essay, and the views expressed later, speak of his maturity and potential. He must presumably have been mulling over this theme for a long time. This essay was highly praised by the Director of Public Instructions, Government of Bombay, in his annual report, and those who had earlier censured him for criticising the British system of administration did not fail to recognize his merits. Professor Alexander Grant of Elphinstone College, being pleased with Ranade's report of year 1862–3 about his studies, remarked, 'I would bring to your notice the remarkable report submitted by Mr. Mahadeo Govind of his work during the past year. This report represents the efforts and achievements of a Hindoo student of superior calibre.'[3]

He became a Fellow of Elphinstone College in 1864, and as part of the duties of his fellowship he was asked to teach the junior classes. During this probationary period he read many books on history and economics, the subjects he loved most, with a view to preparing himself for the task of a history teacher. He made full use of the Elphinstone College Library. Besides the prescribed textbooks, he read repeatedly the works of James Mill, Elphinstone, a translation of Ferishta's *History of the Deccan* and the contributions of Arnold, Merivale, Tacitus, Neibour, Ketley and of course Gibbon on Roman history. Between 1864 and 1866, he was asked to teach the History of the French Revolution, for which he consulted the works of Buckle, Tocqueville, Carlyle, Allison Thier and many others. He had digested the writings of Macaulay, Adam Smith, Edmund Burke, Mackintosh and others, which were required for equipping himself as a teacher of history. He endeavoured to carry the thoughts of these eminent thinkers to the students in his class. He would never say 'no' to any new assignment given to him by his superiors. He was once asked to teach Chapter 44 of Gibbon's *History*, which deals with the evolution of Roman law. While preparing this subject, he realized that without knowledge of Jurisprudence he would not do justice to Chapter 44. Hence he, attended lectures on jurisprudence of the Law College to understand the background of Roman law.

It seems that during this formative period of his career, he had developed certain notions about the writing of history. When he was asked his opinion on a book called *Hindusthancha Samkshipta Itihas* (A Brief History of India), he wrote that those who do not read the books of authentic authors on that subject, would never become successful or popular as authors. He added that unless the author gets a clear picture of the past, it would not be possible for him to distinguish between the facts based on the principle of cause and effect and those that were the results of some casual minor events, leaving no permanent marks on the time scale.[4]

He took his job of teaching quite seriously. But when he found the response of his students to his teaching to be poor he was rather disappointed. He mentioned this in the annual report (1865–6) of the school.[5]

Although he was a great admirer of Shivaji, he would not accept the writings of those who praised the leader to the skies. Thus, while reviewing a book on the Bhonsales of Satara, he wrote:

> After all, it is not just to judge men of the past times in the abstract. One must look upon men and things in the light of contemporary history, and bearing in mind the peculiar circumstances of people who live amidst troublous times. Judged by this charitable (or either just) standard Shivaji was a favourable specimen of the race to which he belonged'.[6]

This is how Ranade was developing his methodology and formulating his ideas about a true Maratha history.

Plan of Writing History

Ranade entered into government service as a Marathi translator in1866, and later on got a place in the judicial department, where he rose to the highest position, that of a justice of the Bombay High Court, in 1893. In spite of his heavy official duties and involvement in social problems, he utilized his spare time in writing stray articles on history, particularly on Shivaji and his times. In 1891, he decided to give some concrete form to his idea of a comprehensive history of the

Marathas, and convened an informal meeting of his friends Balaji Prabhakar Modak, Neelakantha Janardhan Kirtane, and Kashinath Narayan Sane, and others.[7] Justice K.T. Telang, although he did not participate in writing the history of the Marathas, at the behest of Ranade, produced a thought-provoking article on the Marathi *bakhars* entitled 'Gleanings from Maratha Chronicles'.[8] About Telang's essay, Ranade wrote, 'Gleanings from Maratha Chronicles, represents the true spirit in which native historians should treat the past history of their country.'[9] Telang's sudden demise in 1893 was a serious blow to Ranade, who had been depending on him to see his Maratha history through.

However, Ranade's plan of history did not work for various reasons. In the meanwhile, there was an offer from Longmans & Company, the publishers, to write a volume on the Maratha period in their series called 'Epochs of Indian History'. R.C. Dutt wrote on ancient India in this series, but neither Telang nor Ranade could accept this offer. The volumes on the Muslims and the Marathas, though announced by the publishers, failed to get any response from the scholars whom they had approached for the task.

Ranade then addressed himself to the task of writing history, and between 1894 and 1900 he wrote twelve essays on Maratha history, which were later published in a volume in 1900 under the title *Rise of the Maratha Power*. His two other historical writings were the essays on 'Introduction to the Peshwa's Diaries' and 'Currencies and Mints under the Maratha Rule.'[10]

The Genesis of the Rise of the Maratha Power

Rise of the Maratha Power is a collection of twelve essays written from time to time by Ranade. The first two chapters, namely, 'The Importance of Maratha History' and 'How the Ground was Prepared', were based on two lectures delivered by him at the *Vasant Vyakhan Mala*, Pune (Spring Lecture Series) in 1894, and in the same year the theme of the third chapter 'How the Seed was Sown' was presented to members of the Hindu Club, Bombay. His essay on 'Shivaji as a Civil

Ruler' (Ch. VII) was read at the Royal Asiatic Society, Bombay in 1895, and the paper on 'Gingi' or The War of Independence (Ch. IX) was first published in a magazine called *Madras Review* in 1896. 'Saints and Prophets of Maharashtra' (Ch. VIII) first appeared in his society's journal *Sarvajanik Sabha Quarterly* in 1895. The lecture of a scholar, Ramachandra Moreshwar Sane of Barsi, delivered at the Spring Lecture Series, Pune in 1890, inspired him to write the essay, 'Marathas in Southern India' (Ch. XII). He must have written the remaining five chapters later on.

In the very first chapter Ranade discusses the principal features of Maratha history, in which he argues the permanent moral interest of the story of the rise and fall of the Maratha Confederacy. He emphasizes 'that the immediate predecessors of the British Rulers of India were not the Mohamedans as is too often taken for granted, but they were the Native Rulers of the country who had successfully thrown off the Mahomedan Yoke'.[11] Grant Duff had also claimed in the opening sentence of his preface that the Marathas were 'our immediate predecessors in conquest'.[12] However, some present-day historians do not subscribe to this view.

Ranade's entire approach towards the understanding of Maratha history is epitomized in the Introductory chapter itself. He attributes the emergence of Maratha power

> not to the work of one man, or of a succession of gifted men. . . . It was not the outcome of successful enterprise of any individual adventurer. It was the upheaval of the whole population strongly bound together by the common affinities of language, race, religion and literature, and seeking further solidarity by a common independent political existence.

To make his point regarding people's participation in the making of Maratha power more specific, he argues that the political revolution in the Maratha country was preceded, and in fact to some extent, caused by a religious and social upheaval, which moved the entire population.[13]

He then refers to the Maratha institution of confederacy, an experiment in federal government, which enabled the Maratha nation to outlive and grow stronger, which ultimately failed because of the internal tensions. He goes further and suggests that this experiment can be revived under the 'Imperial power of the Queen-Empress of India'.[14]

The subsequent chapters are more or less an elaboration of the ideas expressed in the chapter on the importance of Maratha history, which aims at bringing out the moral significance of its study.

Ranade maintains that the ground for the rise of Maratha power was prepared by nature, partly by the ancient history of the country, partly by the religious revival, but chiefly by the long discipline in arms which the country had undergone under Muslim rule for 300 years (Ch. II). He further tells us how the seed of *swaraj* was sown by Shivaji and his fellow men and how in the course of time their hard work started bearing some fruit. He then makes an assessment of Shivaji as a ruler and tries to impress upon readers that it was not altogether different from the existing system under the British, and also tells us how Shivaji's system of civil government was different from those that preceded or succeeded it in several important respects (Chs. III–IV).

The contribution of the saints and prophets of Maharashtra to the political and socio-religious upheaval in the Maratha country is a favourite theme of Ranade. He finds a parallel between the reform movement of medieval Europe, which strongly protested the authority of the Pope or papal supremacy, and the religious movement in Maharashtra against the domination of the priestly class in medieval society.[15] He also discusses the concept of Maharashtra dharma, a uniting force among the Marathas, and which had been strongly advocated by the saint Ramdas (Ch. VIII).

He discusses at length the heroic resistance, which he calls the War of Independence, offered by the Marathas to the imperial forces that had descended on the Maratha country immediately after the death of Shivaji (1680). This was the most eventful period of Maratha history, which ultimately resulted in establishing order in the Maratha country and consolidating Maratha power under the leadership of Chhatrapati Shahu in the early decades of the eighteenth century (Chs. IX–X).

Ranade was always trying to seek parallels between the British and the Maratha systems. He found some resemblance between the *chauth* of the Marathas and the Subsidiary Alliance system of Wellesley (Ch. IX). He gives us a brief account of the activities of the Marathas in south India since the days of Shivaji with reference to Bellary, Tanjore, North Arcot and other places, the chief centres in the south with which the Marathas were concerned (Ch. XII).

Other Historical Writings

Introduction to Peshwa's Diaries: Ranade and Telang had been trying to get access to the Peshwa Daftar, Pune, since 1883–4, but they could get the necessary permission from the government only in 1890 and 1895. In the meanwhile, the government of Bombay had asked Ganesh Chimnaji Vad, a government official, to select documents for publication. The selected materials could have been published in 32 volumes, but only 15 were published with the help of D.B. Parasnis, P.V. Mawaji and other scholars. The Deccan Vernacular Translation Society of Pune had undertaken the responsibility of the publication as per the norms laid down by the government. Ranade, being the President of the Society, was to write an Introduction to the first volume, but the government informed the society that 'the government would prefer that the selection from the Peshwa's Diaries should be published separately from the paper prepared by the late Honourable Mr Justice Ranade' (1 May 1901). The contention of the government was that, 'It is really an essay written with the object of exhibiting the rule of the Marathas in the most favourable light possible and is coloured throughout with the personal opinion and bias of the author.'[16] Ranade's 'Introduction' was posthumously published separately.

Ranade had some leisure time in 1897–8, which was utilized by him in studying the MS of the Diaries, which covered a period from the careers of Shahu to Bajirao II. After going through the selections carefully he classified the material under such heads as constitution, caste ascendancy, army, navy, forts, public debt, revenue management, remissions, the *kamavisi* system, *ijara* or farming system, village autonomy, wages and prices, taxes-salt, *abkari*, ferries, customs; *jakat* or land customs; justice–civil cases, money suits, watan suits, criminal—murder, treason, dacoity, robbery, adultery, slaves, casting evil spirits, perjury, cow-killing, state prisoners, Police–city kotwals, mints, medicine, military pensions, religious charities, honorific titles, trade, superstitions, etc. These are the main topics that Ranade covered in his Introduction to the Peshwa's Diaries, along with his observations for which illustrations were drawn from the documents.[17]

Currencies and Mints under Maratha Rule: Ranade presented a paper on the above topic to the Royal Asiatic Society in 1894, which was later published in its journal. This paper gives a brief resume of the coins current in the Maratha country and south India and the mints which were issuing them. The occasion was the appointment of the Fowler Commission by the British Parliament in 1898 to make recommendations on the subject of Indian currency, Ranade wrote this paper with the purpose of bringing to the notice of the Commission the fact that gold currency was not new to this country. It would be interesting to know thc circumstances that motivated him to write this paper.

When the East India Company took over the administration of Indian in1818, the Indian currency was in a confused state. It was estimated that no less than 994 different coins of gold and silver of varying fineness and weight were in circulation. In the Bombay Presidency alone 38 gold coins and 127 silver coins were current in the early nineteenth century. As the principle of 'one mint one coin' was not yet developed, the Marathas issued licences to those who were willing to mint coins, both gold and silver.[18]

The constant fluctuations in the market prices of gold and silver, depending on supply and demand, made it difficult for the government to fix the exact ratio between the market value and the official value of gold. The British government appointed several commissions to resolve this problem. The Fowler Commission of 1898 was one such commission.

When Ranade became aware of the government's concern over the problems of Indian currency, he started probing into the past to find out how native ruler had managed currency, namely, the establishment and control of state mints. In this respect, he wrote, 'The study of comparative history can never be better turned to account than when we seek present guidance from the lessons it teaches as to the way in which those who went before us practically dealt with the questions which confront us at the present time.'[19]

After discussing the currency systems of the Mughals and the Marathas, Ranade concluded:

1. Variety of currencies might have been necessary in those days when communication was difficult and authority was decentralized,
2. This variety was due to the tax system of the government which then prevailed, and
3. The most important lesson of history is 'that the statements now so generally made that India was too poor a country for the circulation of gold coins is unsupported by the facts of history. The gold coins were issued and freely circulated, though no attempt was made to regulate their value in relation to silver coins.'[20]

Ranade thus justified the demand of the Indians for gold currency by pointing out the system of currency management that had prevailed in India prior to the British occupation of the subcontinent in 1818.[21]

The Purpose of History

When Ranade's plan to write a comprehensive history of the Marathas in cooperation with his historian friends did not materialize, he abandoned it and decided to select a few themes from Maratha history and write essays, as pointed out before, for the guidance and consideration of future research scholars. He writes:

> Materials for a fuller account of the detailed narrative are being made available by the labours of our native scholars and they will have in time

to be worked up systematically, but the limits assigned to these chapters on Maratha History would of themselves preclude any such ambition. My aim is rather to present a clear view of the salient features of the history from the Indian standpoint, to remove many misapprehensions which detract much from the moral interest and the political lessons of the story, and, above all, to enlist the sympathy of the representatives of the conquering British power in the fortunes of its worsted rival.[22]

This statement about the purpose of history and some other statements made by him in the text of *Rise of the Maratha Power* raise the issue of whether Ranade subscribed to the theory of 'divine dispensation' of British rule advocated by political thinkers such as Raja Rammohun Roy (1774–1833), Gopal Hari Deshmukh (1823–92), Gopal Krishna Gokhale (1866–1915) and other liberal political thinkers. Lokhitwadi, a contemporary of Ranade, supported the existence of British rule in India on various grounds in several of his letters,[23] particularly those of 1848–9, when the last relic of the Maratha power, i.e. the Satara Raj, was lapsed to the British rule, 1848.

While examining the strengths and weaknesses of the Maratha Confederacy, Ranade expresses, his hope that, though the confederacy had failed, the existence of the British rule may in future develop the concept of a 'federated India', distributed according to nationalities and subjected to a common bond of connection with the imperial power of the Queen-Empress of India.[24] His attempts to seek parallels between British institutions of the cabinet system or the Council of the Governer-General and the Ashta Pradhan Mandal of the Marathas, or the Subsidiary Alliance System of Wellesley and the *Chauth-Sardeshmukhi* of the Marathas or the Reformation in Europe and the contribution of Saints and prophets of Maharashtra, create the impression that Ranade was following a policy of appeasement in his historical writings. The impact of Western education, and his inclination towards liberalism, perhaps led him to adopt the policy of 'forgive thy enemy'.

It is true that Ranade did not specifically state anywhere that he advocated or supported 'the divine dispensation' theory 'linking the destinies of India and England'. He was an admirer of the British 'love of order' and 'regulated authority', and believed that British discipline would reconstruct India in several respects. Thus, he indirectly suggested that God was behind the advent of the British in India. While assessing Ranade's views, one has to consider the time and the circumstances in which he was writing these and other essays as well as his participation in reform activities.[25]

It must be remembered here that those who praised British rule were not advocating its 'permanance', but were using it as a model to ensure 'order and discipline' in Indian administration, which had been rotten to the core under both Hindu and Muslim rulers. However, being a liberal in his attitude towards life, he simply advocated the adoption of constitutional methods in a peaceful way to overthrow British rule.

The purpose of his historical writings, as it is often alleged, was not to refute the history of Grant Duff, or to offer a response to his ideas, but rather to create an atmosphere for better understanding the role of the Marathas in the history of India. He emphasized that the rise of Maratha power was due to the genuine efforts on the part of the people of Maharashtra, and that its founder was not a chieftain of a robber state but a leader of the masses. This alone will help us to understand Ranade's sentiment of patriotism, the urge or the purpose behind his historical writings.

Issue Raised in Ranade's Historical Writing

Richard P. Tucker, an American scholar, has broadly discussed some of the major issues raised by Ranade in his historical writings in his essay, 'M.G. Ranade: The Historian as a Liberal Nationalist'. He evaluates the contribution of Ranade to Maratha historiography from a different angle. He maintains that Ranade's classic work, *Rise of the Maratha Power*, is his final and considered judgement on the history of the Marathas, and that it has a vast appeal among the literate Maharashtrian public. He argues that Ranade was not primarily an historian, but a politician and an administrator, and describes his book as is a graphic expression of the conflicts of 1890s', and claims that it is essentially a 'philosophical essay on the identity and character of the Maharashtrian people'. Tucker has analysed the political situation prevailing in Maharashtra when Ranade wrote this book, particularly in the context of his liberal nationalism, and its influence on his presentation of some aspects of Maratha history in his books.[26]

One of the issues raised in the writings of Ranade, according to Tucker, was 'the question where the society's essential dynamism lay: in the persons of great leaders or in the people themselves'. He argues that Ranade's perspective of Shivaji underwent certain changes in the course of time. Ranade departed from the populist fascination for Shivaji and emphasized the 'creative role of the people as a whole more than that of Shivaji or any other single leader'. Ranade maintained, he argues, that the Maratha flowering was an 'upheaval of the whole population strongly bound together by the common affinities of language, race, religion and literature, and seeking further solidarity by a common political existence'. Ranade presumes the unity of the Maratha people and denies their internal tensions. But while seeking the identity of the Maharashtrian people, Ranade was confronted with two dilemmas in Maharashtra's self-image, 'the relations of Hindus and Muslims, and the relations of Brahmins and non-Brahmins'.[27]

Ranade, according to Tucker, resolved the Hindu–Muslim problem by accepting the liberal role of the Muslims in Indian society. He did not want his book to become 'an anti-Muslim document'. He maintained that Islam in the Deccan was marked by 'tolerance and moderation', unlike the passionate Sunni orthodoxy of Aurangzeb, which dominated many Maharashtrian minds as the image of Islam. Ranade believed that social harmony was due to the work of poet-saints, both Hindu and Muslim, of the Maratha country. He says, 'Politics might have communal overtones, but surely not spiritual life.'[28]

Another issue in Maratha history agitating the minds of some historians was the Afzal Khan affair of 1659. The issue was whether the slaying of Afzal Khan was a treacherous murder or an act of self-defence on the part of Shivaji, or, in other words, who struck the first blow? All European authors whose major sources of information were the Persian texts, held Shivaji guilty in this affair. Ranade's deep sympathy for the cause of Shivaji being quite well known, he could not accept this view. Hence he writes that one could never decide who struck first and maintains that both were prepared for such a risk. Tucker calls this as 'an ethical relativism'. Ranade, in fact, pleaded that 'history could be studied for its own sake and for its ability to inspire men, and not become another source of conflict and dispute'.[29] This argument is in tune with his liberalism.

This controversy was later resolved to a reasonable extent by Jadunath Sarkar.[30]

Tucker then examines the other dilemma, that of relations between brahmins and non-brahmins, with which Ranade was confronted. It was believed for a long time that Maharashtrian society was a harmonious balance of different caste interests. Nobody ever questioned the caste of Shivaji's biographer. But when the non-brahmin movement was striking roots in the Maratha country, the writings on Shivaji were also classified: Shivaji as brahmanized and non-brahmanized. Mahatma Jotirao Phule, the founder of Satya Shodhak Samaj, an organization attacking the dominance of the priestly class in society, gave expression to this feeling in his famous 'Shivaji Rajacha Powada' (Ballad of Raja Shivaji), in which Shivaji has been represented as the inspired leader of toiling and the ploughing masses, 'the *bahujan samaj*'.[31]

Ranade, a *chitpavan* brahman by caste, a leader of the Prarthana Samaj and a social reformer, was never a believer in the superiority of any particular caste in the society. When he was invited by the orthodox Brahman Sabha of Mumbai to felicitate him for his membership of the Bombay High Court in 1893, the organizers attributed his elevation to the British recognition of the brahmin virtues. He immediately 'retorted that the virtues of learning, piety and public service were no brahmin monopoly and they were earned by hard effort, not the accidents of birth'. In his famous Introduction to the Peshwa's Diaries, he accused the Brahmin political leaders of the eighteenth century, largely men of his own caste of destroying the hard-earned Maratha unity by systematically favouring their own caste fellows at the expense of the rest of society.[32]

Tucker introduces another point regarding the place of the Marathas in this subcontinent—do they represent a regional nation . . ., or could they be considered the beginning of an all-India nationality.[33] Another problem which is close to this, is the nature of Shivaji's polity: whether the Marathas were a sovereign power, or a feudal state, and whether Shivaji, its founder, remained throughout his life the son of a Jagirdar or rather a chieftain?

It may be pointed out here that historians, both Europeans and Indians, have accorded 'marginal treatment' to Maratha history. The only exceptions among Europeans were, as pointed out earlier, Scott Waring, Sprengel and Grant Duff. It was believed that Maratha history could fit in between the downfall of the Mughals and the rise of the British power in India. It was Ranade among the Indian historians who gave an independent status to Maratha history and emphatically stated that the British wrested power from the Marathas and not from the Muslims as it had often been asserted.

Shivaji declared himself 'Chhatrapati', a soverign ruler, by coronating himself in 1674. As a consequence of this, he adopted the policy of expansion in the south and acquired the territory joining his Maratha country with the newly conquered pockets in the south extending up to Jinji. As a sovereign he concluded treaties with the Bhaganagar state (Hyderabad) and some Maratha independent sardars, and declared war against the Pathan ruler of Bijapur and its allies, the Mughals. He also collected *chauth* from those small powers who sought to avoid his displeasure. He introduced, like his predecessors, a new era called 'Raj Shaka' in 1674, and also issued gold coins, though limited in quantity, called 'Shivarai Hon'. Thus, he fulfilled all those norms that are generally associated with the concept of sovereignty.

The policy of expending Maratha power initiated by Shivaji was subsequently carried further by the Peshwas under Shahu Chhatrapati in the eighteenth century, and the Marathas became a dominant power on the subcontinent, controlling directly or indirectly the territory from the Punjab in the north to Trichinopoly in the south, from Gujarat in the west to

Bengal and Orissa in the east. Contemporary works did acknowledge his sovereignty, though some recent European and American historians deny this historical reality, that Shivaji was a nation-maker and a sovereign Maratha ruler. He did work for the stability of his 'swaraj' and also paved the way for the future expansion of Maratha power. In fact, the term Maratha history is a misnomer. It is indeed a major part of Indian history, dominated by the Marathas.[34]

Tucker has pointed out the ambiguity in the view of Ranade as he was 'faced with severe difficulties in overcoming this dilemma of regional versus all-India nationality'.[35] In this respect, Ranade writes, 'Shivaji did not aspire to found a universal empire under his own direct rule throughout India. He strove to secure the freedom of his own people, and unite them into one nation, powerful for self-defence and for self-assertion also; but the extinction of all other power was not contemplated by him.' In justification of this, he thought that the Bhakti tradition 'made the nation more humane, and at the same time prove to hold together by mutual toleration'.[36]

But the facts do not support this view. Shivaji's coronation, and the Karnataka expedition and the conquest of some areas, clearly indicate his policy of expansion. He was a pragmatic ruler and was not likely to be carried away by the philosophy of the saint-poets while fulfilling his duties as a ruler. Hence, the interpretation put forth by Tucker, is not acceptable. Perhaps the limited sources of information available to him may have led him to think along these lines.

Thus, it can be said that the process of making Maratha power an all-India nationality had already started in Shivaji's times.

After discussing the issues raised by Ranade, Tucker concludes that the *Rise of the Maratha Power* was the culmination of thirty years' thought, in which he had the benefit of many conversations with his active circle of liberal, historically minded associates. His liberal approach pervades all his writings—including history. Ranade felt that there was a need for a persuasive nationalist view of Maharashtrian history. As a political document, the *Rise of the Maratha Power* provided a standard of balance and restraint against which the work of more strident writers in the following generation could be measured'. In conclusion, he says, 'Ultimately, the *Rise of the Maratha Power* was more than either historical monograph or political tract, it was a moral homily on the cultural genius of Ranade's people.'[37]

Ranade as a school boy, as has been noted earlier, had to suffer the wrath of his principal, Sir Alexander Grant, for his essay on Shivaji, but later he was applauded for his essay on Maratha power, which he wrote for his public examination (1859). His book*Rise of the Maratha Power* received similar treatment in the Report of the Director of Public Instruction of Bombay Presidency (1901).[38]

However, H.G. Rawlinson, the principal of the Deccan College, a government institution, and an ardent student of history, gave a contrary opinion on Ranade's book. He writes, 'The late Justice Ranade's brilliant little essay on the Rise of the Maratha Power (1912) is spoilt by the author's exaggerated views on his hero's merits and achievements.'[39] It is quite obvious from this remark that he did not understand the main thesis of Ranade, who considered the rise of the Marathas was the result of the movement of the masses, and not that of one individual. He has shown utmost balance in evaluating the role of Shivaji in the Maratha history.

V.K. Rajwade describes Ranade's brief history of Shivaji as an important contribution to Maratha history mainly because of his discussion of the evolution of society under Shivaji and his times. Any industrious scholar could enumerate with all sincerity many aspects or events of the history of society, but it requires a genius and a man of authority who could bind them together under certain norms of cause and effect and present them in a consistent manner to the reader. Rajwade further argues that though Ranade did not discover many new aspects or events of medieval society, he made good use of the social events inadvertently mentioned by Marathi chroniclers and Grant Duff. He studied this material along with the events mentioned in the lives of the saints of Maharashtra, and prepared a picture of a society of the pre-Shivaji and the Shivaji periods. He had read a number of books on European history with all intensity and formed his opinion that behind the social events of European history there must be some tradition of cause and effect. This helped him to challenge the view of Grant Duff, who maintained Maratha society was not a regulated society. Hence Rajwade concludes that this general theory of the evolution of society—that society is a result of cause and effect—is the only contribution of Ranade in his book.[40]

Except the above-mentioned fact, Rajwade rejects most of Ranade's views mainly on the contribution of saints and prophets and the concept of Maharashtra dharma. He maintains that Ranade's analysis of the saint-poets is baseless and lacks proper research. Ranade failed to examine properly the contributions of the Marathi saints. Ranade's conclusion, based on his comparison between the Bhakti movement and the Protestant movement of Europe, that the Marathi saints were against religious orthodoxy is unacceptable to Rajwade.[41]

Rajwade further says that Ranade could not define properly the concept of Maharashtra dharma, which in no way implies a 'religious upheaval', which Ranade discusses in his essay. It is wrong to equate religious beliefs with a religious upheaval. The nature of religious beliefs in Shivaji's times was entirely different from what Ranade has conceived. Rajwade further says that Ranade's contention that the rise of the Bhakti cult as against the orthodox religion induced the Marathas to shed their weaknesses and prepare their minds for becoming independent, which ultimately resulted in the founding of Maratha power. Rajwade denies this effort to link up cause and effect on the part of Ranade as unscientific.[42] However, it may be noted here that Rajwade's early outburst against the saint-poets of Maharashtra remained a temporary phase, and in his later writings he acknowledged the contribution of the saints, and thereby indirectly supported Ranade.

Among the early Bengali historians who were interested in Maratha history mention may be made of Jadunath Sarkar, and S.N. Sen. But surprisingly Jadunath Sarkar who had paid glowing tributes to the pioneers of Maratha historiography, had not only totally ignored Ranade but had made sarcastic remarks against him at one place. He says, 'The older generation of Maratha scholars like Justice Ranade had put their faith in unauthentic chronicles, formal histories, and later narratives.'[43] It may be pointed out that Sarkar, who had attacked the *bakhars,* had profusely quoted them in his *Shivaji and His Times*. Even Rajwade, who had earlier undermined the importance of chronicles, had later agreed that Maratha history would remain incomplete without any reference to these chronicles and narratives, which represent the ethnic view of history. Sarkar's monumental work on Shivaji, does not make any reference to the *Rise of the Maratha Power*, a classic in historical writings.

Surendra Nath Sen, who had studied the Marathi chronicles and documents, highly praised Ranade's contribution in his book *Administrative System of the Maratha*. He writes,

> Born in Maharashtra, and educated in western method, Ranade combined in him three qualities so indispensable for a historian of the Marathas. He knew the language and traditions of his country, was well conversant with the historical method of the west and had ready access to all papers then available. With true historical instinct he made a delibrate departure from the beaten track and selected a course of his own. His fame today does not rest on the discovery of a new document or an unknown event, but on the surer basis of the right interpretation of the history of his people. . . . Modern research have made some of his conclusions untenable today, but the credit of pointing out a new angle of vision belongs entirely to him.[44]

D.V. Apte (1881–1943), a noted Maratha historian, has discussed the merits and inaccuracies in the historical writings of Ranade.[45] He considers Ranade's greatest contribution was his belief that the British conquered India by defeating the Marathas and not the Muslims. Ranade, he says, emphasized the need to study the fascinating history of the Marathas, who had, surmounted many hurdles during the 150-year period of their rule by adopting all sorts of means and producing a band of courageous leaders and statesmen for the maintenance of Maratha power.

Apte also praises the contribution of Balaji Vishwanath, the first Peshwa, who put forth the idea of uniting all Maratha sardars and creating a confederacy for expanding the Maratha power in the subcontinent.[46]

However, Apte does not agree with Ranade's analysis of the downfall of Maratha power which he makes in his 'Introduction' to the Peshwa's Diaries. He has tried to refute the main contention of Ranade's view that the departure from the system of Shivaji was the root cause of the decline of Maratha power. In support of his statement, Ranade has put forth such factors as the break down of the Ashtapradhan mandal, caste jealousies or distinctions, making public offices hereditary, maintaining mercenary troops, increase in family dissension, and the claim that others were mainly responsible for the extinction of Maratha power.

The refutation of these statements of Ranade by Apte is mainly based on later studies drawing on new sources. Besides, Ranade did not aim at recounting the details of history, but sought to place his ideas for further consideration and research. Thus, Apte's criticism, it can be said, does not in any way belittle the importance of Ranade's ideas, which were in fact original and opened up new vistas for research scholars.

No doubt Ranade, was a great admirer of Shivaji, whom he regarded as a great organizer and a builder of civil institutions, like just Napolean. It would, however, not be appropriate to link Ranade with the Shivaji festival which Lokmanya Tilak started in 1895, as it is quite well-known that both men held divergent views on several political and social questions.[47] It is, therefore, not correct to say that the cult of Shivaji began with Ranade.[48]

Ranade was thus a legend in Maratha historiography. The assessment of his works made by several eminent historians bear eloquent testimony to his influence on future historical writings. However, it may be pointed out here that the suggestions that he had made for the guidance of further studies have not been taken seriously by scholars. Ranade says,

> The selections (from Peshwa's Diaries) cover a period of over a hundred years (1708–1816–17) and they furnish most valuable materials for constructing a true history of the people of Maharashtra during the most eventful period of their annals. Our ordinary *Bakhars* and the works written by English historians like Grant Duff were content chiefly with the narration of political events, and throw little or no light upon the condition of the people, how they lived and thrived . . . These

histories do not also give a clear account of the way in which the work of the Governments was carried . . .,

He then discusses in detail the importance of these documents, which far outweigh in value the narratives of wars and conquests, dynastic changes and revolutions.[49]

Finally, while discussing the causes of the failure of historians to fully engages with historical data, Ranade maintains that 'our failure to realise this higher life brought on the final collapse long before any outside influences were brought to operate upon us'.[50] Through his writing he also emphasized the relevance of history to modern times, and which, according to him, is the principal purpose of historical writings.

NOTES

1. N.R. Pathak, *Nyayamurthi Mahadeo Govind Ranade*, Pune: Neelakantha Prakashan, 2nd edn., p. 15.
2. Ibid., p. 16. 'The felicity and the pleasure (though a little alloyed with pain, when our former power and glory have departed from our nation, when the land knows not its sons for its masters) and yet still great when one sits to write the rise and progress of his own nation. 'Misanthropy may like to brood over the mishaps, which hastened the ruin, the pussillanimity and dissentions, which precipitated the downfall of one's own country. Amidst the sickness so deadly, and destruction so complete as now prevails through the land a warm and a patriotic bosom may prefer to breathe for a time a purer air of more distant ages, when wealth, honour, liberty were the possession of his nation. 'With a mind filled with such thoughts, and throbbing with such pleasure (though it must be owned, not unmixed with pain) it is that I sit to write the essay.' . . .'Thus originated the rise of the Maratha Nation,—a band of robbers (if robbery be the proper name for what Shivaji did) led by a successful chief, laid the foundation of an immense empire, Shivaji was forced to rob for no other plan promised the slightest success under the eaglelike sight and tyranny of Aurangzcb.'
3. Ibid., pp. 15–17.
4. Ibid., p. 45.
5. Ibid., p. 39, I was sorry to find thc majority of the class were content with the manuals. I have ever found it to be true from my own experience as a teacher and student that in the long run there is less waste of time and energy, more of permanent bcnefit and present enjoyment, in reading the largest standard authority upon a particular period of History than in reading half a dozen times the small manuals invariably so dry and only for revision purposes-Quoted.

6. Ibid., p. 46.
7. B.P. Modak (1847–1906), was a science teacher at Rajaram High School, Kolhapur. He wrote, in Marathi, the history of Kolhapur and other southern Maratha states.

   N.J. Kirtane (1844–96), a student of the Deccan College, and a critic of Grant Duff's *History* (1868), edited *Malhar Ramrao Chitnis* and *Life of Shivaji in Seven Chapters*. He helped Ranade in collecting material. Diwan of Dewas State.

   K.N. Sane (1851–1927), edited several Marathi chronicles. He was the editor of *Kavye-itihas Samgraha* (1878–90), a magazine devoted to research in history and literature.
8. Kashinath Trambak Telang (1850–93), a jurist, Justice of the High Court, and orientalist, associated with Indian National Congress. He presented a paper 'Gleanings from Maratha Chronicles', before the Deccan College Union on 17 September 1892, a year before his death. See *Rise of the Maratha Power* (*RMP*) by M.G. Ranade and 'Gleanings from Maratha Chronicles' by K.T. Telang, Bombay University, Bombay, 1961, pp. 136–72. The *RMP* was published (1st edn.) in 1900 by Messers Punalekar & Company, at the Caxton Printing Works, Bombay. A later edition was published by Government of India, Publications Division, 1966.
9. *RMP*, Preface II.
10. Both these essays are included in the Bombay University edition of *RMP*, pp. 173–226. The Editors' Notes to the Introduction to Peshwas Diaries deserve special attention.
11. *RMP*, p. 2.
12. Grant Duff, *A History of the Mahrattas*, ed. S.M. Edwardes, 6th edn., OUP, 1921, p. xxxvi. See also G.W. Steevenes, *India of Yester Years* (1899), rpt. 1984. Steevenes, a visitor to Pune, while examining the case of rebellious Poona with reference to the murders of Rand and Lt. Ayerst in June 1897, observed, 'The Marathas have never forgotten how high they were less than a hundred years ago, and who it was that brought them low. They lost more than others. For others we were a change of masters, them we brought down from masters to slaves. . . . It was from the Marathas and the Sikhs and from Hindus and not from Mussalmans that we actually conquered India . . . other provinces of India were ceded to us or conquered from alien lords, the Marathas lost all in war.' Ch. XXIX, pp. 271–2, *India of Yester Years*, rpt. 1984.
13. *RMP*, pp. 3–5.
14. Ibid., p. 8.
15. Ranade writes, 'There is a curious parallel between the history of the Reformation movement in Western Europe and the struggle represented by the lives and teachings and writing of these saints and prophets who flourished about the same time in Maharashtra', *RMP*, p. 81.
16. A.R. Kulkarni (ed.), *History in Practice*, New Delhi: Books and Books, 1993, p. 132.
17. The critical editorial observations of G.S. Ghurye and R.P. Patwardhan, which compare Ranade's views with present-day studies, in this field, deserve special attention. See *RMP*, pp. 206–15.

   V.K. Rajwade, however, objected to the very editing of the Peshwa Diaries by Vad and his associates. He claims that the documents are not chronologically arranged, and that the glossory attached to it is faulty. In short, all the universally accepted norms of editing historical documents have been violated by the editors of the Diaries. He does not believe that Ranade had given Vad detailed instructions about the method of arranging and printing historical sources, as it is often said that the classification of material published in the Diaries was done in accordance with instructions of Ranade. See *Aithihasik Prastavana* of V.K. Rajwade, published by S.N. Joshi, Pune: Chitrashala Press, 1928, p. 372.

18. A.R. Kulkarni, *Maharashtra in the Age of Shivaji*, Pune: Deshmukh, 1969, p. 235.
19. *RMP*, p. 216.
20. Ibid., pp. 225–6.
21. The Fowler Committee recommended that the ultimate objective for India was to introduce an effective gold standard with a currency based on the principle of the free inflow and outflow of gold, and suggested ways and means for its implementation (see G.B. Jathar and K.G. Jathar, *The Indian Economics*, OUP, 1957, p. 281).

    The British Government did accept the recommendation of the Fowler Committee. However, what eventually came to prevail in India was not a gold standard with a gold currency, but what is known as the Gold Exchange Standard. See Bipan Chandra, *The Rise and Growth of Economic Nationalism in India*, New Delhi: PPH, 1969, p. 277.
22. *RMP*, Preface, p. v.
23. S.R. Tikekar (ed.), *Lokhitwadinchi Shatpatre*, Aundh: Usha Prakashan, 1940. See letter nos. 12, 31, 38, 46, 54, 89, 94, etc.
24. *RMP*, p. 8.
25. B.R. Nanda, *Gokhale: The Indian Moderates and the British Raj*, New Delhi: OUP, 1977, p. 22. On the basis of the 'Miscellaneous Writings of Ranade', Nanda writes 'Under the impact of the forces released by English rule, India was being roused from the stupor of the ages, there were forces at work for social, economic and political reconstruction which could bring her on a level with the advanced countries of the West. In this reconstruction, Ranade saw the guiding hand of God in History.' 'We may smile today at this belief in a Divine dispensation' linking the destinies of India and England. But to the English educated who had grown up in the middle of the nineteenth century, British imperialism did not appear in the same light as it does to us, p. 26.
26. Kulkarni (ed.), *History in Practice*, New Delhi: Books & Books, 1993. See also Richard Tucker, *Ranade and the Roots of Indian Nationalism* Bombay: Popular, 1972.
27. Ibid., pp. 37, 40–1.
28. Ibid., p. 43.
29. Ibid., p. 49.
30. Jadunath Sarkar, *Shivaji and His Times*, Calcutta, 6th edn., 1952, pp. 72–4. He writes, 'The weight of recorded evidence as well as the possibilities of the case supports the view that Afzal Khan struck the first blow and that Shivaji only committed what Burke calls a preventive murder . . . a case of diamond cut diamond.'
31. *Shahiranche Chhatrapati Shivaji Maharaj*, published by Shri Chhatrapati Shivaji Maharaj Smarak Samiti, Mumbai, 1988, pp. 31–46.

32. Kulkarni, op. cit., pp. 45–6.
33. Ibid., p. 50.
34. For a detailed discussion of this point, see *Shivakalin Maharashtra*, by A.R. Kulkarni, Pune: Rajhansa Prakashan, 2nd edn., 1997, pp. 174–96.
35. Kulkarni, op. cit., p. 51.
36. Ibid., p. 50.
37. Ibid., pp. 51–2.
38. S.P. Sen (ed.), *Historians and Historiography in Modern India*, Calcutta, 1973, p. 178. The report says, 'Of these books (which had come to Government for approval) by far the most prominent is the work entitled Rise of the Maratha Power by late Mr. Justice Ranade. Mr. Ranade's peculiar capacity to undertake a historical work of this description will be recognised by all, and it is needless to state that the book is remarkable for its breadth of view, its concise and business like arrangement, and sound common sense. The distinguished author has passed away from amongst us, but this book remains to show at once his mastery over the English language, his spirit of true historical research and his fair and sympathetic treatment of a period of history which is of particular interest to a large part of the population of this presidency.'
39. H.G. Rawlinson, *Shivaji the Maratha: His Life and Times*, Oxford, 1915, Introduction, p. 9.
40. Rajwade, *Aitihasik Prastavana,* op. cit., pp. 358–9.
41. Ibid., p. 419.
42. Ibid., pp. 284–5.
43. Quoted in S.P. Sen, op. cit., p. 178.
44. S.N. Sen, *Administrative System of the Marathas*, Calcutta, 3rd edn., 1976, Introduction, pp. 12–13. Let us take a brief review of the opinions of later historians who disagree with Ranade on the point of role of saint poets in Maratha history. Riyasatkar Sardesai, who otherwise supports Ranade's views, refutes his opinion that the political revolution was preceded, and caused to some extent, by the religious revival. S.P. Sen, op. cit., p. 181.

    Again N.S. Takakhav, in his celebrated book in English, *The Life of Shivaji Maharaj* (Bombay, 1921). He says, 'Mr. Ranade's dissertation about the saints is without any foundation and does discredit to his historical research. He does not seem to have grasped the meaning of the phrase "Maharashtra Dharma". He has fathered upon the saints' ideas which they never even dreamt of it.' Quoted in S.P. Sen, op. cit., pp. 180–1. The able editor of Grant Duff's *History of the Maratha,* OUP, 6th edn., 1921, S.M. Edwardes, makes certain pertinent remarks in this respect. He writes, '. . . one may venture to remark that there is a tendency among some writers to over estimate the influence upon the public mind of Maharashtra of the message of the Marathi poets of the *Bhakti School.* . . . Yet it is doubtful whether the poetry of the saints and writers of the *Bhakti* school ever reached, or made much impression upon, the general mass of the people of Maharashtra . . . one cannot but point out that its influence at the time it was composed, upon the general population of Maharashtra, cannot have been as great as is occasionally pretended, and that its power to mould the public mind did not survive the early days of Maratha political dominance.' Introduction, pp. ixxiii–ixxv.

45. D.V. Apte, 'Ranade Yanchya Marathyanchya Itihasavishayi Vichar', published in *Lekha Samgraha*, edited by Apte, Smarak Mandal, Pune, published by A.V. Prakashan, Pune, 1945, pp. 13–24.
46. This achievement (of Balaji Vishwanath) is his main claim to be regarded as, next to Shivaji, the principal founder of the Maratha Confederacy. *RMP*, op. cit., p. 116.
47. B.R. Nanda, op. cit., p. 83.
48. Sumit Sarkar, *Modern India (1855–1947)*, Macmillan, 1983. 'Ranade's own historical works and articles in a sense began the cult of Shivaji which Tilak took up from 1895. Ranade, however, tried to portray the 17th century revival as a kind of protestant movement inspired by *bhakti* saints, who sought to transcend caste differences', p. 83.
49. *RMP*, op. cit., pp. 173–4.
50. Ibid., p. 205.

13

Riyasatkar Govind Sakharam Sardesai (1865–1959)

Govind Sakharam Sardesai, popularly known as Riyasatkar, was born in a small village, Hasol (Ratnagiri district) on 17 May 1865. He was the first Indian to write a comprehensive history of the Marathas, both in Marathi and English.[1]

After graduating from Elphinstone College in 1888, Sardesai joined the Baroda State Service in 1889 as tutor to the Maharaja, Sayajirao Gaikwad (1863–1938), and continued there in various capacities till his retirement in 1925. This service in the Baroda State led him to select material on various subjects, and reading it out to the Maharaja for his information. He was also supposed to prepare notes for training the princess and members of the royal family. Besides this he acted as personal clerk to the Maharaja, and in that capacity he accompanied the ruler on his visits to Europe, which an experience helped him to widen his circle and meet a number of people, and also enabled him to develop his personality.

Sayajirao, being an enlightened ruler, always encouraged learning and respected intellectuals. Sardesai greatly benefited as a result of these qualities of the Maharaja. With a view to meeting the wishes of the Maharaja, he translated into Marathi some important works such as Machiavelli's *The Prince* (1890) and Seely's *Expansion of England* (1893), which was held as the Bible of British imperialists. He devoted the rest of his life to writing and editing historical works.

It was customary among the royal families in Maharashtra to arrange for the teaching of the history of their ancestors to the younger generation. Sayajirao, in keeping with this tradition, set up a school at the royal palace, with Sardesai as its 'mastersab' to teach history to his son Fatehsingh and other members of the family. Sardesai shouldered this responsibility for nearly twenty-four years, the most creative period in his life. Being a hard-working and self-disciplined person, Sardesai read widely and prepared notes for teaching history to the princes. This preliminary work proved to be the bedrock for his monumental work—the *Riyasats* of the Muslim, Maratha and British rulers covering the period from AD 1000 to 1857. A brief review of his historical writings gives an idea of Sardesai's tremendous effort and sincerity of purpose in presenting a comprehensive history of the Marathas in particular and of Indian history in general.

Historical Writings

Sardesai's main job was to give lessons to his pupils in Maratha history. However, it seems, that he thought that for a better understanding of the role of the Marathas in history, knowledge of the Hindu, Muslim and British regimes in India was also necessary. He, therefore, prepared a tentative plan of writing a complete history of India in four parts: (1) *Ancient History, 4000 BC to AD 1000*; (ii) *Muslim Riyasat, AD 1000 to 1803*; (iii) *Marathi Riyasat, 1600 to 1818*; and lastly (iv) *British Riyasat, 1803 to 1857* under the general title *Hindusthancha Arvachin Itihas*, from which the first part, i.e. the Ancient period, was later on dropped.

He started working on his plan seriously perhaps after 1892. His *Musalmani Riyasat* was published in 1898 in two parts: (1) *Sultan Gharani* and (ii) *Mogal Patshahi*. The first volume covered the period from the rise of Islam (AD 632) to the advent of the Mughals on the Indian scene in 1526. The first volume surveys the early activities of the Muslims in India, from the Sultanate period till the Mughal invasion in 1526. It also deals briefly with the histories of Gujarat, the Bahamanis and their offshoots, and the Vijayanagar Empire. Besides this, it also includes a brief account of the Rajputs of Mewar, Jaipur and Jodhpur states, and a brief review of the administrative and cultural aspects of the history of this period.

The second volume entitled *Mogal Patshahi* covers the period from Babur to Shah Alam, who surrendered to the East India Company in 1803. Though the emphasis is on political history, Sardesai, as in the earlier volume, discusses some other aspects of history. It is interesting to note that he also added an account of foreign travellers of this period such as Terry, Bernier, Thevenot, Fryer, Hamilton and others who had thrown some light on various aspects of Mughal history in their travelogues.

These two volumes covered the history of nearly eight hundred years in about 900 pages, for the first time in Marathi: they were published by 1898, when Sardesai was hardly thirty-three years old, and is a remarkable achievement indeed.

A quick look at the bibliography appended to these two volumes testifies to the immense hard work that Sardesai had put in to equip himself for writing the *Hindustancha Arvachin Itihas* (in 2 vols.) (*Musalmani Riyasat*). He consulted the works of Alberuni, Lanepoole, Rushbrook Williams, Holden, Erskine, Malleson, Beniprasad, Tod and several others who wrote about this period. This being the first book on this subject in Marathi, it was very much appreciated, though when it was first published in 1898 some protests were made against it and it was suggested that it should be banned as some parts of this book hurt the feelings of Muslims. In spite of this, with some minor revisions, it was published five times between 1898 and 1993. This is certainly a major achievement of Sardesai, considering the period in which he was working.[2]

Marathi Riyasat

The initial success of the *Musalmani Riyasat* induced Sardesai to undertake the task of writing and publishing the entire history of the Marathas from their rise to their fall, which was the area of his expertise. This series was known as *Marathi Riyasat*, and its eight volumes were published between 1902 and 1932. They were broadly classified as (a) *Purvardha* (first part) 1 vol.; (b) *Madhya Vibhag* (middle part); 4 vols. and (c) *Uttara Vibhag* (last phase), 3 vols. The three volumes of *Uttara Vibhag* were written and published after his retirement from the Baroda State Service in 1925.[3]

Simultaneously, Sardesai also published the biographies of individual luminaries of Maratha history under different titles such as *Shahaji Raje, Shakakarta Shivaji* (Shivaji the epoch maker), *Ugra Prakriti Sambhaji* (Sambhaji the violent), *Sthirbudhi Rajaram* (Rajaram the stable minded), *Punyashloka Shahu* (Shahu the pious) in four parts discussing the careers of *Peshwa Balaji Vishwanath*, *Peshwa Bajirao, Peshwa Balaji Bajirao* in two parts, *Nigrahak Peshwa Madhavrao*, and lastly *Narayanrao* and *Raghunathrao*, the father of the ill-fated Bajirao II, who surrendered Maratha power to the British.[4]

For the preparation of these volumes, Sardesai consulted the voluminous Marathi source material unearthed by researchers K.N. Sane (1851–1927), Vasudeoshastri Khare (1858–1924), V.K. Rajwade (1863–1926), and D.B. Parasnis (1870–1926), and the selections from the Peshwa Daftar, which he edited between 1929 and 1934. He also studied secondary works in English on Maratha history by European scholars such as Orme, Scott Waring, Grant Duff, Elphinstone and others. Thus, he equipped himself thoroughly for the great task of presenting a history of the Marathas covering its various phases—the rise, growth, decline and extinction—based on available source material.

About his *Marathi Riyasat*, Sardesai says:

> I tried to bring together the scattered, disarranged and uncalandered (even unlisted) mass of historical data, and opinions found in that tongue, and after comparing them with available materials in other languages, to construct a compact critical study of the rise and fall of the modern Maratha State.[5]

He completed the last volume of his *Riyasat* entitled *Uttara Vibhag*—vol. 3 *(1795–1848)* and bade farewell to his readers. He maintained in his address that 'Maharashtra can reclaim its former glory only if it can completely uproot the tendency (*vritti*) sowed by Bajirao II and return to the days of Shivaji'.[6]

British Riyasat

The *British Riyasat*, the last part of his original plan of Indian history, comprises two parts. The first volume gives an account of the early attempts of the Europeans, including the Portuguese, and the Dutch, to capture the trade of India, and the rise of the East India Company and its activities up to the Battle of Plassey (1600–1757). The second volume deals with the intervention of the East India Company in Indian politics and the gradual establishment of its supremacy prior to the Mutiny of 1857, which ultimately paved the way for the transfer of power from the Company to the Crown after 1857, making India a colony of the British Empire (1757–1858).

Sardesai spared no effort to learn everything about the subject on which he was to write. He went through most of the published material in English then available, for instance, Danvers' *History of Portuguese in India*, Sir Alfred Lyall's *British Dominion in India*, Malleson's *History of the French in India*, Kaye's *Administration of the East India Company*, Gibbon's *History of Commerce in Europe*, and many other relevant works. The first volume was published in 1908 and was reprinted in 1933. The second volume appeared in 1939. Both volumes together present the history of the East India Company in India covering a period of 250 years (1600–1858) in nearly 1,100 pages in a simple style.[7]

Thus, Sardesai, in thirty-four years of his long life of ninety-four years produced this monumental work on Indian history covering a period nearly 850 years narrated in nearly 6,000 printed pages.[8]

Life of Nanasaheb Peshwa

The editor of *The Bharat Gaurav Grantha Mala* of Baroda, a series of books narrating the careers of eminent Indians planned along the lines of *the Rulers of India* series, requested Sardesai to write the biography of Balaji (1721–61), the third Peshwa.[9]

Sardesai agreed to do so because of the availability of many of the Peshwa's letters throwing light on various aspects of his career. It was not something new, but simply summarized what he had already written on this Peshwa in two volumes in his *Riyasat* series. But what is noteworthy about it was that he requested a young scholar, T.S. Shejwalkar, to edit this and also write an introduction to this volume knowing fully well that his views on the Peshwa were diametrically opposed to his own. Sardesai believed that a public expression of the differences would ultimately be helpful to the cause of historical writings in general. Sardesai, therefore, published this critical introduction of Shejwalkar along with the text of his book. This is an eloquent testimony of the qualities of head and heart of Sardesai, who could accept praise and criticism in the right spirit. The points raised by T.S. Shejwalkar will be considered later along with the other critics of Sardesai.

Main Currents of Maratha History

Jadunath Sarkar, the life long friend of G.S. Sardesai, was mainly responsible for introducing this unknown Marathi scholar to the non-Marathi-speaking people of India and abroad. After going through Sardesai's book on Peshwa Bajirao I, Sarkar persuaded him to write in English for the benefit of others. He even offered to translate part of his work into English and get it printed in Calcutta without any cost to the author. He writes, 'There is a large field for English histories even in India, and your excellent works should be made available to all the provinces.'[10]

Sarkar utilized his connections in Patna and arranged for Sardesai's lectures at the University of Patna. He asked Sardesai to prepare a series of six or seven lectures in English on some important topics and personalities in Maratha history and the progress made by the Maratha scholars in the field of historical research.

Sardesai worked hard and delivered seven lectures for which he selected topics such as Maharashtra Dharma: Survey of Historical Research in Maharashtra, the Expansion of Maratha Power in the north, the relations between the two great Maratha statesmen of the last phase of Maratha history, namely

Mahadji Shinde and Nana Phadnis, and lastly the causes of the decline and fall of Maratha power. Thus, he presented the major issues of the Maratha period in a nutshell, and expressed his own views on some of the outstanding and debatable questions of Maratha history. These lectures were published under the title *Main Currents of Maratha History* in the same year (1926) by one of the leading publishers of Calcutta.

In his introductory remarks Sardesai observed that his main purpose in delivering these lectures was to acquaint the non-Marathi-speaking people with some aspects of Maratha history based on new evidence available from Marathi sources. He made it clear at the outset that he would speak on the aims and objectives of Maratha policy, explaining what it had achieved and what it had failed to achieve, what good or evil it did to India, and what place it could claim in the history of India as a whole. He also expressed his desire to seek some coordination of effort throughout the country between Maharashtṛa and other parts of India in this important subject of national interest. Our past is a common property which we all have to share equally, he stated.[11]

Thus, through these lectures Sardesai appealed to scholars to study Maratha history in a larger perspective and consider it as part of the history of the Indian subcontinent rather than of a region called Maharashtra.

The second edition of this book was published after a gap of seven years (1933). During this period, Sardesai used the vast treasure of the Pune Archives, as he was working as editor of the selection from the Peshwa Daftar, publication project of historical records sponsored by the Government of Bombay. In the Introduction to the second edition, he reiterated that the main object of these lectures was to interpret Maratha history from a purely Maratha standpoint for the benefit of, those who could not study the original material at first hand owing to their ignorance of the language. He made certain modifications and additions in the text in view of the new material but without disturbing the original plan. He further stated that he had tried to avoid partisanship and to present an impartial reading of Maratha history.[12]

New History of the Marathas

Sardesai must have taken a hint from Sarkar's remark in his 'Foreword' to the first edition of *Main Currents*, noting that 'the wider circles of readers outside Maharashtra require a presentation of the results in English', and hence decided to work on the English edition of *Maratha History*. He claimed that it was not a translation of his Marathi *Riyasat* but a fresh work based on new material. *The New History of the Marathas* in three volumes running into nearly 1,500 pages, was produced between 1946 and 1948. Sardesai was then eighty-three years old.[13]

Sarkar had been very keen since 1916 that Sardesai's work should be rendered into English. He wrote to him:

> Your *Marathi Riyasat*, New Edn. (1915) Vol. I is the thing that deserves translation into English, after being reduced to one half of its size (it was 719 pp. in Marathi) by omitting Rajwade's fantastic etymologies and much of your reflections and greatly compressing the early history of the Deccan and the general history of Mughal Empire . . . which were admittedly mere compilations. The rest of the book is of first-rate historical value.[14]

Perhaps Sardesai followed these guidelines while preparing the text of the *New History of the Marathas*.

After completing his editorial work at the Peshwa Daftar in 1934, Sardesai had some time to spare for this work, though he was associated with Jadunath Sarkar in the selection and publication of the fourteen volumes of the Poona Residency Correspondence between 1936 to 1958. His views on Maratha history by that time had become quite mature because of his better understanding of numerous original Marathi documents and his interaction with many eminent historians like Sarkar and his students. The World War I had given a momentum to the Indian freedom struggle, and historians also played their part by reminding Indians of their glorious past. The Marathas surrendered to the British in 1818, but they had not forgotten their immediate independent past. Sardesai thought that Maratha history was not 'the cherished treasure of a single community or province; it should prove a source of inspiration, wisdom and warning to all India'.[15] This idea perhaps induced him to undertake the writing of the *New History of Marathas*, which he thought would become a source of inspiration to Indian freedom fighters.

In the preface to the first volume of the *New History*, he justified his writing it in English on various grounds. First, this was prompted by the availability of enormous source material since the publication of Grant Duff's *History* in 1826. The progress made by India in historical research, and methodology and the deep social changes that had taken place had brought about a new outlook. Hence, it had become imperative to rewrite Indian history afresh. In support of his stand, he quoted Goethe, who observed:

> History must from time to time be rewritten, not because many new facts have been discovered, but because new aspects come into view, because the participant in the progress of an age is led to the standpoints from which the past can be reviewed and judged in a novel manner.

Second, he thought that the sons of the soil were best qualified to write the history of their own people. In justification of this, he cited Goldwin Smith, who observed 'Each nation in the main writes its own history best. It best knows its own land, its own institutions, the relative importance of its own events, the character of its own great men. Each nation has also its peculiarities of view, its prejudices, its self-love which require to be corrected by the impartial or even hostile view of others.'

Third, he argued that an extreme form of national pride as adopted by historians like V.K. Rajwade had kept many scholars away from using the English language as a medium of expression. This attitude prevented them from reaching out to a larger group of researchers and students of history, all over India and hereby prevented 'Maratha history from becoming a fruitful subject of higher study and criticism in our Universities, and thus speeded up a healthy advance in our knowledge of this subject.' If he had followed the example of Rajwade, Sardesai stated, 'My work too like Rajwade's would have remained unknown to the world ignorant to my native language.'[16]

It is commonly believed that the *New History* is an abridged form of *Marathi Riyasats* translated into English. Sardesai emphatically denied this and asserted, 'It is the first attempt to present a fresh and full treatment of Maratha history in English embodying the results of the latest research.'[17]

He reiterated his purpose of presenting a real picture of the Marathas, who had long been misjudged by their rivals and adversaries and had been painted in the blackest colours both during and after the period of their downfall, as if they had no single good point to their credit. He aimed at producing a true apologia (*kaifiyat*) of the Maratha people and place it before an impartial public.[18]

It can hardly be denied that the efforts made by Jadunath Sarkar in inducing Sardesai to produce this monumental work on the Marathas in English has been commendable.

Sardesai was aware of his limitations about his knowledge of the English language. Once he requested Sarkar to suggest a guide in expanding his English vocabulary and also to acquire a good style. He confessed, 'I find myself much hampered by the difficulty of choosing appropriate words.'[19]

Sarkar promptly recommended that the surest means of acquiring a good style, were (1) to read the best simple English prose for half an hour every morning; (2) to pick up only facts from trashy authors; and (3) to pause and revise frequently in the course of one's own writing.

Sarkar also pointed out to Sardesai that 'he writes too long and too diffusely, and hence your style is bound to suffer. You should compress as much as you could, revise and polish your words.'

He further told him to remember:

> that the elements of a good prose style include not merely the choice of apt phrases, but also the judicious and most effective marshalling of the facts, the order of development of the parts of the theme or proposition you intend to prove, and the proper proportion in the length of the different parts. The true difficulty is to decide what to omit and what to keep, because we cannot give every fact, some must go out, probably many.[20]

During his stay in Kamshet in April 1944, Sarkar revised and discussed Sardesai's manuscript of the three volumes of *New History*. It seems from the correspondence of Sardesai that the original draft of *New History* underwent changes recommended by two experts: (1) V.G. Dighe, who helped him in the initial stages, and (2) Sarkar, who tried to make the text flawless.

Sarkar also took the responsibility of the publication of these volumes of *New History*. He requested Sir V.T. Krishnamachari, the Diwan of Baroda, to get them printed at the expense of the Baroda Government (at an estimated cost of Rs. 6,500) as a memorial to Sir Sayajirao Gaikwad whom Sardesai had served all his life. Krishnamachari accepted this offer, but in the meanwhile he resigned his job in Baroda, and so the proposal could not be implemented.

Sarkar, however, did not give up his efforts of raising funds for publication. He wrote to his student, Rajkumar Raghubir Sinh of Sitamau, 'If the Baroda subsidy fails, should this great work—the ripe fruit of a life of 80 years of toil—be allowed to perish? Somebody is required to advance Rs. 3000 to the press and wait till the money comes back from the sales. Unless the book is an utter failure, this advance will not be a donation, but a loan for 4 to 5 years.'[21]

Sardesai published the final volume of *New History* entitled *Sunset over Maharashtra*[22] (*1792–1848*) in 1948 and bade farewell to his readers with these words: 'Sir Jadunath Sarkar objected to the title of the third volume and suggested that it should be 'The advent of a fresh dawn'. His argument was, 'The so-called Sunset overtook a state and a society, that were rotten to a core. Surely, nature could not have let it continue if the British had not intervened in December, 1802. Repine not over your past, and the dead and the never-to-return past. Look forward and seize the opportunity of the present, plunging into the full rushing stream of modern world-progress and world thought. This is the lesson of Maratha history, when viewed dispassionately in the long perspective.'[23]

Sardesai began his career as a teacher to the members of the royal family of the Gaikwads of Baroda State. Sayajirao, the Maharaja of the state, encouraged him in all his efforts of historical research and writing while he was in the service of the state. The relations of Sardesai with Baroda were somewhat strained over the issue of pension. He had served there for more than thirty-three years and his pension was stopped on flimsy grounds. He was later absolved of all charges, and the successor of the Maharaja, Pratap Singh, the grandson of Sayajirao, restored his pension and relations once again became cordial, and Sardesai was awarded for his historical writings. Sardesai had never forgotton the help and encouragement given by the Maharaja. As a token of gratitude, he dedicated the *New History of the Marathas* to the memory of the Maharaja of Baroda (1875–1939) with these words, 'To whom I have given all my life's years of service and who had led my young steps into the pleasant path of History.'

Sardesai's 'Selections from the Peshwa Daftar'

(A) Marathi Documents

With the conquest of the Maratha territories in 1818, the archives of the Peshwas fell into the hands of the British. The Peshwa Daftar, originally constituted about 13,000 bundles called *Rumals*, consisting of the records of the Peshwas for eighty-eight years from 1729 to 1817. Subsequently, many other records were added to this nucleus, and the number of *Rumals* grew from the original number of 1,300 to 34,972. Of these, 27,332 were in Marathi, 7,482 in English, 29 in Persian, and 129 in Gujarati. As most of the records pertained to the land and its ownership, tenure, transfer, revenue, administration and other allied matters, the collection came to be known as the Alienation Office under the British. It is now known as the Pune Archives.[24]

However, this vast treasure was not open to scholars. One could get access to it only with the permission of the Commissioner of the Central Division, as the office was under his control. With the formation of the Historical Records Commission in 1919, the restrictions on historians and researchers regarding access to the archives were partially removed. As a consequence of this, as has been noted in the chapter on the Archival movement, Jadunath Sarkar, a member of the Commission, in cooperation with G.S. Sardesai, prepared a scheme of the selection and publication of Marathi, English and Persian records preserved in the Alienation Office (Peshwa Daftar), and submitted it to the Bombay Government for consideration. With great efforts, it was decided in 1929 to have these Marathi manuscript records examined and such of their contents as had any historical importance printed by the Bombay Government.

Sardesai was nominated as general editor of the project with a staff of ten assistants (actually six) to be trained and directed by him. A sum of Rs. 10,000 per annum was sanctioned for a period of three years, but when the project was within sight of completion, the Government did not make any provision for the fourth year in its budget. Sarkar was informed by the Government 'that the task would be abandoned and the staff given notice of dismissal on 29 February next, unless public subscriptions were collected before that date for meeting the entire expenditure of this final year'.[25]

Sarkar and Sardesai accepted this challenge, visited many places in the south, made urgent appeals for funds to Maratha Sardars and the enlightened public, and succeeded in raising the sum of Rs. 12,000, required for completing the work in the fourth year.

Sardesai and his team comprising scholars like K.P. Kulkarni, V.G. Dighe, V.S. Bendre, M.V. Gujar, Y.N. Kelkar and others worked hard. They selected a number of Marathi documents, in the Modi script, from the 27,332 Marathi *Rumals*, shortlisted them, transliterated them into the Devanagari script, classified them under different themes, and arranged them in forty-five volumes. These selections included the private papers of individual Peshwas, the Maratha campaigns of Udgir and Panipat, Maratha administration, the private life of Shahu and his Peshwas, the Satara Rajas, the Maratha Sardars, historical families, social life and many other things. This brief reference gives us an idea of the wide net cast by the editors in selecting a variety of documents covering many aspects of Maratha history. This description might induce scholars to consult many more relevant documents by digging into the Pune Archives.

Maximum care was taken to ascertain the date of each printed document. The contents of each was given in one or two lines provided for the guidance of readers, and introduction wherever necessary was also in some volumes. As the first volumes had been printed without indices, Sardesai prepared and published them in a separate volume in 1933.

These forty-five volumes of Marathi records running into approximately 7,800 pages included 8,650 letters covering the period from 1707 to 1848. These volumes were made available to scholars and institutions at a very moderate price varying from 2 annas (3 pence) to Rs. 6–15–0 (11 sh. 6 pence) only. All forty-five volumes in spite of many hurdles were prepared and published between 1929 and 1934. Sarkar compares this achievement of Sardesai with that of Momsen's work on Roman history. From among the large number of documents selected from various *Rumals*, only a few were finally selected and published. The unprinted material has been properly sorted out, rearranged, and preserved in the Pune Archives for the benefit of scholars seeking to undertake further research.[26]

While Sardesai was working on this project, his qualifications were challenged by the Pune scholars, and questions were asked about the caste and qualification of persons selected to help in the Legislative Council.[27]

Sardesai was extremely fatigued during the last stage of the work. In his reply to Sardesai's letter, Sarkar wrote:

> It (fatigue) is not due to old age or physical weakness. It is, I believe, the natural reaction after four years' strenuous exertion at the A.O. (Alienation Office). In the midst of every possible distraction and obstruction from malicious rivals and ignorant, credulous and deluged public that feeds on newspapers. Your wonderful strength of purpose and ingrained habits of methodical work alone have enabled you to reach the completion of the task. And now you have to pay the price for it. The intoxication of work, especially a work on which one has set one's heart, makes us forgetful of everything else—external disturbances, physical fatigue, even the sadness of bereavement.[28]

(B) The Poona Residency Correspondence

After the completion of the Marathi series, Sardesai joined the scheme sponsored by Jadunath Sarkar, known as the Poona Residency Correspondence, and edited five out of fourteen volumes published under this scheme between 1936 and 1958.[29] The Government of Bombay had specifically recorded that both these editors did not claim any remuneration or honorarium or travelling expenses.

One of the purposes of the publication of the *Poona Residency Correspondence* (*PRC*) was to present to the non-Marathi-speaking readers 'fuller and critical accounts of the Maratha activities in India, particularly such information which is not available in Marathi'.

While emphasizng the importance of the *PRC*, Sarkar wrote:

> What enhances the value of these English records is that they supply two elements which are wanting in the despatches written in the Marathi tongue. Their intelligence is far more accurate and widespread than that of the Marathas, and the despatches of the English Residents give a broader survey of Indian politics and a deeper and more intelligent criticism of character and policy than is to be met with in the terse, matter-of-fact Marathi letters. Hence, they enable us to reach the root causes of events and to trace the wider movements of Indian politics in a degree unattainable in the indigenous Persian and Marathi sources.[30]

In his introductions to the Embassies of Malet, Palmer, Close and Elphinstone, Sardesai briefly narrated the life sketch of each Resident and discussed their activities relating to the Poona Court, covering the last phase of Maratha power from 1786 to 1818.

Thus, the publication of forty-five volumes of Marathi documents and five volumes of English records was Sardesai's remarkable contribution to the study of Maratha history.

(C) Mahadji Shinde and Other Papers

Mahadji Shinde and Nana Phadnis were the two Maratha personalities who dominated the political scene of India in the last quarter of the eighteenth century. However, both Sarkar and Sardesai while working on the Peshwa Daftar realized that the important correspondence between these two persons, particularly after 1776 was missing. This was kept by Nana Phadnis in his private archives, and after his death in 1800 his widow transferred the entire collection to her residence at Menavali, a village near Wai (Satara district). Thus, the Menavali Daftar never reached the Pune Archives.

However, Rao Bahadur D.B. Parasnis, about whom a reference has been made earlier, succeeded in getting hold of the Menavali Daftar and except the Mahadji Shinde papers published some of them, through his historical miscellany *Itihas Sangraha*.

Sarkar, as a historian of the Mughals, was keenly interested in the Mahadji papers for his work on the fall of the Mughal Empire. Parasnis had a secret deal with the Shindes of Gwalior regarding the publication of the Mahadji–Nana Phadnis correspondence. He had prepared the text of five volumes, and got them printed in 1915, but did not release them, because he could not settle his terms with the Gwalior Darbar. Sarkar exposed Parasnis[31] and urged the Gwalior Darbar to get them reprinted under the editorial supervision of Sardesai. According to Sarkar, Sardesai was the only suitable person who could edit the papers, correct Parasnis's dates and misreadings, and re-arrange all the letters in strict chronological order.[31]

All these papers, including the ones printed earlier, were arranged, edited and published in one volume entitled *Mahadji Shinde Hyanchi Kagadpatre* (1937). The volume contains 608 letters of primary importance for Maratha history, throwing a flood of new light on the last quarter of the eighteenth century. In his Introduction to this volume, Sarkar revealed the secret behind the recovery of these letters with the help of Sardesai, which had 'at long last been brought out of' Ghosha in a garb worthy of them and made known to students of history.[32]

Rao Bahadur Parasnis had set up a Historical Museum at Satara with financial assistance from the Bombay Government. Sardesai gleaned through the collection of Satara Museum containing a part of Menavali Daftar and published two volumes, first containing 258 and second 424 letters on behalf of the Satara Itihas Samshodhak Mandal in 1940.

(D) Kota Daftar

Sarkar continued his search for the Mahadji Shinde papers throughout his life. Mahadji Shinde had been associated with Rajput politics in the north since 1764–5 when he first attacked the Chief of Kota for *khandani*. Gulgule, a Saraswat Brahmin, who had been appointed as *kamavisdar* for collecting dues from the Chief of Kota. While going through the first two volumes of *Shinde Shahichya Itihasachi Sadhane*, edited by Anandrao Bhausaheb Phalke, a Maratha sardar of Gwalior, Sarkar had made a note of the Gulgule Daftar of Kota possessing Mahadji's many private letters.

Sarkar had started cultivating friendship of the family of Sardar Gulgule of Kota, but he feared that Sardar Anandrao Phalke would object to the involvement of G.S. Sardesai as editor of the Gulgule Daftar. Sarkar approached Sardar Phalke through one of his disciples, Raghubir Sinh, the prince of the Rathod Maharaja of Sitamau, with a request to get the typed copies of the Shinde papers of the Gulgule Daftar but without mentioning the name of G.S. Sardesai.

Chandrakant Gulgule, the scion of the family, who had for sometime been under the influence of A.B. Phalke, ultimately decided to hand over his typed copies to Sardesai for editing.[33] When Sarkar received the typed copies of the Gulgule papers, he wrote to Rajkumar that they were very valuable, and that they would make a richer contribution to Maratha history than V.V. Khare's (1858–1924) *Aitihasik Lekha Samgraha* volumes of original Marathi records of Patwardhan Archives.[34]

Sarkar at last succeeded in getting the typed copies of the Gulgule Daftar and entrusted the job of editing them to Sardesai. While the work of editing was progressing, Sarkar became worried about the costs of printing. He enquired whether Rajkumar would bear half the cost of the printing to induce the publisher to undertake the risk of printing the text. Sarkar was also worried about the advancing age of his friend, for as he wrote, 'I wish to see the work done before Sardesai (now approaching his 82nd year) and myself (in my 76th year) leave the earthly scene.'[35]

He negotiated with the Bombay Government for making a deal with the heir of Gulgule, but these talks did not bear any fruit. Sardesai was nominated as the General President of the Indian History Congress of the Jaipur Session of 1951. Sarkar thought that Sardesai would be very happy to say something, if possible, about the publication of the Gulgule papers, the sole remaining collection of first-class records on Maratha history, as yet denied to scholars.[36]

While the negotiations were going on with the Gulgules, Sardesai continued to work quietly on arranging the Gulgule papers chronologically to avoid any delay.[37]

The Kota Daftar contains twenty-three bundles making a total of 4,407 papers, out of which 1,756 were selected for printing by Sardesai. But not a single volume appeared before both veteran historians died. On 10 May 1958, Sardesai's ninety-second birthday, Sarkar assured him, 'If I enjoy my present health, I shall see these volumes through the press, even when your eyes and brain are no longer available. Rely on me.'[38] But that was not to be. Perhaps before this letter reached the ailing Sardesai, Sarkar himself passed away, on 19 May 1958. Sardesai survived him by nineteen months, and expired on 29 November 1959. Thus, the chapter of the publication of the Kota Daftar, for which both historians had struggled since 1935, was closed forever.

Besides these major editorial works, Sardesai also edited some documents published by K.N. Sane in his *Kavyeitihas Samgraha* (1930), *Geneologies of Historical Families* (1957), *Shivaji Souvenir* (1927), and *Parmanand Kavyam* (1952) on behalf of the Gaikwad Oriental Series, Baroda.[39]

Making of a Historian

Sardesai was born at a time when the Indian National Congress had launched the freedom movement against British rule. As student volunteer he had witnessed the first session of the Congress held in Bombay in 1885. The nationalist Maratha historians and researchers, who were denied access to the historical source material preserved in the government archives, raised their voice against the restrictions imposed on them. The Marathas had not forgotten their immediate past, a time when they had been masters of the country and the British had wrested political power from them in the early nineteenth century.

As has been noted earlier, Sardesai got the necessary impetus for his historical studies in the Baroda State Service, where his main job was to teach history to the royal family. Sardesai was not a trained but a self-made historian. The exchange of letters between Sarkar and Sardesai spread over a period of fifty years (1907–58) gives us an idea of his endeavours in getting suggestions for further reading, fixation of dates of certain events (chronology), identification of locations of certain places, and in general seeking corroboration of information that he had collected from Marathi sources, with other contemporary sources in different languages. A glance at the bibliographies appended to his historical writings and the references to books and authorities he consulted mentioned in his autobiography—*Mazi Samsar Yatra*—give us an idea of his equipment as a historian and researcher.[40]

It seems that he developed his methodology and philosophy of history in the very course of writing history itself. He has mentioned two books on the scientific aspects of history, namely, Fredric Harrison's *Meaning of History* and G.J. Renier's *History: Its Purpose and Method*, which he read perhaps in the last phase of his life.[41] He was deeply impressed by the 'illuminating little book' (i.e. Renier) and felt satisfied that 'it agrees so well with what I have long thought and felt'.[42] For his historical writings, particularly his method and style, Sardesai relied on the major works of great historians, both foreign and Indian, the suggestions he received from senior people, either through personal discussions or correspondence, and comments from his critics.

It seems that the autobiography of Gibbon, the great historian of the Roman Empire, had a tremendous impact on him. He was simply amazed to note how Gibbon could write the history of nearly 1,500 years after twenty year's hard work in spite of poor health and adverse circumstances, which hastened his death when he was hardly fifty-seven years old. Gibbon's *History of the Decline and Fall of the Roman Empire*, in spite of its shortcomings, is read by generation after generation of Englishmen as a classic. The same can be said, in a limited sense, about the popularity of the works of Sardesai among Marathi readers.

Sardesai always followed the principle that the historian should not be rigid in his views, he should not approach historical research with preconceived notions, he must revise his opinion as and when new facts, or convincing interpretation of old facts, come forward. He cites his own example in this respect. In his earlier *Riyasat*, published in 1920, he did not give much prominence to the career of Peshwa Bajirao I for want of convincing evidence. He was publicly criticized for the shortcomings in his writings on Bajirao I. But when he found numerous new records about Bajirao I while compiling 'Selections from the Peshwa Daftar', he revised his views about this 'fighting Peshwa' on the basis of this new authentic material in its subsequent editions.[43]

Sardesai did not allow caste or religion to influence his historical writings. He would not unduly praise Nana Phadnis, a brahmin like him, or belittle Mahadji Shinde, a Maratha by caste, while assessing their roles in history. He strictly observed objectivity and impartiality in his writings. A booklet on *Pan-Islamism*, published in 1910 by Mushir Husain Kidwai, a nationalist Muslim, believed Sardesai, would be very useful for establishing Hindu–Muslim unity in India. He raised certain doubts about Kidwai's book and sought clarifications from him. Kidwai candidly replied, criticizing the attitude of Indian Muslims who had moved far away from the true teaching of Islam (10 September 1910).[44]

It appears from his correspondence that Sardesai kept himself abreast of modern trends in historiography and did not hesitate to express his views. He contacted Philip V.N. Myers, an American historian, to ascertain from him whether he agreed with Freeman's view that history consists virtually in the experience of European nations. Myers wrote to Sardesai (18 January 1921) that he did not accede to Freeman's view and agreed with Sardesai that much larger space should be given to peoples of the far east in the general histories, and that India, China and Japan would in the future receive recognition as important factors in universal history. He wrote further, 'As you very justly observe, the great war has indeed revealed to the world the oneness of humanity and will, without doubt, mark the beginning of a new great age of Internationalism.'[45]

This shows how Sardesai resented the Eurocentric view of history and pleaded for an all pervasive universal history.

Justice M.G. Ranade was a source of inspiration to Sardesai. He met Ranade one evening in 1899 in Bombay and spent nearly three hours with him discussing Maratha history, after which he felt that what Panini's *Ashtadhyai* is to Sanskrit, Ranade's *Rise of the Maratha Power* is to Maratha history—a source of inspiration.[46]

He was in correspondence for several years with contemporary scholars such as C.V. Vaidya, Rajaramshastri Bhagwat, D.B. Parasnis, T.S. Shejwalkar and many others about whom he had his own opinions. He describes C.V. Vaidya as a prolific writer without depth. He examined *Riyasats*, but did not make any fundamental suggestion. His *Shivaji* (1931) could not replace Sarkar's and nobody knows about him now.[47]

C.A. Kincaid, who wrote *Maratha History* in three volumes (1918–25) in collaboration with D.B. Parasnis, used to get a good deal of help from Sardesai through correspondence. He was full of praise for his *Riyasats* and other writings.[48]

In his Presidential address to the Indian History Congress, Jaipur Session, 1951, Sardesai expressed his views on history. To him the authentic history is the story of civilized human societies as told by earnest students of the subject. He described the historian's task:

> If posterity is to accept and cherish his story, the narrator must practice intellectual integrity. He must not delude. . . . History becomes a generalised account of the personal stories of men united in bodies for some public purpose. The value of the historical narrative is constantly tested by the degree to which it fits in with the evidence gathered up to that time, but still more by the integrity which he brings to bear on his treatment of his subject as an intellectual worker.[49]

It is interesting to note that half a century back he suggested the founding of some sort of an 'intellectual Labour Exchange Bureau' for the dissemination of historical knowledge to all concerned people. He further suggested that the Indian History Congress should supply a selective and critical bibliography indicating the primary sources, instead of putting our 'mere indiscriminate all-embracing catalogues of books'. He pleaded for some positive work 'spreading freely fresh knowledge to the rising generation of our students'.

He maintained that a nation or race is judged at the bar of history not by its military conquests, but by what its members had done to expand the human mind, promote the happiness and power of the human race, or console the hearts of unborn generations. These are the imperishable gifts of history. The true historian rises above racial prejudice, provincial patriotism, and religious bigotry.[50]

Motivation Behind the Writing of a Maratha History

Sardesai's views on the purpose, method, and importance of Maratha history are expressed in his brief introductions to his *Riyasats*, *New History of the Maratha's* and in his correspondence, particularly with Jadunath Sarkar.

He was deeply impressed with historian J.L. Motley's book *The History of the Rise of the Dutch Republic* (1856).[51] In his preface to the *New History* vol., he wrote, *The History of the Rise of the Dutch Republic*, particularly the remark of the author that 'the spectacle of a brave nation, inspired by the soul of one great man and rising against an overwhelming despotism will always speak to the heart from generation to generation motivated me to write *The Rise of the Maratha Power*. While reading the book, he must have noticed some parallels in the histories of both the countries, the Dutch and the Marathas.

It was during the Second World War, when the freedom movement was at its height, that Sardesai felt it was the special need of the hour for the nation to know the history of the struggle for freedom launched by the Marathas in the past.

Sardesai was a pragmatist in his approach to history. He believed in the principle of relevance of history. Every nation needs its past history to devise its policies for the present. All controversies are created by history and they could be resolved only by a better understanding of history. There is no absolute truth in history. History is often written as per the demands of the present. Earlier, the histories of India had been written by administrators with a definite motive, that is, to create a favourable opinion about the new rulers of the subcontinent, namely the British. The main purpose of history is to identify the causes of our failure and try to remove them and aim at resurrection, like the Phoenix. He did not agree with historian V.K. Rajwade, the life-long collector of source material, who maintained that the time was not yet ripe for presenting a connected account of Maratha history. He was not prepared to wait forever collecting all possible sources—an endless task—and then write history. History, he said, grows gradually, like other subjects. Research and the writing of history based on the findings of research should continue without a halt.[52]

He maintained that Maratha History was no longer the cherished treasure of a single community or province. Rather, it should prove a source of inspiration, wisdom and warning to all Indians. If history has any relevance for the present, he believed then, the lives of Shivaji, Bajirao I, Mahadji Shinde and others, 'convey a moral which modern India will be the wiser for taking to its heart'.

While emphasizing the relevance of Maratha history in modern times, Sardesai stated:

> If the true function of history is to impart wisdom of the past for the benefit of the present to warn a nation in the days of prosperity against the hidden dangers of creeping deterioration, as also to stimulate its courage and call forth its recuperative energy in times of adversity—then India cannot afford to ignore the lessons which Maratha History has left behind in its short but eventful career.[53]

He further stated: 'Maratha Government with all its faults inspired the people under its rule with a living sense of unity and cooperation without which no self-rule is attainable.'

One finds the influence of Justice Ranade on Sardesai in his treatment of Maratha history. One may not agree entirely with Sardesai's arguments, but at the same time admire his deep involvement in the subject of his choice.

Sardesai made Maratha history his life's mission because he believed that the 'Marathas had long been misjudged by their rivals and adversaries and painted in the blackest colours both during and after the period of their downfall, as if they had no single good point to their credit.' He therefore aspired to produce through his historical writings a true 'apologia' (*kaifiyat*) of the Maratha people and place it before an impartial public. He pleaded for a scientific investigation of this subject by a 'trained mind endowed also with the constructive vision of a true historian'.[54]

Kamshet Meet

With a view to promoting the 'constructive vision of a true historian', Sardesai, with the help of his historian friends, had created a platform for holding regular meetings of like-minded scholars at his residence at Kamshet.[55] This came to be known as 'Kamshet Meet'.

In 1938, Sardesai invited some historians, scholars and students to visit his 'hermitage' during the days of the Dasara festival—a sort of informal gathering—the Kamshet Meet as Jadunath Sarkar calls it. Sardesai writes to Sarkar who presided over the first Kamshet Meet that while we are here, will have quiet heart-to-heart talks, consultations and deliberations through night and day as we sit together and devote practically all our time to the subject. We will handle only a few subjects, not ambitious spectacular plans, for the world at large, but practical items for those who wish to sit down and start work at once. A new school of ardent workers young novices, is fast coming into being as in politics, we must encourage such workers and separate them from the old figure heads.[56] (Obviously the reference is to the historians of the Pune School.)

Invitations were sent to all the concerned people. But the historians of Pune such as T.S. Shejwalkar, D.V. Potdar, D.V. Apte, N.C. Kelkar unanimously decided in a meeting that the Kamshet Parishad was invited by a few people and a recognized institution like Bharat Itihas Samshodhak Mandal should not send its representative.[57]

Critics of Sardesai

Sardesai, the 'Hermit of History' who was quietly working in his hermitage at Kamshet, was not without rivals or critics. He was criticized at a personal level both as a historian and an editor of historical documents. However, this criticism or personal attacks did not prevent him from his pursuit of history writing and research. In this connection, he wrote to Sarkar: 'I have always been of the opinion that we cannot avoid evil-doers in this world. You are forced to deal with them. So I leave them to their fate. They may or may not reap the consequences of their evil actions. That is not my lookout. I shall be content if I do my duty properly.'[58]

The Pune School of historians, particularly the members of the BISM, a premier historical research institute founded by V.K. Rajwade in 1910; but he had to quit it because of internal feuds. In fact, both Sarkar and Sardesai were life members of the Mandal, but they were not accepted as experts on Maratha history. Sarkar was rejected because he did not know the Modi script, which was used for Marathi historical documents, and Sardesai because he was not a historian, but a compiler (*sankalankar*) and because his *Riyasats* are not histories but 'story books'.

The opposition to both men became severe when the two historians came together to promote the cause of Maratha history, and the Government of India appointed Sarkar a Honorary Member of the Historical Records Commission to explore the possibility of making available in print the Marathi Records preserved in the Alienation Office (Peshwa Daftar), Pune. After reviewing the Daftar, Sarkar recommended the appointment of G.S. Sardesai, a man who enjoyed his confidence, as the editor of the Selections from the Peshwa Daftar, ignoring the Pune School of historians. This hurt the ego of BISM members, and a campaign against the scheme, particularly regarding the selection of documents, its working, accusations of casteism in selecting assistants, the qualifications of the editor, the procedure of compilation and publication and so on, was launched. The Pune School even induced some members of the Bombay Legislative Council to raise some of the above-mentioned issues in the Council.

However, the British administrators handled this issue with determination and 'nothing came out of the fireworks in the Legislative Council, only the petty-mindedness of those who were behind all the uproar, on a relatively small matter, was exposed. On this issue, Sarkar simply remarked, 'The caravan goes on even though the dogs on the road-side bark.'[59]

While appreciating the editorial job of the Peshwa Daftar, Sarkar wrote to Sardesai:

> Your own University, and every university where Maratha History is taught should recognize your work and confer on you the honorary degree of D.Litt. In Europe true scholars are honoured even more surely and quickly. But here, half the Senate and the Board of History are blissfully ignorant of the present state of research and names of research workers in Maratha History and the other half are consumed by jealousy of your achievements and would thwart every attempt to recognise your scholarship.[60]

However, it may be noted here that the Pune University (founded in 1948–9) recognized Sardesai's merits as an outstanding Maratha historian and conferred on him the Honorary D.Litt. in 1955. It was really a great triumph for Sardesai, who had earlier been ridiculed and ignored by the Pune historians, who now participated and witnessed the honour bestowed upon this great son of the soil.

A noteworthy Bengali historian of the Marathas, Surendra Nath Sen, of whom Sarkar was very critical, did not appreciate the achievements of Sardesai as the editor of the Peshwa Daftar. In his Presidential address to the Indian History Congress, in 1944, he described Sardesai's work as a pitfall and snare, being an indifferently printed source-book and opined that it was much better to leave the archives unpublished and refer the beginner to the manuscript source.[61]

Sen was too harsh in his attack on Sardesai, who was quite aware of the shortcomings in the *Selections*, particularly the problem of incorrect dates, which he had corrected and submitted to the Government in 1944. Nevertheless, research scholars and students of history welcomed this voluminous work of Sardesai as a pioneering work and an inducement to further research in Maratha history.

Critical Assessment of Sardesai's Historical Writings

One finds two sets of critics and reviewers of Sardesai's work, particularly *Riyasats* and *New History of the Marathas*. It is interesting to note that most of the Marathi reviewers of Sardesai's work have indulged in fault-finding, whereas others have appreciated his work as a great contribution to Maratha history.

Y.N. Kelkar, a researcher in Maratha history and an assistant to Sardesai in his work in the Peshwa Daftar project, launched a virulent attack on him. He wrote a series of eight articles in the *Kesari*, the leading Marathi newspaper of Pune, between 1930 and 1932, on Sardesai's *Riyasats*. He pointed out several shortcomings and mis-statements in the *Riyasats* and tried to expose him as a historian of the Marathas. However, he did not condemn him, like others as compiler—*sankalankar* but paid him compliments for his efforts which nobody had done so far, and maintained that the *sankalankar* is equally important as *samshodhak* (researcher).

Nevertheless, he pointed out that Sardesai's writings suffer from many defects such as repetition, loose construction, overuse of quotations which are often unnecessary, contradictory statements, and plenty of other mistakes.[62] He accused him of borrowing, or rather summarizing, the summaries of Vasudeoshastri Khare (who was also condemned by some as a 'summarizer' (*saramshakar*), who had through his introduction to his series *Aitihasik Lekha Samgraha* practically covered the history of the Peshwas of the post-Panipat period. But Sardesai, while refuting this charge, remarked that he did not reach any where close to the level of Khare's writings.[63]

Kelkar says further that Sardesai's *Riyasats* are so far the only ones to present the entire history in simple language, and that the common man will read it as an authentic history of the Marathas. He argues that so long as no competent person comes forward and produces a faultless history of the Marathas, one cannot avoid pinpointing the defects, mistakes and doubts, which occur in abundance in the *Riyasats*. Sardesai endeavoured throughout his life to collect passages from others, link them up and produce a history.[64]

He says further that nobody can confidently rely on Sardesai's history as it is not flawless, authentic and balanced. However, he gives full credit to Sardesai for his effort and tireless energy, although criticizing him for lacking the skill to present the huge amount of information and for writing not a history in the proper sense of the word, but rather a tool to understand the real history. He stated that Sardesai's admirers may say that he erected the edifice or temple of Maratha history, but declared that his *Riyasats* are no more than a collection of raw material, a godown of a building contractor. Kelkar further remarks that Sardesai simply collected the details, perhaps waiting for a Gibbon to come forward and complete his task of writing a scientific history of the Marathas.[65]

Sardesai did not respond to this newspaper criticism. He simply said that he did not gain anything by this series of articles written in bad taste, which had crossed the limits of decency and had done more harm to the subject.[66]

T.S. Shejwalkar of the Deccan College, Pune reviewed the *New History of the Marathas* in the *Journal* of the Bombay University. According to Sardesai, Shejwalkar was a young man with sharp intelligence, but very whimsical and pessimistic. However, Sardesai established contact with him and even asked him to write an introduction to his book *Nanasaheb Peshwyanche Charitra*, despite knowing fully well his anti-Peshwa views.

While reviewing his book, Shejwalkar writes,

> What he has done in his *New History* is merely to refashion his old chapters with the help of new material without changing the base, as it ought to have been done. His present work is, therefore, merely putting his old developed thoughts into English garb, and pouring them out before the sympathetic reader. We cannot, therefore, apply the hard canons of historical criticism to his *New History of the Marathas*.'[67]

He says that Sardesai did not think closely on the various episodes of Maratha history, and depended on others for their assessments, and thus became a mouthpiece of their views. Shejwalkar was here indirectly referring to Jadunath Sarkar, the enemy of the Pune School.[68]

Shejwalkar concludes his review with these pungent remarks, 'His work became a sort of guide to all and sundry sources of Maratha history, chronologically and topically arranged. He was acclaimed as the historian of the Marathas by one and all (Shejwalkar here was obviously referring to Jadunath Sarkar who called him the greatest living Maratha historian. A.C. Banerjee and other scholars shared his opinion). This made Sardesai think himself as a good historian. . . .' His work has come to be a good illustration of the scissors and paste type of history which is 'not really history at all' as Collingwood says, 'But the author,' he adds, 'cannot be seriously condemned on this count, because (to quote Collingwood again) until lately it was the only kind of history in existence and a great deal of the history people are still reading today and even a good deal of what people are still writing belongs to this type.'

Shejwalkar sounds a note of warning to the readers of Sardesai, who consider him an authority on Maratha history, that they should know that he was first 'a tutor by profession who had cultivated the knack of telling what he wanted to tell in an easy style'. His main charge was that Sardesai had no grounding in the constitutional aspect of history and this accounts for his treating 'history as a day to day flow of events'. Thus, he concludes 'Sardesai's *New History of the Marathas* is a structure without its steel/framework or a body without its spine.

In the end, he says something good about the book. 'In spite of its serious flaws, it will go a long way to supply the complete story of the Marathas to the men outside Maharashtra for sometime to come, till a better and new history is presented by some higher mind.'

Shejwalkar applied the same method in evaluating Sardesai's Maratha biography of Balaji Bajirao alias Nana Saheb Peshwa (1740–61). He raises a number of questions such as: Was Nana Saheb a statesman? Can he be compared with Shivaji the Great? What is his place in the history of the world? Was he able to prevent the English from striking their roots in India? Did he understand the time-spirit? The entire tone of his criticism is negative. It was a reflection of his preconceived hatred of the Peshwas.[69]

An anonymous reviewer in the *Times of India*, 22 March 1949 declared: 'His (Sardesai's) work based on first-rate contemporary Marathi, English and other languages and gives a much better picture of Maratha politics and should be able to dispel many misconceptions.' L.B. Gokhale, of the *Sunday Leader*, Allahabad, 23 January 1949, after summing up the contents of vols. II and III of the *New History*, congratulates the author for presenting a correct picture of the Marathas who portrayed during the British period in the blackest colours and who had even been branded as a race of bandits.

The *Evening News of India*, Bombay, in its write-up on Sardesai on the eve of the publication ceremony of the third volume of the *New History*, wrote: 'His books both in English and Marathi are well documented, pleasant to read and easy to follow. They are free from prejudices which it is said often mar the otherwise good work done by scholars in Maharashtra.' M.M. Datto Vaman Potdar, of the BISM, Pune presided over this publication ceremony, and the speakers who participated paid tributes and highly praised his energy and modesty for undertaking this painstaking work (14 October 1948).

A student of the Maratha period in an article, 'Fresh Light on Maratha History', points out one great drawback, and that is its almost complete preoccupation with political and military incidents to the almost total exclusion of all others. In spite of these limitations and omissions, the book deserved to be welcomed. He added: 'This work as a whole is of permanent value, and forms a notable contribution to historical literature relating to the Maratha period of our history.'[70]

Y.R. Gupte, a research scholar of Maratha history, in his review of the first volume of *New History* brings out the importance of this work in a series of three articles, but disagrees with the author on some matters, in particular with his views on the purpose of Shivaji's state and the discussion on the work of Rajaram during the period of the Maratha War of Independence (1689–1707).[71]

Honours Won

Sardesai not only received some brickbats for his work, but also won some bouquets.

The number of letters he received for his *Riyasat* from common people speak volumes for his public recognition. The

Government of Bombay expressed its admiration for his patience, sincerity and devotion to work in spite of the virulent attack inside the Council of Legislature and outside by the Poona school of historians challenging his qualifications and competence to work on the selection of documents from the Peshwa Daftar. At the behest of Jadunath Sarkar, the Government conferred on him first the title of Raosaheb in 1932 and a higher title, Rao Bahadur in 1937.[72]

Sardesai did not attend the award distribution function where the title of Raosaheb was conferred on him. While congratulating Sardesai, the Governor of Bombay said, 'You have deserved higher honours and I hope they will follow in due course.' Lord Brabourne the Governor of Bombay (1933–7), had personally visited the Peshwa Daftar in 1934 and acquainted himself with Sardesai's work. On 10 May 1937, Lord Brabourne wrote to him, 'I am delighted to see your name in the list of coronation awards and I write to congratulate you very much indeed on the honour that has been conferred upon you by the Viceroy.' Thus, Sardesai, as promised earlier, received a higher title—Rao Bahadur in 1937 from the Government of India.[73] The highest title that he was given was the Padma Bhushan, awarded by the President of India in 1957.

Jadunath Sarkar was very pleased to see Sardesai being conferred the title of Rao Bahadur. He wrote, 'It is a great point scored by us authors, that Govt. have gazetted you as "historian". This is for the first time they have recognised a historian qua historian.'[74]

Nor did the princely states forget Sardesai's immense contributions to Maratha history. The Chhatrapati of Satara presented him the robes of honours, called *Sade Teen Vastre*.[75] On 2 January 1934, in a grand ceremony held at Satara which lasted for three days, Jadunath Sarkar and his wife attended. Sardesai turned seventy years old on this occasion, and was very pleased to receive this honour from the descendent of the house of Chhatrapati Shivaji.

Baroda, where Sardesai had spent the most formative period of his life, did not lag behind in honouring him. The overwhelming enthusiasm of the citizens and the members of the royal family, including Maharani Chimnabai, the widow of

Sayajirao, and Maharani Shanta Devi, wife of Pratap Sinh, knew no bounds. Sardesai was very touched by this. He writes, 'I had no idea that such deep feelings existed in Baroda towards my humble self.'[76] Sardesai was not willing to accept any present from the reception committee. He requested that the cheque of Rs. 5,000 offered by Maharani Chimnabai be sent to the Rajwade Samshodhan Mandal, Dhule, and that the rest of the money collected be returned to those from whom it had been collected but the committee did not agree to these suggestions. The committee presented him a silver casket worth Rs. 1,000 and it was decided that the balance should be used towards further work in history as per his advice. The ceremony, held on 2 March 1947, was presided over by Shanti Devi, the Maharani of Baroda.

The Chief of Bhor, Pant Sachiv, honoured Sardesai with a *Mahavastra* in 1952.

Various research institutions also came forward to honour him. The Rayagad Smarak Mandal, an organization of the BISM, on the occasion of his seventy-first birthday offered him the presidentship of the death anniversary of the Shivaji Maharaj ceremony, in 1935, in which historians of Pune, including D.V. Potdar, D.V. Apte and others participated. However, Sardesai did not relish the Pune ceremony as he did the Satara one. He says the former was artificial, whereas the latter was spontaneous.[77]

The Rajwade Samshodhan Mandal, Dhule, with which both Sardesai and Sarkar had been associated since its inception (1915), honoured him with the title of *Itihas Martand* (literally the Sun of History) in a ceremony organized in Dhule on 19 January 1946. The chief justice of the Bombay High Court, Sir Leonard Stone, presided over this ceremony. Incidentally, the appellation *Itihas Martand* was attributed to Sardesai by Rajwade himself in one of his earlier letters addressed to him.[78]

Jadunath Sarkar was very happy to learn about this function at Dhule. He wrote to his disciple, Rajkumar Raghubir Sinh:

> It is a happy news that the Rajwade Mandal of Dhulia has done the right thing by welcoming Sardesai, indeed. They have really honoured themselves by honouring him. Evidently, there is none in the Bombay University to think of Maratha History and its highest living workers.[79]

Sarkar had a different plan of honouring Sardesai, and had been seriously thinking about it since 1937. He thought that presenting a felicitation volume comprising learned articles by eminent scholars in the field would be the highest honour that could be bestowed on a scholar. A committee was set up under the chairmanship of Shri Bhaskarrao Jadhav with S.R. Tikekar, a common friend of both Sarkar and Sardesai. Sarkar immediately asked Tikekar, to plan and edit two felicitation volumes, one in English and one in Marathi, entitled *Sardesai Commemoration Volume*, and *Sardesai Smriti Grantha* respectively. He prepared a list of learned scholars from all over India, to contribute to the volumes.[80] He had asked Tikekar to exclude from the two volumes such papers as were not first-rate in originality nor of enduring value. 'We wish that scholars for a generation to come will consult these volumes as invaluable, and not toss them away after reading like railway book-stall novels. . . . It is quality and not quantity that counts in the world of scholarship.'

The memorial volumes were to be presented in a ceremony intended to honour Sardesai. Sarkar had planned all the details of the ceremony. He prepared a panel including in it the names of, Dr Paranjape, Vice-Chancellor, Mr Chandavarkar, Chancellor, Bombay University and Mr Jayakar, Judge, Federal Court. In case none of them was available, he suggested the name of the Pant Pratinidhi of Aundh, 'a tower of learning as well as a sympathetic friend of long standing'.

He also suggested that Pune historians like Potdar, Shejwalkar, Gunjal and Sardar Muzumdar, who had abused Sardesai in the Legislative Council, be excluded from the list of invitees. He was not very much in favour of donations, particularly from the Maharaja of Baroda. He writes, 'Money is not the supreme consideration in the world, least of all has it been so in the life of a man like Nana (Sardesai). There is such a thing as self-respect and you have forgotten it.' He suggested that the memorial volumes should be presented to Sardesai in one large (or two medium) sandalwood caskets, artistically decorated with branches and leaves. Gold or silver caskets would be a mockery to a man like Sardesai, whose whole life has upheld the ideal of plain living and high thinking.

According to him, the best presents to Sardesai from his friends would be English (and some Sanskrit) books of value on history or biography, not necessarily confined to India. He submitted his own list of books to be presented to Sardesai.

He chalked out a detailed plan for the ceremony, from the opening song to the closing song in Marathi, and finally tea and refreshments.[81]

The two volumes were prepared on time and were released by the Rt. Hon M.R. Jayakar at the St. Xavier's College, Bombay on 1 October 1938. Jadunath Sarkar, Rajkumar Raghubir Sinh, Dr. Qanungo, and Pandit Jayachandra Vidyalankar paid glowing tributes to Sardesai on this occasion.

The Maharashtra Sahitya Parishad suggested his name for the Presidentship of its Annual Conference (Marathi Sahitya Sammelan) twice, but once he lost to V.D. Savarkar and second time when he was elected for the Ahmednagar session of the conference, but being disgusted with the method of selection adopted by the Sahitya Parishad, he rejected this honour. D.V. Potdar, whose name was second in order of preference was declared as President in his place.[82]

The newly established Pune University conferred the Hon. D. Litt. degree on him, along with Dhondo Keshav Karve and Homi Modi in 1951. M.R. Jayakar, the Vice-Chancellor, presided over this convocation. In the same year, Sardesai was nominated as the General President of the Indian History Congress for its Jaipur Session, and thereby he got the highest recognition as a historian of merit from this national organization of historians.

SARDESAI AND SARKAR: A UNIQUE FRIENDSHIP

Much has already been said earlier about the relationship of these two historians of India in their pursuit of historical research. The friendship between them which started with a personal letter from Sarkar in 1904 remained uninterrupted for fifty-four long years till the death of one of them, namely Jadunath Sarkar in 1958. It is a unique friendship in the historical world, because both respected each other without compromising their individuality. The enormous correspondence between them not only throws light on their personal matters, but also gives a lot of information about historical events of medieval India, fixing their dates and identification of places, about the source material and their publication/ guidance for further research, raising queries and seeking answers and several other things. The personal letters reveal the sharing of experiences of joy and sorrows that they encountered during their life, appreciations and criticism.

The editor H.R. Gupta aptly remarks about these letters: 'Consider the duration, continuity and range of this correspondence with enormous learning and a light touch expressing firm convictions and containing the exploits two self-reliant scholars.'[83]

It cannot be denied that Sarkar played a major part in making Sardesai a great historian. Sarkar was of great help to Sardesai in giving shape to his historical works. He spared no efforts in bringing him into the limelight and presenting him as a historian of merit and not as a mere compiler, as some of his Marathi colleagues used to call him. He gave him every help, supplying him with books, suggestions, and instructions, correcting his manuscripts, particularly of the *New History of the Marathas*, procuring funds for publication, and in getting him recognition from the government and learned people.

In his own way Sardesai also helped Jadunath Sarkar by supplying information about Marathi sources, particularly for his *History of Aurangzeb* and *Fall of the Mughal Empire*. Their annual meetings at Kamshet or Darjeeling helped them to promote historical research. It was because of Sardesai that Sarkar could visit different historical places in Maharashtra connected with Mughal history and identify their locations. Thus, their mutual help in a way enriched the historical research of the medieval period, particularly, the seventeenth and eighteenth centuries. Sardesai writes to Sarkar about their mutual correspondence, 'Your own letters to me, all of which I have preserved carefully, are valuable in so far as they record a complete account of historical research in Maharashtra during the last 30 years and as you have doubtless preserved my letters, the two collections together will form a guide to future workers.'[84]

Epilogue

Sardesai had no pretensions about his abilities as a historian. He was proud of his presentation of the entire history both in Marathi and in English. At the same time he was quite humble about his achievements as can be seen from his 'Farewell' to the third volume of his *New History*, published in 1948.

About the title *New History*, he tells his readers, 'that title need not be taken to claim for it the rank of definitive standard authority' on the Maratha history. He explained his main purpose in producing this work on Maratha history:

> My aim has been much humbler, to pour out to the sympathetic reader all that an ordinary son of Maharashtra has thought and felt, as he studied and pondered on the storied past of his life of more than four score years. In spite of the long list of my historical works, I do not claim to be a scholar or even a trained historian, but only an eager, tireless worker. Call this my final work, if you like, the table talk of an ardent seeker after knowledge.[85]

He respected authority, and was loyal to it, but never compromised with it on the issue of self-respect. As a servant of the Baroda State, he remained loyal to his master Sayajirao throughout his life, but when he asked him to write his biography, Sardesai politely refused it on the ground that he, being his paid servant, could not make a fair assessment of his career. Besides, he argued, the real assessment of an individual is made only after his death. At the same time, he offered to compile his letters and other papers for his future biographer, and he did publish in a volume the correspondence of the Maharaja. As a consequence of this, he fell in grace, and hence offered for voluntary retirement. But the Maharaja was not prepared for that. He told him, 'You must not leave me. You must die here, in my palace.' But Sardesai had no interest in continuing in the state, and he resigned in 1925. The Maharaja accepted this decision, but ordered that Sardesai's pension should be cut by 60 per cent.[86] In spite of all this, being a loyal servant and grateful to the Maharaja, he dedicated his life's treasure—*New History*—to the Maharaja only.

It seems that when he was working in the Peshwa Daftar there were some difference, of opinion between him as editor and the Commissioner of the Central Division over the title of vol. 14 of the selections from the Peshwa Daftar. The editor suggested that the title of the volume should be either 'Maratha Conquests in the North' or 'Expansion of the Maratha Empire in the North'. The Commissioner, being the head of the Alienation office, however suggested that it should be 'The Incursions of the Marathas into the North or Northern India'.

Sardesai refused to accept this fundamental change, and resented this sort of direct interference in the interpretation of history. He was not prepared to forego his liberty as editor and wrote to the Government, 'While on the one hand I must not divulge any official information on the papers in the Alienation Office, I have on the other hand a certain duty to perform towards that large expectant public in India who are interested in historical research. . . . By agreeing to do research work here, I think I do not lose my individual liberty to say what I think right.'[87] The Bombay Government yielded, and volume 14 was entitled *Maratha Conquest in the North*.

Sardesai was equally loyal and grateful to his dear friend, Jadunath Sarkar, whom he always considered as a superior authority on Maratha history. He did not hesitate to admit that a major portion of the whole of Maratha history had been reconstructed by him. He writes, 'If you have not sacrificed money and labour of life, Maratha history could not have progressed to what it is, in spite of Rajwade and others.'[88] To him, Sarkar's *Shivaji* would now (in 1946) be the last word on the subject, 'comprehensive enough to stand as an immortal monument of your scholarship and genius'.[89] He admits without reservation that 'he cannot claim even to be a glow worm before the Sun, i.e. Jadunath Sarkar.[90]

Sarkar paid glowing tributes to Sardesai's achievements in these words: 'If human life is to be measured, not by the number of years spent on earth, not by the amount of riches piled up and pleasure enjoyed, nor by the din of popular applause that acclaims a man, but by enduring achievements—then the life of Govind Sakharam Sardesai has not lived been in vain.'[91]

NOTES

1. G.S. Sardesai was also known as Mavalankar, after Mavalange, a village in the Ratnagiri district of Maharashtra. Govindrao Sardesai was born on 17 May 1865, and married to Laxmibai Kirtane on 29 February 1884. He had two sons: Shamkant (1899–1925) and Shri Vatsalanchan (1903–15) settled in Kamshet (Pune district) after retirement in 1925. Wife died in 1943; led a lonely life for sixteen years. Died on 29 February 1959 at the age of 94.
2. *Musalmani Riyasat*, pts. I and II
   Saw four editions in his lifetime, between 1898–1928–59. Reprinted and published by Popular Prakashan as 5th edn. in 1993.
3. *Marathi Riyasat*, *Poorva Vibhag* upto 1707 (1901–85); *Madhya Vibhag*, 4 vols. (*1707–1774*) (1920–1925); *Uttara Vibhag* (*1774–1848*) (1929–32).
   These three parts of *Riyasats* are published in eight volumes by Popular Prakashan, Mumbai, edited by S.M. Garge between 1988–92. These *Riyasats* were made available now thanks to the generosity of the Gaikwads of Baroda for the benefit of students of history.
4. These biographical sketches were published between 1935 and 1958.
5. Sardesai, *New History of the Marathas* (*NHM*), vol. I, Preface, p. 7.
6. Sardesai, *Uttara Vibhag*, vol. 3, 1932, *Shevatacha Nirop* (Farewell), p. 5.
7. *British Riyasat* in 2 vols.: vol. I (*1600–1757*); vol. 2 (*1757–1848*), published in 1923 & 1939 respectively. 2nd edn. published by Popular Prakashan, Bombay, 1993.
8. Sardesai, *NHM*, vol. III, Preface, p. ix.
9. Sardesai, *Nanasaheb Peshwyanche Charitra*, with Introduction by T.S. Shejwalkar, Bombay, 1926.
10. Unpublished, from S.R. Tikekar's Collection, letter from Sarkar, 21 August 1925.
11. Sardesai, *Main Currents of Maratha History*, Calcutta, 1926, 1st edn., Introduction.
12. Sardesai, Preface to 2nd edn., 1933.
13. In an All India Radio talk in 1957, two years prior to his death, he said, 'The most satisfactory event in my life is that I could present both in Marathi and English the complete and up-to-date history of the Marathas to my readers. I am now prepared for the last voyage.' Quoted in Arvind Tatake's Marathi book *Samshodaka Saptarshi*, Pune, 1962, p. 70.
14. H.R. Gupta (ed.), *Life and Letters of Sir Jadunath Sarkar*, vol. I, Punjab University, 1958 (henceforth referred to as Gupta, vol. I), pp. 135–6, 9 August 1916.
15. Sardesai, *NHM*, vol. I, Preface, p. 5.
16. Ibid., p. 7, D.V. Apte, a well-known Maratha research scholar, does not agree with this reasoning of Sardesai about writing Maratha history in English. He asks, 'Should we write to convince people that Maratha history was great, and if we do not get such certificate from them, should we then take it that it does not deserve that status?'
    Dattopant Apte Lekh Samgraha, Pune, 1945, p. 24.
17. Sardesai, *NHM*, vol. I, Preface, p. 8.

18. Ibid., p. 8.
19. Gupta, vol. I, p. 335, 22 January 1943.
20. Ibid., p. 233, 29 January 1943.
21. V.G. Khobrekar and S.R. Tikekar (eds.), *Making of a Princely Historian*, Bombay, vol. III, p. 160, 28 May 1975. (Here Offer referred to as 'price').
22. The first volume was entitled as *Shivaji and His Line* (*1600–1707*), Bombay 1946, and the second, *The Expansion of Maratha Power* (*1707–1772*), Bombay, 1948, and the third, *Sunset over Maharashtra*, Bombay, 1998.
23. *NHM*, vol. III, op. cit., p. 522.
24. For details see *Handbook to the Records in the Alienation Office, Poona*, compiled by G.S. Sardesai in 1933. See its Foreword by Jadunath Sarkar, pp. 1–12. Its Marathi translation by Hari Ramchandra Guruji and Vishwanath Govind Dighe, Bombay, 1934.
25. Tikekar (ed.), *Sardesai Commemoration Volume*, Bombay, 1938 (henceforth referred to as *Comm. Vol.*), p. 299.
26. About the publication of forty-five volumes within minimum time, Sarkar writes, 'It is an achievement that recalls to our memory the huge corpus of documents on Roman History published under the guidance of Momsen and it stands as an enduring monument to the devoted labour and wide accurate learning of this son of Maharashtra'
Comm. Vol., pp. 299-30.
27. *Proceedings of the Legislative Council*, printed in 1930, by G.N. Majumdar, S.K. Bole, N.E. Navale, N.R. Gunjal. See also S.R. Tikekar, *Jadunath Sarkar and Riyasatkar Sardesai* (Marathi), p. 39.
28 J. Gupta, p. 168, 27 March 1933.
29. Volumes of *Poona Residency Correspondence* edited by Sardesai under the general title *Poona Affairs are*
Vol. 2: *Malet's Embassy (1786–1792)*, 1939.
Vol. 6: *Palmer's Embassy (1797–1801)*, 1939.
Vol. 7: *Col. Close's Embassy (1801–1810)*, 1940.
Vol. 12: *Elphinstone's Embassy*, pt. I *(1811–1815)*, 1950
Vol. 13: *Elphinstone's Embassy*, pt. II *(1816–1818)*, 1958.
30. *Poona Residency Correspondenc*, vol. I, Introduction, p. iv.
31. J.N. Sarkar, *House of Shivaji*, Calcutta, 3rd edn., 1955, pp. 318–21.
32. Sardesai (ed.), *Mahadji Shinde Hyanchi Kagadpatre*, Gwalior, 1937. Foreword by Jadunath Sarkar, pp. 1–10, Sardesai's remark on pp. 13–16
33. Princely, p. 149, 22 February 1943.
34. Ibid., p. 158, 28 May 44.
35. Ibid., p. 192, 3 March 1946
36. Ibid., p. 252, 4 July 1951.
37. Ibid., p. 264, 29 October 1953.
38. Tikekar, *NHM*, vol. III, pp. ix-x.
39. For a complete list of his publications see the Appendix to this chapter.
40. Sardesai, *Mazi Samsar Yatra*, Dhavale, Bombay, 1956, pp. 137-76.
41. Ibid., p. 169.
42. *Indian History Congress Proceedings* (*IHCP*), 1951, p. 3.
43. *Samsar Yatra*, op. cit., p. 138.
44. Ibid., pp. 163–4. Kidwai was a follower of Gandhiji. 'He wrote to Sardesai', 'The Musalmans of India have fallen into wrong hands. Their

Leaders are either blind or they are object villians. It gives me a headache to see my religion and my co-religionist both disgraced. I feel for India and cannot bear so selfishly sacrificed' (10 September 1910).

45. Ibid., pp. 164–5, E.A. Freeman, a British historian of the nineteenth century, author of *The Norman Conquest* and *Methods of Historical Study*. Historian of the Ancient world—Athens to Rome. Central theme is unity of history—continuity from Greece to Medieval and Modern Europe. A hero-worshipper and propagandist' G.P. Gooch, *History and Historians of the Nineteenth Century*, London: Longmans, 1961, pp. 323–8.
46. *Yatra*, op. cit., p. 145.
47. Ibid., pp. 159–60.
48. Ibid., pp. 147–54. About Sardesai's *Riyasats*, he writes, 'It is the one work in the Marathi language which shows, besides eloquence and style in abundance, the true historical method of dealing with facts and presenting them in a readable form' (23 November 1921).

    About his English he writes, 'It was a matter of genuine surprise and still greater admiration to find that your English was in no way inferior to your Marathi', 6 February 1927.
49. *IHCP*, 1951, p. 4.
50. Ibid., p. 12.
51. J.L. Motley—a nineteenth century historian of the United States, How he was driven to the history of the Dutch Republic, he says 'I did not first make up my mind to write a history, and then cast about for a subject. My subject had taken me up, drawn me in, and absolved me into itself.' The choice of the subject was a master stroke. His work was based on the archives of Belgium, Holland and Germany. Gooch, p. 389.
52. *Lok Shikshan*, a Marathi journal, Sardesai's article, 'Rashtriya Itihas, Artha, Vyapti ani Bhumika'(National History: Its Meaning, Scope and Approach), December 1932.
53. *NHM*, vol. I, Preface, p. 5.
54. Ibid., pp. 8, 6.
55. Kamshet, a village, situated on the bank of the Indrayani river, about 48 km. north-west of Pune. Sarkar writes, 'The rural peace and seclusion of place, its settings amidst the hills of the Chat range, and the rivulet that fringes it, and its bracing temperate climate justify him in calling it his 'hermitage' (*ashram*), Tikekar (ed.), *Sardesai Commemoration Volume*, Dhavale, Bombay 1938, p. 297. Here lived the Hermit of History till he breathed his last in 1959.
56. Gupta, vol. I, p. 318, 31 July 1938.
57. See *BISM Quarterly*, vol. I, July 1938, pp. 41–2.
58. Gupta, vol. I, 4 May 1930, p. 289.
59. Tikekar, *On Historiography*, Bombay: Popular, 1964, pp. 43–8.
60. Gupta vol. I, p. 176, 1 May 1934.
61. Quoted by Presidential Address, *IHCP*, 1952, p. 4. Surendra Nath Sen, without mentioning the name of the editor or the title of the Selection of Documents, remarked in his Presidential Address to the Indian History Congress, Madras Session, 1945,

    'A few years back a series of about 40 volumes of vernacular records was published under the auspices of a provincial Government. The editor finished his task with phenomenal expedition and the printing and get-up of the series suffers from inaccuracies and inadequacies of all sorts and has been scathingly condemned by a competent scholar as 'a pitfall and shame'. An expert familiar with the script and general character of these records may easily spot the wrong reading, the inaccurate chronology and the faulty translation, the inadequate introduction may not prove a handicap to them, but for one competent scholar at least a dozen neophytes will be handing these volumes and their needs and requirements would not be left out of account when the original sources are edited. It is much better to leave the archives unpublished and refer the beginner to the manuscript sources than to present him with an indifferently edited source book bearing on the title page a name calculated to inspire unquestioning confidence', pp. 17–18 of the Presidential Address. (The references to 'a provincial Government', 'editor', and 'an expert' mean indirectly 'Bombay government', 'G.S. Sardesai', and 'a Historian' from the Pune School, probably D.V. Potdar.) Sarkar had suspected much earlier that Surendra Nath Sen had joined hands with the Pune historians in undermining the contribution of Sardesai to *Maratha History*. He wrote to Sardesai,

'You have now seen . . . (Dr Surendra Nath Sen) in his true colours? With his elementary knowledge of the Marathi language and scanty collection of Marathi printed letters, he has presumed to run down your Main Currents, and why? Is it to curry favour with the . . . (Potdar) gang? His ludicrous mistranslations from Marathi and Portuguese made known to the general public of Bombay would add to the mirth of the scholarly world.' Gupta, vol. I, p. 152, 22 April 30. *N.B.* From the published letter the names of Sen and Potdar were dropped but the original letter mentions these names, as can be seen from S.R. Tikekar's collection.

62. Y.N. Kelkar, *Bhutavar Bhraman* (Marathi), Pune, 1940, pp. 86–8.
63. *Samsar Yatra*, op. cit., p. 266.
64. Kelkar, op. cit., p. 260.
65. Ibid., p. 264.
66. *Samsar Yatra*, op. cit., p. 162.
67. *Journal of the University of Bombay*, July 1949.
68. See G.H. Khare, *Nivadak Lekh*, 'Whether Marathas Crossed Attock', Pune, 1972, pp. 149–57.
69. Sardesai, *Nanasaheb Peshwe Hyanche Charitra*, Mumbai, 1926. See Introduction to this volume by T.S. Shejwalkar.
70. *Hindustan Review*, May–June 1949, pp. 307–8.
71. Views of Shri Y.R. Gupte published in the Marathi daily of Pune are summarized by D.N. Darshane in the periodical *Maharashtra*, April 1946, pp. 117–18.
72. *Samsar Yatra*, op. cit., pp. 172–5.
73. Sardesai's name was originally recommended for a raobahadurship in 1932, but as the quota of the title for that year had been completed, the lesser title of raosaheb was conferred on him in 1932. Sardesai was about to reject it, but Sarkar, who had obtained an assurance from the Government that the mistake would be rectified the next year, persuaded him not to do so as it might hamper the Peshwa Daftar work *Samsar Yatra*, op. cit., pp. 181–4.

74. Gupta, vol. I, op. cit., 5 November 1940, p. 224.
75. *Sade Teen Vastre*: presentation of three and half pieces of rich cloth to a distinguished person. The dress material comprising this honour are one dhoti, a silk garment, one *shela* (scarf), one *pagote* (head dress), and a half *kinkat* (a bundle of multicoloured high-quality cloth for a belt).
76. Gupta, vol. I, op. cit., 21 March 1947, p. 351.
77. *Samsar Yatra*, op. cit., pp. 186–8.
78. Ibid., pp. 196–9.
79. *Princely*, op. cit., 28 January 1946, p. 191.
80. The learned scholars invited were Pandurang Pissurelencar, H.G. Rawlinson, Srinivaschari, E. Thomson, H.R. Gupta, C.A. Kincaid, R.N. Salatore, V.G. Dighe, Qanungo, N.K. Sinha, A.L. Srivastav, S.M. Katre, P.K. Gode, Dr. Balkrishna, S.N. Sen, Nilakantha Shastri, Bagchi and many others.
81. All these details of the function are taken from the private file of S.R. Tikekar, the editor, and are unpublished letters from 30 January 1938 26 February 1938. Now preserved in vol. I, Maharashtra State Archives, Bombay.
82. *Samsar Yatra*, op. cit., p. 203.
83. H.R. Gupta (ed.), *Life and Letters of Sir Jadunath Sarkar*, Punjab University, Hoshiarpur, 1958, pp. 370. It contains 625 letters of Sarkar and over 700 of Sardesai. See Gupta's Introduction, pp. 14–15.
84. Ibid., p. 336, 4 May 1943.
85. *NHM*, vol. III, 'The Author's Farewell', p. 5.
86. *Samsar Yatra*, op. cit., pp. 107–12.
87. A.R. Kulkarni, *History in Practice*, New Delhi: Books & Books, 1993, p. 146.
88. Gupta, vol. I, op. cit., pp. 348, 353.
89. Ibid., p. 348, 15 June 1946.
90. Ibid., p. 352, 15 June 1946.
91. *Commemoration Volume*, p. 304.

APPENDIX

Books by G.S. Sardesai

English

(A) 1. *Main Currents of Maratha History*, 1st edn., 1926, 2nd rev. edn., 1933, 3rd edn., 1949.

2. *New History of the Marathas: Shivaji and His Times*, Vol. I: (1600–1707), 1st edn., 1946, 2nd edn., 1957, 3rd edn., 1971.
Vol. II: *The Expansion of the Maratha Power (1707–1772)*, 1st edn., 1948, 2nd edn., 1958.
Vol. III: *Sunset Over Maharashtra (1772–1848)*, 1st edn., 1948, 2nd edn., 1968.

Munshiram Manoharlal, New Delhi reprinted all the three volumes in 1986.

Edited Books (English)

(B) 1. *Shivaji Souvenir*, a collection of articles in English, Marathi, Gujarati and Hindi.
A Souvenir of the Shivaji Tercentenary Celebrations, 1927.

(C) *Poona Residency Correspondence*:

Vol. 2: (*1786–1747*), 1936.
Vol. 6: (*1747–1801*), 1939.
Vol. 7: (*1801–1810*), 1940.
Vol. 12: (*1811–1815*), 1950.
Vol. 13: (*1816–1818*), 1958.

Marathi

Hindustancha Arvachin Itihas, Two Parts:

Part I (1) *Musalmani Riyasat*, 2 vols.

Vol I: *Sultan Ghazani* (up to 1526). 1st edn., 1898, 2nd edn., 1910, 3rd edn., 1927, 4th edn., 1959, and 5th edn., 1993.

Vol. II: *Mugal Badshahi* (*1526–1803*), 1st edn., 1898, 2nd edn., 1910, 3rd edn., 1928, 4th edn., 1958 and 5th edn., 1993. The 5th edn., was published by Popular Prakashan, Bombay.

Part II (2) Three Parts:

I Poorva Vibhag
II Madhya Vibhag
III Uttara Vibhag

Part II: *Marathi Riyasat*: 8 vols. Divided into three Parts.

(1) *Poorva Vibhag*, 1 vol.
(2) *Madhya Vibhag*, 4 vols.
(3) *Uttara Vibhag*, 3 vols.

Poorva Vibhag, vol. I (upto 1707), 1920, 1921.

Madhya Vibhag

Vol. I: (*1700–1740*), 1920, 1925.
Vol. II: (*1740–1750*), 1921.
Vol. III: (*1750–1761*), 1922.
Vol. IV: (*1761–1774*), 1925.

Uttara Vibhag

Vol. I: (*1774–1783*), 1929.
Vol. II: (*1784–1795*), 1929.
Vol. III: (*1795–1848*), 1932.

(All eight volumes were edited by S.M. Garge and published by Popular Prakashan, Bombay, between 1988 and 1992.)

Part III: *British Riyasat*: 2 vols.

Vol. I: (*1600–1757*), 1923.
Vol. II: (*1757–1858*), 1939.

(Both the volumes are reprinted by Popular Prakashan, Bombay, 1993.)

Part IV: *The Poorva Vibhag* and *Madhya Vibhag* were completely recast in biographical sections between 1935–54 in eleven small volumes.

(1) *Shahaji Raje*, 1935.
(2) *Shakakarta Shivaji*, 1935.
(3) *Ugraprakriti Sambhaji*, 1935.
(4) *Sthirabuddhi Rajaram*, 1936.
(5) *Peshwa Balaji Vishwanath*, 1942.
(6) *Punyashloka Shahu*.
(7) *Peshwa Balajirao*, Part I, 1944.
(8) *Peshwa Balajirao*, Part II, 1953.
(9) *Nigrahak Mashavrao*, 1954.
(10) *Apeshi Narayanrao*, 1958.
(11) *Duragrihi Raghunathrao*, 1958.

Edited Works

(1) *Selections from the Peshwa Daftar*, 45 vols., 1930–4.
(2) *Aitihasik Patra Vyavahar* (in collaboration), 1933.
(3) *Aitihasik Patrabodha* (*1596–1819*), 1939 and 1962.
(4) *Aitihasik Gharanyachya Vamshavali*, 1957.
(5) *Satara Itihas Samshodhak Mandal Aitihasik Lekhamala* (in collaboration), 1940.
(6) *Mahadji Shinde Hyanchi Kagadpatre*, 1937.
(7) *Kavyetihas Samgrahatil Aitihasik Patre*, Yadi Vagaire, 1930.
(8) *Selected Letters of H.H. the Maharaja Sayaji Rao Gaekwar*, vol. I: (*1886–1901*), Baroda, 1923.
(9) *Parmanand Kavyam* (Sanskrit), Gaikwad Oriental Series, 1952.

14

Sir Jadunath Sarkar (1870–1958): Historian of Medieval India

Sir Jadunath Sarkar[1] was basically a historian of the Mughal period, particularly of Aurangzeb and the later Mughals. The award of the prestigious Premchand Roychand Fellowship of the Calcutta University (1897) introduced him to the field of research in history, and as a part of the condition of the fellowship he produced his first monograph entitled *India of Aurangzeb: Its Topography, Statistics and Roads* in 1901.

This initial research work on Aurangzeb introduced Jadunath Sarkar (JNS) to the wider field of research in Mughal history, which became the mission of his life. Consequently, in the course of time he produced a number of research works on the last phase of Mughal India and other related subjects, including Maratha history.[2]

The latter half of the seventeenth century was dominated by the careers of two extraordinary personalities, namely, the Mughal Emperor Aurangzeb and Chhatrapati Shivaji representing the nascent Maratha power. Shivaji posed a great challenge to Aurangzeb in his Deccan policy, which ultimately ruined him and led to the disintegration of the Mughal Empire. Though a historian of the fall of the Mughal Empire and of Aurangzeb, JNS could not ignore the Marathas, and he therefore took stock of their activities in general and of Shivaji in particular in order to present his research in its proper perspective. This is how JNS entered the field of research on Shivaji and his successors and the downfall of Maratha power.

JNS's two major works on Maratha history are *Shivaji and His Times*, first published in 1919, and enlarged and reprinted five times up to 1952, and *House of Shivaji*, which ran into three editions in his lifetime between 1940 and 1955. Besides, he was directly or indirectly instrumental in publishing the source material on Maratha history, as pointed out earlier in the chapter on G.S. Sardesai, by convincing the state government and research institutions of the need to do so. This service of JNS has certainly helped in promoting research in Maratha history and raising it to the national level.

When JNS was exploring Persian and other European sources for his works on the Mughals in the north, another scholar in Maharashtra, G.S. Sardesai, was struggling to present a picture of Indian history of the medieval and the modern periods in the regional language, that is, Marathi. However, for a fairly long time these two scholars did not know each other. It was by sheer accident that JNS once met Shri Gopalrao Deodhar (1849–1935), a member of the Servants of India Society, founded by Gopal Krishna Gokhale, the political leader, in the Khudabaksh Oriental Library, Patna in 1904. JNS casually asked him whether he, that is JNS, could get any help from Maharashtra for his study of Aurangzeb, and Deodhar, without hesitation, recommended G.S. Sardesai to him. JNS needed a Marathi scholar who could guide him to the original Marathi sources and Sardesai was looking for a friend who could lead him to the Persian sources.

> Thus JNS and Sardesai could complement each other's work. The huge correspondence between the two scholars speaks volumes for their unique friendship, which lasted for more than half a century. It is said that in the history of India this is the first time that two great historians working in the same field collaborated so intensively and so well.[3]

The contribution of JNS to the study of Maratha history can be gleaned through his extensive correspondence with Sardesai and his pupil Rajkumar Raghubir Sinh of Sitamau.[4] The exchange of letters between JNS and Sardesai particularly throws much light on the discovery and authenticity of certain sources known to them, resolving controversies regarding the authenticity of documents, fixing the dates of certain events, the identification of historical places, and interpretation of certain facts, discussion on research activity in the fields of Mughal and Maratha history with reference to collecting, editing and publishing historical documents, and many other allied topics. It also reveals how they shared their joys and sorrows, personal and professional problems, besides telling us about the hints and guidance given to research scholars regarding methodology and research problems.[5] The practical hints given by the guide to his pupil concerning the reading and writing of his postgraduate thesis in JNS's correspondence with Rajkumar indicates their excellent *guru-chela* relationship.[6]

Shivaji and His Times

As JNS's involvement in the study of Aurangzeb grew deeper, particularly when he was writing on his southern policy, he inevitably become interested in the study of Shivaji, who proved to be a great threat to the implementation of the Mughal emperor's southern policy.[7] This led JNS to the study of the land and people of Maharashtra, where Shivaji, the founder of the Maratha kingdom, was born.[8]

While working on vol. IV of the *History of Aurangzeb (1645–1689)*, JNS could not avoid taking stock of the activities of Shivaji and his sons. He wrote four chapters dealing only with the Marathas, running into 239 pages in this volume. Similarly, he devoted a small chapter in vol. V, the central theme of which was the Deccan ulcer.

While analysing the factors leading to the rise of Maratha power under the leadership of Shivaji, JNS became his admirer. He writes '. . . the imperishable achievement of his life was the welding of the Maratha into a nation, and his most precious legacy was the spirit that he breathed into his people . . . No other Hindu has shown such capacity in modern times.' He adds, 'He taught the modern Hindus to rise to the full stature of their growth.'[9]

However, this brief account of Shivaji and his times, included in his major study of Aurangzeb, did not satisfy him. It seems that while preparing for vol. IV he began working simultaneously on Shivaji, and consequently both the works, *Aurangzeb,* vol. IV; and *Shivaji and His Times*, were published in 1919.

Research Methodology

JNS is considered a pioneer among Indian scholars who introduced a scientific basis for research in medieval Indian history. He laid great emphasis on the authenticity of historical statements and their corroboration with each other. It would be interesting to note his views on writing 'history that will live', the purpose of the collection of historical data, the function of a historian, the problems of interpretation and other things as expressed in the exchange of letters between him and his friend Sardesai.[10]

He was keen on identifying the places referred to in the sources that he consulted. He took trouble to visit those places whenever necessary. About the location of places in Maharashtra, he writes, 'Maharashtra has been my second house, I have paid more than forty visits to it, and travelled to its hamlets and forts far away from rail and bus routes.'[11] His correspondence with Sàrdesai makes several references to their visits for purposes of identifying certain historical places. With the help of large-scale survey maps, he located many places connected with Mughal and Maratha history.[12]

He consulted all possible repositories or archives concerned with his study, mostly by paying from his personal resources or by obtaining the relevant material through his friends or the government. As a nominated member of the Historical Records Commission, he exerted his influence in getting the historical material deposited in the State Archives or research societies, and published whenever possible. In this respect, his efforts in promoting the publication of Marathi, English and Persian records of the Maharashtra Archives with the help of his friend Riyasatkar Sardesai are highly commendable.

Sources for Maratha History

JNS for his *Shivaji and His Times* discussed and evaluated the sources consulted by him for each edition of his monumental work. It would be, interesting to analyse the Introductions he wrote to his editions of *Shivaji* from 1919 onwards for a better understanding of his views about the sources and the methodology he adopted for evaluating them.

In his first edition of *Shivaji*, JNS explains how his work was different from that of Grant Duff's book *A History of the Mahrattas*, the only authority on Maratha history published in 1826. JNS maintains in his Preface to the first edition that many Persian sources, besides Khafi Khan, were unknown to Grant Duff, who relied too much on the uncritical and often deliberately false *Chitnis bakhar* written 183 years after Shivaji's birth. He further argues that for his biography of Shivaji, he preferred the *bakhar* of Krishnaji Anant Sabhasad, a contemporary of Shivaji, and a mass of Marathi material from Pune and Satara, as well as chronicles that 'have been carefully edited with variations of readings and notes'. He claims that the English and Dutch Factory Records were examined in great detail by him and every useful bit of information had been collected from them.

Two other minor additions made by him to the existing state of information are as follows:

1. exact positions of all places mentioned; and
2. a detailed chronology that would help to correct Grant Duff's numerous inaccuracies in this respect.[13]

Editions of *Shivaji*

JNS was constantly engaged in revising and enlarging his *Shivaji* in the light of new source material that had come forward since the publication of the first edition in 1919 to the fifth and last edition in 1952 during his lifetime. The prefaces, the additions, the appendices to relevant chapters, the critical bibliography of the sources, the corrections of chronology, and many other things, testify to his deep involvement in the subject and his efforts to provide the correct information to the maximum number of readers about the 'hero and his times'.

JNS' *Shivaji*, apparently attracted the attention of scholars, and just within a year he brought out an enlarged edition, in June 1920. In this edition, he critically examined the evidence for the Javil (1656) and Afzal Khan (1659) episodes, discussed fully the nature of the Marathi sources, and attempted a comparative estimate of the value of evidence of the English, Persian and Marathi records. He gave an account of the very first battle between the English and the Marathas for the first time, and Shivaji's letter of protest to Aurangzeb against the revival of *jaziya*. He added notes on the extent of Shivaji's dominions in 1648, 1655, 1660 and 1674–5. He also wrote a long note on his personal appearance and his extant portraits, and produced the most authentic portrait of Shivaji obtained from the British Museum.[14]

The third edition, thoroughly rewritten and enlarged, was published after a gap of nine years, in 1929. About this edition JNS writes, 'In this edition more than half of the narrative has been entirely rewritten and expanded and elsewhere too, so many old statements and views have been modified as the result of a fresh study of the subject, that in its present form the book has practically become a new one.'

It differs from the earlier two editions in the following respects: (1) Total rejection of the nineteenth-century fabrications such as *Saptaprakarnatmak Charitra of Shivaji* by Chitnis (*bakhar*), *Shivadigvijaya* (*bakhar*) by Nadurbarkar, *Brihadishwar Inscription of Tanjavur*, etc.; (2) Cautious and selective use of the middle part of the eighteenth century sources such as *The 91 Qalmi bakhar* of Malkare-Waqnis in its different recensions; (3) The full use of contemporary French and Portuguese sources for the first time; and (4) Additions of all the four portraits known to be contemporary.

JNS claims that in this new edition a fresh and detailed study of the old material in the light of newly acquired sources has been made. His reflections on them, which have resulted in several minute corrections and changes in the details of the narrative, and his own opinions about certain persons and events, have been incorporated in the narration.

He further maintains that the three classes of sources, namely (1) contemporary French and Portuguese manuscript sources; (2) the skeleton chronologies (the *shakavalis*); and (3) Persian authorities other than Khafi Khan, which were unknown to Grant Duff, and which now fill up many gaps in our present knowledge, have proved Grant Duff's narrative of Shivaji's career obsolete and erroneous in many places.[15]

One of the important features of this third edition is the addition of a critical bibliography of the authorities on the history of Shivaji. It examines the authenticity of the *bakhars*, *shakavalis* (i.e. the chronologies), the new material produced in the nineteenth century, the laudatory poetic works, and the value of European source material. It also gives details of source material available in Indian and foreign languages.[16]

The fourth edition of *Shivaji*, published in 1948 after a long gap of nearly nineteen years, gave JNS an opportunity to study and incorporate new source materials, particularly the Jaipur records, of 'unique value' relating to Shivaji which were made available only after 1939, the Portuguese sources, and the writings published by the two schools of the Shivaji birth tercentenary.

The 91 Qalami bakhar, published in 1930, with all its versions had been extensively utilized in this edition for revisions in statements or information, wherever necessary.[17]

The last edition of *Shivaji* appeared in Sarkar's lifetime, in 1952. He mentions in the Preface that he added a full description of Shivaji's ships and naval bases, and examined a Muslim historian's statement that Afzal Khan first struck Shivaji out of pride to prove himself a *bahadur*; the succession intrigues in the Maratha court before and after Shivaji's death; the dispute between Shivaji and his step-brother Vyankoji, and many other things. He used in this edition the fragmentary Sanskrit work of Parmanand, edited by G.S. Sardesai, and new Portuguese source material made available by Chevalier Pandurang S.S. Pissurelencar.[18]

A Sketch of a Book on Shivaji

It appears from the correspondence between Sarkar and Sardesai that JNS had prepared a 'sketch' of a book on Shivaji. It does not mention the date and place of the letter, but from the internal evidence it appears that it was written some time in 1929, after the publication of the third edition of his *Shivaji* and was addressed to Sardesai.[19] One does not know whether he had supplied this information at the behest of Sardesai (for which no reference is found in the correspondence) or whether he had written it on his own, suggesting some improvement to him in his *Marathi Riyasat*, vol. II, relating to the life of Shivaji (*Shakakarte Shivaji*). While examining the Marathi sources for his second edition of *Shivaji* (1920), JNS commented on Sardesai's *Marathi Riyasat,* vol. I, 2nd edn, 'a painstaking and accurate compilation, and a guide to sources, but lacks knowledge of all original sources except Marathi'.[20]

Whatever may be the purpose of this letter or 'sketch', it gives us some idea of JNS's approach to the study of Shivaji and his times. The 'sketch' begins with a historical background and the dark future of the Maratha race and Hindus in general, and points out how Shivaji appeared as a saviour (on this scene) and how he founded a state and established a military system wherein lies his greatness. His concluding remark is 'the last constructive genius of the Hindu race'.[21]

Further, he emphasizes Shivaji's civil and military organization and makes a very pertinent remark on his religious policy. He writes, 'His religious toleration was a wonder in that age. Indian nationality is possible and enduring only when there are equal rights for all and a fair field and no favour or, as the French Revolution of 1789 declared, "Career open to talent" only. This is the supreme ideal of the Modern State. Shivaji realized it 250 years ago.'[22]

Sarkar and the Shivaji Movement

When JNS was preparing his biography of Shivaji, the Shivaji movement or the public celebrations of Shivaji's birthday, launched by Lokamanya Tilak in 1895 as a weapon to mobilize public opinion against colonial rule, was at its highest popularity. In the initial period, it was confined to Maharashtra, but it was introduced in Bengal in the year 1902, and it became popular when Lord Curzon proposed the partition of Bengal in 1905. The person responsible for introducing the Shivaji movement in Bengal was Sakharam Ganesh Deuskar (1869–1912), who was a Maharashtrian by birth but who had settled in Bengal. He wrote both in English and Bengali about the Marathas in local periodicals, and being a follower of Tilak he took the lead in celebrating the Shivaji festival in Bengal in 1902. Tilak attended the Shivaji festival in 1906, which helped the Bengali leaders to organize public opinion against the British decision to partition Bengal.[23]

Though an admirer of Shivaji as a nation builder, JNS as a historian did not want legends about Shivaji to be circulated among the people and nor did he want the Shivaji 'myth' to be developed by fabricating or distorting historical documents. In the preface to the first edition of his *Shivaji*, JNS wrote, 'I have considered it necessary in the interest of historical truth to give every fact, however small, about him, that has been ascertained on unimpeachable evidence and to discuss the probabilities of the others.' He maintained that as 'the Marathas were only one among the many threads in the tangled web of Deccan history in the seventeenth century, his book is more than a mere biography of Shivaji; it frequently deals with the contemporary history of these three Muslim states, namely, the Mughal Empire, Bijapur and Golconda.'[24] He, therefore, gives his work the title *Shivaji and His Times* and examines sources from all relevant languages.

Sources for the History of Shivaji: Marathi Sources

JNS declared in all his editions of *Shivaji* from 1919 to 1952 that 'the only contemporary sources of a truly historical nature relating to Shivaji's and Shambhuji's times that now survive are in English, Persian, Portuguese and Rajasthani languages and *none in Marathi*'.[25] His dissatisfaction with Marathi sources is expressed in candid words in the bibliographical notes that he appended to the editions of *Shivaji*. His contention is that as the Marathas during the last phase of the royal period, particularly from 1671 to 1689, were more busy with the sword than the pen, no literature proper and no long history or biography was produced then, and as regards the state papers, they might well have existed, but must have been destroyed by the Mughals who occupied the Maratha forts and cities during the period of the war of independence (1689–1707).[26]

The Sabhasad *bakhar*, compiled by a contemporary of Shivaji, Krishnaji Anant Sabhasad, at Jingi in 1697, is based, he remarks, 'on the half obliterated memory of an old man, who had no independent source of information or state papers. It, therefore, occupies the third rank and in point of accuracy and authenticity its position is lower still'.[27]

In contrast, JNS is full of praise for English, Portuguese, Persian and Rajasthani documents. He described the English factory records as having 'the supreme merit of having been preserved in the original manuscript without any later garbling or interpretation'. The Portuguese records are rated as 'of first rate authenticity within their own limited sphere and their relations with Shivaji and his neighbours'. The Persian and Rajasthani sources, according to him, 'are of unrivalled authenticity and importance for the history of Shivaji. . . . All these are absolutely contemporary and ungarbled . . . their authors were accurate, matter-of-fact observers or realists, while the Marathi, Hindi and Sanskrit writers on our subject are mostly found to be neurotics.'[28]

In view of these drawbacks of the Marathi chronicles, JNS remarks, 'It may be patriotic to prefer the Marathi accounts always long posterior to the events and very often full of legends and garbled or entirely false traditions to the accurate and contemporary Persian and English sources, but it would not be honest history.' 'In short,' he writes, 'their gossipy character and poor literary merit at once mark them out for worthless collections of modern traditions. They are not history in any sense of the term.'[29]

However, he accepted the Sabhasad *bakhar* as the most valuable Marathi account of Shivaji and described it as 'the only source of information from the Marathi side'.[30]

Another *bakhar* that deserves some attention, according to JNS, was *The 91 Qalmi bakhar*, which was published in 1930, although he could not use it for his third edition (1928–9) as he was not earlier aware of its existence. He considered it as a much less legendary work than the Chitnis *bakhar* (1810), and therefore he accepted it as a source worthy of attention. [31]

He rejects most of the Marathi *bakhars* as they are 'mostly copied from the Sabhasad *bakhar* and padded them with Sanskrit quotations, miracles, and several other things which do not fit into a historical work.' Even the Chitnis *bakhar*, written 150 years after the death of Shivaji, derived, he maintained, all its true facts from Sabhasad. He vehemently rejected the *Shivadigvijay* (about which numerous references are made in his correspondence with Sardesai), edited by P.R. Nandurbarkar and L.K. Dandekar (Baroda, 1939), the authorship of which is attributed to Khando Ballal (1715), the son of Balaji Avaji Chitnis, the Secretary of Shivaji. He pointed out numerous historical anachronisms, instances of rhetorical padding and digressions in this *bakhar*.[32]

Shakavalis

It was customary among the families of the nobles in Maharashtra to maintain records of the important historical events in which they were directly or indirectly involved. They are known as *shakavalis* or chronologies. These skeleton chronologies generally mention the date and other relevant details of an event with which the members of the family had been associated. They were maintained 'partly through family pride and partly from the practical necessity arising from litigation'. They are sometimes compared with the ancient Roman family chronicles.[33]

The Jedhe *Shakavali* is one such *shakavali*, which gives a number of events of the seventeenth century for knitting the political history of Shivaji's time. The Jedhe family of Kari (Pune district) played an important role in mobilizing the

Marathas under the leadership of Shivaji in his efforts at founding the Maratha State.[34]

There are some other *shakavalis*, for instance, those of Shivapur Deshpande, Gadadhar Prahlad, the Pratinidhi of Shahu, Ghodegaonkar and so on—all these Maratha families involved in political life of Maharashtra in the seventeenth and eighteenth centuries.[35]

In the initial stages of his research JNS had a high opinion about the Jedhe *Shakavali*. He writes:

> Zedhe chronicle is the most valuable and authentic contemporary record of Shivaji and his ancestors. Exact dates are given in every case. It was published in 1918, and hence the idea of deliberate modern fabrication cannot be suggested. There are some evident mistakes, which we can detect with the help of the English and Persian sources, but they were due to the copyist and not to any deliberate fabrication. Contains some correct dates which no forger could have known.[36]

In spite of this recommendation of the Jedhe *Shakavali*, JNS has hardly used it in his *Shivaji*, particularly for narrating the events after the Afzal Khan episode. In fact, he had fully translated it into English for the benefit of non-Marathi research scholars, which is incorporated into *Shivaji Souvenir*, edited by G.S. Sardesai.[37]

D.V. Apte, in his critique of JNS' *Shivaji*, points out that he could have fruitfully utilized the *shakavali* for confirming the dates which he has taken from English and Persian sources in a general way. But he must have found it complicated to convert these Hindu calendar dates into the Christian calendar. In this respect, JNS remarks, 'The dates are given (in the *shakavali*) in the Hindu-lunisolar era of the Deccan and defy conversion to the Julian calendar except approximately.' He, it seems, therefore avoided the use of the Jedhe *Shakavali* in his treatment of Shivaji after the Afzal Khan episode.[38]

Birth Date Controversy

The fixation of the birth date of Shivaji became a controversial issue among the historians of Maharashtra. One group called the 'old school' supported the second day of the bright half

(*Shuddha*) of the month Vaishakha of Shaka 1549, equivalent to 6 April 1627, and the other group called the 'new school' advocated the third day of the dark half (*vadya*) of the month of Falgun of Shaka 1551, equivalent to 19 February 1630. While fixing the year AD1627, the 'old school' followed mainly the Chitnis *bakhar*, whereas the 'new school', with the help of newly discovered source material, namely the Jedhe *Shakavali*, the Thanjavur inscription called *Brihadishwara Shilalekha*, Paramananda's *Shivabharat*—all these contemporary sources arrived at a complete agreement with one another and defended strongly the conclusion that the year AD 1630 is the authentic year of Shivaji's birth.[39]

JNS had doubted the authenticity of the Jedhe *shakavali* and of Parmanand's *Shivabharat* which, according to him, 'held by the ignorant as a historical source of first rate authenticity' but he considered it as a laudatory poem written by a court flatterer, 'a literary beggary carried to nauseating lengths by the brahman court poet, beating Abul Fazl in his exaggerated praise of his patron' and rejects it as 'worthless'.[40] JNS, therefore, supported the old school, adhering to the year 1627.

It is really strange that JNS, who had earlier condemned and totally rejected the Chitnis *bakhar*, now accepted it in fixing the date of Shivaji's birth. He had even convinced Sardesai about it.[41]

Marathi documents: JNS maintains that Marathi documents should not be accepted without proper scrutiny; only those should be considered that are beyond doubt. As regards the documents published by V.K. Rajwade, both political and private, JNS states that 'till their authenticity is established, they cannot be used'. He further remarks, '*Marathyanchya Itihasachi Sadhane*, edited by V.K. Rajwade, vols.VIII and XV–XXIV contain a few political letters and a vast mass of private legal documents and charters of Shivaji and his times. Some of them are clearly forgeries made to deceive the Inam Commission and other judicial bodies. Some others seem to have been faked to support "popular" history or family prestige.'[42]

The documents published by the Bharat Itihas Samshodhak Mandal (BISM), Pune, in its annual proceedings and other publications and by others are put in the same class as above and are not used by JNS in his *Shivaji*. Again, *Ajnapatra, a Royal Edict on Maratha State Policy* by Ramachandra Pant Amatya has been declared by him as 'not a genuine document by a contemporary of Shivaji, throws no real light'. Similarly, *Tanjavarcha Shilalekh*, an inscription in Marathi (2,652 lines in print carved in Dec. 1803 at the instance of Sarfoji Raje II (1717–1832) in the Brihadishwar temple of Thanjavar (printed in Rajwade's *Marathyanchya Itihasachi Sadhane,* vol. IX (1906), according to JNS is an 'utterly worthless modern concoction of the history of Shahaji and Shivaji, evidently for exalting the junior Bhonsale branch, (the House of Tanjore)'.[43] It possesses all the merits and demerits of a *bakhar*, but as it is based on Parmanand's *Shivabharat*, the Marathi scholars consider it useful for knitting the story of Shahaji and Shivaji. But as JNS holds both the *bakhar* and *Shivabharat* as not 'honest' sources of history, he rejected them totally.

In short, it can be said that JNS does not hold the Marathi *bakhars*, the published documents, the Inscription of Thanjavur, and Parmanand's *Shivabharat* as authentic sources for the narration of the history of Shivaji and his times. He, therefore, came to the conclusion that the only authentic and reliable sources for the history of Shivaji are available only in Persian, Rajasthani and European languages and 'none in Marathi'.[44]

Reaction to JNS *Shivaji* in Maharashtra

It cannot be denied that it was JNS who presented the life of Shivaji in its proper perspective to non-Marathi readers in India and abroad. It was, however, received with mixed feelings in Maharashtra. His friend Sardesai once wrote to him, 'I am anxious that your *Shivaji* should now be the last word, comprehensive enough to stand as an immortal monument of your scholarship and genius.'[45]

The Poona group of historians mainly objected to JNS's under-estimation of Marathi sources throughout his work on Shivaji, from 1919 to 1952. Chhatrapati Shivaji is a highly revered historical person in Maharashtra, and therefore even the reference to him as 'Shiva' by JNS in his earlier editions of Shivaji was strongly resented by the Marathi people.[46]

The Poona group of Historians doubted his knowledge of Marathi particularly of the historical documents written in the Modi script, though Sardesai had certified that 'his knowledge of Marathi is thorough and accurate'.[47] According to D.V. Potdar, a reputed Maratha historian, JNS had working knowledge of Marathi, but he did not study Marathi literature intensively. His study had, therefore, become often one-sided. As he could not read original Marathi documents in the Modi script, his opinion on the Marathi document—whether it is 'forged' or 'real'—cannot be accepted without proper scrutiny.[48]

Another Marathi scholar, D.V. Apte, puts forward this question: if JNS was convinced that there were no contemporary Marathi documents for reconstructing the career of Shivaji, he should have, like Rajwade, declared that the time was not yet ripe to write a true and honest history of Shivaji, and should not have indulged in writing about Shivaji and his times if he claims to be an 'honest' historian. As JNS depended entirely on Persian and English sources, he has been regarded by Marathi scholars, as the modern incarnation of Grant Duff.[49]

JNS is rather uncharitable in his criticism of Marathi documents and their authors, whom he calls 'neurotics', not properly equipped for writing, persons who could wield a sword but not a pen, who did not hold any position in *politics*. The authors, particularly of the chronicles, were well versed in contemporary literature and had developed a style of their own for *bakhar* writing. They held positions at the royal court as Sabhasad (member), Chitnis (secretary), Waqnavis (news writers) and so on. The *shakavalis* were often properly dated and could be corraborated with other sources. In fact, early English historians like Scott Waring (1810) had found Marathi chronicles more authentic than Persian *tawarikhs*.[50]

Chronicles are deficient in some respects but they represent the ethnic view of Maratha history, and therefore cannot be altogether ignored or totally rejected. In fact, most of the historians of the Marathas who have condemned *bakhars* as 'gossiping' accounts have nevertheless used them whenever it suited their purpose. Grant Duff and JNS are no exception to this.

JNS who considered the Chitnis *bakhar* as uncritical and deliberately false, and preferred the Sabhasad *bakhar* to it, could not avoid the temptation of following the Chitnis as well as *Shivadigvijaya* while narrating the account of Shahaji's release from the custody of the Adilshah in 1649.[51]

Sarkar condemns the use of all legends, but could not resist the temptation of making the occasional use of the same. For instance, it is said that Tanaji Malusare sacrificed his life while capturing the fort of Kondana from the Mughals in 1670, and Shivaji therefore renamed the fort as 'Sinhagad', after the lion-heart who had won it. However, it has been pointed out that Kondana has been referred to as Sinhagad in an authentic Marathi letter of Shivaji of the year 1663 (Rajwade, vol. 8: 12), and that the name Sinhagad appears four times in that letter.[52]

G.S. Sardesai's Reaction

When Sardesai found that JNS's *Shivaji* was mercilessly criticized in *Maratha* and the *Kesari* newspapers and by scholars like D.V. Apte, he was puzzled why 'the vociferous section of Maharashtra' was furious against JNS, and also with him, either for siding with him or not trying to check his pen. He was convinced that the history of Shivaji owed a great deal to JNS. He writes, 'Had the Persian and foreign sources not been brought to light, we would have no true account of him (Shivaji) even now. You have made Shivaji a human figure in the world. All the episodes from Afzal Khan onwards are entirely your creation, whatever Maharashtra might say.'[53]

Sardesai expresses his personal gratitude and his opinion about the Poona School in one of his letters to JNS.[54]

When the people of Pune understood the importance of JNS' work, they decided to offer him honorary membership of the BISM, which he politely declined.[55]

It seems that once the people of Pune had thought of bringing out a biography of Shivaji in English by way of a reply to JNS work. When Sardesai heard about it, he wrote to him immediately stating that it would be a futile attempt.[56]

C.V. Vaidya's *Shivaji*

Chintaman Vinayak Vaidya of BISM did write a biography of Shivaji in English entitled *Shivaji, the Founder of Maratha Swaraj* in 1931. In justification of his book, Vaidya writes in the introduction, 'Though written by a Maratha and an admirer [of Shivaji], it tries to keep the balance of a judge's mind in apportioning blame or praise. I hope that a life should be written by an admirer and a countryman, who naturally takes a favourable view of his hero's motives and in judging of moral and political justification, the *writer* must maintain an impartial attitude.'[57]

The book was supported by the BISM, but while recommending this book D.V. Potdar, its Secretary, writes in his note, 'The book is not so much an exhaustive and authorised life of the great Shivaji as a presentation and interpretation of the same.'[58]

JNS did not care to take notice of this book. When Sardesai promised to get a copy of it, he wrote, 'You may send me C.V. Vaidya's *Shivaji* and I shall send back to you a list of glaring mistakes in it with evidences.'[59]

The book did not fulfil any expectations as it did not even go into a second edition.

Indictment Against JNS

1. The Poona school declared that JNS was not a researcher but a historian. He collected material from the Jaipur and other archives relating to Jahangir, Shahjahan and Aurangzeb, of which an account was published by his friend in the *Indian Historical Quarterly* of September 1934. He did make use of most of the material in his historical works, but a major portion remained unused. Had he paid attention to editing and publishing the material, it would have been of much help in furthering historical research. It would have been also possible to verify the statements made by him in his own works. He did not pay much attention to even the published Marathi documents nor did he try to compare them with the Persian and other documents on the same subject.[60]

2. A charge was brought against JNS by some scholars that his *Shivaji* had caused some historians in other parts of India to hold an adverse opinion or to create a misunderstanding about the Marathas in general.

Saiyid Tafazzul Daud Sayeed Khan, a pleader of Sultanpur (Oudh) and a research scholar from Aligarh University, wrote a book entitled *The Real Shivaji*, which was published in Allahabad in 1935. It represents a study in communal rivalry in pre-independent India. Sayeed Khan claims that he had formed his opinion about Shivaji only by reading JNS' works, and that he has submitted his thesis for the consideration especially of those 'who are of Professor Sarkar's mode of thinking'. As he accepts Sarkar's opinion that the sources consulted by the Maharashtra scholars are unauthentic, he does not regard their writings as reliable. He says, 'As to the Maratha school, we are separated as poles asunder from each other' (p. 45). He admits that his conclusions are mainly based on Sarkar's writings. He continues, 'In fact, mine is only the logical corollary of his (JNS) work. I am saying what ought to have formed a part of his own conclusions' (p. 12). Sayeed Khan's main thesis is that Shivaji was not a person whom Hindus should worship, and that secondly, Maratha scholars are engaged only in 'discovering documents endlessly which are worse than useless' and 'are sources of danger' (p. 44).

It is pertinent to note the reaction of JNS to the book. In his letter to Sardesai he writes, 'I shall take with me the disgusting volume entitled *The True Shivaji* written by a Mohammedan graduate of Aligarh, to show you to what lengths malignity and ignorance can go. It is, I consider the natural reaction against the chauvinistic brag of Savarkar and even Rajwade, about the purely imaginary Hindu Pat Padshahi' (20 October 1936).

The book was proscribed by the Government of India because of the fury of public reaction against it.[61]

Another Muslim historian Zahir Ud'din Faruki, the author of *Aurangzeb and His Times* (1935) does not accept JNS' views on Aurangzeb, but endorses what he writes about Shivaji, particularly his opinion on the Marathi sources.[62]

In short, the non-Marathi scholars blindly followed JNS' views on Marathi sources in their own works.

Sardesai on JNS

Sardesai, however, did not agree with the Marathi scholars who were very harsh in their criticism of JNS' *Shivaji*. To Sardesai it was 'the last word on the subject'. He says, 'I realize the excellent services you have rendered to Maratha history . . . some of your chapters are worth their weight in gold. I have never read anything more ennobling, more reasoned and more thoughtful' (8 July 1934). In another letter he writes, 'I have always believed that a major portion of the whole of Maratha History, has been reconstructed by you. If you have not sacrificed money and labour of a life, Maratha History could not have progressed to what it is in spite of Rajwade and others' (19 September 1941).[63]

While summing up his contribution to Maratha history, Sardesai writes, 'In his treatment of Maratha history, he is calm and dispassionate, severely just and possessed of enough fire and firmness to inspire and admonish a brave nation about an unfulfilled political destiny in the eighteenth century.'[64]

Assessment by other Historians

JNS was awarded the Sir James Campbell Gold Medal for his work *Shivaji and his Times* by the Royal Asiatic Society, Bombay in 1926. His *Shivaji* was highly acclaimed by British historians including V.A. Smith, who had accused Shivaji of being a 'robber chieftain'. About JNS' *Shivaji*, he writes, 'A conscientious presentation of recorded facts, a bold and deliberately provocative book meriting the closest study.' Another critical historian, Henry Beveridge, who held him as the Bengali Gibbon, writes, 'All his books are good, but perhaps the best of them is the *Life and Times of Shivaji*.'[65]

Sir Richard Temple writes, 'This new historical study by Mr. Sarkar has come out at an opportune time and I have no hesitation in saying also in an opportune manner. This book is indeed history treated in the right way and in the right spirit.'[66]

K.R. Qanungo, one of Sarkar's students, observes, 'He has rehabilitated Shivaji in all his real glory in the heart of every patriot throughout this subcontinent.'[67]

Sarkar's Views on Some Other Historians of the Marathas

1. *M.C. Sprengal (1746–1803):* The German historian who was the first European to attempt the—history of Marathas, JNS wrote to Sardesai, 'The book is worthless, because the writer has merely translated some catch-penny English brochure produced during the first Maratha War. He could not have had access to the true sources. Read the French motto on Rajwade's first volume.—No document, no history.'[68] (16 September 1944).
2. *Dr Balkrishna*: Sarkar had gone through the first volume of Dr Balkrishna's *Shivaji, the Great*, but he had some doubts about the *Mudhol Firmans,* which he had used for the history of Shahaji. He, therefore, asks Sardesai to enquire about them. He writes, 'But I doubt how far Balkrishna is correct and to what extent he has succumbed to the wishes entertained by the Raja of Mudhol. If there be any hoax in it, it ought to be speedily exposed. Otherwise all that matter will go down as accurate and unchallenged history in the eyes not only of the Poona School of noisy history, but outside also'[69] (25 June 1952).
3. *C.A. Kincaid*: About *The History of Marathas* written by C.A. Kincaid in collaboration with D.B. Parasnis in three volumes, JNS simply remarks, 'Kincaid's three volumes have succeeded in merely spoiling the market for better books'[70] (19 June 1946).

House of Shivaji

JNS' other major contribution to Maratha history is his *House of Shivaji*, a book first published in 1940. Its second edition, with some additional chapters, appeared in 1948, with minor additions in some chapters and rearrangements and corrections in many places. The third and last edition was published in 1955 in a much enlarged form by adding new chapters and documents. It included, as he writes, 'all the material is acquired by me. Besides a new chapter on Malik Ambar, it includes biographies of the four eminent historical research pioneers, Rajwade, Sane, Khare and Parasnis.'[71]

It was, according to him, 'a companion volume to his studies in Mughal India'.[72] His work on Mughal history and the two volumes on Shivaji thus cover practically the entire history of the Marathas from their rise to the beginning of their decline with the signing of the Treaty of Bassein in 1803. Thus, according to Sardesai, JNS raised the status of Maratha history as an independent discipline in the history of the Indian subcontinent.

JNS makes a critical analysis of the factors responsible for the decline and fall of the Maratha Empire. While writing the last chapter of the *Fall of the Mughal Empire*, he wrote to Sardesai, 'Its subject is even truly the fall of the Maratha Empire.' He added 'I can say that I have written it, not with the ink, but with my heart's blood . . . the imbecility and vices of the rulers, the cowardice of their generals, and the selfish treachery of their ministers. It is a tale which makes every true son of India hang his head down in shame' (15 May 1950 night).[73] This letter speaks of his intense emotional involvement in the history of the Marathas. He says the same causes that he traced in the *Fall of Mughal Empire* are applicable to the fall of Maratha power. He admired the achievements of Shivaji, but at the same time makes a revealing analysis of the causes of his failure to build an enduring State. The national glory and prosperity, he writes:

> resulting from the victories of Shivaji and Bajirao I created a reaction in favour of Hindu orthodoxy. It accentuated caste distinction, and ceremonial purity of daily rites, which ran counter to the homogeneity and simplicity of the poor and politically depressed early Maratha Society. Thus his (Shivaji's) political success sapped the main foundation of that success. In proportion as Shivaji's ideal of a Hindu Swaraj was based on orthodoxy, it contained within itself the seed of its own death.[74]

He believed that the Marathas invited political ruin by their failure to evolve a liberal society. He also emphasizes that the Maratha rulers neglected the economic development of the state, and that they had to wage wars as a normal method of supply. The Maratha state became a government that lives and grows only by wars of aggression—a '*krieg staat*' He added one more factor leading to their fall—they trusted in too much 'finesse' and 'intrigue'. They could not always abide by their treaty obligations.[75]

The above-mentioned factors leading to the extinction of Maratha power, particularly the neglect of economic development that led the Maratha state to becoming a war state, may be applicable to the fall of Maratha power in the eighteenth century in a general way, but certainly not to the period of Shivaji, whom JNS considers 'not only the maker of the Maratha nation but also the greatest constructive genius of medieval India'.[76] An intensive study of contemporary and near-contemporary Marathi source material, and its reinterpretation, would certainly help to refute the charges levelled by him against the royal period. They would clearly and decisively prove that the charges that the Maratha state had no stable basis, or that it had no normal sources for growth within itself, or that it was a simply a war state, are not tenable as they are not supported by the source material in Marathi.[77]

Was JNS a Biased Historian?

However, in spite of this critical assessment of the Maratha State, one could hardly dare to accuse JNS of being a biased historian having some preconceived notions about the Marathas. Objectivity in historical research is certainly an ideal thing, but it is difficult to find such an ideal historian. The question is to find out whether or not the bias is of the right kind, whether it affects the approved scientific basis of study.

K.R. Qanungo, in his assessment of JNS as a historian remarks:

> It may be said that a certain amount of bias and warmth for Shivaji . . . is perhaps noticeable in Jadunath. But this bias is in the right

> direction and an echo of the sentiment of contemporary India, for the defenders of their religion and honour against Aurangzeb's aggressive bigotry and intolerance. . . In his *Fall of the Mughal Empire*, his bias turns against the Marathas, particularly the ruling Chitpavan Brahmans. . . The Abdali and Nasir-ud-daulah have received higher admiration and praise from the historian who admires fact, valour and efficiency, wherever they are found. The historian does not share the grief of Maharashtra after the catastrophe of the third battle of Panipat because the historian has nothing to choose between the Peshwa and the Abdali.

On the basis of these facts Qanungo concludes that Sir Jadunath possesses 'all the sterner virtues of a historian which dominate his "human values" not to the detriment of truth. He lives today, like Ranke in the nineteenth century as the greatest historian of India beyond comparison.'[78]

NOTES

1. Sri Jadunath Sarkar was Born on 10 December 1870 in village Karachmaria (now in Bangladesh) into a Kayastha zamindar family.
   Premchand Roychand Fellow, 1897; married Kadambini Chaudhuri in 1893; had three sons and seven daughters. Served in colleges at Calcutta, Benares, Cuttack, and Patna from 1893 to 1926; Vice-Chancellor, Calcutta University (1926–8), knighted in 1929, died 19 May 1958.
2. His major works are:
   (A) *Mughal History*
      1. *Anecdotes of Aurangzeb and Historical Essays*, 1912.
      2. *Studies in Mughal India*, 1919.
      3. *History of Aurangzeb*, in 5 vols., 1912–24.
      4. *Mughal Administration*, 1920.
      5. *A Short History of Aurangzeb*, 1930.
      6. *Studies in Aurangzeb's Reign*, 1933.
      7. *Fall of the Mughal Empire*, in 4 vols., 1932–50.
      8. *Masir-i-Alamgiri*, edited and translated into English, 1949.
      9. *Later Mughals*, William Irvine's incomplete work, edited and continued with an additional three chapters, 1922.
      10. *Ain-i-Akbari*, vols. II and III, translated into English by Col. H.S. Jarrett, corrected and further annotated by JNS, published in 1948 and 1949.

   His other major works are:
   (B) *Maratha History*
      1. *Shivaji and His Times*, April 1919. Followed by editions in June 1920, December 1928, February 1948, December 1952, February 1961. Longmans published its first impression in 1973. This book has been translated into Marathi, Hindi and Bengali.

2. *House of Shivaji*, May 1940, followed by editions in May 1948 and April 1955. Longmans reprinted in 1973.
3. 'Shivaji: A Study in Leadership', lecture delivered in Sholapur, 1930.
4. *Shivaji's Visit to Aurangzeb at Agra*, translation of Dingal Letters, Pune, 1963.

(C) *Editorial Work*

English Records of Maratha History: Poona Residency Correspondence, with G.S. Sardesai.

Vol. I, *Mahadji Scindia and North Indian Affairs (1785–1794)*, 1936.

Vol. VIII, *Daulatrao Scindia and North Indian Affairs (1794–1799)*, 1936.

Vol. XIV, *Scindia's Affairs (1810–1818)*, 1951.

(D) *Persian Records of Maratha History*

1. Vol. I, *Delhi Affairs (1761–1788)*, 1953.
2. Vol. II, *Scindia as Regent of Delhi (1787 and 1789–91)*, 1959. published by the Maharashtra State Archives.
3. *Nusha-i-Dilkasha*, English translation by JNS, Government of Maharashtra, 1972.
4. The following Persian works are translated by JNS and are available in the Maharashtra State Archives Bulletins:
   No. 2: *Ibratnama* by Faqir Khair-Uddin.
   No. 5: *Tarik-i-Shah Alam* by Munna Lal.
   For a detailed bibliography of JNS's contribution to medieval Indian history, see:
   (a) A.C. Banerjee, *Jadunath Sarkar*, New Delhi: Sahitya Akademi, 1989, pp. 86–90.
   (b) Kiran Pawar, *Sir Jadunath Sarkar: A Profile in Historiography*, New Delhi: Books & Books, 1985, pp. 194–9.
   (c) H.R. Gupta (ed.), *Life and Letters of Sir Jadunath Sarkar*, vol. I, Hoshiarpur, 1958, pp. 108–24. Hereafter referred to as 'Gupta'.

3. Gupta, op. cit., p. 13.
4. V.G. Khobrekar and S.R. Tikekar (eds.), *Making of a Princely Historian*, Bombay, 1975. Hereinafter referred to as *Prince*.
5. About this exchange of letters, Sardesai writes to JNS: 'Your own letters to me, all of which I have carefully preserved, are valuable in so far as they record a complete account of historical research in Maharashtra during the last 30 years and as you have doubtless preserved my letters, the two collections together will form a guide to future workers, if a selection could be published, when easy times come dealing with the various problems of research, the difficulties that were encountered and overcome' Gupta, op. cit., p. 336. (4 May 1943).
6. *Prince*, op. cit., pp. 12, 13.
7. 'The political paradox makes Aurangzeb's reign an object of supreme interest to the student of political philosophy no less than to the student of Indian History.' JNS quoted in S.R. Tikekar, *On Maratha Historiography*, Bombay, 1964, p. 4.
8. JNS, *Shivaji*, op. cit., pp. 1–13.

9. The four chapters are:
   1. Rise of the Maratha Power, p. 27.
   2. Shivaji (1660–1669), p. 30.
   3. Shivaji (1670–1680), p. 30.
   4. Reign of Shambhuji, p. 65.

   Banerjee, *Jadunath Sarkar*, 1989, op. cit., pp. 34–5.
10. Writing a history that will live requires not only mere industry (a copyist's industry) in collecting material, but what is far higher—extensive reading (not narrow specialised study), power of deep thinking and connecting together the near and the distant things, Indian and foreign (by way of comparative estimate and liberal interpretation), and a certain advance in age. . . . The true historian's function is that of the stomach in digesting and extracting the vital juice from the new food stuff passed down the throat' (Gupta, op. cit., p. 169, JNS to Sardesai, 27 March 1933).
    'When a historian quotes a document within inverted commas, he ought to give it faithfully word for word. But if he doctors the language to suit his theory, he will be charged with dishonesty' (Gupta, p. 259, JNS to Sardesai, 3 September 1947).
    'My sole interest is in the discovery of truth from unassailable sources, and I am not so vain as to feel hurt if any statement in a book of mine is contradicted by later discovered (or published) sources. For unless such continued supersession is welcomed, progress in human knowledge would be impossible' (Gupta, p. 239, JNS to Sardesai, 25 August 1943).
    'True, interpretation must differ according to the writer's personality, but the basis of the conclusion must be unquestionable facts (as established by the latest research) and not mere conjecture. Moreover, the interpretation must be such as to convince an impartial outsider' (Gupta, p. 252, JNS to Sardesai, 19 June 1946).
11. Sarkar, *House of Shivaji*, op. cit., p. 334.
12. Gupta, op. cit., p. 20 and its fn and p. 21.
13. Sarkar, *Shivaji and His Times*, 2nd edn., Calcutta, 1920.
    Preface to 1st edn., April 1919, p. 6.
14. *Shivaji*, 1920, op. cit., pp. 7–8.
15. *Shivaji*, 3rd edn., 1928, Preface, pp. iii–v.
16. Ibid., pp. 406–18.
17. *Shivaji*, 1973, pp. iv–v.
18. Ibid., p. vi.
19. Gupta, op. cit., pp. 187–8.
20. *Shivaji*, 1920, op. cit., p. 454.
21. This conclusion is repeated in further editions of *Shivaji* and *House of Shivaji*. See *Shivaji*, 5th edn., 1952, p. 388. *House of Shivaji*, 3rd edn., p. 115.
22. Gupta, op. cit., p 188
23. Anil Samarth, *Shivaji and the Indian National Movement*, Bombay, 1975, pp. 63–70.
24. *Shivaji*, 1920, op. cit., p. 7.
25. *Shivaji*, 1952 edn., p. 391.
26. *Shivaji*, 1928, 3rd edn., p. 407.
27. This opinion about the Sabhasad *bakhar* is repeated in almost all the editions, from the 2nd to the 5th.
    Shivaji, 1920, 2nd edn., p. 446. *Shivaji*, 1952 edn., p. 392.

28. *Shivaji*, op. cit., 1973, p. 395.
    About the writers of the non-Marathi sources, JNS remarks: 'Their writers belonged to a higher intellectual type than the Marathi chroniclers. . . . These so-called bakhars are evidently the production of some ignorant, credulous, dull-brained writers and not the work of any clever minister or scholarly author' 2nd edn., 1920, pp. 446, 448. See also 3rd edn., 1928, p. 412.
29. *Shivaji*, 1920, p. 447.
30. Ibid., pp. 449–50.
31. The edition of this *bakhar*, first published by V.S. Wakaskar of Baroda in 1930, brings together all the different recensions of the text, originally printed by D.B. Parasnis in the *Bharatvarsha*, V.K. Rajwade in the *Prabhat*, and K.N. Sane in the *Kavyetihas Samgraha*) together with the English translation of another version called the *Rairi bakhar* made by Lt. Frissell in 1906, and the translation of the Persian manuscript called *Tarikh-i-Shivaji* by JNS and published in *Modern Review*, 1907.
32. *Shivaji*, 1952, pp. 391–2.
33. R.P. Patwardhan and H.G. Rawlinson (ed.), *Source Book of Maratha History* Calcutta, rpt., 1978, pp. 31–2.
34. Kulkarni (ed.), *Jedhe Shakavali and Karina*, Pune, 1999, see Introduction, pp. 11–36.
35. D.V. Apte and S.M. Divekar (eds.), *Shivacharitra Pradeep*, Pune, 1925, pp. 50–70.
36. JNS, *Shivaji*, 1920 edn, p. 452, *Source Book*, op. cit., p. 31.
37. G.S. Sardesai (ed.), *Shivaji Souvenir*, Mumbai, 1928, pp. 1–44. See Kulkarni, op. cit., pp. 295–322.
38. Divekar and Apte (eds.), *Parmanand Shivabharat*, 1927, p. 56.
39. Sardesai wrote to JNS: 'The Poona workers have during the last few years made a terrible confusion in their enthusiasm to prove the correctness of 1630 date. Mr. Apte alone has written and printed over 800 pages on this subject, i.e. the Introduction of *Shivabharat*, *Shivacharitra Pradeep*, *Shivacharitra Sahitya*, etc., not to mention the newspaper controversies, which are still raging. After reading all this enormous literature one gets completely bewildered about the real state of things. I hope you will be able to clear the path for us all once and for all.' (15 Novenber 1928), Gupta, op. cit., pp. 283–4.
40. *Shivaji*, 1952, edn., p. 394.
41. 'I am getting more and more convinced that the 1630 date of Shivaji's birth must have been purposely fabricated' (12 June 1927), Gupta, op. cit., p. 278.
42. *Shivaji*, 1928, 3rd edn., p. 414.
43. Ibid.
44. Gupta, op. cit., p. 348 (15 June 1946).
45. In this respect Sardesai once requested JNS: 'I have to make a personal suggestion. When you print your new edition of "Shivaji" please do change "Shiva" into "Shivaji". The former is an insulting appellation.' (21 February 1927), Gupta, op. cit., p. 277.
46. Ibid., p. 23.
47. D.V. Potdar, *Olakha* (Marathi), Pune, 1961, pp. 45–53.
48. D.V. Apte Introduction to *Shivabharat*, op. cit., p. 52.

49. Their (Maratha) historians (some will deny them the name) write in plain, simple and unaffected style. . . . Victory and defeat are briefly related. . . . They do not endeavour to bias or mislead the judgement but are certainly greatly deficient in chronology and in historical reflections. *History of the Mahrathas*, by Edward Scott Waring, London, 1810, Preface, pp. ix–x. Quoted in A.R. Kulkarni, *James Cuninghame Grant Duff*, Pune, 1971, p. 127.
50. *Shivaji*, 1920, 2nd edn, p. 41. 'Sarkar has rejected the *Shivadigvijaya bakhar* as a modern, Prabhu concoction intended by some modern gossipy old man, well read in Sanskrit, but not in *tawarikhs*, to glorify Kayastha families as the greatest and most loyal helpers of Shivaji. This sort of propaganda sickens me.' JNS to Sardesai, 19 August 1947, Gupta, op. cit., p. 258.

    See also *Shivaji*, 1952 edn, p. 39. It may be noted here that JNS as relied on those sources such as Jedhe's *Shivabharat* that he had declared unauthentic and worthless. D.V. Apte has pointed out that Ranadullah Khan, who was held responsible for Shahaji's release, was not alive in 1649. *Shivabharat*, op. cit., Introduction, p. 52.
51. JNS, *Shivaji*, 2nd edn., p. 15, 3rd edn, p. 23, 5th edn., p. 19. D.V. Apte, ibid., p. 53. James Mill in his *History of India*, vol. II (1826 edn.) makes a similar statement, p. 358.
52. *Shivaji*, 1952 edn., p. 166. D.V. Apte, Introduction to *Shivabharat*, p. 54.
53. Gupta, op. cit., 21 February 1927, p. 277.
54. 'The study of Shivaji's times has now made me quite at home on the subject. I can rewrite Shivaji without the least help of the . . . (Poona) people. It is the extremely hostile attitude of these people which has retarded the progress of history in the University and with Government. They are extremely jealous of other workers and would rather damage all other work in the hope of pushing on their own hobbies. But they are now thoroughly exposed' (14 April 1927). Gupta, op. cit., pp. 277–8. About the teaching of history in Maharashtra, JNS's Draft Report on the selection of a Professor of History at the Deccan College deserves some attention. See Gupta, op. cit., pp. 218–19.
55. 'I have declined the honorary membership of the Bharat History Society as it is neither of real benefit to them, nor an honour to allow my name to be borne on the rolls of such a mushroom society' 15 November 1952, Gupta, op. cit., p. 269.
56. 'No scholar in Poona who can write decent English, studied Shivaji, so at the most some one will translate the Marathi version into English. This means there will be no genuine spirit in the work. And your book (3rd edn.) appearing something like a year in advance before their celebration (tercentenary of Shivaji's birth) will have taken the wind out of their bags.' 25 November 1928, Gupta, op. cit., pp. 284–5.
57. C.V. Vaidya, *Shivaji, the Founder of Maratha Swaraj*, Pune, 1931, Preface, pp. iii–iv.
58. Ibid., Foreword, p. 1.
59. Gupta, op. cit., p. 362.
60. D.V. Apte Smarak Mandal (ed.), *Dattopant Apte Lekh Samgraha*, Pune, 1945, pp. 57–8.

61. For details, see Apte, op. cit., in n. 60, pp. 55–6, Gupta, op. cit., p. 196, and Anil Samarth's article, 'The Real Shivaji', in *Chhatrapati Shivaji*, ed. N.H. Kulkarni, op. cit., pp. 99–108.
62. D.V. Apte, op. cit., p. 56. Faruki writes about the Marathi sources, 'But many documents have been discovered recently and they are spurious (p. 351).' This is based on JNS, 1st edn. of *Shivaji*, p. 30. See also C.H. Philips (ed.), *Historians of India, Pakistan and Ceylon*, op. cit., p. 303.
63. Gupta, op. cit., pp. 309 and 398.
64. Quoted, in *History in Practice*, ed. A.R. Kulkarni, op. cit., p. 96.
65. Gupta, op. cit., p. 61.
66. *Shivaji*, 1920 edn., Appendix, *Works of JNS.*
67. Gupta, op. cit., p. 62.
68. Ibid., p. 248. For details on M.C. Sprengel, see D. Rothermund's article, 'Matthias Christian Sprengel', in *History in Practice*, op. cit., pp. 1–12.
69. Gupta, op. cit., p. 298.
70. Ibid., p. 252 and Sardesai's letter to JNS enquiring about the authenticity of Nadir Shah's letter to Bajirao I, 2 November 1940, p. 328.
71. JNS, *House of Shivaji*, 3rd edn., Calcutta, 1955, Preface, pp. iii–iv
72. Gupta, op. cit., JNS's letter to Sardesai, 28 June 1939, p. 209.
73. Ibid., p. 265
74. *Shivaji*, 1952, edn., pp. 374–5.

    About Shivaji, Rabindranath Tagore's remarks in this respect, as quoted by JNS, are: 'He wanted to make this heterogeneous society triumphant over all India! He wove ropes of sand, he attempted the impossible. It is beyond the power of any man, it is opposed to the divine law of the universe to establish the *swaraj* of such a caste-ridden, isolated, internally torn sect over a vast continent like India.' Ibid., p. 375.
75. Banerjee, op. cit., pp. 36–7.
76. The historian of Shivaji, at the end of a careful study of all the records about him in eight different languages, is bound to admit that Shivaji was not only the maker of the Maratha nation but also the greatest constructive genius of medieval India. States fall, empires break up, dynasties become extinct, but the memory of a true 'hero as king' like Shivaji remains an imperishable historical legacy for the entire human race:

    The pillar of a people's hope,
    The centre of a world's desire,

    to animate the heart, to kindle the imagination and to inspire the brain of succeeding ages to the highest endeavours. *House of Shivaji*, 3rd edn., p. 115.
77. Kulkarni, *Maharashtra in the Age of Shivaji*, 2nd edn., Pune, 2002, pp. xix–xxiii.
78. Gupta, op. cit., pp. 72–3. For a discussion on JNS's view on the Maratha disaster at Panipat, see Banerjee op. cit., pp. 67–8.

15

Surendra Nath Sen (1890–1962)

Among the Bengali historians of the Marathas, Surendra Nath Sen[1] enjoys a unique place for various reasons. He was the first historian who broke new grounds in the hitherto neglected areas of Maratha history, namely administrative and military history. He believed firmly in the efficacy of Marathi sources for the study of Maratha history, and therefore spared no effort to learn the language. As a nationalist historian, he became deeply involved in the study of the Marathas. Among the nationalist historians from Bengal, particularly those specializing in Maratha history, a reference has to be made to B.D. Basu's book, *Story of Satara* (1922), which attacked the British annexation of Satara State in 1848.

Sen entered the field of Maratha history at the behest of Sir Asutosh Mookerjee, who had a plan to prepare a selection, in a handy form, of all the useful documents on Maratha history and translate them into English for the benefit of non-Marathi-speaking students of Maratha history.

Sen, with a view to implementing the suggestion of Sir Asutosh, started working on the translation of the Marathi chronicle Sabhasad *bakhar*, the most important Life of Shivaji, by his contemporary Krishnaji Anant Sabhasad, written in the 1690s. Being the history of Shivaji narrated by a contemporary Maratha, it is considered by most historians to be an authentic document. Besides this, Sen also included in this volume, entitled, *Siva Chhatrapati*, the translations of extracts from two other chronicles, namely, *Sivadigvijaya* and Chitnis *bakhar*, dealing with the life of Shivaji, but written much later, after Shivaji's death, i.e. in the nineteenth century. Besides these translations, this volume includes three notes and appendices, which indicate the deep interest of Sen in the study of the sources on Maratha history.

His devotion to Maratha history can be seen from the preface to his pioneering work, *The Administrative System of the Maratha,* first published in 1923. He states very briefly that Maratha power extended from sea to sea and remarks that this last Hindu empire of India passed away after a chequered existence of 170 years.

He was puzzled by the common belief among people that this vast empire had existed by plunder and robbery and that the Maratha generals were 'robbers, plunderers and scoundrels'. He wondered how such an empire could last for a century and a half by robbery and plunder alone. M.G. Ranade, in his classic work *Rise of the Maratha Power*, had also raised the same question and tried to absolve the Marathas from this baseless charge.

Sen carried further this argument by citing the examples of Maratha civil and military institutions, that had made the Maratha state endure for such a long time. He writes:

> The Marathas were not mere robbers and plunderers. From their original documents I found that they had an excellent set of regulations for their own empire. Further investigations convinced me that these regulations and administrative institutions were not their own inventions. They had inherited them from their Hindu and Muhammadan predecessors. The administrative system of the Marathas is thus of surpassing interest.

He further states: 'It helps us to understand the growth of present British Indian administrative institutions, partly engrafted as they are on older Hindu and Muhammadan systems.'[2]

Mountstuart Elphinstone, who was in charge of the territories conquered from the Peshwas, had a good opinion of the existing administrative system of the Marathas, and therefore tried to avoid the introduction of Western ideas or innovations. He was at once an imperialist and a liberal. He thought that British authority in its formative period could be promoted only by avoiding the introduction of Regulations in the newly conquered Maratha territory, and tried to preserve as much as he could the Maratha system that had served the Marathas well. His contemporary, Sir Thomas Munro, also subscribed to this view of Elphinstone.[3]

The intensive study of the Maratha administration over a period of five years or so, and the publication of the results in 1923, involved Sen in further research in Maratha history. Initially, he was attracted to the career of Shivaji as a military leader when he first read Romesh Chandra Dutt's novel, *Maharashtra Jeevan Prabhat*.[4] Perhaps this induced him to undertake research in the military system of the Marathas.

Sen was well acquainted with Marathi sources, as can be seen from his book *Siva Chhatrapati*, mentioned above, and his critical analysis of the sources consulted for Shivaji's administrative system. In his preface to the *Military System of the Marathas*, he writes, 'Nearly ten years ago, I began a study of the civil institutions of the Marathas with a view to exploring the causes of the rapid expansion of their empire and its speedy collapse. The Maratha empire was primarily a military organization and its civil institutions were closely connected with its military system.' This conviction led him to study military system. In his work *The Military System of the Marathas* (1928), Sen seeks to trace the roots of the fall of Maratha power in the revival of feudalism after the death of Sambhaji and also examines their institutions such as the *chauth* and *sardeshmukhi*, their military organization with special reference to the navy and the role of the Angres, the admirals of the Marathas, and many other aspects.

In the course of this study, Sen realized that as the Marathi and other indigenous sources did not throw much light on the subject, particularly on 'maritime history', and one has 'to rely almost entirely on foreign sources'. He therefore examined as far as possible all the manuscript records available in London, Paris, Lisbon, Evora and Goa, and also some rare old publications. He has thus brought out, perhaps for the first time, the importance of the study of the Portuguese language for a better understanding of Maratha history.[5]

Sen, as a true historian, was a firm believer in the principle that 'the historian works with the documents' and he was constantly in search of documents. There is no substitute for documents: 'no documents, no history'.[6] Sen was evidently a follower of the German historian Ranke, who believed in 'the necessity of founding historical construction strictly on contemporary sources.'[7]

Sen, as we have seen, began his studies with the translation of some Marathi chronicles as part of Asutosh Mookerjee project, who paid Rs. 500, perhaps, as seed money, to work on Maratha history. With the setting up of the Historical Records Commission in 1919, a boost was given to the publication of historical documents for the benefit of research scholars. The Government as part of the Commission's programme published, *A Source Book of Maratha History,* vol. I, edited by H.G. Rawlinson and R.P. Patwardhan, in 1929. It included English translations of some Sanskrit, Marathi, and Persian sources as well as extracts from the accounts of foreign travellers mainly pertaining to Shivaji's period.[8]

Sen excluded all the sources included in 'A *Source Book* and instead selected some foreign sources, mainly Portuguese, French and Dutch dealing with the career of Shivaji, translated and published them in a volume entitled *Foreign Biographies of Shivaji* in 1927.[9] He selected the writings of foreigners because, as he explains, Shivaji's fame had reached Europe while he was still alive. His heroic exploits, daring deeds and clever stratagems had found a fitting place in the accounts of contemporary English, French, Dutch, Portuguese and Italian writers long before the name of the Marathas became known to the world outside. Sen was quite aware of some shortcomings in the accounts of the foreigners, yet he says, 'In spite of their obvious defects, no serious student of Maratha history can afford to ignore the testimony of these European writers.'[10]

One can understand the importance of this observation if one visits the European archives, where rich archival material is preserved in the Records offices of Lisbon, the Hague, London, and Paris. Maratha history would remain incomplete without the intelligent use of sources in the Portuguese, the

Dutch and the French languages. This volume includes the Life and History of Shivaji written by contemporary Europeans such as Cosme da Guarda, Jean de Thevenot, Barthelemy Carré, François Martin, François Valentine, as well as a few extracts from Dutch and English records.

Besides this, while working as Director of the National Archives, Sen published another volume on important foreign source material—the travelogues of the French travellers of the medieval period, namely, Thevenot and Carré. The translations of their travel accounts into other European languages, had omitted the Indian parts. As head of the National Archives of India, Sen deemed it necessary to translate the impressions of these two French travellers about India. He published the English translation under the title, *Indian Travels of Thevenot and Careri* from the National Archives of India, in 1949.[11]

Besides these major works, Sen also contributed a few papers to journals mainly dealing with sources pertaining to Maratha history. They were published in a book form under the title, *Studies in Indian History* by the University of Calcutta in 1930. This volume contains a monograph running to more than a hundred pages on historical records at Goa. With a view to going through the original sources, Sen took lessons in Portuguese from Braganza Cunha of Calcutta University and then visited the Goa archives and published his *Report on the Historical Records at Goa* in 1925. This document is indeed useful for the study of the relations between the Marathas and the Portuguese in the seventeenth century. His discussion on the origin of *chauth* based on unpublished Portuguese records in the Goa archives throws much light on this medieval practice of exacting money from the weaker powers by force. It helps to reconstruct the maritime activities of the Marathas on the west coast, particularly those of the Angres. The purpose of this *Report*, as Sen has pointed out, was 'to indicate what new light the Portuguese records (both published and unpublished) can throw on Indian history'. He states, 'History cannot afford to ignore the original Portuguese sources, and as very few of these records have hitherto been published, the Portuguese archives still offer a fruitful field for study and research to all students of modern Indian history.'[12]

It is really unfortunate that this suggestion of Sen has not been taken seriously by researchers in Maratha history. However, after the formation of an international seminar on Indo-Portuguese Studies in 1978 by a group of interested scholars both Indian and Portuguese—periodic sessions are held and their proceedings are published.[13]

Besides this long report on the Goa Archives, and other articles on the Karnatak Expedition and on Hyder Ali and Tipu Sultan, Sen has made available a full translation of a Portuguese document called *Marquis of Alorna's Instructions*. The Marquis of Alorna was the Viceroy of Portuguese India for six years, and after his retirement he wrote a brilliant resumé about the annexation of certain territories, which is known as the New Conquest.[14]

Assessment

Sen was a patriot, and a nationalist historian. As a young man he had participated actively in the Swadeshi movement led by the Congress. Perhaps this induced him to study the role of the Marathas in Indian history as the most appropriate theme for research.

A resumé of his contributions to Maratha history reveals that his approach to history was institutional rather than biographical. The translations of Marathi, Portuguese, French and Dutch sources attracted him to the career of Shivaji, no doubt, but he did not pursue the traditional path of writing a biography of this Maratha hero. He studied these indigenous and foreign sources to grasp the system—administrative and military—which made the Marathas an important power for nearly two hundred years in the history of India.

Sen worked very hard between 1920 and 1930, but afterwards, during the last three decades of his life, he could not undertake any additional major research work on Maratha history other than those mentioned above. His shift from Calcutta to Delhi, first as record keeper of the Imperial Records (later renamed the National Archives of India), and afterwards as Vice-Chancellor of University of Delhi, meant that he was preoccupied with much administrative work, and he found hardly any time for substantial research work in history.

His last major work was on 1857, an assignment from the Government, which he accepted and completed within only one and a half years.

He associated himself with the Indian History Congress practically from its inception. He was its Secretary, and also its General President. In his presidential address, he emphasized the role of the historian in politics. He maintained,

> The politician may safely rely on the patriotism and good sense of the historian, but he must not forget that the historian is by profession and training an investigator. It is his business to reconstruct and, where necessary, to reinterpret the past. His judgement is unbridled except by logic, but his imagination is fettered by the available sources. Beyond the extent of evidence, he cannot go. History has no sermon to preach, no philosophy to deliver, and no moral to point.

This summarizes his approach to historical studies and reveals his firm belief in the importance of archival material.[15]

Sen was one of the prominent members of the Indian History Congress who organized the plan for the publication of a *Comprehensive History of India* in twelve volumes under the auspices of the Congress. He agreed to edit vol. IX (1712–72) but could not make any progress due to his many preoccupations.

Sen, it is true, could not do any major work on Maratha history after 1920. But his pioneering work on the administrative and military system of the Marathas, and his translations of Marathi and foreign sources for the benefit of research scholars, have assured for him a permanent place in Maratha historiography. A.C. Banerjee, while assessing the work of Sen's, has aptly remarked:

> Every student of Indian history in the seventeenth, eighteenth and nineteenth centuries must acknowledge his debt to his work. Later research will supplement and correct his conclusions, but it is unlikely that they will ever be entirely superseded. They stand on the granite foundations of a critical exploration of source-materials and uncompromisingly dispassionate interpretation of facts.[16]

Follow up

As noted earlier, Sir Asutosh Mookerjee, the then Vice-Chancellor of the University of Calcutta, envisaged regional histories of the Marathas, the Sikhs and the Rajputs as the major research projects in the Postgraduate Department of History. Sen came forward to pursue research in Maratha history, and by his commendable work set an example for the younger generations to follow.

The torch lighted by Sen was carried forward by his students in the course of time. Pratul Chandra Gupta's monograph 'Bajirao II and the East India Company' (1939), his doctoral thesis from the University of London, threw light on the last phase of Maratha history. Anil Chandra Banerjee, another student, produced a biography of Peshwa Madhavrao I (1943). This book was critically reviewed by a competent Maratha historian, T.S. Shejwalkar, who pointed out that besides consulting the known sources, 'Banerjee had also plunged into the still un-tapped archives and brought forth new material for use in his work which can be considered as his distinct contribution to the world of scholarship.'[17]

After a long gap a young Bengali scholar, Sailendra Nath Sen, also brought up in the tradition of S.N. Sen, produced two major works, namely, *Anglo–Maratha Relations, 1772–1785* (1961) and *Anglo–Maratha Relations, 1785–1796* (1974), covering the post-Panipat period. He is currently working on a project entitled 'Fall of the Maratha Empire', covering the last phase of Maratha history, from the Battle of Kharda in 1796 to the Third Anglo–Maratha War in 1818. It mainly discusses the part played by the component parts of the Maratha confederacy like the Peshwa, the Shinde, the Holkar, the Bhonsale, and the Gaikwad as an organic whole in the broad canvas of Indian political development. Thus, the four volumes on the history of the Marathas in chronological sequence, from 1772 to 1818, form a valuable supplement to Jadunath Sarkar's four-volume study *Fall of the Mughal Empire*.

The younger generation of scholars is also taking a keen interest in Maratha history. Upendra Narayan Chakravorty wrote a well-researched monograph, *Anglo–Maratha Relations and Malcolm, 1798–1830* (1979). Pranjal Kumar Bhattacharya analysed the inner workings of British diplomacy carried out by successive British Residents at the Poona Court in his work *British Residents at Poona, 1788–1818* (1984). Another Bengali scholar, Sudhindra Nath Qanungo, produced a biographical study of Yashwantrao Holkar, *Jaswantrao Holkar: A Golden Rogue* (1965), an unfortunate appellation which perhaps the subject does not deserve.

The military history of the Marathas has always retained its aura even among the new generation of scholars. *The Journal of James Young*, a British artillery officer of the East India Company during the Second Maratha War, has been reproduced with valuable notes by P.D. Khanna in his book, *The Second Maratha Campaign (1804–1808): Diary of James Young* (1990). Anthony S. Bennel, a retired official of the British Ministry of Defence and a scholar of Corpus Christi College, Oxford University, made a penetrating study of Arthur Wellesley (later Duke of Wellington), who played a pivotal role in defeating the Marathas in 1803–5 in his book *The Making of Arthur Wellesley* (1997).[18]

Anirudha Ray of University of Calcutta, who is well acquainted with the French sources of Indian history, has written an exhaustive introduction to the 2nd revised edition (1977) of Sen's *Foreign Biographies of Shivaji* and reviewed a number of books on Maratha history. His book entitled *Trade, Politics and Plunder, The Marathas in Cambay (1725–1825)* will be shortly published from Delhi.

Notes

1. Born on 29 July 1890 at Mahilwada (now in joined the Bangladesh); joined Robertson College, Jabalpur, 1915; Postgraduate Department of Calcutta University, 1917; became the Asutosh Mookerjee Professor of Medieval and Modern History, 1931; Keeper of Imperial Records, Delhi, 1939; Professor of History, University of Delhi, and Vice-Chancellor, 1950; President of the Indian History Congress, Madras Session, 1944;

Visiting Professor, Wisconsin University, 1957–8; D.Litt., University of Delhi, 1947 and Oxford, 1958; died on 30 October 1962.

Siva Chhatrapati was published by the University of Calcutta in 1920. Sen was then holding the Premchand Roychand Student Fellowship of the University, and Mookerjee was then the President of the Postgraduate Department. In his note of dedication, Sen compares Mookerjee with Shivaji.

About the translations of the *bakhars*, Riyasatkar Sardesai writes, 'I have compared the translation with the original and am glad to say that it is faithful, elegant and yet quite simple.' To K.N. Sane on the whole the work of translation seemed to have been well done. S.N. Sen, *Studies in Indian History*, Calcutta, 1930. See Appendix 'Opinions', p. 11.

2. S.N. Sen, *Administrative System of the Marathas*, Calcutta, 1976, Preface, p. 2. The first edition appeared in 1923 and it was reprinted in 1925 without much revision.
3. Kenneth Ballhatchet, *Social Policy and Social Change in Western India*, Oxford: OUP, 1957, pp. 30–1. 'The present system is probably not bad in itself as the country has prospered under it notwithstanding the feebleness and corruption with which it was administered. . . It suits the people whom indeed it has helped to form, and it probably is capable of being made tolerably perfect by gradual improvements introduced as they appear to be called for.' Elphinstone wrote to the Governor-General of India on 18 June 1818. Quoted in Ballhatchet, *Social Policy*, pp. 30–1.

   Munro held similar views about the haste of the British administrators in introducing the Regulations in India. He wrote to Elphinstone on 12 May 1818: It is too much regulations that ruins everything. Englishmen are as great fanatics in politics as Mohamedans in religion. They suppose that no country can be saved without English institutions. The natives of this country have enough of their own to answer every useful object of internal administration.' G.R. Gleig, *The Life of Major General Sir Thomas Munro*, London, 1830, vol. III, p. 252.
4. S.R. Tikekar, 'Dr. Surendra Nath Sen', *Nav Bharat* (a Marathi journal), year 17, vol. 2, November 1963, p. 48.
5. S.N. Sen, *The Military System of the Marathas*, Calcutta, 1979, rpt., Preface, pp. vii–viii. The first edition appeared in 1928, and the second revised edition in 1958. In the Preface to this new edition, Sen writes, 'The monograph was written in 1926. I long hesitated to publish it for it was submitted as a thesis and disapproved by the examiners, Sir Verney Lovett and Mr. N.C. Seddon, both retired ICS men. I then sought the advice of the late Professor Dodwell and the book was sent to press under his advice.' 3 September 1958.

   This book was first submitted to the Calcutta University in 1926, when Sir Jadunath Sarkar was the Vice-Chancellor (1926–8). It was rumoured that as the candidate (Sen) had pointed out a mistake committed by Sarkar in his reading of some English and Marathi documents, the thesis had been rejected by the University. Sen and Sarkar were both great scholars of Maratha history, and Sen had admitted in the Preface to the first edition of this *Siva Chhatrapati* that he was indebted to Prof. Sarkar, who had not only revised his manuscripts, and had given him many valuable suggestions, but had also placed his entire library at his disposal.

(See S.R. Tikekar, *Nav Bharat*, op. cit., p. 53, and the Preface to *Siva Chhatrapati*, op. cit., p. ix.)

See also Sarkar's letter to G.S. Sardesai, dated 22 April 1930, published in *Letters on Jadunath Sarkar*, vol. I, ed. H.R. Gupta, Chandigarh, 1958, p. 152, in which, without mentioning the name of Sen, it is stated: 'His ludicrous mistranslations from Marathi and Portuguese, if made known to the general public of Bombay, would add to the mirth of the scholarly world.'

See also Sen's Preface to his *Foreign Biographies of Shivaji*, in which he writes about Jadunath Sarkar's translation of Carré's *Histoire de Sevagy and Suite de L'histoire de Sevagy* (History of Shivaji and Sequel to the History of Shivaji). He says, 'Unfortunately, his translation is not only incomplete, but sometimes inaccurate', p. xvi, 7 October 1927.

6. C.H.V. Langlois and C.H. Seignbos, *Introduction to the Study of History*, London, rpt, 1966, p. 17 (original in French, translated by G.G. Berry, first published in London in 1898).
7. G.P. Gooch, *History and Historians of the Nineteenth Century*, London: Longmans, rpt, 1961, p. 92.
8. H.G. Rawlinson and R.P. Patwardhan (eds.), Bombay, 1929. It is being reprinted under the scheme of reprinting rare books sponsored by the Indian Council of Historical Research (ICHR), and published bv K.P. Bagchi, Calcutta, 1978.
9. S.N. Sen, *Foreign Biographies of Shivaji*, first published in 1927 and reprinted in 1977 under the Reprint Scheme of the ICHR mentioned in n. 8.
10. Ibid., Introduction, p. 1.
11. Tikekar, op. cit., p. 50.
12. S.N. Sen, *Studies in Indian History*, Calcutta, 1930, p. 117.
13. The first session of this seminar was held in Goa in 1978 and was followed by seminars in Lisbon, Macao, Cochin, etc. It is still continuing its activities.
14. S.N. Sen, *Studies in Indian History*, op. cit., pp. 185–243.
15. *Proceedings of the Indian History Congress*, Madras Session, 1944, Presidential Address, p. 11.
16. S.P. Sen (ed.), *Historians and Historiography in Modern India*, p. 358.
17. T.S. Shejwalkar, 'Peshwa Madhav Rao I: A Review', *Deccan College Research Bulletin*, vol. 4, 4 June 1993, pp. 363–75.
18. Thc author is greatly indebted to Prof. Shailendra Nath Sen of Kolkata for his note on the publications of Bengali scholars on Maratha history, on which the last section of this chapter is based.

16

Maratha Historiography in the Twentieth Century

The groundwork for historical research prepared by pioneering research scholars like K.N. Sane, V.V. Khare, V.K. Rajwade, D.B. Parasnis and many others who unearthed documents from historical families; the provocative writings of British historians; the direction in historical writings given by M.G. Ranade and later by G.S. Sardesai and others, bore fruit in the twentieth century. The attentions of historians and researchers from various parts of the subcontinent was drawn to the historical role of the Marathas from whom the British had wrested political supremacy of this subcontinent, and they were induced to search for regional source material to throw some light on the activities of the Marathas.

The availability of source material, both published and un-published, the vast literature produced by the saint-poets of medieval Maharashtra, the rich cultural heritage of the province, and the struggle of the Marathas against European colonialism, induced many western and Asian scholars to explore this field.

Thus, we find a large number of scholars, both Indian and foreign, studying various aspects of Maratha history in the twentieth century. It is difficult to offer even a brief survey of the various works produced in the regional and foreign languages on Maharashtra, its history and culture. Nevertheless, an attempt is made here to trace the trends of Maratha historiography in the preceding millennium.[1]

Trends in Maratha Historiography

The favourable atmosphere created by several factors gave a filip to historical research in the twentieth century. The foundation of historical societies for the collection of historical documents and research, the establishment of new regional universities and autonomous funding agencies at the government level, the liberalization of government policies regarding the use of archival material in the state archives, the facilities for getting material from foreign archives, and many other factors contributed to the promotion of historical research in India in a major way.

In Maharashtra, there were attempts to produce historical biographies of heroes like Shivaji, Sambhaji, Rajaram, Tarabai, Peshwa Bajirao I, Madhavrao Peshwa, Mahadji Shinde, Holkar, and many others. A few historians wrote on major political events such as the Battles of Panipat, Kharda, and Bassein, and the Anglo-Maratha Wars. Others examined various aspects of Maratha history like administration, civil and military organization socio-economic conditions, and political history of the various regions of Maharashtra.

The Marathas had established their political sway either directly or indirectly over many parts of the subcontinent. Research scholars from areas that had been under Maratha influence, particularly Bengal, Rajasthan, Gujarat, and Karnataka, examined, with the help of regional sources, the impact of Maratha rule over their respective areas. This has certainly widened the horizon of Maratha historiography. The bibliography appended to this book gives an idea of the growth of historical writings on Maharashtra from many angles.

The Comprehensive History of the Marathas

However, we hardly find any major attempt at writing a comprehensive history of the Marathas except perhaps the three-volume, *History of the Marathas* by C.A. Kincaid and D.B. Parasnis (1918–25), *A New History of the Marathas* by

G.S. Sardesai (1946–8), and in a limited way by R.V. Nadkarni in his book, *The Rise and Fall of the Maratha Empire* (1966). In addition, a few works in Marathi were produced mainly to meet the requirements of the universities in Maharashtra.

Kincaid and Parasnis

Charles Alexander Kincaid (1870–1954) was an administrator like Grant Duff, and perhaps the last British administrator-historian of the Marathas. He joined the Indian Civil Service in 1891 and retired in 1926. This coincided with a period of great activity in the field of research in Maratha history. This was an age of research scholars like Sane, Khare, Rajwade, Parasnis and historians like Jadunath Sarkar and G.S. Sardesai. During his service of three and a half decades in the Bombay Presidency in various capacities as a civil administrator, an agent for the Deccan Sardars, and a High Court Judge, Kincaid learned more about the land and people of Maharashtra, and perhaps this induced him to follow the tradition of his predecessors such as Elphinstone, Grant Duff, Malcolm and others in studying the history and culture of the people of the region under their control.

How C.A. Kincaid developed an interest in the history of the people under his charge, and why he undertook the stupendous task of writing the history of the Marathas, can be understood by examining his correspondence with his co-author, D.B. Parasnis (1870–1926), and G.S. Sardesai, whose advice he sought on many issues concerning the Marathas. This correspondence of Kincaid may be compared with the similar exchange of letters between Elphinstone and Grant Duff, referred to earlier.

Kincaid was associated with Satara first as Assistant Judge (1845–97) and again as District Judge for a brief period in 1913–14. During his stay in Satara, he cultivated friendship with the research scholar and publisher D.B. Parasnis, which continued till he retried from the Indian Civil Service in 1926. The correspondence between the two reveals Kincaid's interest and desire to write a new history of the Maratha people in collaboration with his new friend D.B. Parasnis. Kincaid had cultivated the art of writing by contributing articles regularly to newspapers like the *Times of India*, *Hindustan Review* and so on, for his Anglo-Indian friends, particularly on Maratha folklore and literature.

When Kincaid decided to work on Maratha history, two histories written by British administrators, namely of Scott Waring (1810) and Grant Duff (1826), were available. Kincaid, however, considered Scott Waring's *History* to be 'worthless because of the inadequate material at his disposal'. Grant Duff's *History*, according to him, 'though a valuable work, it had two grave defects, namely, (1) it was written without any regard for the feelings of the race whose story the author related, and (2) it lacked artistic arrangements and it was more a chronicle than a history'.[2]

D.B. Parasnis, to whom he expressed these views, immediately suggested that he should take up the task of writing a new account and offered him help by placing at his disposal the documents and papers from his own collection. To this. Kincaid promptly replied, 'You have kindly suggested that I should re-write the history of your splendid nation', which he decided to attempt (16 September 1913, p. 87). Kincaid wrote to Parasnis: 'The idea has long been in my mind and I have finally decided with your invaluable help to attempt it.' While emphasizing the need for a new history, Parasnis impressed on him that Grant Duff had been unfair to the Marathas and assured him that if he went through the material that he had collected, he would form a different opinion.[3]

Kincaid was quite pleased with this assurance from Parasnis for whom he had the highest admiration and was sure that he would not deliberately mislead him. He agreed to take up the arduous task of writing Maratha history on Parasnis's firm assurance and promise to give him all the necessary material.[4]

Kincaid's original plan was to narrate the history of the Marathas in two volumes: the first, the rise of Maratha power up to the death of Shahu, and second, 1749–1818. During the period of his leave of absence in England, in November 1913, he started working seriously on his plan. He wrote to Parasnis, his colleague and co-author, that he was 'hard at work at our History', and explained to him the progress he had made. Both men continued their correspondence in spite of the difficulties in communication caused by the First World War. Kincaid was keen on getting the study published by Oxford University Press (OUP) in England because he thought that by publishing it in India he might lose the English market. He writes, 'But I do not think that the England market is worth much. The English people are far too anxious about the War to be interested in a history of distant people'[5] (11 March 1918).

He was quite hopeful that the Government of Bombay could be induced to extend its financial support by purchasing a few copies of the book. But the Government was thinking in another way. Sir P.R. Cadell (1871–1961), a civil servant of the Bombay Presidency, reported that the book might be used by the extremists as a weapon against the Government. The Bombay Government therefore, refused any support to this 'nation-oriented history'. Its argument was, 'If the book is a good work, it will sell without the Govt. assistance. If it does not sell, this fact will prove that it may not be a good book and therefore undeserving of Govt. assistance.'[6]

This attitude of the Bombay Government was a setback for Kincaid. He wrote to Parasnis, 'The trouble is that the Oxford University Press may not care to publish the work now that Government will not guarantee the purchase of any copies. In that event, I shall have to publish it at my own expense.'[7]

However, the OUP accepted Kincaid's work and the first volume of *Maratha History* was published in August 1918. It was well received in India by the nationalists because it glorified their hero Shivaji, who was absolved of all charges of treachery in the Javali and Afzal Khan episodes.[8]

In the first volume, Kincaid traced the history of the Marathas from the Satvahanas to Shivaji, with a chapter on Tukaram and Ramdas. He was full of praise for Shivaji. He wrote, 'In all history there is no such example of modesty in the face of continued success.'[9] He dedicated the book to the Maratha people. In his preface, he referred to the prominent research scholars since the time of Grant Duff, and expressed his indebtedness to D.B. Parasnis. He confessed that he could not have single-handedly accomplished so great a work without the aid of Parasnis, whose 'vast knowledge, untiring industry and unrivalled collection of Marathi documents entitled him to a share in the success of the book'.[10]

Kincaid's *History*, however, did not make any advance over the study of Grant Duff, and it hardly crossed the level of a chronicle, and was rejected by Indian historians.

His first volume, however, was well received in India, and after this initial success, Kincaid started working on the second volume from 1919. After some contemplation, he thought that his original plan needed some revision, and with the consent of his co-author—Parasnis—he redrafted it. The second volume, according to his new plan, would end with the death of Balaji Bajirao alias Nanasaheb Peshwa. He wrote to Parasnis that Panipat was a good point to stop as it undoubtedly marked the decline of Maratha power (2 September 1919). For this volume, he got some Portuguese material from Goa and collected some data from foreign sources. He worked very hard and completed by April 1921, the draft of the second volume.[11]

Parasnis went through this 'draft' and recommended that Kincaid should consult the *Riyasat* of Sardesai on this subject. Kincaid started corresponding with Sardesai in 1921, which continued up to 1932. Sardesai replied to all his queries, but was surprised to note that the information that Kincaid required could easily have been supplied to him by his co-author. He suspected that Parasnis was interested only in securing some monetary gain from Kincaid rather than eliciting scientific history of the Marathas from him. After going through the suggestion made by Sardesai, Kincaid wrote, 'I am afraid I have had to change a good deal of the 'draft' in the light of your Riyasat'[12] (15 June 1921).

Kincaid was full of praise for Sardesai in his correspondence with him. He considered the *Riyasats* as most 'charming and delightful' and the most valuble contribution to Maratha history in modern times. He wrote to Sardesai that he was trying to put the Maratha case fairly before the English public and to destroy the venomous atmosphere created by Grant Duff and his school through his works on Maratha history (5 July 1921).[13]

The second volume was published in September 1922, but it did not sell like the first, and the publisher had to incur some loss.

Kincaid had a different plan about the third volume of his *History*, covering the long period from the death of Shahu to the end of the Chitpavan Age. He suggested that Parasnis should write it first in Marathi, which could later be translated by him into English. Parasnis agreed to this arrangement, but somehow could not follow it through. As Kincaid was eager to get rid of this work, he had no alternative but to start working on it himself. He writes, 'Had I any idea of the labour that awaited me, I should not in 1913 have so light-heartedly undertaken the task of writing the history of your nation (19 June 1922). Kincaid completed the draft of the third volume, and passed it on to Parasnis. He made some suggestions, which were carried out, and it was then sent to OUP. Thus, the three volumes of the *History* running into 880 pages took nearly eleven years to complete; they were published between 1918 and 1925.[14]

In the Preface to the third volume, Kincaid tried to solicit the favour of Indian readers. He writes, 'I have compressed into too small a space the reign of Bajirao II. This I have done deliberately. My work is primarily for Indian readers and to them the glorious period of the Maratha kingdom will, I think, prove more interesting than the decline and fall. Maratha pre-eminence ended with the death of Madhavrao II.'[15]

It is quite obvious from this confession that Kincaid intended to impress on Indian readers that he cared more for the sympathies of the Marathas than his predecessors, particularly Grant Duff.

In spite of their sincere efforts, the *History* of Kincaid and Parasnis failed to impress historians and discerning students of Maratha *History*. It could not supersede Grant Duff, as they had expected. It did not find a place in the university curriculum. Of the three volumes of his *History*, the last two did not finish their first editions; only the first volume dealing mainly with the Shivaji period saw a second edition after eight years, in 1926, and a reprint by an Indian publisher appeared in 1968.

How much help did Kincaid receive from his Marathi co-author Parasnis in securing authentic sources? Though he expressed his appreciation of Parasnis's assistance in his letters and autobiography, it appears that Parasnis's help was negligible. It has been, rightly remarked that the Indian collabor ator's share is less than the title page.[16]

Critical Assessment of Kincaid's *History*

Rajwade held a poor opinion about the research abilities of Kincaid. In his review of Kincaid's book *The Tale of the Tulsi Plant and other Studies* (1909), he remarked that the Briton had no knowledge of history, his statements were baseless, his information limited, his work lacked research, that his writing was neither classical nor elegant prose, but rather was peurile and jejune.[17]

British historians were not prepared to pardon Kincaid for his new interpretation of the Javali and Afzal Khan episodes absolving Shivaji from these two acts, namely, the 'murder of Chandrarav More of Javali' and the 'assassination of Afzal Khan'. According to them, they were 'treacherous and condemnable' acts on the part of Shivaji. Henry Beveridge, in his review of the book, writes, 'Such one-sidedness is excusable in a Maratha, but we expect more mental solidarity from a British.'[18]

Another British historian, P.E. Roberts, writes:

> Charles's *History* has many merits and contains some new matter and presents a correct and readable account of the Maratha history, but it cannot be said that it is, either by reason of important contributions to knowledge, force and dignity of style or grasp of historical principles, of absolutely first-rate importance, nor is it likely to supersede, though it may certainly claim to supplement the standard work of Grant Duff.[19]

It has been pointed out by Kincaid's critics that he did not adhere to the high standards of historical writing because basically he was a story teller and was inexperienced in undertaking work of this kind, which required tenacity and sustained study.[20]

Aroon Tikekar in his well-researched monograph on Kincaid, while evaluating him as a historian, opines that

> he did not take history in its pure aspect for he was not so much infatuated by the science of history. He looked at history from a literary angle. Three prominent aspects of his writings on historical subjects related to Maratha history are: first, he popularized Maratha history to the extent possible for him, second his sympathies were always with the local people, and third, he was basically a story-teller who successfully employed historical material to interest Anglo-Indian readers in the land as well as the people of the Deccan.[21]

Kincaid's *History of the Maratha People* is a product of the collaborative methodology, which has its own limitations. It always suffers from the domination of the stronger partner. Though this 'history' has D.B. Parasnis's name along with that of C.A. Kincaid, the writing is entirely that of Kincaid whose concept of history is to 'tell a story'. Parasnis was surely the better historian, as has been pointed out in Part II of this book, but his role in the preparation of this history was confined to supplying material to Kincaid, or at best getting important Marathi historical documents translated into English for Kincaid, as can be seen from their mutual correspondence. In this entire episode, Parasnis received a raw deal. Neither did he get much money, nor could he claim the co-authorship as the writing is in the first personal singular, obviously that of Kincaid. He got a bad name for a 'bad' history. Kincaid's concept of history was wrong. His *History of the Maratha People*, therefore, is a substandard work. It is conceived as the 'story-telling' of the Marathas, and hence it is unworthy of being called a serious historical work.

R.V. Nadkarni

R.V. Nadkarni of Mumbai attempted an overall view of Maratha history in his book, *The Rise and Fall of the Maratha Empire* (1966).[22] It is not a comprehensive history of the Marathas arranged chronologically, but rather an attempt to explain the rise and fall of the Maratha empire in terms of Maratha society's economic and social development in the seventeenth and eighteenth centuries. Nadkarni argues that the Marathas succeeded in establishing their supremacy after the Muslims, but they failed against the British, who had a superior economic and social organization.

Nadkarni tried to interpret the historical facts of the Maratha movement by focusing attention on socio-economic factors. He maintained that Ranade in his classic work *Rise of the Maratha Power* considered only the social and religious factors, and ignored altogether the economic factors. While commenting on the works of the two leading historians of the medieval period, namely Sardesai and Sarkar, he remarked that they are 'inadequate and sometimes misleading'.[22]

V.S. Bendre

Vasudeo Sitaram Bendre (1893–1986), the founder of the Itihas Samshodhak Mandal, Mumbai, undertook the arduous task of writing the entire history of the House of Shivaji. He began with the reassessment of the history of Sambhaji (1960) and tried to remove the charges levelled against him by the Marathi Chroniclers. He then presented the history of Shivaji's ancestors, Maloji and Shahaji (1967). It was followed by a two volume biography of Shivaji (1973) and finally an analytical history of the period of Rajaram, the second son of Shivaji (1975). Besides this there are about 58 small books on various historical subjects to his credit.

Stewart Gordon

Stewart Gordon, an American scholar, produced a general book on the Marathas on similar lines as above, entitled, *The Marathas (1600–1818)* in the New Cambridge History of India (1993).[23] In a compact volume of about 200 pages, Gordon made 'an attempt to allow the Maratha polity to stand on its own as a significant part of India's history'.

He analyses the extant source material from the point of the view of the legacy of the Maratha policy with reference to the profound effects it had on revenue administration, law, education, trade patterns, migration, and the economic and social make-up of central India, Gujarat and Maharashtra.

Gordon's main purpose is to review the Maratha polity created by Shivaji from different aspects as, first, a rising out of the regional consciousness of Maharashtra, second, the Hindu response to oppressive Muslim rule, and lastly, as a brave attempt to change the nature of Hindu society and better the lot of its poorest members. He raises a number of questions in this context and tries to find answers in the existing source material by looking at it from different angles.[24]

As a fresh and objective look at Maratha history, Gordon's book is a good contribution to Maratha historiography.

Biographies of Shivaji

Shivaji formed the nucleus of Maratha historiography in the twentieth century, and there was a flood of literature, both historical and fictional, on the founder of Maratha power. A brief resumé of this literature is necessary in order to understand the trends in Maratha historiography in modern times. Nationalism, regionalism, communalism, and above all opportunism have prompted many to write on Shivaji. One need not expect much research in most of these works, but a rehash of whatever has been done by predecessors. The life of Shivaji has been interpreted from different ideological points or in justification of the author's own pet themes. A modern American historian in this respect observes, 'In the last ten years, Shivaji and the Maratha polity have assumed importance in yet another political struggle. Within Maharashtra, the struggles among, Brahmins, non-Brahmins, and untouchables have focused attention on the social reform aspect of Shivaji's reign. In his person, as a Maratha, he has become a symbol of non-Brahmin power. More interestingly, Marxist and untouchable writers have seized on his attempts to decrease the power of the independent landed elites as both consciousness of the need to end caste discrimination and a commitment to the task.'[25]

Let us briefly review the historical and fictional works available on Shivaji.

Historical

Hugh George Rawlinson (1880–1957)

Rawlinson, a member of the Indian Educational Service, was Principal and Professor of English at the Deccan College, Pune (1923–33). Being fascinated by the career of Shivaji, a hero of the people of the region where he was serving, produced a book on Shivaji in 1926. He is credited with writing the first Anglo-Indian monograph on Shivaji.

It appears from his Introduction, that Rawlinson consulted most of the Marathi *bakhars* (wherever English translations were available), a few published documents in the *Itihas Samgraha* by D.B. Parasnis, ballads, Muslim histories of the Deccan, travellers, accounts, and the works of early historians like Orme, Scott Waring, Grant Duff and so on.

He also consulted Justice Ranade's 'brilliant little essay on the rise of the Maratha power' (Bombay, 1912), which, according to him, was spoilt by the author's exaggerated views on his hero's merits and achievements. He made a general observation on the historians of Shivaji in these words, 'English writers on Shivaji generally speak of Shivaji as an assassin and freebooter. Indian authors run to the opposite extreme in palliating his faults and magnifying his achievements.' The objective of the historian, as conceived by Rawlinson in his biography of Shivaji was, 'Nothing extenuate, nor aught set down in malice' (p. 10).[26]

N.S. Takakhav

Takakhav of the Wilson College, Mumbai wrote a biography of Shivaji (1921) not as an independent research work but rendering in English of the original Marathi study of K.A. Keluskar, a teacher at the Wilson High School, Mumbai.[27]

This English rendering was done perhaps with the motive of reaching out to a larger public and thereby removing all the prejudices and misunderstanding created by those who wrote in English, namely Grant Duff, Rawlinson, Sarkar and Kincaid. Some leading members of various Hindu communities had founded the Shri Shivaji Literary Memorial Committee in 1924. Its office bearers, who were mainly drawn from the Maratha community, prepared a circular letter dated 15 September 1925 addressed to libraries in India, with a request to accept a copy of this book gratis. The object of this letter was to place before the English reading public an authentic story of Shivaji Maharaj, and to accomplish it 'the Committee purchased 4,000 copies of the English biography of N.S. Takakhav for the distribution of them among the English libraries and other educational institutions of all kinds'.

Takakhav, in his Preface to the book, writes, 'The name of Shivaji stands forth in bold relief as the author of a momentous national revival that changed the destiniy of India.' He lamented that the fact the 'Rulers of India' series did not include Shivaji in its scheme. With a view to justifying that his own work was an advance over the earlier three major works, namely those by Rawlinson, Sarkar and Kincaid, Takakhav endeavours to identify their shortcomings.[28]

Takakhav claims that in his work Shivaji is depicted as the director and entrepreneur of the greatest movement for the assertion of national liberty and independence that India had known in pre-British times (p. iii).[29]

C.V. Vaidya

C.V. Vaidya, a prominent member of the Poona School of historians, at the behest of the Chief of Aundh, decided to write a biography of Shivaji in English, perhaps to replace Sarkar's *Shivaji*. But it did not succeed in superseding Sarkar's study. Vaidya based his work mainly on Parmanand's *Shivabharat* and the Marathi sources then available. There is hardly anything new in this book, but the ten appendices attached to this volume dealing with various aspects of Shivaji's administration and personal life deserve some attention.

Balkrishna (1882–1940)

Balkrishna was trained as a historian at the London University. His work *Commercial Relations between India and*

England (1924) was well received by scholars in India and Europe. He joined the Rajaram College, a premier institute established by the Kolhapur State Government, in 1922, and since then he developed an interest in the history of Maharashtra, particularly of Shivaji. After eighteen years of strenuous labour he produced his magnum opus *Shivaji the Great* in two volumes, each having two parts (1932). The chief merit of this book is that it uses Dutch sources *in extenso* preserved in Batavia and The Hague in addition to material preversed in the archives in London, Goa, Bombay, Pondicherry, Madras, Tanjore, Satara and so on. He considered it 'necessary to turn the torchlight of foreign contemporary writings and records on the vernacular literature to pick up the grains of truth lying scattered here and there'.

However, as already noted earlier, his use of the Mudhol *farmans* in establishing the ancestory of Shivaji has been doubted by Sarkar and Sardesai.

About the objective of this work, Balkrishna writes in his foreword:

> My object has been to present the positive side of the character of Shivaji, the founder of the Maratha kingdom, and examine the charges levelled against his personality . . . the life of such a unique liberator of his people, a great nation builder and an immortal fighter for the freedom of his country must be source of inspiration to all.

However, this work could not replace Sarkar's *Shivaji.* It did not see its second edition. Dr Pawar, while assessing the merits of this work, thinks that the book could have been more readable had it been planned differently. In his opinion, it was a history-cum-source book and unfortunately the source material overshadowed the historical narration. He felt that it could better be used as a source book for the period it covered.[31]

Besides these major works on the House of Shivaji, a number of biographies in Marathi and English narrate the inspiring career of Shivaji, as a nation builder. A few of them are cited in the note to this chapter.[32]

Fictional Writings on Shivaji

The character and achievements of Shivaji influenced novelists, poets, and playwrights in various parts of this subcontinent besides Maharashtra. Literary personnel from Bengal, Andhra Pradesh, Tamil Nadu, Karnataka, Gujarat, Punjab, Bundelkhand, Orissa, Assam, Uttar Pradesh, and Bihar have richly contributed to fiction on Shivaji. Shivaji has thus become a national figure.[33]

As a part of the Swadeshi and freedom movements, attempts were made by nationalists and writers to revive the memory of the past through historical and popular fiction. Bengal took the lead in this respect. Romesh Chandra Dutt, the well-known economic historian and a civil servant of the British period, wrote two historical novels, *Maharashtra Jiban Prabhat* and *Rajput Jiban Prabhat*, on the careers of Shivaji and Jai Singh respectively. As regards the purpose of his novels he says:

> My sole object has been to narrate the glories of the past and the greatness of our national heroes. If I had succeeded in kindling a single spark of love and admiration for our national heroes then not in vain did I take up my pen.

Rabindranath Tagore in his two poems 'Pratinidhi' (1897) and 'Shivaji Utsav' (1904), hailed Shivaji's achievements because underlying them was his farsighted vision of uniting the whole of India.[34]

Literary works on Shivaji in other parts on India were motivated by the same impulses that moved R.C. Dutt and Rabindranath Tagore. In Gujarat, several biographies of Shivaji were written during the British period K.V. Laxman Rao of Andhra Pradesh wrote *Sri Shivaji Charitram* (1914). In Orissa, we have 'Chhatrapati Shivaj', a play written by Raghunath Panda. In Assam, Atul Chandra Hazarika's drama on the same theme depicted the struggle for freedom. In Punjab, Lala Lajpat Rai, wrote *Shivaji, the Maratha*.

Maharashtra has produced a number of writers of historical fiction such as Hari Narayan Apte, Nath Madhav, V.V. Hadap, N.S. Inamdar, Ranjit Desai, Captain Belwalkar and many others.

Trimbak Shankar Shejwalkar (1895–1963)

T.S. Shejwalkar[36] has carved out a unique place for himself in Maratha historiography for his bold and unconventional views on many issues connected with the history of the Marathas. He was brought up in the tradition of earlier historians like V.K. Rajwade, V.V. Khare, and D.V. Apte. However, Shejwalkar emerged as an independent thinker and objective historian, who wrote to establish the relevance of history. In fact, his monographs are very few, but his interpretative historical writings are numerous. He was a prolific writer, tackling a variety of subjects both historical and contemporary. As editor of the learned Marathi periodical *Pragati*, he made a valuable contribution to educating people in various matters of public interest.[37]

Shejwalkar was very critical about the historical writings of his predecessors, including Ranade, V.K. Rajwade, Vasudeoshastri Khare, G.S. Sardesai and others. It is true that he had great respect for them, but he also had the courage of his convictions to differ with them publicly. He divided Maratha history into the Age of Shivaji and the Age of the Peshwas. He was a powerful protagonist of the Age of Shivaji, and a severe critic of the Age of the Peshwas, who, according to him had departed from the path of Shivaji and thereby brought about the ruin of Maratha power.

He made his debut in the field of Maratha history by writing a critical introduction to Sardesai's book *Nanasaheb Peshwe Yanche Charitra* (1926) at the instance of the author himself. Sardesai, being keen on knowing the views of the young historian, persuaded Shejwalkar to evaluate, in his own way, his book, and this large hearted senior historian included it as it was in his book.[38] Shejwalkar's views about Balaji Bajirao alias Nanasaheb Peshwa were diametrically opposite to those of Sardesai, who extolled his achievements and placed him next to Shivaji. This interpretation was overthrown by Shejwalkar, who cited historical evidence in support of his own views. He maintained that history would not be worth reading if it conceals demerits. History should not be taken as entertainment, but as a useful and necessary science.[39] With this honest method of differing with an established historian, Shejwalkar entered in the field of historiography commanding great respect.

Shejwalkar was also critical about the achievements of Balaji Vishwanath, the first Peshwa of Shahu (1713–20), who was given the credit of getting the Three Sanads of *Swaraj*, *Sardeshmukhi*, and *Chauthi-Babati*, which are considered as constituting the Magna Charta of the Maratha dominion'[40] Shejwalkar, being a defender of Tarabai's party, however, considered them as 'nothing short of the shackles of slavery in as much as they acknowledge the Emperor's supreme power'.[41]

A similar line of argument about the Age of the Peshwas is seen in his noteworthy monograph *Nizam-Peshwe Sambandha* (1954).[42] Shejwalkar's main charge against the Peshwas, particularly regarding their relations with the Mughal Subedar of the Deccan, Nizam-ul-mulk, that they never declared with confidence their national policy, which was always unstable. The Mughal Emperor became widely acceptable as the ruler of India and the Nizam struck his roots in the Deccan because of the Peshwa rule in the Deccan over a century. The credit of eradicating the Peshwas goes ultimately to the British, who wrested power from the Marathas,[43] or the Peshwas, for as Elphinstone's Report (1819) says, 'The Territories Conquered from the Peshwas.'

Of course, he admits that the Peshwas alone cannot be blamed for the calamities that this subcontinent had to face in the past. But the achievements of rulers are not judged by the motives behind their act; they may be noble, but history always takes into account the overall effects of the rulers' policies, and in this test, the Peshwas had failed miserably.[44]

One of the major charges against this book is that Shejwalkar did not properly consult the Persian sources, and mainly relied on Marathi sources and the historical writings of Marathi scholars. As a result, his discussion and analysis are incomplete and one-sided.[45]

Shejwalkar's most well-known monograph is *Panipat-1761* (1946), an episode in Maratha history that hastened the downfall of Maratha power.[46] In this well-documented and well-argued monograph, he makes a critical and comparative analysis of the published and unpublished sources relating to this episode and also points out the shortcomings in the writings of V.K. Rajwade, Jadunath Sarkar and others on this event.[47] Shejwalkar maintains that 'the work has entailed a reconstruction on the basis of the revaluation of the old material with the help of new material filling in the gaps, and a closer study of the positive background of geography'.[48] He does not accept the verdict of Sarkar on the role of the Marathas in the Battle of Panipat. He writes:

> When a responsible historian of India like Jadunath Sarkar charges the Marathas with being 'lesser breeds beyond the law' (*Fall of the Mughal Empire*, vol. II, p. 291), one does not know how to characterize such a statement and what standard of conduct and morality he wants to apply. He seems to belong to that category of historians-cum-moralists 'who justify providence by the event and hold nothing so deserving as success'.[49]

Shejwalkar maintains that Sarkar had treated:

> The subject from a wrong angle as a part of the history of the Mughal Empire. He has overlooked important relevant material. His interpretation of the material used is incorrect, not to say inadequate. He betrays insufficient knowledge of the Marathi language and the expertness in using the material in that language. An unsympathetic critic must, at least, be fully and correctly acquainted with the subject he writes upon . . . and these conditions are unfortunately not fulfilled by Sir Jadunath Sarkar's very brilliant presentation in masterly English.'

Shejwalkar ultimately gave up criticizing Sarkar and decided to 'write out the whole piece myself in my own manner . . . which unconsciously assumed the form of a reply to Sarkar's writing'.[50]

Shejwalkar, in his monograph on Panipat, gives the historical background in the introductory chapter, followed by a detailed account of the Battle of Panipat, from the begnning to the end based on authentic documents, and fieldwork and maps wherever necessary, to explain the movements of the contending parties. It is a monumental work, placing Shejwalkar among the ranks of the prominent historians of the Marathas. He emphatically stated that the roots of the Maratha disaster should not be traced to the failure of some personalities like Malharrao Holkar, or Govindpant Bundele, as V.K. Rajwade has done, but should be attributed to the very administrative system of the Marathas. According to him, Panipat was a national disaster.

He analyses the constitutional basis of the Panipat campaign, and maintains that the Marathas did not wage the war for aggrandisement but for the defence of a principle—India for Indians, and governed by Indians. . . . 'There are many Marathas—perhaps the majority—who think it better to have lost the Empire than to have followed a line of conduct after the manner of a Clive, or Najib or Abdali.'[51]

Shejwalkar was a great admirer of Shivaji, and he had a plan to write a biography of his hero. Maratha Mandir, a private organization based in Mumbai, was in search of a competent scholar who could write an authentic biography of Shivaji, and they considered Shejwalkar, on his terms, as the most suitable person for such an assignment. He prepared an ambitious plan, and between 1959 and 1963 he wrote the Introduction, gave details of the work, and made critical notes on the sources to be consulted. Maratha Mandir, published this study running into about 650 pages, as a tribute to the great historian, who expired on 28 November 1963, leaving this ambitious project incomplete.[52] Shejwalkar was a prolific writer. He had a plan to write the history of Konkan, but could not give effect to it. He managed to write a historical background of Konkan, which can serve as a guide to research scholars. He also edited documents relating to Nagpur Affairs in two volumes while he was in the service of the Deccan College. His many writings are available in volumes of his collected works.[53]

Further Research Activity

A survey of the contributions by eminent historians—both Indian and foreign—to Maratha historiography has been made in the preceding pages. It is necessary to review briefly the research activity in Maharashtra undertaken by the research institutions and scholars associated with them. The pioneering work of Sane, Rajwade, Khare and Parasnis in the field of the collection, selection and publication of source material, and in writing research papers, was carried forward by a band of devoted scholars, in various research institutions and universities.

It has already been noted that the restrictive policy of the colonial government had instigated many nationalist historians to collect historical material through research institutions. The historian Rajwade took the lead in this and founded the Bharat Itihas Samshodhak Mandal (BISM) in 1910 with the help of a handful of research-minded friends. BISM in the course of time collected a huge amount of records and other source material from historical families, and published a number of research papers and monographs. Rajwade's contemporaries, Sane, Vasudeoshastri Khare, and D.B. Parasnis, were also doing similar work on their own. With a view to commemorating the achievements of Rajwade, the history-conscious people of Dhule, set up in his name the Rajwade Samshodhak Mandal in 1927. A number of research institutes were set up in the twentieth century in various parts of Maharashtra.[54]

Maharashtra has perhaps taken the lead, both at the private and government levels, in the collection and publication of source material. Jadunath Sarkar in this respect writes,

> The legitimated pride in their real and immediate past has prompted the Marathas to preserve, collect, edit and publish their historical records in a voluminous size and a high level of successful attainments, not one-tenth of which can be seen in any other Indian province, not even in the imperial cities of the Mughals or the antique capitals of Rajput princes.[55]

The erstwhile government of the Bombay Presidency did publish a number of documents, mainly from the Peshwa Daftar, but they had their own limitations. It has been rightly pointed out that the government publications suffered from two major drawbacks:

> Firstly, as the majority of them are published in the British period, only documents of a 'non-controversial nature' were published and many crucial and important documents were set aside. Secondly, the process of selection of documents adopted by the editors and policy-makers hampered many kinds of research, for instance, documents relating to economic history of Maharashtra, etc.[56]

After independence, a 'New Series of Selections from the Peshwa Daftar' was started in 1957 under the editorship of P.M. Joshi, but this did not achieve much. Only two volumes—*Expansion of the Maratha Power (1707–61)* and the *Revival of the Maratha Power (1761–73)*—were published in 1957 and 1962 respectively. A third volume entitled *Aithihasik Sadhane,* edited by S.V. Avalaskar, appeared later.

The Maharashtra Board for Literature and Culture, an autonomous body sponsored by the Government of Maharashtra, published nine volumes of French Records relating to Maratha history, translated into English by V.G. Hatalkar (1980–5) and Portuguese Records relating to Portuguese–Maratha Relations, collected by P.S.S. Pissurlencar and translated into English by P.R. Kakodkar.

The Government of Maharashtra had an ambitious plan of publishing an authentic and official history of Chhatrapati Shivaji, but it could not succeed in this venture. However, the Gazetteer Department of Maharashtra planned a project of writing the History of Maharashtra from Ancient to Modern Times in four volumes. The Department has so far published three volumes in this series.[57]

Research Scholars

P.S.S. Pissurlencar

Pandurang Sakharam Shenvi Pissurlencar, an expert in Portuguese historical documents, added new dimensions to the research in medieval history, particularly to the history of the Marathas and the Deccani rulers. Jadunath Sarkar has aptly summarized his contribution to historical research in these words: 'You are doing capital work in filling up, with your researches on a corner of Indian history in which you are the emperor.'[58] As Director of the Historical Archives of Goa, and through his contacts with the Lisbon Archives, he brought to the notice of Indian historians many important Portuguese documents useful for the study of the political and economic history of Portuguese India. He delivered a series of lectures under the auspices of the University of Pune, in 1964, on Portuguese–Maratha relations in the medieval period.[59] Pissurlencar had no formal education, nor had he any training in historiography. However, in view of his mastery over the Portuguese sources the Lisbon University conferred on him the honorary, Doctorate Degree in 1956. He was a self-made historian. Like Sardesai, he, too, cultivated friendship with Jadunath Sarkar, whose constant encouragement enabled him to develop as a research scholar and historian of the medieval period.

Research Work of the BISM

It is somewhat difficult to present a detailed account of the research work of the BISM done by its research scholars, including Datto Vaman Potdar (1890–1979), Dattatraya Vishnu Apte (1881–1943), Shankar Narayan Joshi (1889–1964), Ganesh Hari Khare (1901–90), Dinkar Vishnu Kale (1898–1980), and Y.N. Kelkar (1903–2002) to mention only a few.

M.M. Datto Vaman Potdar, a disciple of Rajwade, was associated with the BISM right from its inception, and was mainly responsible for its organization and development in his capacity as secretary and later as president. He edited some volumes of historical documents and contributed articles to the BISM's quarterly journal.

D.V. Apte, S.N. Joshi and G.H. Khare were the lifetime workers of the BISM whose tireless energy and sacrifice made the organization, one of the leading research centres of medieval history of India.

Apte was an ardent follower of Rajwade and was adept at fixing the correct dates of events because of his knowledge of mathematics and astronomy. He wrote an analytical introduction to Parmanand's *Shivabharat*, and compiled a most valuable volume called *Shivacharitra Pradeep*, wherein he discarded the date of Shivaji's birth as advocated by Sardesai and Sarkar, and on the basis of accurate calculations and authentic evidence declared that the third day of the second half (*Vadya*) of the month of Falgun, or 19 February 1630, was the correct date of Shivaji's birth.

S.N. Joshi served the BISM for a fairly long period. He was competent in deciphering old Marathi documents in the Modi script. He wrote several articles and monographs on the administration of village communities, social conditions of the Maratha period, and many other topics. His editions of the Marathi *Bakhars*, particularly the *Life of Shivaji* by Krishnaji Anant Sabhasad, compilation of *vamshavalis* (chronologies), and indices of historical documents are highly useful to research workers.[60]

G.H. Khare gained expertise in Persian sources, which were not intensively studied by many Marathi scholars. He was adept in the technical aspects of research, namely, accuracy in reading historical documents, his knowledge of correct spelling, particularly of Persian words, fixing the correct dates of documents, establishing the authenticity of documents by examining internal and external evidence, and the proper editing of documents. His book *Samshodhakacha Mitra* (1951) is a useful guidebook for those interested in research in Maratha history. He published six volumes of the *Aitihasik Parsi Sahitya*, a Marathi translation of Persian documents, namely, *farmans* and *akhbarats* between 1934 and 1973. G.H. Khare, was the only known Maratha historian to have developed proficiency in many other ancillary disciplines such as numismatics, epigraphy, iconography, and etymology, which are immensely useful for the proper understanding of medieval Indian history.[61]

Y.N. Kelkar, another noteworthy research worker of BISM, brought to the notice, of scholars the importance of ballads (*pawadas*), and also edited them with introductions. The compilation of a dictionary of historical terms appearing in the documents called *Aitihasik Shabdakosh*, a critical evaluation of the Bassein campaign of 1739, and a critical assessment of Sardesai's *Marathi Riyasats* are some of his remarkable contributions to Maratha history.[62]

Among other research scholars at BISM, mention may be made of Krishnaji Vasudeo Purandhare, editor of three volumes of *Purandhare Daftar* and co-editor of a few volumes of documents. Shantaram Vishnu Avalaskar, the editor of

Sources of Konkan History, and many other scholars have enriched the historical literature on Maratha history by their efforts.

M.V. Gujar, A.G. Pawar, S.M. Garge and others have made available to us a rich collection of sources relating to the history of Karvir, i.e. Kolhapur State.[63]

Lastly, the interest shown by foreign scholars in the study of various aspects of Maharashtra society and culture by interpreting the existing source material from different angles has immensely helped to enhance Maratha historiography. Hiroshi Fukazawa and Hiroyuki Kotani of Japan, like Richard Tucker, Stewart Gordon, Frank Conlon, Eleanor Zelliot, Anne Feldhaus of the USA, Dietmar Rothermund and Günther-Dietz Sontheimer of Germany, Kenneth Ballhatchet, Frank Perlin, Rosalind O'Hanlon of England, Guy Delury of France, André Wink of the Netherlands, Irina Glushkova of Russia, Jim Masselos of Australia, I.J. Catanach of New Zealand, and other young scholars, are working on various aspects of Maharashtra society and culture. The International Conference on Maharashtra: Society and Culture, formed by Narendra K. Wagle of Canada and Günther-Dietz Sontheimer of Germany in 1984, through its bi-annual conferences held in the USA, Europe, Australia, Japan and India, provides a good platform for interaction between Indian and foreign scholars. Since 1984 the conference has organized eleven sessions. The efforts of these scholars are highly commendable.[64]

NOTES

1. For details on Maratha historiography, see the following works:
   (1) S.P. Sen (ed.), *Historians and Historiography of Modern India*, Calcutta: Institute of Historical Studies, 1973.
   (2) C.H. Philips (ed.), *Historians of India, Pakistan and Ceylon*, Oxford: OUP, 1961.
   (3) Kavita Bhalerao, *Marathyancha Itihasachi Granthasuchi* (Marathi), Bombay: Popular, 1997.
   (4) Arvind Tatake, *Samshodhak Saptarishi* (Marathi), Pune: Inamdar, 1962.
2. Aroon Tikekar, *The Kincaids*, New Delhi: Promilla, 1992, p. 87.
3. Ibid., p. 87. It is interesting to note that earlier Parasnis had praised Grant Duff's *History* 'as the most noble book . . . the paramount

authority on the subject of Maratha history' (*J.B.B. RAS*, nos. 60–2, vol. 22, *1904–7*, p. 171. Quoted in A.R. Kulkarni, *James Cuninghame Grant Duff*, fn 42, p. 236.

4. C.A. Kincaid, *Forty-Four Years A Public Servant: An Autobiography*, Oxford: OUP, 1934, p. 178.
5. Tikekar, op. cit., p. 91.
6. Johannes H. Voigt, 'British Policy Towards Indian Historical Research,' *IESHR*, Delhi, vol. 3, no. 2, June 1965.
7. Tikekar, op. cit., p. 91.
8. Ibid., pp. 91–2.
9. C.A. Kincaid, *A History of the Maratha People*, vol. I, rpt., Delhi, 1968, pp. 275–6.
10. Tikekar, op. cit., p. 87.
11. Ibid., pp. 92–4.
12. G.S. Sardesai, *Mazi Samsar Yatra*, op. cit., pp. 147–8.
13. Ibid., pp. 149–51, letters praising Sardesai's *Riyasats*.
14. Tikekar, op. cit., pp. 94–8.
15. Kincaid, op. cit., vol. 3, 1925. See Preface.
16. Tikekar, op. cit., pp. 101–2.
17. Rajwade, *Lekh Samgraha*, vol. 3, 1940, p. 52.
18. Tikekar, op. cit., p. 104.
19. Ibid., pp. 111–12.
20. Ibid., p. 108.
21. Ibid., p. 118.
22. R.V. Nadkarni, *The Rise and Fall of the Maratha Empire*, Bombay, 1966, p. 10. This is his MA thesis, his revised version submitted to the Bombay University.
23. Stewart Gordon, *The Marathas (1600–1818)*, New Delhi: Cambridge University Press, 1993. *Marathas, Marauders and State Formation in Eighteenth Century, India*, New Delhi: OUP, 1994, is a collection of articles on history. 'The Slow Conquest: Administrative Integration of Malwa into the Maratha Empire (1720–1760)', pp. 23–63, is an important article in the abore book.
24. Gordon, *The Marathas*, op. cit., p. 79.
25. Ibid., p. 6.
26. H.G. Rawlinson, *Shivaji: His Life and Times*, OUP, 1915, pp. 7–10.

    Professor Rawlinson also wrote *An Account of the Last Battle of Panipat and of the events Leading to it* (OUP, 1926), in which he defended Bhau's policy and the Maratha efforts in these words: 'The Bhau Saheb did not commit a tithe of the blunder of both Wellington and Napoleon in the Waterloo campaign. He lost, not because he was a bad General but because his opponent was a better one' (Introduction, pp. ix–xiii).

    When the OUP gave volume III of Kincaid's *History* to Rawlinson for his opinion, he wrote violently against it. 'Mr. Rawlinson, who formerly used to be pro-Hindu, has now become very anti-Hindu and especially anti-Maratha' (Kincaid to Parasnis, 6 September 1924), Tikekar, op. cit., p. 266.
27. N.S. Takakhav, *The Life of Shivaji Maharaj: The Founder of the Maratha Empire*, Bombay, 1921. This is mainly an English rendering of K.A. Keluskar's original Marathi work entitled *Kshatriya Kulavatans Chhatrapati Shivaji Maharaj* (Bombay, 1907) and dedicated to the Chhatrapati

Shahu Maharaj of Kolhapur, a staunch supporter of Mahatma Jotiba Phule, the founder of Bahujan Samaj. In his Introduction, Keluskar blames the intellectuals of Maharashtra for not writing on Shivaji. He complains that the organizers of the 'Kesari Fund' had been claiming since 1895 that some persons were engaged in writing on Shivaji, but that nothing tangible had come out in the last twenty-five years or so. In view of this, Keluskar himself undertook the responsibility of writing a biography of Shivaji and published it in 1907. The reprints appeared in 1921 and 1965. There is hardly any original research in it.

28. He writes that Mr Kincaid reviewed the work of Shivaji as fragments of *The History of the Maratha People*, that Sarkar discoursed upon *Shivaji and his Times* and often forg the hero while discoursing upon his times, that Rawlinson's, work avowedly a monograph and was too meagre in its scope to comprise the life work of a great hero like Shivaji. Kincaid's *History* and Sarkar's *Shivaji* stood at two opposite extremes of historical method and style. The one was romantic in conception and uncritical in method, the other was hypercritical in method and sceptical in its intellectual outlook. Sarkar's sympathies were anywhere except with Shivaji and his gallant companions. Shivaji had fallen into the background.
29. Ibid., p. vii.
30. C.V. Vaidya, *Shivaji, the Founder of the Maratha Swaraj*, Pune: Author, 1931.
31. S.P. Sen (ed.), *Historians*, op. cit., article by A.G. Pawar on Balkrishna, pp. 158–64.
32. A select bibliography of Marathi works on Shivaji and his house:

V.S. Bendre, *Shri Chhatrapati Shivaji Maharaj*, 2 vols., Mumbai, 1972 (1250 p.). Sources quoted in extensive.

——, *Chhatrapati Sambhaji* (726 p.), Mumbai, 1971. In defence of Sambhaji

——, *Maloji Raje and Shivaji Raje*, Pune: Author, 1967 (636 p.).

——, *Rajaram Maharaj*, Mumbai, 1975 (555 p.)

D.V. Kale, *Chhatrapati Shivaji Maharaj* (3rd edn.), Pune: Pune University, 1971. Brief but authentic.

V.K. Bhave, *Yugapravartak Shivaji Maharaj*, Pune: Bhare Prakashan, 1955.

——, *Shivaji and Shiva Kal*, Pune: Kale, 1957.

S.M. Pagadi, *Shiva Charitra*, New Delhi: NBT, 1989.

——, *Shivacharitra: Ek Abhyas*, Kolhapur: Shivaji University, 1971.

B.M. Purandhare, *Raja Shiva Chhatrapati*, 2 vols., Pune, 1967. A popular work reprinted in several editions.

Jayasingrao Pawar, *Shivaji and Shivakal*, Mumbai, 1978.

G.S. Sardesai, *Shakakarta Shivaji*, Mumbai, 1935.

——, *Raja Shivaji*, Mumbai, 1958.

V.S. Vakaskar, *Shivaji ani Shivakal*, Mumbai, 1930 (translation of Jadunath Sarkar's *Shivaji and his Times*).

T.S. Shejwalkar, *Shri Shiva Chhatrapati* (Introduction, plan of work, sources of the proposed *Life of Shivaji* and a few relevant research papers), Bombay, 1964.

Kamal Gokhale, *Shivaputra Sambhaji*, Pune: Navakamal, 1981.

Besides these major works, there are also a number of small pamphlets on Shivaji published by Narhar Kurnudkar, Sharad Joshi, Govind Pansare, Jayant Gadkar, Sharad Patil and others.

33. N.H. Kulkarni (ed.), *Chhatrapati Shivaji*, New Delhi: Shivaji Samarak Samiti, 1975, pp. xvii–xxxvii.
34. Ibid., p. 25.
35. Ibid., pp. 20–98.
36. Shejwalkar was born on 25 May 1895 at Kasheti (Ratnagiri district,); he graduated from Bombay University and submitted his this is 'Influence of Muslim Culture on Hindu Culture', for the M.A. degree in 1919, but it was not approved; editor of *Paragati*, a Marathi periodical (1929–32), Reader in Maratha History, Deccan College, Pune; died on 28 November 1963.
37. For details about his character, achievements, and numerous articles, and books, see the following two books in Marathi:
    (1) Sarojini Vaidya, *Tryambak Shankar Shejwalkar, Vyaktitva Ani Kartutva (1895–1963)*, Bombay: Rajya Marathi Vikas Samstha, 1995.
    (2) Sushama Paudwal, *Tryambak Shankar Shejwalkar, Suchi*, Bombay: Rijya Marathi Vikas Samstha, 1996.
    (3) Narhar Kurundkar, *Magowa*, Pune, 1967, pp. 152–202.
38. G.S. Sardesai, *Nanasaheb Peshwe Yanche Charitra*, Bombay, 1926. Introduction by T.S. Shejwalkar, pp. 1–36.
39. Ibid., p. 36 (Introduction).
40. G.S. Sardesai, *New History of the Marathas*, vol. II, Bombay, 2nd edn., 1953, p. 53.
41. Ibid., p. 69.
42. T.S. Shejwalkar, *Nizam-Peshwe Sambandh (18th Century)*, Pune: Pune University, 1954, rpt., 1963.
43. Ibid., pp. 146–7.
44. Ibid., p. 162.
45. Sarojini Vaidya, op. cit., pp. 251–3.
46. T.S. Shejwalkar, *Panipat, 1761*, Pune: Deccan College, 1946.
47. Ibid., pp. 121–7.
48. Ibid., Preface, p. v.
49. Ibid., p. 125. It seems that Sarkar did not appreciate the charges levelled by Shejwalkar against his treatment of Panipat in vol. II of *The Fall of the Mughal Empire*. He wrote to Sardesai, 'On taking stock of the charges, I find that Shejwalkar, of his 14 years 'strenuous and exclusive labour' on the Panipat campaign of four months—against the entire North India History for 17 years treated in my second volume—has been able to correct me on four small points.' H.R. Gupta, op. cit., p. 266, 19 October 1950.
50. Ibid., Introduction., pp. v–vi.
51. Ibid., pp. 123 and 125.
52. T.S. Shejwalkar, *Sankalpeet Shivacharitrachi Prastavana Arakhada va Sadhane*, Bombay: Maratha Mandir Prakashan, 1964.
53. H.V. Mote (ed.), *Shejwalkaranche Lekh*, vol. I, Bombay: Mote Prakashan, 1940.
    Ibid., vol. II, Bombay: Mote Prakashan, 1959.
    Ibid., vol. III, Bombay: Mote Prakashan, 1977. For details, see *Shejwalkar Suchi*, op. cit., pp. 19–33.

54. For details see the following books:
V.G. Khobrekar, *Maharashtrateel Daftar Khane*, Bombay, 1968.
(1) C.N. Parchure and M.S. Kanade (eds.), *Bharat Itihas Samshodhak Mandal, Prakashit Lekh, Sadhane, etc., Suchi*, Pune, 1981.
55. Jadunath Sarkar, *House of Shivaji*, 3rd edn., Calcutta, 1965, p. 338.
56. Stewart Gordon, *The Marathas*, OUP, 1993, p. 5.
57. Govt. of Maharashtra, Gazetteer Department:
Part I *Ancient Period*, ed. H.D. Sankalia and A.S. Altekar, (eds.), Bombay, 1962.
Part II *Medieval Period*, by B.G. Kunte, Bombay, 1967.
Part III *Maratha Period*, ed. V.G. Dighe, Bombay, 1967.
58. S.P. Sen (ed.), *Historians and Historiography in Modern India*, Calcutta, 1973, p. 385. For details, see B.S. Shastry, on P.S.S. Pissurlencar, pp. 385–95 in the volume.
59. P.S.S. Pissurlencar, *Portuguese–Marathe Sambandha*, Pune, 1967.
60. S.N. Joshi, *Arvachin Maharashtretihaskalateel Rajyakarbharacha Abhyas*, Part I, Pune, 1960.
——, *Kulabkar Angre Shakaval*, Pune, 1939.
——, *Chhatrapati Shivaji Maharaj Yanchi bakhar*, Krishnaji Anant Sabhasad Virachit (ed.), 1960.
——, *Bhausahebanchi bakhar* 3rd edn, 1972.
Mantratama Nana Phadnis Shakavali, Pune, 1950.
——, *Shivakalin Shakavali*, Pune, 1937.
——, *Shivakalin Patra Sar Samgraha*, vols. 1–3, Pune, 1930.
61. G.H. Khare, *Dakshinchya Madhya yugin Itihasachi Sadhane*, vol. I, Pune, 1930.
——, *Mandalateel Nani*, Pune, 1933.
——, *Marathyanchya Itihasachi Vistrut Shakavali*, vol. I, Pune, 1977.
——, *Nivadak Lekh*, vols. I and II, Pune, 1972, 1976.
——, *Maharashtrachi Char Daivate*, Pune, 1958.
——, *Murti Vidnyan*, Pune, 1939.
——, *Samshodhakacha Mitra*, vol. I, Pune, 1951.
——, *Hingane Daftar*, vol. 2, Pune, 1947.
G.H. Khare and A.R. Kulkarni (eds.), *Marathyancha Itihas*, vols. 1–3, Pune, 1984–6.
G.H. Khare and S.N. Joshi (eds.), *Aitihasik Marathi Sadhane*, Pune, 1983.
62. Y.N. Kelkar, *Itihasatil Sahali*, vols. 1 and 2, Pune, 1951.
——, *Aitihasik Powade Kinva Marathyancha Kavyamaya Itihas*, vols. 1, 2, and 3, Pune, 1928–69.
——, *Aitihasik Shabda Kosh*, vols. 1 and 2, Pune, 1962.
——, *Vasaichi Mohim*, Pune, 1937.
——, (ed.) *Holkaranchi Kaifiyat*, Pune, 1954.
63. For details, see C.N. Parchure and M.S. Kanade (eds.), *Prakashit Lekh, Sadhane, etc., Suchi*, Pune: BISM, 1981 and Kavita Bhalerao, *Marathyanchya Itihas sach*, Grantha Suchi, Bombay: Popular, 1997.
64. For details of the contribution of these scholars, see the Bibliography. For details of the International Conference on Maharashtra: Society and Culture, see *Intersections: Socio-Cultural Trends in Maharashtra*, edited by Meera Kosambi, New Delhi: Orient Longman, 2000.

Epilogue

The survey of the historical writings on the Marathas from the seventeenth century onwards by both Indian and Western historians, mainly Europeans, undertaken in this volume is an eloquent testimony to the significance of the role of the Marathas in the history of the Indian subcontinent, particularly in the medieval and modern periods. As the Marathas had established their sway, directly or indirectly, almost all over India, their history no longer remained a regional history, but became the history of India as a whole. This is the main reason why foreign and non-Marathi historians were attracted to the study of the rise, growth and fall of the Marathas.

G.W. Steevens, a British visitor to Pune in 1897–8, was amazed by the courage and daring of the Chapekar brothers who had killed two British officers, Rand and Ayerst, on 22 June 1897; the officers were returning from Government House at Ganeshkhind in Pune after attending a party organized to celebrate the Diamond Jubilee of Queen Victoria. Steevens made a note of this incident in his book.[1] He writes:

> You must remember that it was from the Marathas and not from the Mussulmans that we actually conquered India . . . other provinces in India were ceded to us, or conquered from their alien lords. The Marathas lost their all in war. . . . The Marathas had never forgotten how high they were less than a hundred years ago, and who it was that brought them so low. They lost more than others, and they feel the loss more. For others we were a change of masters, them we brought down from

masters to slaves. . . . They were gallant warriors, they were also patriots, devotees and a people of an extra-ordinary acuteness of intellect. His Empire, his nationality, his religion, his honour, his beautiful language . . . . We have taken away his all.

Jadunath Sarkar, who considered Maharashtra as his second home, in a way endorses the opinion of G.W. Steevens quoted above. In his brilliant essay,[2] he writes: 'No other Indian race has produced such a galaxy of leaders in war and learning as Maratha history records'. He further remarks:

The Marathas have a historic advantage of unique importance in the India of today. Their near ancestors had faced death in a hundred battle-fields, had led armies and debated in the chamber of diplomacy, had managed the finances of kingdoms, and grappled with the problems of empire, they had helped to make Indian history in the immediate and not yet forgotten past. The memory of these things is a priceless asset to their race.

While analysing the Maratha character in the context of the geographical conditions of the region, which play a significant role in Indian history, Sarkar observes, 'They develop self-reliance, courage, perseverance, a stern simplicity, a rough straight forwardness, a sense of equality, and consequently pride in the dignity of man as man'.[3]

This pride in their past led Maratha intellectuals to preserve their history by collecting the indigenous source material necessary for reconstructing a consistent and rational account of the role of Marathas in Indian history. In this respect Jadunath Sarkar writes:

The legitimate pride in their *real* and immediate past has prompted the Marathas to preserve, collect, edit and publish their historical records in voluminous size and a high level of successful attainment not one-tenth of which can be seen in any other Indian province—not even in the imperial cities of the Mughals or the antique capitals of the Rajput princes. To this success many learned men of unsurpassed industry and self-abnegation have contributed. Among the dead, I shall mention only Kashinath Narayan Sane, Vishwanath K. Rajwade and V.V. Khare. No other race in India has produced their equal.[4]

The political framework of the Marathas is more or less researched and presented by now. However, there are many more aspects that still remain to be explored. For instance, the study of village communities, which have been rightly described by Elphinstone as 'little republics having nearly everything they can want within themselves', based mainly on regional records, has a larger scope for micro-studies with the help of numerous records preserved in the Jamav section of the Pune Archives (formerly known as the Peshwa Daftar or Alienation Office). The study of Marathi literature produced from the thirteenth century onwards would enable scholars to present a reliable picture of social, cultural and other aspects of medieval and modern Maharashtra.

It is really very gratifying to note that because of the availability of adequate source material, scholars both Indian and foreign are nowadays attracted to Maharashtra for research in the social sciences.

Why should one study Maratha history? This is a pertinent question which deserves some consideration. British administrators of the nineteenth century studied it purely from a practical point of view. Grant Duff, Political Agent and Collector of Satara, wrote for the first time a comprehensive history of the Marathas (1826) because British administrators believed in the axiom that if one wants to govern a people, one must know the people and one could know them only through their histories. The missionaries working in western India also studied some aspects of the history of Maharashtra in order to understand the way of life of the local people, particularly their social and religious life, with a view to establishing the superiority of their own religion over the religious beliefs and practices of the natives.

M.G. Ranade, in his classic work *Rise of the Maratha Power*, however, did not approve of such a mundane motive behind the study of the Marathas. In his above-mentioned treatise, he emphasized the moral significance of the study of Maratha history. While pointing out the importance of such a study, he maintained

> that the *Rise of the Maratha Power* was due to the first beginnings of what one may well call the process of nation-making. It was not the outcome of the successful enterprise of any individual adventure. It was an upheaval of the whole population strongly bound together by the

common affinities of language, race, religion and literature and seeking further solidarity by a common independent political existence.[5]

Perhaps this new direction shown by Ranade induced other scholars from various parts of the world to study the language, literature, religion and other cultural aspects of this region, elements that have imparted an independent identity to Maharashtra in the history of India.

Notes

1. G.W. Steevens, *India of Yester Years*, London, 1899, rpt., 1964, pp. 271–3.
2. J.N. Sarkar, *House of Shivaji*, Calcutta: M.C. Sarkar and Co., 3rd edn., 1955, pp. 334–9.
3. Idem, *Shivaji and His Times*, Calcutta, M.C. Sarkar and Co., 1973, pp. 6–7.
4. Idem, *House of Shivaji*, op. cit., p. 338.
5. M.G. Ranade and K.T. Telang, *Rise of the Maratha Power*, Bombay: Bombay University, 1961, pp. 3–4.

Bibliography

Acharya, K.A., *Maratha-Rajput Relations from* AD *1720–1795*, Akola: Author, 1978.

Alam, Muzaffar, *Crisis of Empire in Mughal North India*, Bombay: OUP, 1986.

Apte, B.K., *History of Maratha Navy and Merchantships*, Bombay: Maharashtra State Board for Literature and Culture, 1973.

Apte, D.V. and M.R. Paranjape, *Birth Date of Shivaji*, Pune: Maharashtra Publishing House, 1927.

Avalaskar, S.V., *Rayagadchi Jeevan Katha*, Pune: Maharashtra State Board for Literature and Culture, 1974.

——, *Angrekalin Ashtagar*, Pune: BISM, 1940.

Atre, T.N., *Gaogada*, Mumbai: H.V. Mote Prakashan, 3rd edn., 1959.

Attwood, D.W. (ed.), *City, Country and Society in Maharashra*, Toronto, 1988.

Balkrishna, *Shivaji, The Great*, vol. I (pts I & II); vol. II (pts. I & II), Bombay: D.B. Taraporewala, 1932.

Banaji, D.R., *Bombay and the Siddis*, London: Macmillan, 1932.

Banerjee, A.C., *Peshwa Madhavrao I*, Calcutta: A Mukherjee, 2nd edn., 1968.

Basu, B.D., *Story of Satara*, Calcutta: Modern Review Office, 1922.

Ballhatchet, K., *Social Policy and Social Change in Western India (1817–1830)*, Oxford: OUP, 1957.

Bearce, G.D., *British Attitude Towards India*, Oxford: OUP, 1961.

Bendre, V.S., *Sadhan Chikitsa*, Pune: PPH, 1976.

——, *Downfall of Angre's Navy or a Contemporary Narrative of the Siege of Gherta*, Bombay: BMGS, 1967.

——, *Maloji Raje ani Shahaji Maharaj*, Pune: Author, 1967.
——, *Shri Chhatrapati Shivaji Maharaj*, vols. I & II, Bombay: Author, 1972.
——, *Chhatrapati Sambhaji Maharaj*, Bombay: PPH, 2nd edn., 1971.
——, *Rajaram Maharaj* etc., Bombay: PPH, 1975.
Bhalerao, Kavita, *Marathyanchya Itihasachi Granth Suchi*, Mumbai: Popular Prakashan, 1997.
Bhat, B.V., *Shivajichi Rajniti*, Dhule: Rajwade Samshodhan Mandal, 1941.
Bhattacharya, P., *Residents at Pune Court (1780–1818)*, Calcutta: PPH, 1986.
Bhave, V.B., *Shri Shivakavya* (Marathi translation of *Sanskrit Shivakavya* of Purushottam Kavi (1887), Pune: BISM, 1943.
Bhave, V.K., *Shivaraj va Shivakal* (Shivakalin Maharashtra), Pune: N.V. Kale, 1957.
——, *Peshwe Kalin Maharashtra*, 1st edn., 1935, Pune: Author, rpt., 1976.
——, *Yugapravartak Shivaji Maharaj*, Pune: Y.B. Bhave, 1955.
——, *Musalman Purva Maharashtra*, vols. I & II, Pune: Bhave Prakashan, 1946–7.
Bhave, V.L., *Afzalkhanacha Vadha*, Pune: Bharat Swayamsevak Mandal, 1921.
Birje, W.L., *Who Are Marathas?*, Bombay: N.S. Press, 1896.
Broughton, Thomas D., *Letters in a Maratha Camp in the Year 1809*, London: Archibald Constable, 1892 rpt.
Buckland, C.E., *Dictionary of Indian Biography*, London: Swams, 1906.
Burton, R.G., *Mahratta and Pindari War*, New Delhi: Seema Publications, 1975.
Burway, Mukund Wamanrao, *Devi Ahilyabai Holkar*, Indore: Holkar State Press, 2nd edn., 1922.
——, *Life of H.H. Maharaj Tukojirao Holkar II, Ruler of Indore (1835–1886)*, Indore: Holkar State Press, 1925.
——, *Life of Ranoji Sindhia: Founder of Gwaliar State*, Bombay: Author, 1917.
——, *Life of Subhedar Malhar Rao Holkar, Founder of the Indore State*, Indore: Holkar State Press, 1930.
——, *Mahadji Sindhia*, Indore: Author, 1921.
Chakravorty, U.N., *Anglo-Maratha Relations and Malcolm: 1798–1830*, New Delhi: Associated, 1979.
Chandra, Satish, *Eighteenth Century*, Calcutta: K.P. Bagchi, 1989.

——, *Parties and Politics at the Mughal Court*, New Delhi: PPH, 1972.

Choksey, R.D., *A History of British Diplomacy at the Court of the Peshwas*, Pune: Author, 1951.

——, *Mountstuart Elphinstone*, Bombay: Popular Prakashan, 1971.

——, *Period of Transition (1818–1826)*, Pune: Author, 1945.

——, *Raja Pratapsinh of Satara (1839–1848)*, Pune: BISM, 1974.

——, *The Aftermath 1818–1826*, Bombay: New Book Co. Ltd., 1950.

Colebrooke, T.E., *Life of Honourable Mountstuart Elphinstone*, vols. I and II, London: J. Murray, 1884.

Cotton, J.S., *Mountstuart Elphinstone* (Rulers of India Series), Oxford: OUP, 1892.

Deodhar, V.N., *Nana Phadnis and the External Affairs of the Maratha Empire*, Bombay: Popular Prakashan, 1964.

Desai, Sudha, *Social Life in Maharashtra under the Peshwas*, Bombay: Popular Prakashan, 1980.

Desai, W.S., *Bombay and the Marathas upto 1774*, New Delhi: Munshiram Manoharlal, 1970.

Deshmukh, Sharada, *Shivakalin va Peshwekalin Stree Jeevan*, Pune: T.M. Vidyapeeth, 1973.

Deshmukh, Vijay, *Shakakarta Shivaji*, vols. I and II, Chhatrapati Seva Pratishthan, Nagpur: 1984.

Deshpande, A.M., *John Briggs in Maharashtra*, Delhi: Mittal, 1987.

Deshpande, G.K., *Deliverance or the Escape of Shivaji, the Great from Agra*, Pune: Author, 1929.

Deshpande, P.N., *Chhatrapati Shivaji Maharaj Yanchi Patre*, Dhule: Sushma Prakashan, 1983.

Dhabu, D.G., *Kulabkar Angre Sarkhel*, Alibag: Author, 1939.

Dhere, R.C., *Musalman Marathi Santkavi*, Pune: Dnyanraj Prakashan, 1967.

——, *Shikhar Shinganapur Shri Shambhu Mahadeo*, Pune: Shri Vidya Prakashan, 2001.

Dighe, V.G., *Peshwa Bajirao I and Maratha Expansion*, Bombay: Karnatak Publishing House, 1929.

Divekar, S.M. (ed.), *Kavindra-Parmand Krita: Shri Shivabhakat*, Pune: Author, 1927.

Divekar, V.D., *Survey of Material in Marathi on the Economic and Social History of India*, Pune: BISM, 1981.

Douglas, James, *Bombay in West India, 2 vols*, London: Sampson Law, Marston & Co., 1893.

Duff, James Cuninghame Grant, *A History of the Maharattas*, vols I & II, edited with Introduction by S.M. Edwardes, London: OUP, 6th edn., 1921.

Dutta, Ramesh C., *Sivaji*, Allahabad, 1944.

East India Company, London, *Case of Deposed Raja of Satara*, London: EIC, 1884.

Elphinstone, Mountstuart, *History of India,* London, 1889, 7th edn.

——, *Territories Conquered from the Paishwa*, Delhi: Oriental Publishers, rpt., 1973.

Elliot, F.A.H., *Rulers of Baroda*, Baroda: Baroda State Press, 1934.

Feldhaus, Anne (ed.), *Images of Women in Maharashtra Society*, Albany: SUNY, 1998.

Forbes, John, *Case of Raja of Satara at a Court of Directors, held on Wednesday, 8th April 1840*, 1840.

Forrest, Sir G.W. (ed.), *Selections from the Letters*, Despatches, and other State Papers Preserved in the Bombay Secretariat, Maratha Series, vol. 1, Bombay, 1885.

Fukazawa, Hiroshi, *The Medieval Deccan*, New Delhi: OUP, 1991.

Gadre, N.K., *Maharashtra Mahodayacha Purvaranga*, Mumbai: Maharashra State Samshodhak Mandal, 1971.

Garge, S.M., *Karveer Riyasat*, Pune: Rane Prakashan, 1980, 2nd edn.

——, *Karveer Riyasatichi Kagatpatre*, vols 1–4, Kolhapur: New Palace, 1982.

——, *Hindurao Ghorpade*, Pune: Dastane, 1983.

George, S.M. and S.H. Vartikar, *Kapshikar Senapati Ghorpade Gharanyachi Itihas*, Kolhapur: New place, 1974.

Gavali, P.A., *Peshwekalin Gulamgiri va Asaprushata*, Kolhapur: Prachar Prakashan, 1990, 3rd edn.

Gense, J.H. and D.R. Banaji, *Gaikwads of Baroda*, vols. 1 & 10.

——, *Third English Embassy to Poona*, Bombay: D.B. Taraporvala, 1934.

Ghorpade, M.Y., *Grand Resistance: Murarirao Ghorpade and the eighteenth Century Deccan*, New Delhi: Ravi Dayal, 1992.

Ghosh, Pradeep Kumar, *Mountstuart Elphinstone's Embassy and Poona Affairs*, Lucknow: P.K. Ghosh, 1977.

Glushkova, Irina and Anne Feldhaus (eds.), *House and Home in Maharashtra*, New Delhi: OUP, 1998.

Gokhale, B.G., *Poona in the Eighteenth Century*, New Delhi: OUP, 1988.

Gokhale, Kamal, *Chhatrapati Sambhaji*, Pune: Navakamal, 1978.
——, *Shivaputra Sambhaji*, Pune: Navakamal, 1981.
Gordon, Stewart, *The Marathas (1600–1818)*, New Delhi: Cambridge University Press, 1993.
——, *Marathas, Maraudars and State Formation in Eighteenth-Century India*, New Delhi: OUP, 1994.
Godbole, K.B., *Mountstuart Elphinstone Yanche Charitra*, vols I and II, Mumbai: Damodhar Saralaram, 1911–12.
Graham, D.G., *Statistical Report of the Principality of Kolhapur*, Bombay, 1854.
Grewal, J.S., *Muslim Rule in India: The Assessment of British Historians*, Calcutta: OUP, 1970.
Gribble, J.D.B., *A History of the Deccan*, 2 vols, London, 1896.
Guha, J.P. (ed.), *James Grant Duff: History of the Mahrattas*, vol. I, New Delhi: Associated, 1971.
Guha, Sumit, *The Agrarian Economy of the Deccan, 1818–1941*, New Delhi: OUP, 1993.
Gulavani, H.G., *Hukumatpanah*, Kolhapur: Rajprasad, 1994.
Gune, V.T., *Judicial System of the Marathas*, Pune: Deccan College, 1953.
——, *Survey and Calendar of Marathi Documents 1600–1818*, Calcutta: K.P. Bagchi, 1996.
Gupta, Bhagwandas, *Life and Times of Maharaj Chhatrasal Bundela*, New Delhi: Radiant, 1980.
Gupta, Hari Ram (ed.), *Marathas and Panipat*, Hoshiarpur: Punjab University, 1961.
——, *Life and Letters of Sir Jadunath Sarkar*, Hoshiarpur: Punjab University, 1958.
Gupta, K.S., *Mewar and Maratha Relations*, Delhi: S. Chand, 1971.
Gupta, P.C., *Bajirao II and the East India Company*, Bombay· Allied, 2nd edn., 1964.
——, *The Last Peshwa and the English Commissioners*, Calcutta: S. Sarkar, 1944.
Hardas, Balshastri, *Chhatrapati Shivaji*, vols. 1–4, Pune: Kale Prakashan, 1984.
Hatalkar, V.G. (ed.), *French Records Relating to History of Marathas*, vols. 1–9, Bombay: Maharashtra State Board for Literature and Culture, 1980.
——, *Relations between the French and the Marathas (1608–1815)*, Bombay: Bombay University, 1958.
Herwadkar, R.V., *Marathi Bakhar*, Pune: Venus, 1975.

——, *Peshwyanchi Bakhar*, Pune: Venus, 1972.

——, *Sambhaji Maharaj ani Thocele Rajaram yanchi Charitre*, Pune: Venus, 1972.

——, *Saptaprakarnatmak Charitra*, Pune: Venus, 1967.

Hockley, *Pandurang Hari or Memoirs of a Hindoo*, London: Chatto & Windus, 1891.

Hope, John, *House of Scindea*, London: Longman, 1863.

Hume, *Raja of Satara*, pts I and II, London: House of Commons, 1843.

Israel, Milton and N.K. Wagle (eds.), *Religion and Society in Maharashtra*, Toronto, 1987.

Jadhav, Rangubai-Saheb, *Mogal Mardini Tarabai Karveer Rajya Samsthanika*, Belgaum: The Belgaum Printing & Publishing House, 1946.

Joshi, A.B. and Chandorkar Aba, *Shivshahicha Lekhanalankan*, Pune: Author, 1934.

Joshi, P.M. (ed.), *Expansion of Maratha Power (1707–61)*, Bombay: Govt. Central Press, 1957.

——, *Revival of Maratha Power (1761–1772)*, Bombay: Govt. Central Press, 1962.

Joshi, P.S., *Chhatrapati Sambhaji (1657–1689)*, Delhi: S. Chand, 1980.

Joshi, S.N., *Nana Phadnis Shakavali*, Pune: BISM, 1950.

——, *Arvachin Maharashtretihasateel Rajya Karbharacha Abhyas*, pt. I, Pune: Pune University, 1960.

——, *Marathekalin Samaj Darshan*, Pune: Anath Vidyarthi Griha Prakashan, 1960.

Joshi, V.V., *Clash of Three Empires*, Allahabad: Kitabistan, 1941.

Kadbadi, B.R., *History of Peshwai* (Telugu), Dharwar, 1904.

Kadam, V.S., *Maratha Confederacy (A Study in its Origin and Development)*, Delhi: Munshiram Manoharlal, 1993.

Kakodkar, P.R. (tr), *Portuguese and the Marathas*, Bombay: Maharashtra State Board for Literature and Culture, 1975.

Kamalapur, J.N., *Deccan Forts: Study in the Art of Fortification in Medieval India*, Bombay: Popular Prakashan, 1961.

Kamble, B.R. (ed.), *Studies in Shivaji and his Times*, Kolhapur: Shivaji University, 1982.

Kantak, M.R., *First Anglo-Maratha War: The Last Phase (1780–83)*, Pune: Deccan College, 1989.

——, *The First Anglo-Maratha War (1774–1783)*, Bombay: Popular Prakashan, 1993.

——, *A Military Study of Major Battles*, Bombay: Popular Prakashan, 1993.

——, *Rajwade and His Thoughts*, Pune: BISM, 1990.

Kantak, M.R. and G.T. Kulkarni (eds.), *Battle of Kharda*, Pune: Deccan College, 1980.

Karaka, D.F., *Shivaji: Portrait of an Early Indian*, Bombay: Times of India Press, 1969.

Karandikar, S.L., *Rise and Fall of the Maratha Power*, vol. I (*1620–1689*), Pune: S.S. Karandikar, 1969.

Karkaria, R.P., *Death of Shivaji and Other Essays*, Bombay: Times of India Press, 1906.

——, *Shivaji and Pratapgad Tragedy*, Calcutta: Calcutta Review, 1894.

Karve, Iravati, *Maharashtra: Land and its People*, Bombay: Govt. of Maharashtra, 1986.

——, *Marathi Lokanchi Samskriti*, Pune: Deshmukh, 1962.

Kavade, P.B., *Chhatrapati Shivaji Maharajyanche Charitra*, Pune: Dadasaheb Patnis, 1961.

Keer, Dhananjay, *Shahu Chhatrapati, Royal Revolutionary*, Bombay: Popular Prakashan, 1976.

Kelkar, N.C., *Marathe va Ingraj*, Pune: Modern Book Depot, 1918, 5th edn., 1963.

Kelkar, N.C. and D.V. Apte (ed.), *Shivaji Nibandhavali*, 3 vols., Pune: BISM, 1930.

Kelkar, Y.N., *Vasaichi Mohim* (*1737–1739*), Pune: Author, 1937.

——, *Vasudeo Shashtri Khare: Thor Itihas Samshodhak*, Miraj: Miraj Vidyarthi Sangh, 1956.

——, *Aitihasik Pawade Kinva Marathyancha Kavyamaya Itihas*, vol. I, 1928, vol. 2, 1944, vol. 3, 1969, Pune: T.M. Vidyapeeth.

——, *Marathi Shahir ani Shahiri Vyangmaya*, Pune: Pune University, 1974.

——, *Aitihasik Shabda Kosh*, vols. 1 and 2, Pune: Thokal Prakashan, 1962.

Keluskar, K.A., *Life of Shivaji Maharaj*, Pune: Varada Books, 1919, 4th edn.

Khalap, V.A., *Gomantakateel Samudayik Malkichi Gram Sanstha-Padhati*, Pune: N.V. Khalap, 1955.

Kharbas, D.S., *Maharashtra and the Marathas: Their History and Culture: A Bibliographical Guide to Western Language, Material*, Boston, 1971.

Khan, Saiyid T.D.S., *Real Shivaji*, Allahabad: Popular Press, 1935.

Khare, G.H. (ed.), *Aitihasik Parsi Sahitya*, vols. 1–6, Pune: BISM, 1934–73.

——, *Mandalatil Nani*, Pune: BISM, 1933.

——, *Marathyanchya Itihasachi Vistruta Shakavali*, vol. I, Pune: BISM, 1977.

——, *Maharashtrachi Char Daivate*, Pune: BISM.

——, *Samshodhakacha Mitra*, vol. I, Pune: BISM, 1951.

——, *Shahaji-Shivaji Sambandha*, Pune: Author, 1979.

——, *Nivadak Lekh*, vol. I, 1971, vol. II, 1972, Pune: Author.

——, *Select Articles*, Pune: Author, 1973.

Khare, Vasudeo Shastri, *Adhikar Yoga*, Pune: Modern Book Depot, 1908.

——, *Ichalkaranji Samsthancha Itihas*, Pune: Arya Bhushan Press, 1913.

Khare, Yashwant (ed.), *Harivamsachi Bakhar*, Pune: Arya Bhushan Press, 1909.

——, *Himat Bahadur Chavan Gharanyacha Itihas*, Kolhapur: L.D. Diwan, 1967.

——, *Nana Phadnisache Charitra*, Miraj: Y.V. Khare, 1927.

—— (ed.), *Aitihasik lekh Samgraha*, vols. 1–15, Miraj: Author, 1897–1948.

Khobrekar, V.G., *Maharashtrateel Daftar Khane*, Bombay: Maharashtra State Board of Literature and Culture, rpt. 1968.

——, *Marathyanchya Swaryanche Mukkam (1708–1820)*, Bombay: Itihas Sanskriti Mandal, 1977.

——, *Ingraji Sattevirudha Maharashtrateel Sashastra Uthava*, Bombay: Popular Book Depot, 1959.

Kincaid, C.A. and D.B. Parasnis, *History of the Marathas*, vol. I, 1918, vol. II, 1922 and vol. III, 1925, London: OUP.

Kincaid, David, *Shivaji, the Founder of Maratha Empire*, Delhi: Discovery Publishing House, 1984.

Kincaid, Dennis, *Grand Rebel*, London: Kollins, 1937.

Kinderslay, A.F., *Handbook of Bombay Govt. Records*, Bombay: Govt. of Bombay, 1921.

Kishor, Brij, *Tarabai and Her Times*, Bombay: Asia Publishing House, 1963.

Kosambi, Meera (ed.), *Intersection: Socio-Cultural Trends in Maharashtra*, New Delhi: Longmans, 2000.

Kotani, Hroyuki, *Western India in Historical Transition*, New Delhi: Manohar, 2002.

Kothekar, S.V., *Gaikwads of Baroda and East India Company*, Nagpur: Nagpur University, 1977.

Kulkarni, A.R., *Maharashtra in the Age of Shivaji*, Pune: Deshmukh & Co., 1969; 2nd rev. edn., Pune: Prabha Prakashan, 2002.

——, *The Marathas (1600–1848)*, Delhi: Books & Books, 1996.

——, *Medieval Maharashtra*, Delhi: Books & Books, 2000.

——, *Medieval Maratha Country*, Delhi: Books & Books, 1996.

——, *Maharashtra: Society and Culture*, Delhi: Books & Books, 2000.

—— (ed.), *History in Practice*, Delhi: Books & Books, 1993.

——, *Jedhe: Shakavali & Kavina*, Pune: Mansanman, 1999.

——, *Ajnapatra*, Pune: Mansanman, 2003.

——, *Vallabha's Parasram Charitra* (co-ed. N.K. Wagle), Bombay: Popular Prakashan, 1976.

——, *Region, Religion and Nationalism* (co-ed. N.K. Wagle), Bombay: Popular Prakashn, 1999.

——, *History of Modern Deccan*, vol. I (co-ed. M.A. Nayeem), Hyderabad: Govt. of Andhra Pradesh, 2000.

——, *Medieval Deccan History* (P.M. Joshi Felicitation Volume, co-eds M.A. Nayeem and T.R. deesouza), Bombay: Popular Prakashan, 1996.

——, *Marathyancha Itihas*, vols 1–3 (co-ed. G.H. Khare), Pune, 1984.

——, *James Cuninghamme Grant Duff* (Marathi), Pune: Pune University, 1970; (Hindi), New Delhi: Granthshilpi, 2003.

——, *Shivakalin Maharashtra* (Marathi), 2nd edn., Pune: Rajhansa, 1997.

——, *Shivajike Samayka Maharashtra* (Hindi), New Delhi: Granthshilpi, 2000.

——, *Peshwe Bakhar* (co-eds V.M. Kulkarni and A.N. Deshpande), Pune: Deshmukh & Co., 1963.

——, *Ashi Hoti Shivashahi*, 2nd edn., Pune: Rajhansa, 2000.

——, *Punyache Peshwe*, 2nd edn., Pune: Rajhansa, 2000.

——, *Company Sarkar* (East India Company), 2nd edn., Pune: Rajhansa, 2000.

Kulkarni, G.T., *Mughal-Maratha Struggle: Twenty-five Fateful Years (1682–1707)*, Pune: Deccan College, 1983.

Kulkarni, N.H. (ed.), *Chhatrapati Shivaji: Architect of Freedom*, New Delhi: Chhatrapati Shivaji Smarak Samiti, 1975.

Kulkarni, Sumitra, *Satara Raj (1818–1848)*, Delhi: Mittal, 1995.

Kulkarni, V.B., *Portrait of a Patriot*, Bombay: Longmans, 1963.

Kumar, Ravinder, *Western India in the Nineteenth Century: Study in the Social History of Maharashtra*, London: R. & Kegan Paul Ltd., 1968.

Lele, Jayant (ed.), *Tradition and Modernity in Bhakti Movement*, Leiden, 1981.

Loch, W.W., *Dakhan History: Musalman and Maratha (AD 1300–1818)*, Delhi: Asian Education Service, 1989.

MacDonald, A., *Memoir of the Life of the Late Nana Farnavis*, Oxford: OUP, 1927.

Mahajan, T.T., *Industry, Trade and Commerce during Peshwa Period*, Jaipur: Pointer, 1989.

——, *Maratha Administration in the Eighteenth Century*, New Delhi: Commonwealth, 1990.

——, *Shivaji and His Diplomats*, New Delhi: Commonwealth, 1991.

Mahaley, K.L., *Shivaji, the Pragmatist*, Nagpur: Vishwa Bharati, 1971.

Maharashtra State Gazetteers, *History*, pt. III: *Maratha Period* by V.G. Dighe, Bombay Govt. of Maharashtra, 1967.

Mahamai, S.K., *The Sawants of Sawantwadi and the Portuguese*, New Delhi: Concept, 1981.

Majumdar R.C., *Historiography in Modern India* Bombay: OUP, 1970.

Majumdar, R.C. and V.G. Dighe (eds.), *Maratha Supremacy*, vol. 8, Bombay: Bhartiya Vidya Bhavan, 1977.

Malcolm, (Sir) John, *Political History of India*, 2 vols, London: John Murray, rpt. 1970.

Malgoankar, Manohar, *Chhatrapatis of Kolhapur*, Bombay: Popular Prakashan, 1971.

——, *Kanhoji Angrey: Maratha Admiral, an account of his battle with the English*, Bombay: Asia Publishing House, 1959.

——, *Puars of Dewas Senior*, Bombay: Longmans, 1963.

Malik, Zahir Uddin, *Reign of Muhammad Shah, 1719–1748*, Bombay: Asia Publishing House, 1977.

Mankar, J.L., *Life and Exploits of Shivaji*, Bombay: Nirnayasagar Press, 1886.

Marshal, P.J., *The Eighteenth Century in India's History: Evolution or Revolution*, Oxford: OUP, 2003.

Mate, M.S., *Maratha Architecture AD 1650–1850*, Pune: University of Pune, 1959; 2nd edn., Pune: Mansamman, 2003.

Modak, B.P., *Chronological Tables Containing Corresponding Dates of the Hindu, Mohomedan and Christian Eras from*

AD 1728–1889 – Modak-Jantri, Kolhapur: Vidya Vilas, 1989.

Muddachari, B., *Mysore-Maratha Relations in the Seventeenth Century*, Mysore: University of Mysore, 1969.

——, *Resistance of Mysore to the Maratha Expansion*, Mysore: University of Mysore, 1970.

Nadkarni, R.V., *Rise and Fall of the Maratha Empire*, Bombay: Popular Prakashan, 1966.

Nagrale, N.N., *Peshwa Maratha Relations and Malhar Rao Holkar*, Jaipur: Publication Scheme, 1989.

Nairne, Alexander Kyd, *Konkan: Historical Sketch*, Bombay: Bombay Government, 1875.

Natu, V.R., *Madhavrao Urfa Mahadji Shinde Yanche Charitra va Karkirda*, Belgaum: Author, 1894.

Nayeem, M.A., *External Relations of the Bijapur Kingdom (AD 1489–1686)*, Hyderabad: Bright Publishing House, 1974.

——, *Mughal Administration of Deccan under Nizamul Mulk Asf Jah (1720–1748)*, Bombay: Jaico, 1985.

Nicolson, W.N., *Statement of the Case of Raja of Satara, etc.*, London, 1845.

Nightingale, P., *Trade and Empire in West India (1784–1800)*, Cambridge: Cambridge University Press, 1970.

O'Hanlon, Rosalind, *Caste, Conflict and Ideology: Jyotiba Phule and Low Caste Social Protest in the Nineteenth Century*, Cambridge: Cambridge University Press, 1985.

Orme, Robert, *Historical Fragments of the Mughal Empire of the English Concerns in Indostan from the year MDCLIX*, London: F.W. Wingrave, 1805 (2nd edn.).

Oturkar, R.V. (ed.), *Peshwekalin Samajik va Arthik Vyavahar*, Pune: BISM, 1950.

Owen, Sydney, *India on the Eve of the British Conquest: Historical Sketch*, London: M. Allen, 1872.

Padhye, P. and S.R. Tikekar, *Aajkalcha Maharashtra*, Bombay: Bharat Gaurav Granth, 1935.

Pagadi, Setu Madhavrao, *Chhatrapati Shivaji*, Pune: Continental, 1974.

——, *Shri Chhatrapati ani Tyanchi Prabhaval*, Pune: Continental, 1976.

——, *Shiva Charitra: Ek Abhyas*, Kolhapur: Shivaji University, 1971.

——, *Mogal–Maratha Sangharsha*, Pune: Chitrashala, 1964.

——, *Hindawi Swaraj ani Mogal*, Pune: Venus, 1966.

——, *Shiva Charitra*, Delhi: NBT, 1989.
——, *Marathe va Nizam* (Urdu-Persian Sadhane), Bombay: Mumbai Marathi Granth Samgrahalaya, 1961.
——, *Mogal Darbarchi Batmipatre*, 3 vols., Mumbai: Mumbai Marathi Granth Samgrahalaya, 1978–9.
——, *Maharashtra Karnatakateel Suvarnakal*, Bombay: Parchure, 1989.
——, *Eighteenth Century Deccan*, Bombay: Popular Prakashan, 1963.
——, *Studies in Maratha History*, vol. II, Kolhapur: Shivaji University, 1971.
——, *Tamas Nama*, Bombay: Popular Prakashan, 1967.
Palsokar, R.D., *Shivaji, Great Guerrilla*, Pune: Author, 1973.
Panse, M.G., *Yadavkalin Maharashtra*, Pune: Pune University, 1963.
Parab, K.P., *Marathyanchi Bakhar* (tr. of Grant Duff's *Maratha History*), Bombay: Javaji Dadaji, 1892.
Parasnis, D.B., *Brahmendra Swami Yanche Charitra*, Bombay: Babaji Sakharam, 1900.
Pawar, A.G., *Studies in Maratha History*, vol. I, Kolhapur: Shivaji University, 1971.
——, *Tarabai Papers*, Kolhapur: Shivaji University, 1971.
——, *Tarabai, Ramraja and Peshwa Balaji Bajirao*, Kolhapur: Shivaji University, 1972.
Pawar, Jaysingrao (ed.), *Chhatrapati Sambhaji*, Kolhapur: Manjushri, 1990.
——, *Maharani Tarabai*, Kolhapur: Tarabai Vidyapeeth, 1975.
——, *Santaji Ghorpade*, Kolhapur: Manjushree, 1987.
——, *Rajarshi Shahu Maharaj*, Kolhapur: Maharashtra Itihas Prakashan, 2000.
Pawar, Kiran, *Sir Jadunath Sarkar: Profile in Historiography*, Delhi: Books & Books, 1985.
Pearson, M.N., *Coastal Western India: Studies from the Portuguese Records*, Delhi: Concept, 1981.
——, *New Cambridge History of India*, vol. I: *Portuguese in India*, Bombay: Orient Longmans, 1987.
Phalke, A.B., *Shindeshahichya Itihasachi Sadhane*, vols. 1-6, Gwalior: Shinde Charitable Trust, 1929–35.
Phadke, Y.D. et. al. (eds.), *Shivachhatrapati Itihas ani Charitra*, vol. I (*1300–1650*), Bombay: Macmillan, 2001.
Philips, C.H. (ed.), *Historians of India, Pakistan and Ceylon*, Oxford: OUP, 1961.

Pinge, S.M., *Yuropiyanacha Marathicha Abhyas va Seva*, Bombay: Author, 1960.

Pingulkar, V.P., *Sawantwadi Samsthancha Itihas*, Sawantwadi: Author, 1919.

Pissurlencar, P.S.S., *Portuguese-Marathe Sambandha*, Pune: Pune University, 1967.

——, *Marathyanchya Itihasachi Sadhane, Portuguese Daftar*, vol. 2, Bombay: Maharashtra State Board of Literature and Culture, 1974.

Pitre, K.G., *Second Anglo-Maratha War (1802–1805)*, Pune: D. Ramchandra, 1990.

Potdar, D.V., *Marathi Itihas ani Itihas Samshodhan*, Pune: V.P. Nene, 1935.

Purandare, K.V., *Chimaji Ballal Urfa Chimaji Appa*, Pune: Author, 1948.

Priyolkar, A.K., *Goa Re-Discovered*, Bombay, 1967.

——, *Goa Inquisition*, Bombay: Author, 1961.

Raddi, S.V., *Shivaji*, Bombay: R.M. Press, 1921.

Raeside, Ian, *Decade of Panipat (1751–61)*, Bombay: Popular Prakashan, 1984 (translation of *Bhausahebanchi Bakhar*).

Rai, Lala Lajpat, *Shivaji, the Great Patriot*, 1st published in Urdu in 1896, revised in 1923. Translated into English and edited by R.C. Puri, Delhi, 1980.

Raghubir Sinh, *Malwa in Transition or a Century of Anarchy (1698–1765)*, Bombay: D.B. Taraporewala, 1936.

——, *Treaty of Bassein and the Anglo-Maratha War in the Deccan (1802–1804)*, Calcutta: Gouranga, 1951.

Ranade, M.G., *Rise of the Maratha Power*, Bombay: Bombay University, 1st edn., 1900, rpt., 1963.

——, *Introduction to the Peshwa's Diaries*, pp. 173–215.

Ranade, Ramabai (ed.), *Miscellaneous Writings of the Late Honourable Mr Justice M.G. Ranade*, Bombay: Manoranjan Press, 1915.

Ranade, Rekha, *Sir Bartle Frere and his Times*, New Delhi: Mittal, 1990.

Rawlinson, H.G. (ed.) *Battle of Panipat*, Oxford: OUP, 1926.

——, *Concise History of the Indian People*, Oxford: OUP, 1940.

——, *Shivaji, the Maratha: His Life and Times*, Oxford: Clarendon Press, 1915.

Rawlinson, H.G. and R.P. Patwardhan, *Source Book of Maratha History*, vol. I, pt. II, Bombay, 1929, rpt., Calcutta, 1978.

Rothermund, Dietmar, *The German Intellectual Quest for India*, New Delhi: Manohar, 1986.

Roy, M.P., *Origin, Growth and Suppression of the Pindaris*, New Delhi: Sterling, 1977.

Salvi, P.G., *Chhatrapati Shivaji*, Pune: Venus, 1983.

Sahasrabudhe, S.A., *Thorle Madhavrao Peshwe*, Mumbai: Thorale Madhavrao Peshwa Charitra Prakashan Mandal, 1938.

Samant, Bal, *Shivkalyan Raja*, Bombay: Parchure, 1998.

Samant, Shrinivas, *Vedha Mahamanavacha*, Pune: Deshmukh, 1965.

Samarth, Anil, *Shivaji and the Indian National Movement*, Bombay: Somaiya, 1975.

Sankpal, Bapuji, *Bakhar Vangmaya: Udgam ani Vikas*, Pune, 1982.

Sarda, Har Bilas, *Shivaji: Sisodia Rajput*, Ajmer: Vedic Yantralaya, 1935.

Sardesai, G.S., *Historical Geneologies*, Bombay: Maharashtra State Board of Literature and Culture, 1957.

——, *Main Currents of Maratha History*, Bombay: Dhavale, 1933.

——, *New History of the Marathas*, 3 vols. 1st edn., Bombay: Phoenix, 1946.

—— (ed.), *Parmananda Kavya of Kavindra*, Baroda: Oriental Institute, 1952.

——, *Shivaji Souvenir*, Bombay: Dhavale 1927.

——, *Nanasaheb Peshwe Charitra*, Bombay: Bharat Gaurav Granthmala, 1926.

——, *Musalmani Riyasat*, 2 vols. (upto 1526, and 1526 to 1803), 5 edns. between 1898 and 1993, Bombay: Dhavale.

——, *Marathi Riyasat*, 8 vols, 1st edn., 1902–1932, new edn in 8 vols., Bombay: Popular Prakashan, 1988–92.

——, *British Riyasat*, vol. I (*1600–1757*), Bombay, 1923, 1992, vol. II (*1757–1858*), Bombay: Popular, 1992.

—— (ed.), *Selections from Peshwa Daftar*, 45 vols., Bombay: Bombay Govt., 1930–4.

——, *Mahadji Shinde Hyanchi Kagad Patre*, Gwalior, 1937.

Sarkar, Jadunath, *Fall of the Mughal Empire*, 4 vols., 2nd edn., Calcutta: M.C. Sarkar, 1949.

——, *History of Aurangzeb*, 5 vols., Calcutta: M.C. Sarkar, 19248.

——, *Shivaji and His Times*, 6th edn., Calcutta: M.C. Sarkar, 1961.

——, *Shivaji: Study in Leadership*, Pune: International Book Service, 1950.

——, *House of Shivaji*, 3rd edn., Calcutta: M.C. Sarkar, 1953.

Saxena, R.K., *Maratha Relations with the Major States of Rajputana (1761–1818)*.

Sen, Sailendra Nath, *Anglo-Maratha Relations during the Administration of Warren Hastings (1772–1785)*, Calcutta, 1961.

——, *Anglo-Maratha Relations (1785–1796)*, Bombay: Popular Prakashan, 1974.

Sen, Surendra Nath, *Administrative System of the Marathas*, Calcutta: K.P. Bagchi, 3rd edn., 1976.

——, *Anglo-Maratha Relations*, Calcutta: Firma K.L. Mukhopadhya, 1961.

——, *Military System of the Marathas*, Calcutta: K.P. Bagchi, 2nd edn., 1979.

—— (ed.), *M.M. Professor D.V. Potdar Sixty-First Birthday Commemoration Volume*, Pune: BISM, 1950.

——, *Early Career of Kanhoji Angria and other Papers*, Calcutta, 1941.

——, *Foreign Biographies of Shivaji*, Calcutta: K.P. Bagchi, rpt., 1977.

——, *French in India (1763–1816)*, Calcutta: Firma K.L. Mukhopadhya, 1958.

——, *Indian Travels of Thevenot and Careri*, New Delhi: NAI, 1949.

——, *Siva Chhatrapati*, vol. I, Calcutta: University of Calcutta, 1920.

——, *Studies in India History*, Calcutta: University of Calcutta, 1930.

Sen, S.P., *Historians and Historiography in Modern India*, Calcutta: Institute of Historical Studies, 1973.

Sharma, S.R., *Founding of Maratha Freedom*, Bombay: Orient Longman, 1964.

——, *Maratha History Re-examined (1295–1707)*, Bombay: Karnatak Pub., 1944.

Sharma Sri Ram, *Religious Policy of the Mughal Emperors*, 3rd edn., Bombay: Asia Publishing House, 1972.

Shejwalkar, T.S., *Panipat—1761*, Pune: Deccan College, 1956.

——, *Shri Shiva Chhatrapati* (Proposed Life of Shivaji—Introduction, Plan and Sources), Bombay: Maratha Mandir, 1964.

—— (ed.), *Nagpur Affairs*, vols. I and II, Pune: Deccan College, 1954.

Sherwani, H.K. and P.M. Joshi (eds.), *History of Medieval Deccan*, Hyderabad: Govt. of Andhra Pradesh, 1973 and 1975.

Shiva Charitra Karyalaya, *English Records on Shivaji (1659–1692)*, Pune: BISM, 1931.

Shrivastava, V.S., *Advents of Marathas in Bundelkhand (1729–1792)*.

——, *Elements amongst Marathas*, Pune: Aitihasik Gaurav Granthamala, 1952.

Shivade, Sadashiv, *Jwalatjjwantejas Sambhaji Raja*, Pune: Author, 2000.

——, *Maharadni Yesubai*, Pune: Padmagandha, 2004.

Singh, Gulcharan, *Battles of Panipat*, New Delhi: Army Educational Stores, 1966.

Sinha, H.N., *Rise of the Peshwas*, vol. I, Allahabad: Indian Press, 1931.

Sinha R. and J. Sarkar, *Shivaji's visit to Aurangzeb at Agra*, Calcutta: Indian History Congress, 1963.

Srinivaschari, C.K.S., *History of Gingee and its Rulers*, Annamalainagar: Annamalai University, 1943.

——, *Maratha Rule in the Carnatac*, Annamalainagar: Annamalai University, 1944.

Srinivasan, C.K., *Bajirao the First: The Great Peshwa*, Bombay: Asia Publishing House, 1961.

Stein, Burton, *Thomas Munro*, New Delhi: OUP, 1989.

Sunthankar, B.R., *Nineteenth-Century History of Maharashtra*, vol. I (*1818–1857*), Pune: Subhadra Saraswat, 1988.

Subramanian, K.R., *Maratha Rajas of Tanjore*, New Delhi: Asia Educational Service, 1985.

——, Maratha Rule in Carnatiac, Annamalainagar: Annamalai University, 1944.

Swaminathan, K.D., *Nayaks of Ikkevi*, Madras: P. Varadachari, 1957.

Takakhav, N.S., *Life of Shivaji Maharaj: Founder of the Maratha Empire*, Bombay: Manoranjan Press, 1921.

Temple, Richard, *Shivaji and the Rise of the Maharattas*, Calcutta: Sushil Gupta, 1953.

Thakore, Balwantrai K., *Account of the First Madhavrao Peshwa*, Bombay: University of Bombay, 1897.

Thakur, V.W., *Life and Work of Shree Devi Ahilya Bai Holkar*.

Tikekar, Aroon, *The Kincaids*, New Delhi: Promilla, 1992.

Tikekar, S.R., *On Historiography*, Bombay: Popular Prakashan, 1964.

—— (ed.), *Sardesai Commemoration Volume*, Bombay: Dhavale, 1938.

Tone, W.H., *Some Institutions of the Maratha People*, Asiatic Annual Register, 1799.

Vaidya, C.V., *Shivaji, the Founder of Maratha Swaraj*, Pune: Author, 1931.

——, *Aitihasik Nibandha*, Pune: Author, 1931.

Vaidya, S.G., *Peshwa Bajirao II and the Downfall of Maratha Power*, Nagpur: Pragati Prakashan, 1976.

Vaish, Devi Charan, *Rise of British Power and Fall of the Marathas*, Lucknow: Upper India Publication, 1972.

Varadarajan, Lotika (ed.), *India in the Seventeenth Century, 1670–1694*, New Delhi: Manohar, vol. I, pt. I, 1981; vol. II, pt. II, 1983.

Varma, D.G., *History of Bijapur*, Delhi: Kumar Brothers, 1974.

Varma, O.P., *Yadavas and Their Times*, Nagpur: Vidarbha Samshodhan Mandal, 1970.

Varma, Shanti Prasad, *Study in Maratha Diplomacy*, Agra: Aggarwal, 1956.

Varma, Sushama J., *Mountstuart Elphinstone in Maharashtra (1801–1827)*, Calcutta: K.P. Bagchi, 1981.

Vashishta, H.B., *Land Revenue and Public Finance in Maratha Administration*, New Delhi: Oriental Pub., 1975.

Vinchurkar, S.R., *Brief History of Vinchurkar Family*, Pune: Author, 1914.

Vishvanath, R.G., *Memorial to Her Majesty the Queen from H.H. Suguna Bai Saheb, Rani of Sattara*, Bombay: Union Press, 1874.

Vivekanand Kendra Patrika, *Shivaji in Stories*, Madras: Vivekanand Prakashan Kendra, 1973.

Vriddhagirisan, V., *Nayaks of Tanjore*, Annamalainagar: Annamalai University, 1942.

Wagle, N.K. (ed.), *Writers, Editors and Reformers: Social and Political Transformation of Maharashtra 1830–1930*, New Delhi: Manohar, 1999.

——, *Images of Maharashtra: A Regional Profile of India*, London: Curzon, 1980.

Walimbe, R.S., *Ekonisavya Shatakatil Maharashtrachi Samajik Punarghatana*, vol. I, *1800–1845*, Pune: Author, 1963.

Warder, A.K., *An Introduction to Indian Historiography*, Bombay: Popular Prakashan, 1972.

West, Edward W., *Memoir of the States of the Southern Maratha Country Drawn up for Govt.*, Bombay: Bombay Govt., 1869.

Wheeler, J. Talboys, *Summary of Affairs of Maratha States (1627–1856)*, Jaipur: Publication Scheme, 1989.

Wiggins, K.W. and K.K. Maheshwari, *Maratha Mints and Coinage*, Nasik: Indian Institute of Research in Numismatic Studies, 1980.

Wills, C.V., *British Relations with the Nagpur State in the Eighteenth Century*, Nagpur: Author, 1926.

Wilson, H.H., *Glossary of Judicial and Revenue Terms*, New Delhi: Munshiram Manoharlal, rpt., 1968.

Woodruff, P.W., *The Men Who Ruled India*, vols. I & II, London: Jonathan Cape, 1953.

Yusuf, Husain, *Nizam-ul-Mulk Asaf Jah*, Bombay: Asia Publishing, House, 1963.

Zastaupil, Lynn, *John Stuart Mill and India*, California, 1994.

Index